Hibernate Search
in Action

Hibernate Search
in Action

EMMANUEL BERNARD
JOHN GRIFFIN

MANNING

Greenwich
(74° w. long.)

For online information and ordering of this and other Manning books, please visit
www.manning.com. The publisher offers discounts on this book when ordered in quantity.
For more information, please contact:

Special Sales Department
Manning Publications Co.
Sound View Court 3B   fax: (609) 877-8256
Greenwich, CT 06830   email: orders@manning.com

⊗ Recognizing the importance of preserving what has been written, it is Manning's policy to have
the books we publish printed on acid-free paper, and we exert our best efforts to that end.
Recognizing also our responsibility to conserve the resources of our planet, Manning books are
printed on paper that is at least 15% recycled and processed without elemental chlorine.

/▌▌ Manning Publications Co.   Development editor: Nermina Miller
      Sound View Court 3B   Copyeditor: Linda Recktenwald
      Greenwich, CT 06830   Typesetter: Dottie Marsico
                                         Cover designer: Leslie Haimes

ISBN 1-933988-64-9

Printed in the United States of America

1 2 3 4 5 6 7 8 9 10 – MAL – 14 13 12 11 10 09 08

To Iwona
For her infinite support and patience.

—EB

To Judy, my wife
Thank you for giving me up for a year.
I love you forever.
And to my buddies Clancy and Molly.

—JG

contents

preface

I joined an e-commerce company in 2000, nothing unusual I suppose. We were quite annoyed by the quality of Amazon's search engine results compared to ours. A few years later, we reimplemented our search engine from scratch using Lucene. That's where I learned that a good search engine is 50% kick-ass technology and 50% deep understanding of the business and the users you serve. Then I sailed different seas and joined the Hibernate team and, later on, JBoss Inc.

It must be Destiny that a few years later I worked on unifying Hibernate and Lucene. Hibernate Search's design has been influenced by the work on Java Persistence and JBoss Seam: ease of use, domain model-centric, annotation-driven and focused on providing a unified experience to the developer. Hibernate Search brings full-text search to Hibernate application without programmatic shift or infrastructural code.

Search is now a key component of our digital life (Google, Spotlight, Amazon, Facebook). Virtually every website, every application, has to provide a human-friendly, word-centric search. While Google addresses the internet, Spotlight searches your desktop files, Amazon focuses on products, and Facebook finds people. I firmly believe Lucene's flexibility is a key differentiator for developers building business-centric search engines. This has also influenced the design on Hibernate Search: While Hibernate Search relieves you of the burdens of indexing and retrieving objects, we made sure that all the flexibility of Lucene is accessible to you, especially when you build queries.

I am thrilled to see the rapidly growing community around Hibernate Search and nothing is more rewarding than hearing people saying: "I wish I knew about Hibernate Search six months ago."

EMMANUEL BERNARD

At JavaOne 2007 I attended a presentation titled "Google Your Database!" and heard Emmanuel present his full-text search framework Hibernate Search. I had been working with Lucene, Hibernate Search's engine, for over a year and a half and when Emmanuel invited anyone to help collaborate, I jumped. After Emmanuel's presentation we had time only to exchange email addresses. That was the last time I saw him in person until JavaOne 2008 where we at least got to hang out together for an evening. Email and IM are amazing things.

We have two other active project committers now and I have to admit it never ceases to amaze me that four people: Emmanuel in Atlanta, Georgia; myself in a little town in Utah; Sanne Grinovero in Rome, Italy; and Hardy Ferentschik in Stockholm, Sweden, can produce and maintain a framework like Hibernate Search.

JOHN GRIFFIN

acknowledgments

We never really like to enumerate names because invariably someone is left off the list and may be offended, but for a work of this magnitude anything less would be a disservice to the individuals.

- *Nermina Miller*—I remember thinking–a long time ago it seems—"We have to have what?!?! by when?!?! But we finished ahead of schedule and no small thanks to you. You are an amazing psychologist who managed to get the best out of us.
- *Michael Stephens*—I remember our first phone call where we talked for a good hour about full-text search and how it is changing the world we know. Thanks for inviting us to write this book.
- *Sanne Grinovero*—Not only are you an excellent contributor to Hibernate Search but one of the most tireless technical proofreaders I have ever met. Do you ever sleep?
- *Elizabeth Martin*—You kept us moving even through corrupted files, were a pleasure to work with, and have the coolest email address I have seen in a long time.
- *Karen Tegtmeyer*—I really do not know how you handle the pressure of getting reviewers, not just for us but for the many other Manning books. The range of knowledge and selection of people that reviewed our book was a direct cause of our not slacking in any way during our writing. What do you threaten these people with to get them to actually turn in their reviews? And then some of them come back and do it again?!

- *All of the Reviewers*—Thank you very much to: Erik Hatcher, Otis Gospodnetìc, Hung Tang, Alberto Lagna, Frank Wang, Grant Ingersoll, Aaron Walker, Andy Dingley, Ayende Rahien, Michael McCandless, Patrick Dennis, Peter Pavolovich, Richard Brewter, Robert Hanson, Roger D. Cornejo, Spencer Stejskal, Davide D'Alto, Deepak Vohra, Hardy Ferentschik, Keith Kin, David Grossman, Costantino Cerbo, and Daniel Hinojosa. You kept us honest and did not let anything slip through. You improved the book a great deal.
- *The MEAP Contributors*—This was one of the most interesting parts of writing this book. We had a very active MEAP and it really helps to know that there are a lot of people interested in what you are doing and are hungry for information on your work.
- All the contributors and users of Hibernate Search. This book would be meaningless without you.

Emmanuel would also like to thank his fellows and friends at JBoss–Sacha Labourey, Gavin King and Christian Bauer–for warning him that writing a book will be harder than he can imagine (they were dead on), but nevertheless letting him do it. Many thanks to Bruno Georges, his manager, for supporting him on this endeavor all along. Bruno has a rare quality as a manager: Present when you need him, out of your way the rest of the time. Emmanuel also thanks Hardy Ferentschik and Sanne Grinovero for pushing Hibernate Search 3.1 out while he was working on the book. He sends a special thanks to Iwona who literally supported him during this whole year and to his parents, they know why.

John would also like to thank Spencer Stejskal for having a math degree and agreeing to review chapter 12. This Bud, eh, I mean that chapter is dedicated to you. In addition, Professor David Grossman of the Illinois Institute of Technology was extremely gracious to allow us to use his "gold silver truck" example to aid in the explanation of document ranking. He would also like to again thank Hardy Ferentschik and Sanne Grinovero for being patient with him and Emmanuel for allowing him to be his co-author.

about this book

Hibernate Search is a library providing full-text search capabilities to Hibernate. It opens doors to more human friendly and efficient search engines while still following the Hibernate and Java Persistence development paradigm. This library relieves you of the burdens of keeping indexes up to date with the database, converts Lucene results into managed objects of your domain model, and eases the transition from a HQL-based query to a full-text query. Hibernate Search also helps you scale Lucene in a clustered environment.

Hibernate Search in Action aims not only at providing practical knowledge of Hibernate Search but also uncovering some of the background behind Hibernate Search's design.

We will start by describing full-text search technology and why this tool is invaluable in your development toolbox. Then you will learn how to start with Hibernate Search, how to prepare and index your domain model, how to query your data. We will explore advanced concepts like typo recovery, phonetic approximation, and search by synonym. You will also learn how to improve performance when using Hibernate Search and use it in a clustered environment. The book will then guide you to more advanced Lucene concepts and show you how to access Lucene natively in case Hibernate Search does not cover some of your needs. We will also explore the notion of document scoring and how Lucene orders documents by relevance as well as a few useful tools like term highlighters.

Even though this is an "in Action" book, the authors have included a healthy amount of theory on most of the topics. They feel that it is not only important to know "how" but also "why." This knowledge will help you better understand the design of Hibernate Search. This book is a savant dosage of theory, reference on Hibernate Search and practical knowledge. The latter is the meat of this book and is lead by practical examples.

After reading it, you will be armed with sufficient knowledge to use Hibernate Search in all situations.

How to use this book

While this book can be read from cover to cover, we made sure you can read the sections you are interested independently from the others. Feel free to jump to the subject you are most interested in. Chapter 2, which you should read first, will give you an overview of Hibernate Search and explain how to set it up. Check the road map section which follows for an overview of *Hibernate Search in Action.*

Most chapters start with background and theory on the subject they are covering, so feel free to jump straight to the practical knowledge if you are not interested in the introduction. You can always return to the theory.

Who should read this book

This book is aimed at any person wanting to know more about Hibernate Search and full-text search in general. Any person curious to understand what full text search technology can bring to them and what benefits Hibernate Search provides will be interested.

Readers looking for a smooth and practical introduction to Hibernate Search will appreciate the step-by-step introduction of each feature and its concrete examples.

The more advanced architect will find sections describing concepts and features offered by Hibernate Search as well as the chapter about clustering to be of interest.

The regular Hibernate Search users will enjoy in-depth descriptions of each subject and the ability to jump to the chapter covering the subject they are interested in. They will also appreciate the chapter focusing on performance optimizations.

The search guru will also enjoy the advanced chapters on Lucene describing scoring, access to the native Lucene APIs from Hibernate Search, and the Lucene contribution package.

Developers or architects using or willing to use Hibernate Search on their project will find useful knowledge (how-to, practical examples, architecture recommendations, optimizations).

It is recommended to have basic knowledge of Hibernate Core or Java Persistence but some reviewers have read the book with no knowledge of Hibernate, some with knowledge of the .Net platform, and found the book useful.

Roadmap

In the first part of the book, we introduce full-text search and Hibernate Search.

Chapter 1 describes the weakness of SQL as a tool to answer human queries and describes full-text search technology. This chapter also describes full-text search approaches, the issues with integrating them in a classic Java SE/EE application and why Hibernate Search is needed.

Chapter 2 is a getting started guide on Hibernate Search. It describes how to set up and configure it in a Java application, how to define the mapping in your domain model. It then describes how Hibernate Search indexes objects and how to write full-text queries. We also introduce Luke, a tool to inspect Lucene indexes.

PART 2 focuses on mapping and indexing.

Chapter 3 describes the basics of domain model mapping. We will walk you through the steps of marking an entity and a property as indexed. You will understand the various mapping strategies.

Chapter 4 goes a step further into the mapping possibilities. Custom bridges are introduced as well as mapping of relationships.

Chapter 5 introduces where and how Hibernate Search indexes your entities. We will learn how to configure directory providers (the structure holding index data), how to configure analyzers and what feature they bring (text normalization, typo recovery, phonetic approximation, search by synonyms and so on). Then we will see how Hibernate Search transparently indexes your entities and how to take control and manually trigger such indexing.

PART 3 of *Hibernate Search in Action* covers queries.

Chapter 6 covers the programmatic model used for queries, how it integrates into the Hibernate model and shares the same persistence context. You will also learn how to customize queries by defining pagination, projection, fetching strategies, and so on.

Chapter 7 goes into the meat of full-text queries. It describes what is expressible in a Lucene query and how to do it. We start by using the query parser, then move on to the full programmatic model. At this stage of the book, you will have a good understanding of the tools available to you as a search engine developer.

Chapter 8 describes Hibernate Search filters and gives examples where cross-cutting restrictions are useful. You will see how to best benefit from the built-in cache and explore use cases such as security filtering, temporal filtering, and category filtering.

PART 4 focuses on performance and scalability.

Chapter 9 brings in one chapter all the knowledge related to Hibernate Search and Lucene optimization. All areas are covered: indexing, query time, index structure, and index sharding.

Chapter 10 describes how to cluster a Hibernate Search application. You will understand the underlying problems and be introduced to various solutions. The benefits and drawbacks of each will be explored. This chapter includes a full configuration example.

PART 5 goes beyond Hibernate Search and explores advanced knowledge of Lucene.

Chapter 11 describes ways to access the native Lucene APIs when working with Hibernate Search. While this knowledge is not necessary in most applications, it can come in handy in specific scenarios.

Chapter 12 takes a deep dive into Lucene scoring. If you always wanted to know how a full-text search engine order results by relevance, this chapter is for you. This will be a gem if you need to customize the scoring algorithm.

Chapter 13 gives you an introduction to some of Lucene's contribution projects like text highlighting, spell checking, and so on.

Code conventions

All source code in listings and in text is in a `fixed-width font just like this` to separate it from normal text. Additionally, Java class names, method names, and object properties are also presented using fixed-width font. Java method names generally don't include the signature (the list of parameter types).

In almost all cases the original source code has been reformatted; we've added line breaks and reworked indentation to fit page space in the book. It was even necessary occasionally to add line continuation markers.

Annotations accompany all of the code listings and are followed by numbered bullets, also known as cueballs, which are linked to explanations of the code.

Code downloads

Hibernate Search and Hibernate Core are open source projects released under the Lesser GNU Public License 2.1. You can download the latest versions (both source and binaries) at http://www.hibernate.org.

Apache Lucene is an open source project from the Apache Software Foundation released under the Apache Public License 2.0. Lucene JARs are included in the Hibernate Search distribution but you can download additional contributions, documentation and the source code at http://lucene.apache.org.

The source code used in this book as well as various online resources are freely available at http://book.emmanuelbernard.com/hsia or from a link on the publisher's website at http://www.manning.com/HibernateSearchinAction

Author Online

Purchase of *Hibernate Search in Action* includes free access to a private web forum run by Manning Publications where you can make comments about the book, ask technical questions, and receive help from the lead author and from other users. To access the forum and subscribe to it, point your web browser to http://www.manning.com/HibernateSearchinAction or http://www.manning.com/bernard. This page provides information on how to get on the forum once you're registered, what kind of help is available, and the rules of conduct on the forum.

Manning's commitment to our readers is to provide a venue where a meaningful dialog between individual readers and between readers and the authors can take place. It's not a commitment to any specific amount of participation on the part of the authors, whose contribution to the AO remains voluntary (and unpaid). We suggest you try asking the authors some challenging questions lest their interest stray!

The Author Online forum and the archives of previous discussions will be accessible from the publisher's website as long as the book is in print.

About the authors

EMMANUEL BERNARD graduated from Supelec (French "Grande Ecole") then spent a few years in the retail industry as a developer and architect. That's where he started to be involved in the ORM space. He joined the Hibernate team in 2003 and is now a lead developer at JBoss, a division of Red Hat.

Emmanuel is the cofounder and lead developer of Hibernate Annotations and Hibernate EntityManager (two key projects on top of Hibernate Core implementing the Java Persistence(tm) specification) and more recently Hibernate Search and Hibernate Validator.

Emmanuel is a member of the JPA 2.0 expert group and the spec lead of JSR 303: Bean Validation. He is a regular speaker at various conferences and JUGs, including JavaOne, JBoss World and Devoxx.

JOHN GRIFFIN has been in the software and computer industry in one form or another since 1969. He remembers writing his first FORTRAN IV program in a magic bus on his way back from Woodstock. Currently, he is the software engineer/architect for SOS Staffing Services, Inc. He was formerly the lead e-commerce architect for Iomega Corporation, lead SOA architect for Realm Systems and an independent consultant for the Department of the Interior among many other callings.

John has even spent time as an adjunct university professor. He enjoys being a committer to projects because he believes "it's time to get involved and give back to the community."

John is the author of *XML and SQL Server 2000* published by New Riders Press in 2001 and a member of the ACM. John has also spoken at various conferences and JUGs.

He resides in Layton, Utah, with wife Judy and their Australian Shepherds Clancy and Molly.

About the title

By combining introductions, overviews, and how-to examples, the *In Action* books are designed to help learning and remembering. According to research in cognitive science, the things people remember are things they discover during self-motivated exploration.

Although no one at Manning is a cognitive scientist, we are convinced that for learning to become permanent it must pass through stages of exploration, play, and, interestingly, retelling of what is being learned. People understand and remember new things, which is to say they master them, only after actively exploring them. Humans learn in action. An essential part of an *In Action* guide is that it is example-driven. It encourages the reader to try things out, to play with new code, and explore new ideas.

There is another, more mundane, reason for the title of this book: our readers are busy. They use books to do a job or to solve a problem. They need books that allow them to jump in and jump out easily and learn just what they want just when they want it. They need books that aid them *in action*. The books in this series are designed for such readers.

About the cover illustration

The illustration on the cover of *Hibernate Search in Action* is captioned "Scribe" and is taken from the 1805 edition of Sylvain Maréchal's four-volume compendium of regional dress customs. This book was first published in Paris in 1788, one year before the French Revolution. Each illustration is colored by hand.

The colorful variety of Maréchal's collection reminds us vividly of how culturally apart the world's towns and regions were just 200 years ago. Isolated from each other, people spoke different dialects and languages. In the streets or the countryside, they were easy to place—sometimes with an error of no more than a dozen miles—just by their dress. Dress codes have changed everywhere with time and the diversity by region, so rich at the time, has faded away. It is now hard to tell apart the inhabitants of different continents, let alone different towns or regions. Perhaps we have traded cultural diversity for a more varied personal life—certainly a more varied and faster-paced technological life.

At a time when it is hard to tell one computer book from another, Manning celebrates the inventiveness and initiative of the computer business with book covers based on the rich diversity of regional life of two centuries ago, brought back to life by Maréchal's pictures.

Part 1

Understanding Search Technology

In the first two chapters of *Hibernate Search in Action*, you will discover the place of search in modern applications, the different solutions at your disposal, and their respective strengths. Chapter 1 covers the reasons behind the need for search, introduces the concepts behind full-text search, and describes the types of full-text search solutions available. Going closer to the Java developer's mind, chapter 1 also explains some of the problems that arise with integrating the object-oriented domain model and full-text search. Once you are equipped with this background, chapter 2 will guide you through your first steps with Hibernate Search.

After reading this part of the book, you will understand the concepts behind full-text search and benefits of this technology. You will also discover some issues that may arise when integrating full-text search in an object-oriented world and will learn how to set up and start using Hibernate Search in your Java applications.

State of the art

Search is a quite vague notion involving machine processes, human processes, human thoughts, and even human feelings. As vague as it is, search is also a mandatory functionality in today's applications, especially since we're exposed to and have access to much more information than we used to. Since the exposure rate doesn't seem to slow down these days, searching efficiently, or should we say finding efficiently, becomes a discriminatory element among applications, systems, and even humans. It's no wonder your customers or your users are all about searching.

Unfortunately, integrating efficient search solutions into our daily applications isn't an easy task. In Java applications, where the domain model of your business is described by an object model, it can be particularly tricky to provide "natural" search capabilities without spending a lot of time on complex plumber code. Without breaking the suspense of this chapter, we'll just say that Hibernate Search helps you build advanced search functionalities in Java-based applications (functionalities that will not shy against the big contenders in this field like Google or Yahoo!). But even more important, it relieves the application developer from the burdens of infrastructure and glue code and lets him focus on what matters in the end, optimizing the search queries to return the best possible information.

Before jumping into the details of Hibernate Search, we want you to understand where it comes from and why this project was needed. This chapter will help you understand what search means today when speaking about interacting with an information system (whether it be a website, a backend application, or even a desktop). We'll explore how various technologies address the problem. You'll be able to understand where Hibernate Search comes from and what solutions it provides. Take a comfortable position, relax, and enjoy the show.

1.1   *What is search?*

> *Search*: transitive verb. To look into or over carefully or thoroughly in an effort to find or discover something.

Whenever users interact with an information system, they need to access information. Modern information systems tend to give users access to more and more data. Knowing precisely *where* to find *what* you're looking for is the edge case of search, and you have practically no need for a search function in this situation. But most of the time, *where* and *what* are blurrier. Of course, before knowing where to look, you need to have a decent understanding of what you're looking for.

Surprisingly, some users barely know what they're looking for; they have vague (sometimes unorganized) ideas or partial information and seek help and guidance based on this incomplete knowledge. They seek ways to refine their search until they can browse a reasonably small subset of information. Too much information and the gem are lost in the flow of data; too little and the gem might have been filtered out.

Depending on typical system usage, the search feature (or let's call it the *reach* feature) will have to deal with requests where what is looked for is more or less clear in the user's mind. The clearer it is, the more important it is for the results to be returned by relevance.

NOTE WHAT IS RELEVANCE? *Relevance* is a barbarian word that simply means returning the information considered the most useful at the top of a result list. While the definition is simple, getting a program to compute relevance is not a trivial task, mainly because the notion of usefulness is hard for a machine to understand. Even worse, while most humans will understand what usefulness means, most will disagree on the practical details. Take two persons in the street, and the notion of usefulness will differ slightly. Let's look at an example: I'm a customer of a wonderful online retail store and I'm looking for a "good reflex camera." As a customer, I'm looking for a "good reflex camera" at the lowest possible price, but the vendor might want to provide me with a "good reflex camera" at the highest retail margin. Worst-case scenario, the information system has no notion of relevance, and the end user will have to order the data manually.

Even when users know precisely what they're looking for, they might not precisely know where to look and how to access the information. Based on the *what*, they expect the information system to provide access to the exact data as efficiently and as fast as possible with as few irrelevant pieces as possible. (This irrelevant information is sometimes called *noise*.)

You can refine what you're looking for in several ways. You can categorize information and display it as such, you can expose a detailed search screen to your user, or you can expose a single-search text box and hide the complexity from the user.

1.1.1 Categorizing information

One strategy is to categorize information up front. You can see a good example of this approach in figure 1.1. The online retail website Amazon provides a list of departments and subdepartments that the visitor can go through to direct her search.

The categorization is generally done by business experts during data insertion. The role of the business expert is to anticipate searches and define an efficient category tree that will match the most common requests. There are several drawbacks when using this strategy:

- Predefined categories might not match the search criteria or might not match the mindset of the user base. I can navigate pretty efficiently through the mountain of papers on my desk and floor because I made it, but I bet you'd have a hard time seeing any kind of categorization.
- Manual categorization takes time and is nearly impossible when there's too much data.

However, categorization is very beneficial if the user has no predefined idea because it helps her to refine what she's looking for. Usually categorization is reflected as a navigation system in the application. To make an analogy with this book, categories are the table of contents. You can see a category search in action figure 1.1.

Unfortunately, this solution isn't appropriate for all searches and all users. An alternative typical strategy is to provide a detailed search screen with various criteria representing field restrictions (for example, find by word and find by range).

1.1.2 Using a detailed search screen

A detailed search screen is very useful when the user knows what to look for. Expert users especially appreciate this. They can fine-tune their query to the information system. Such a solution is not friendly to beginner or average users, especially users browsing the internet. Users who know what they are looking for and know pretty well how data is organized will make the most out of this search mode (see, for example, the Amazon.com book search screen in figure 1.2).

Figure 1.1   Searching by category at Amazon.com. Navigating across the departments and subdepartments helps the user to structure her desires and refine her search.

For beginners, a very simple search interface is key. Unfortunately it does add a lot of complexity under the hood because a simple user interface has to "guess" the user's wishes. A third typical strategy is to provide a unique search box that hides the complexity of the data (and data model) and keeps the user free to express the search query in her own terms.

Figure 1.2   A detailed search screen exposes advanced and fine-grained functionalities to the user interface. This strategy doesn't fit beginners very well.

1.1.3 Using a user-friendly search box

A search box, when properly implemented, provides a better user experience for both beginning and average users regardless of the qualification of their search (that is, whether the *what* is vaguely or precisely defined). This solution puts a lot more pressure on the information system: Instead of having the user use the language of the system, the system has to understand the language of the user. Proceeding with our book analogy, such a solution is the 21st-century version of a book index. See the Search box at Amazon.com in figure 1.3.

Figure 1.3   Using one search box gives freedom of expression to users but introduces more complexity and work to the underlying search engine.

While very fashionable these days, this simple approach has its limits and weaknesses. The proper approach is usually to use a mix of the previous strategies, just like Amazon.com does.

1.1.4 Mixing search strategies

These strategies are not mutually exclusive; *au contraire*, most information systems with a significant search feature implement these three strategies or a mix or variation of them.

While not always consciously designed as such by its designer, a search feature addresses the *where* problem. A user trying to access a piece of information through an information system will try to find the fastest or easiest possible way. Application designers may have provided direct access to the data through a given path that doesn't fit the day-to-day needs of their users. Often data is exposed by the way it's stored in the system, and the access path provided to the user is the easiest access path from an information system point of view. This might not fit the business efficiently. Users will then work around the limitation by using the search engine to access information quickly.

Here's one example of such hidden usage. In the book industry, the common identifier is the ISBN (International Standard Book Number). Everybody uses this number when they want to share data on a given book. Emmanuel saw a backend application specifically designed for book industry experts, where the common way to interact on a book was to share a proprietary identifier (namely, the database primary key value in the company's datastore). The whole company interaction process was designed around this primary key. What the designers forgot was that book experts employed by this company very often have to interact outside the company boundaries. It turned out that instead of sharing the internal identifiers, the experts kept using the ISBN as the unique identifier. To convert the ISBN into the internal identifier, the search engine was used extensively as a palliative. It would have been better to expose the ISBN in the process and hide the internal identifier for machine consumption, and this is what the employees of this company ended up doing.

1.1.5   *Choosing a strategy: the first step on a long road*

Choosing one or several strategies is only half the work though, and implementing them efficiently can become fairly challenging depending on the underlying technology used. In most Java applications, both simple text-box searches and detailed screen searches are implemented using the request technology provided by the data store. The data store being usually a relational database management system, an SQL query is built from the query elements provided by the user (after a more or less sophisticated filtering and adjustment algorithm). Unfortunately, data source query technologies often do not match user-centric search needs. This is particularly true in the case of relational databases.

1.2   *Pitfalls of search engines in relational databases*

SQL (Structured Query Language) is a fantastic tool for retrieving information. It especially shines when it comes to restricting columns to particular values or ranges of values and expressing data aggregation. But is it the right tool to use to find information based on user input?

To answer this question, let's look at an example and see the kind of input a user can provide and how an SQL-based search engine would deal with it. A user is looking for a book at her favorite online store. The online store uses a relational database to store the books catalog. The search engine is entirely based on SQL technology. The search box on the upper right is ready to receive the user's request:

```
"a book about persisting objects with ybernate in Java"
```

A relational database groups information into tables, each table having one or several columns.

A simple version of the website could be represented by the following model:

- A `Book` table containing a title and a description
- An `Author` table containing a first name and a last name
- A relation between books and their authors

Thanks to this example, we'll be able to uncover typical problems arising on the way to building an SQL-based search engine. While this list is by no mean complete, we'll face the following problems:

- Writing complex queries because the information is spread across several tables
- Converting the search query to search words individually
- Keeping the search engine efficient by eliminating meaningless words (those that are either too common or not relevant)

- Finding efficient ways to search a given word as opposed to a column value
- Returning results matching words from the same root
- Returning results matching synonymous words
- Recovering from user typos and other approximations
- Returning the most useful information first

Let's now dive into some details and start with the query complexity problem.

1.2.1 Query information spread across several tables

Where should we look for the search information our user has requested? Realistically, title, description, first name, and last name potentially contain the information the user could base her search on. The first problem comes to light: The SQL-based search engine needs to look for several columns and tables, potentially joining them and leading to somewhat complex queries. The more columns the search engine targets, the more complex the SQL query or queries will be.

```
select book.id from Book book left join book.authors author where
    book.title = ? OR book.description = ? OR author.firstname = ? OR
    author.lastname = ?
```

This is often one area where search engines limit the user in order to keep queries relatively simple (to generate) and efficient (to execute). Note that this query doesn't take into account in how many columns a given word is found, but it seems that this information could be important (more on this later).

1.2.2 Searching words, not columns

Our search engine now looks for the user-provided sentence across different columns. It's very unlikely that any of the columns contains the complete following phrase: "a book about persisting objects with ybernate in Java." Searching each individual word sounds like a better strategy. This leads to the second problem: A phrase needs to be split into several words. While this could sound like a trivial matter, do you actually know how to split a Chinese sentence into words? After a little Java preprocessing, the SQL-based search engine now has access to a list of words that can be searched for: *a, about, book, ybernate, in, Java, persisting, objects, with.*

1.2.3 Filtering the noise

Not all words seem equal, though; *book, ybernate, Java, persisting,* and *objects* seem relevant to the search, whereas *a, about, in,* and *with* are more noise and return results completely unrelated to the spirit of the search. The notion of a noisy word is fairly relative. First of all, it depends on the language, but it also depends on the domain on which a search is applied. For an online book store, *book* might be considered a noisy word. As a rule of thumb, a word can be considered noisy if it's very common in the data and hence not discriminatory (*a, the, or,* and the like) or if it's not meaningful for the search (*book* in a bookstore). You've now discovered yet another bump in the holy quest of SQL-based search engines: A word-filtering solution needs to be in place to make the question more selective.

1.2.4   *Find by words...fast*

Restricted to the list of meaningful query words, the SQL search engine can look for each word in each column. Searching for a word inside the value of a column can be a complex and costly operation in SQL. The SQL `like` operator is used in conjunction with the wild card character `%` (for example, `select ... from ... where title like '%persisting%' ...`). And unfortunately for our search engine, this operation can be fairly expensive; you'll understand why in a minute.

To verify if a table row matches `title like '%persisting%'`, a database has two main solutions:

- Walk through each row and do the comparison; this is called a *table scan*, and it can be a fairly expensive operation, especially when the table is big.
- Use an index.

An *index* is a data structure that makes searching by the value of a column much more efficient by ordering the index data by column value (see figure 1.4).

To return the results of the query `select * from Book book where book.title = 'Alice's adventures in Wonderland'`, the database can use the index to find out which rows match. This operation is fairly efficient because the title column values are ordered alphabetically. The database will look in the index in a roughly similar way to how you would look in a dictionary to find words starting with *A*, followed by *l*, then by *i*. This operation is called an *index seek*. The index structure is used to find matching information very quickly.

Note that the query `select * from Book book where book.title like 'Alice%'` can use the same technique because the index structure is very efficient in finding values that start with a given string. Now let's look at the original search engine's query,

Book table

Id	title	description
1	The Da Vinci Code	Detective novel basing the plot ...
2	Alice's adventures in Wonderland	Classic of the nonsense literature ...
...	...	...
234	Economics for Dummies	Introductory book demystifying ...
235	The real history behind the Da Vinci Code	Uncover reality behind ficiton ...

Index on title

title	id
Alice's adventures in Wonderland	2
Economics for Dummies	234
The Da Vinci Code	1
The real history behind the Da Vinci Code	235

Figure 1.4   A typical index structure in a database. Row IDs can be quickly found by title column value, thanks to the structure.

where title like `'%persisting%'`. The database cannot reuse the dictionary trick here because the column value might not start with *persisting*. Sometimes the database will use the index, reading every single entry in it, and see which entry has the word *persisting* somewhere in the key; this operation is called an *index scan*. While faster than a table scan (the index is more compact), this operation is in essence similar to the table scan and thus often slow. Because the search engine needs to find a word inside a column value, our search engine query is reduced to using either the table scan or the index scan technique and suffers from their poor performance.

1.2.5 Searching words with the same root and meaning

After identifying all the previous problems, we end up with a slow, complex-to-implement SQL-based search engine. And we need to apply complex analysis to the human query before morphing it into an SQL query.

Unfortunately, we're still far from the end of our journey; the perfect search engine is not there yet. One of the fundamental problems still present is that words provided by the user may not match letter to letter the words in our data. Our search user certainly expects the search engine to return books containing not only *persisting* but also *persist, persistence, persisted,* and any word whose root is *persist.* The process used to identify a root from a word (called a *stem*) is named the *stemming* process. Expectations might even go further; why not consider *persist* and all of its synonyms? *Save* and *store* are both valid synonyms of *persist.* It would be nice if the search engine returned books containing the word *save* when the query is asking for *persist.*

This is a new category of problems that would force us to modify our data structure to cope with them. A possible implementation could involve an additional data structure to store the stem and synonyms for each word, but this would involve a significant additional amount of work.

1.2.6 Recovering from typos

One last case about words: *ybernate.* You're probably thinking that the publication process is pretty bad at Manning to let such an obvious typo go through. Don't blame them; I asked for it. Your user will make typos. He will have overheard conversation at Starbucks about a new technology but have no clue as to how to write it. Or he might simply have made a typo. The search engine needs a way to recover from *ibernate, ybernate,* or *hypernate.* Several techniques use approximation to recover from such mistakes. A very interesting one is to use a phonetic approach to match words by their phonetic (approximate) equivalent. Like the last two problems, there's no simple approach to solving this issue with SQL.

1.2.7 Relevance

Let's describe one last problem, and this is probably the most important one. Assuming the search engine manages to retrieve the appropriate matching data, the amount of data might be very large. Users usually won't scroll through 200 or 2000 results, but if they have to, they'll probably be very unhappy.

How can we ensure data is ordered in a way that returns the most interesting data in the first 20 or 40 results? Ordering by a given property will most likely not have the appropriate effect. The search engine needs a way to sort the results by *relevance*.

While this is a very complex topic, let's have a look at simple techniques to get a feel for the notion. For a given type of query, some parts of the data, some fields, are more important than others. In our example, finding a matching word in the title column has more value than finding a matching word in the description column, so the search engine can give priority to the former. Another strategy would be to consider that the more matching words found in a given data entry, the more relevant it is. An exact word certainly should be valued higher than an approximated word. When several words from the query are found close to each other (maybe in the same sentence), it certainly seems to be a more valuable result. If you're interested in the gory details of relevance, this book dedicates a whole chapter on the subject: chapter 12.

Defining such a magical ordering equation is not easy. SQL-based search engines don't even have access to the raw information needed to fill this equation: word proximity, number of matching words per result, and so on.

1.2.8   *Many problems. Any solutions?*

The list of problems could go on for awhile, but hopefully we've convinced you that we must use an alternative approach for search engines in order to overcome the shortcomings of SQL queries. Don't feel depressed by this mountain of problem descriptions. Finding solutions to address each and every one of them is possible, and such technology exists today: full-text search, also called free-text search.

1.3   *Full-text search: a promising solution*

Full-text search is a technology focused on finding documents matching a set of words. Because of its focus, it addresses all the problems we've had during our attempt to build a decent search engine using SQL. While sounding like a mouthful, full-text search is more common than you might think. You probably have been using full-text search today. Most of the web search engines such as Google, Yahoo!, and Altavista use full-text search engines at the heart of their service. The differences between each of them are recipe secrets (and sometimes not so secret), such as the Google PageRank™ algorithm. PageRank™ will modify the importance of a given web page (result) depending on how many web pages are pointing to it and how important each page is.

Be careful, though; these so-called web search engines are way more than the core of full-text search: They have a web UI, they crawl the web to find new pages or existing ones, and so on. They provide business-specific wrapping around the core of a full-text search engine.

Given a set of words (the query), the main goal of full-text search is to provide access to all the documents matching those words. Because sequentially scanning all the documents to find the matching words is very inefficient, a full-text search engine (its core) is split into two main operations: indexing the information into an efficient format and searching the relevant information from this precomputed index. From the definition, you can clearly see that the notion of *word* is at the heart of full-text search; this is the atomic piece of information that the engine will manipulate. Let's dive into those two different operations.

1.3.1 Indexing

Indexing is a multiple-step operation whose objective is to build a structure that will make data search more efficient. It solves one of the problems we had with our SQL-based search engine: efficiency. Depending on the full-text search tools, some of those operations are not considered to be part of the core indexing process and are sometimes not included (see figure 1.5).

Let's have a look at each operation:

- The first operation needed is to gather information, for example, by extracting information from a database, crawling the net for new pages, or reacting to an event raised by a system. Once retrieved, each row, each HTML page, or each event will be processed.

- The second operation converts the original data into a searchable text representation: the *document*. A document is the container holding the text representation of the data, the searchable representation of the row, the HTML page, the event data, and so on. Not all of the original data will end up in the document; only the pieces useful for search queries will be included. While indexing the title and content of a book make sense, it's probably unnecessary to index the URL pointing to the cover image. Optionally, the process might also want to categorize the data; the title of an HTML page may have more importance than the core of the page. These items will probably be stored in

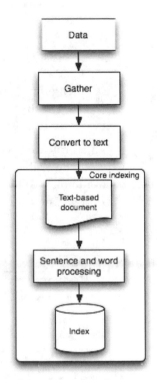

Figure 1.5 The indexing process. Gather data, and convert it to text. From the text-only representation of the data, apply word processing and store the index structure.

different *fields*. Think of a document as a set of fields. The notion of fields is step 1 of our journey to solve one of our SQL-based search engine problems; some columns are more significant than others.

- The third operation will process the text of each field and extract the atomic piece of information a full-text search engine understands: words. This operation is critical for the performance of full-text search technologies but also for the richness of the feature set. In addition to chunking a sentence into words, this operation prepares the data to handle additional problems we've been facing in the SQL-based search engine: search by object root or stem and search by synonyms. Depending on the full-text search tool used, such additional features are available out of the box—or not—and can be customized, but the core sentence chunking is always there.

■ The last operation in the indexing process is to store your document (optionally) and create an optimized structure that will make search queries fast. So what's behind this magic optimized structure? Nothing much, other than the index in the database we've seen in section 1.2, but the key used in this index is the individual word rather than the value of the field (see figure 1.6). The index stores additional information per word. This information will help us later on to fix the order-by-relevance problem we faced in our SQL-based search engine; word frequency, word position, and offset are worth noticing. They allow the search engine to know how "popular" a word is in a given document and its position compared to another word.

While indexing is quite essential for the performance of a search engine, searching is really the visible part of it (and in a sense the only visible feature your user will ever care about). While every engineer knows that the mechanics are really what makes a good car, no user will fall in love with the car unless it has nice curvy lines and is easy

Book table

Id	title
1	The Da Vinci Code
2	Alice's adventures in Wonderland
...	...
234	Economics for Dummies
235	The real history behind the Da Vinci Code

Full text index

Word	id	freq.	position
adventures	2	1/3	2
alice	2	1/3	1
code	1	1/3	3
	235	1/6	5
da	1	1/3	1
	235	1/6	4
dummies	234	1/2	2
economics	234	1/2	1
vinci	1	1/3	2
	235	1/6	5
wonderland	2	1/3	3

Figure 1.6   **Optimizing full-text queries using a specialized index structure. Each word in the title is used as a key in the index structure. For a given word (key), the list of matching ids is stored as well as the word frequency and position.**

to drive. Indexing is the mechanics of our search engine, and searching is the user-oriented polish that will hook our customers.

1.3.2 Searching

If we were using SQL as our search engine, we would have to write a lot of the searching logic by hand. Not only would it be reinventing the wheel, but very likely our wheel would look more like a square than a circle. Searching takes a query from a user and returns the list of matching results efficiently and ordered by relevance. Like indexing, searching is a multistep process, as shown in figure 1.7. We'll walk through the steps and see how they solve the problems we've seen during the development of our SQL-based search engine.

The first operation is about building the query. Depending on the full-text search tool, the way to express query is either:

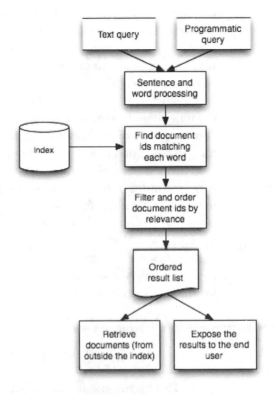

Figure 1.7 Searching process. From a user or program request, determine the list of words, find the appropriate documents matching those words, eliminate the documents not matching, and order the results by relevance.

- *String based*—A text-based query language. Depending on the focus, such a language can be as simple as handling words and as complex as having Boolean operators, approximation operators, field restriction, and much more!

- *Programmatic API based*—For advanced and tightly controlled queries a programmatic API is very neat. It gives the developer a flexible way to express complex queries and decide how to expose the query flexibility to users (it might be a service exposed through a Representational State Transfer (REST) interface).

Some tools will focus on the string-based query, some on the programmatic API, and some on both. Because the query language or API is focused on full-text search, it ends up being much simpler (in complexity) to write than its SQL equivalent and helps to reduce one of the problems we had with our SQL-based search engine: complexity.

The second operation, let's call it *analyzing*, is responsible for taking sentences or lists of words and applying the similar operation performed at indexing time (chunk into words, stems, or phonetic description). This is critical because the result of this operation is the common language that indexing and searching use to talk to each other and happens to be the one stored in the index. If the same set of operations is not applied, the search won't find the indexed words—not so useful! This common language is the cornerstone of full-text search performances (another problem we had with our SQL-based search engine).

Based on the common language between indexing and searching, the third operation (finding documents) will read the index and retrieve the index information associated with each matching word (see figure 1.8). Remember, for each word, the index could store the list of matching documents, the frequency, the word positions in a document, and so on. The implicit deal here is that the document itself is not loaded, and that's one of the reasons why full-text search is efficient: The document does not have to be loaded to know whether it matches or not.

The next operation (filtering and ordering) will process the information retrieved from the index and build the list of documents (or more precisely, handlers to documents). From the information available (matching documents per word, word frequency, and word position), the search engine is able to exclude documents from the matching list. More important, it is able to compute a score for each document. The higher its score, the higher a document will be in the result list. A lengthy discussion about scoring is available in chapter 12, but in the meantime let's have a look at some factors influencing its value:

- In a query involving multiple words, the closer they are in a document, the higher the rank.
- In a query involving multiple words, the more are found in a single document, the higher the rank.
- The higher the frequency of a matching word in a document, the higher the rank.
- The less approximate a word, the higher the rank.

Depending on how the query is expressed and how the product computes score, these rules may or may not apply. This list is here to give you a feeling of what may affect the score, therefore the relevance of a document. This last part has solved the final problem faced by our SQL-based search engine: ordering results by relevance.

Once the ordered list of documents is ready, the full-text search engine exposes the results to the user. It can be through a programmatic API or through a web page. Figure 1.8 shows a result page from the Google search engine.

Sounds like we've found the perfect solution to address our problem. Now let's have a look at the kind of full-text search solutions on the market.

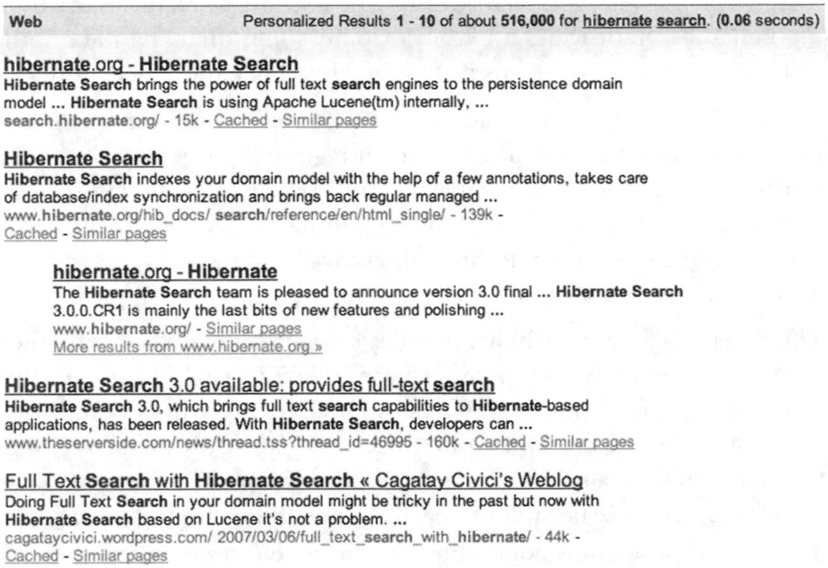

| Web | Personalized Results **1 - 10** of about **516,000** for <u>hibernate</u> <u>search</u>. (0.06 seconds) |

hibernate.org - Hibernate **Search**
Hibernate Search brings the power of full text **search** engines to the persistence domain
model ... **Hibernate Search** is using Apache Lucene(tm) internally, ...
search.**hibernate**.org/ - 15k - <u>Cached</u> - <u>Similar pages</u>

Hibernate Search
Hibernate Search indexes your domain model with the help of a few annotations, takes care
of database/index synchronization and brings back regular managed ...
www.**hibernate**.org/hib_docs/ **search**/reference/en/html_single/ - 139k -
<u>Cached</u> - <u>Similar pages</u>

    hibernate.org - **Hibernate**
    The **Hibernate Search** team is pleased to announce version 3.0 final ... **Hibernate Search**
    3.0.0.CR1 is mainly the last bits of new features and polishing ...
    www.**hibernate**.org/ - <u>Similar pages</u>
    <u>More results from www.hibernate.org »</u>

Hibernate Search 3.0 available: provides full-text **search**
Hibernate Search 3.0, which brings full text **search** capabilities to **Hibernate**-based
applications, has been released. With **Hibernate Search**, developers can ...
www.theserverside.com/news/thread.tss?thread_id=46995 - 160k - <u>Cached</u> - <u>Similar pages</u>

<u>Full Text **Search** with **Hibernate Search** « Cagatay Civici's Weblog</u>
Doing Full Text **Search** in your domain model might be tricky in the past but now with
Hibernate Search based on Lucene it's not a problem. ...
cagataycivici.wordpress.com/ 2007/03/06/full_text_search_with_hibernate/ - 44k -
<u>Cached</u> - <u>Similar pages</u>

Figure 1.8   Search results returned as a web page: one of the possible ways to expose results

1.3.3   *Full-text search solutions*

A variety of full-text search solutions are available. Depending on their focus, they might better fit different needs. Some go beyond the core part of full-text searching and all the way up to exposing the results in a web page for you. Three main families of solutions exist:

- An integrated full-text engine in the relational database engine
- A black box server providing the full-text service
- A library providing a full-text engine implementation

Let's explore these three classic approaches.

FULL TEXT IN RELATIONAL DATABASES

Integrating full-text search with the relational engine sounds like a very appealing solution when full-text searches aim at targeting data stored in the database. When the objective is to enhance SQL queries of our application with full-text search capabilities, this solution is a serious contender. Let's go through some of the benefits:

- *Less management duplication*—Because both your data and your index are handled by the same product, administering the system should be quite simple. (Note that some full-text-search relational integration is not that integrated and requires a different backup-and-restore process.)
- *Data and index are always synchronized*—Because a database knows when you update your data, keeping the index up to date is very easy. Note that not all products shine in that regard.

- *Mixing SQL queries and full-text queries*—The authors think this is the most appealing benefit; SQL provides a lot of flexibility when querying data. Enhancing it with full-text-search keywords makes the querying experience more integrated.

Performance-wise, these products differ greatly depending on the quality of the full-text search engine and the complexity of the integrated query (SQL and full-text).

Recent versions of the main databases tend to include a full-text search module. Oracle DB, Microsoft SQL Server, and MySQL, to name a few, embed such a module. As shown in figure 1.9, your application talks only to the database.

This solution unfortunately suffers from some problems:

- The first problem is scalability. In today's application architecture, the database tends to be the most critical path where scalability cannot be as easily achieved as in other tiers. Full-text indexing and searching can be quite intensive in terms of CPU, memory, and input/output. Do we really want to spend database resources on such a feature set as depicted in figure 1.9? Will it be a problem in the future, and how fast will we reach the scalability limit?

- The second problem is portability. Unfortunately, there is no standard today to express a full-text query. Relational vendors have extended SQL to support the ability to express those kind of queries, every single one in its own way. The end result for the user is the inability to build an application compatible with multiple relational backends. Even if the user is committed to a migration effort, the features themselves are not standard, and their behavior might change from one product to another (if they are even present in both).

- The third problem is flexibility. Depending on the relational engine, indexing can be more or less flexible. Generally speaking, flexibility is not the strong point of such engines. Flexibility is key to adapting your search engine to your business needs and to fulfilling your user's requests. Flexibility is needed both at indexing time (how you want your data to be prepared) and at searching time (what kind of full-text operations are available).

Full-text search engines embedded in a relational database are best for people who specifically target searching on the data embedded in their database, who don't

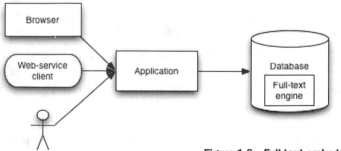

Figure 1.9   Full-text embedded in a relational database

expect the requirements to go too far, who aren't ready to invest a lot in development time, and of course who aren't concerned about database portability. Scalability is another concern for some implementations.

APPLIANCE SOLUTIONS

On the other side of the full-text search spectrum are fully dedicated products whose focus is mainly on searching heterogeneous content on a website, intranet, or the information system in general. As shown in figure 1.10, they serve as the central indexing and searching service. Thanks to their focus, they tend to have very good performances both at indexing time and for processing queries. The best-known example today is the Google Search Appliance, but the giant is not the only one on this market.

Such a tool is deployed on a dedicated server (included or not) and crawls your website, your intranet, and the content of your documents (stored in a content management system or elsewhere) in the background, pretty much like Yahoo! and Google.com do for the web. Those tools are very interesting for the out-of-the-box experience they provide. Beyond the core indexing and searching capabilities that belong to full-text search, these products usually provide some or all of those functionalities:

- Crawling for websites, CMS, wikis, and databases
- Indexing a variety of document formats such as presentations, spreadsheets, and text documents
- Providing a unified web page to search this content and render the results

Black box solutions really shine when you aim at finding data across the enterprise and when they are stored in a variety of areas. Maintenance of these solutions is usually quite low because of their out–of-the-box focus. Most products come with an administration interface. They're not primarily focused on providing a business-

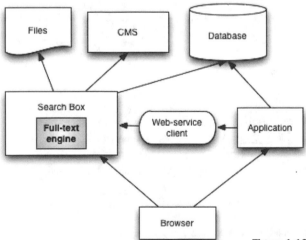

Figure 1.10   Server dedicated to full-text search

oriented search capability of a specific application and might lack the flexibility and refinement to do so. Another differentiator you need to look at is the variety of connectors: You might need to manually code access to your information system through some custom connector API if available connectors are lacking or are too generic. For commercial products, pricing may vary, but a price per document indexed or per index size is quite common.

NOTE   Apache Solr™, a product based on Apache Lucene™, is a hybrid product in between the appliance and the library category. It takes care of a lot of the administration but exposes the indexing and searching through an XML-based API.

Let's now explore the last approach: search libraries.

LIBRARIES

A full-text search library is an embeddable full-text engine that you can use in your application. This solution is by far the most flexible of the three when the search feature aims at being integrated into an application. Your application will call the library APIs when indexing a document or when searching a list of matching results. The query expressiveness and flexibility is the strong point of such solutions: The application developer can decide which full-text feature will be exposed and which data specifically will be searchable (and potentially manipulate this data before indexing) and is free to decide how a user will express his query (which user interface, which natural language, and so on). Flexibility when indexing is also quite strong since the application developer decides when and what to index and has control over the structure. The application is at the center of the full-text experience, as figure 1.11 shows.

Depending on the richness and the popularity of the library you choose, it may be able to read complex formats such as PDFs or Word documents (either as part of the core product or as third-party plug-ins).

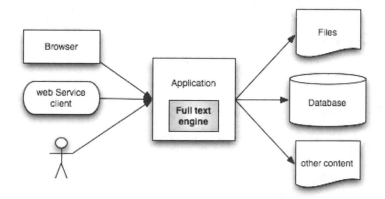

Figure 1.11   Library providing a full-text search engine implementation

Unfortunately, flexibility comes at a price. You need to be able to integrate the full-text library into your application, as shown in figure 1.11. While it's very easy for a new application, it might be more difficult for an application that has reached the end of its life (or close to it) or for an application for which you don't have the source code. While developers are willing to spend time working on integrating the search phase, they often find it harder to integrate the necessary indexing phase. Said differently, developers would rather avoid the burdens of infrastructure code. But as you've seen previously, both operations (indexing and searching) are integral parts of a full-text search engine.

Among the libraries available to you, Apache Lucene™ is probably the most popular. Lucene is an open source library from the Apache Software Foundation initially written and still maintained in Java. Because of its popularity, Lucene has subsequently been ported in different languages (C, C++, C#, Objective-C, Perl, PHP, Python, and a few more). Lucene is also noticeable because this library is at the core of Hibernate Search; this is not the last time you'll read about Lucene in this book.

Now that we know the three main full-text solutions, the hard part is in front of us. Which one should we choose?

WHICH ONE SHOULD I CHOOSE?

The answer is, "It depends." For each solution, we've tried to give you the most common use case and the strong and weak points. Each product on the market fits more or less in one of those categories, but some will sit in between. Instead of giving you a definitive answer, let's have a look at some of the questions you should answer before deciding to go for one product:

- Do I need to search data from one database or from multiple sources?
- Do I want to slightly improve an existing search feature, or do I want to fully benefit from a full-text search engine?
- How much (in time and money) will this solution cost me?
- Can I modify or influence the scoring (prioritize) algorithm to fit my needs? Do I care?
- Can I express a search by phrase, approximation, range, exclusion, weak inclusion, mandatory inclusion, and so on?
- Can I index nontextual data? What about my own data format?
- What is the maintenance cost?
- How fast is indexing? How fast is searching? How about after 1, 10, or 100 million records?
- How much integration and customization do I need for my business rules?
- How well integrated does a search need to be with my user interface?

This list of questions is not exhaustive. Both authors have used Lucene extensively in their applications and like the flexibility and performance it provides. They also think that the way to implement the best search engine focused on your business needs is to use the library approach. They also were ready to pay the price of flexibility and dig more into the code. This is the approach described in this book. Hibernate Search and this book are focused on reducing as much as possible the overhead paid for the flexibility gained when using Lucene and Hibernate.

NOTE   HOW DOES HIBERNATE SEARCH COMPARE TO XYZ? During the book development, people have asked for a comparison between Hibernate Search and other approaches on the market. The authors have decided to resist doing that for a couple of reasons:

- Nobody is equally knowledgeable on all products; this makes comparisons unfair.
- Products evolve rapidly, making such comparison obsolete quickly.
- We believe that this chapter has given you the fundamentals to understand full-text search and a grid to make your own choices—a cleaner approach, we think.

The next section will focus on problems and difficulties of integrating Lucene into domain model–centric applications. This will help you understand the reasons behind Hibernate Search.

1.4   *Mismatches between the round object world and the flat text world*

Full-text search seems to be the magic bullet for our search solution when search is driven by a human input. It solves many of the problems we had with an SQL-based solution: performance, complexity to express the query, search by approximation, phonetic search, and ordering by relevance. And if we focus on the library solution, which is the one that seems to provide the most flexibility for achieving our goals, we'll be able to extend our application with a custom search engine that will increase user productivity. But how hard will it be to add such a solution into an application?

To answer this question, we'll take a typical Java application and try to integrate Lucene. Our typical Java application is a web application (it could very well be a rich client application) that uses Hibernate to persist a domain model into a relational database.

NOTE   A domain model is the object representation of a data model; it represents the business domain of an application. This model, which is fairly close to the relational model, is mapped to the database thanks to an object-relational mapper (ORM) such as Hibernate in our application. This object model is at the heart of your application and is used by different modules to interact with the data.

This journey will show us three fundamental problems:

- The structural mismatch
- The synchronization mismatch
- The retrieval mismatch

People used to ORMs might find the idea of mismatch quite familiar. This is not surprising since we try to exchange information from an object model to an index model, as ORMs do from the object model to the relational model.

1.4.1 The structural mismatch

Lucene represents a record (an entry) as a `Document`. A `Document` is an API that can receive as many fields as pleases you. Each field has a name and a value. This value is a string. A full-text search engine like Lucene does not know a lot of types. The only type it understands is string. We need to find a way to convert the rich and strongly typed domain model in Java to a string-only representation that can be digested and indexed by the full-text search engine (see figure 1.12). While this is fairly easy for some types, it can be pretty questionable for others.

Date is one example. When doing a search query on a date or date range, we don't always need the date with its full precision up to the millisecond. Perhaps providing a way to store only the date up to the day or the hour could make sense. Date is not the only type with problems; number is another one. When comparing numbers, mathematical common sense tells us that 23 is lower than 123. Not for Lucene! Remember, everything is a string, and in the string world, 23 is indeed higher than 123 because the lexical order of 2 is higher than 1. Beyond built-in Java types, custom classes like `Address` or `MoneyAmount` also have to be somewhat translated into a string representation in the index.

Let's explore our domain model a bit more. Some entities have relationships with each other. In a relational model, these relations are represented by foreign keys, while in an object model, they are pointers from one object to another. Unfortunately, Lucene doesn't support the notion of relation between documents, as shown in figure 1.13. The consequence is quite strong and means that Lucene does not support the notion of `JOIN` (as in SQL). We need to find a workaround to build queries that rely on constraint to related entities or documents, like returning the list of matching orders where one item has *Alice* in the title and the customer lives in Atlanta.

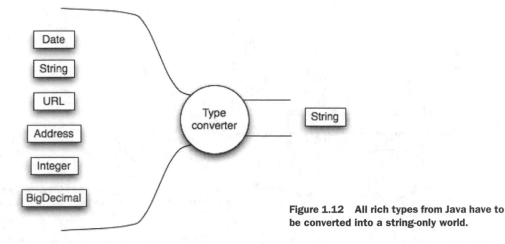

Figure 1.12 All rich types from Java have to be converted into a string-only world.

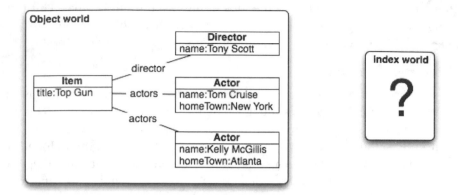

Figure 1.13　**The notion of relationship between entities is not available in a full-text index such as Lucene. How can a query on associated objects be expressed?**

To integrate the conversion from the object model to the index model, we need to write some boilerplate code.

1.4.2　*The synchronization mismatch*

Converting the data is one part of the problem; the system also has to keep the data synchronized between the database and the index. Remember, Lucene isn't part of the relational engine and doesn't know when the data is updated. Thanks to its high-level knowledge, the application layer knows when data is changed. The application could be responsible for updating the index when it updates a database row, as shown in figure 1.14.

This solution is a bit fragile, especially if data is updated in multiple areas in the system. Missing one or two update routines might have unfortunate consequences

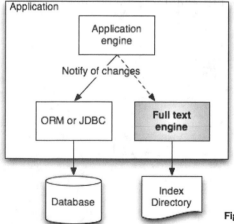

Figure 1.14　**Every change made to the database by the application has to be made to the full-text index as well.**

and be very hard to track down. Likewise, if you make use of the update-by-cascade feature provided by ORMs, it can be fairly hard to know which object is deleted, updated, or created in a whole object graph.

> **Why not get rid of the database?**
>
> A lot of the problems encountered are due to the fact that data has to be maintained in both the full-text index and the database. Why not store all the data in the Lucene index and remove the database from the equation?
>
> A database is a very complex system that guarantees some very important properties while you're playing with your data. Data is accessible and updatable by many concurrent users as if they were the only one playing around. Modern relational databases have become very good at ACID (atomicity, concurrency, isolation, durability) concurrency and offer scalability unattained by other storage systems. Beyond concurrency and referential integrity, relational databases have years of known records of stability in keeping data safe.
>
> Every major development platform has access to the main relational databases. Maybe you're rewriting an old COBOL application in Java. Your data and databases hosting it will most likely outlive your application. Compatibility is key; don't jeopardize it.

Our integration process now has to take care of the synchronization between the two data structures, one way or another.

1.4.3 The retrieval mismatch

Once the data is properly converted to the index and kept synchronized with the database, we need to think about doing what we planned from day one: finding information. The full-text search engine will return a list of matching documents through a Lucene-specific API. A document is essentially a map of field names and field values. The developer has two choices: Accept an untyped version of its domain model (the map) and adjust the code to deal with two different models depending on the search method (full-text versus SQL), or convert the document back to the domain model. In addition to having to write the code to convert the index data back into an object model, some problems will arise: The index needs to store the same amount of data as the database, potentially wasting Lucene performance. You also need to be sure that the text version of the data can be converted back into its original type. This system also needs to implement lazy loading.

Lazy loading

Lazy loading is a technique heavily used in ORMs to avoid loading too much information into memory. Without lazy loading, loading an object means loading the object and all its associated objects recursively. Provided that the entities have rich relationships, this could mean loading the whole database into memory. To avoid that, an ORM will load only the object or object graph up to a certain level. This level is defined statically or dynamically by the developer. If the program reaches one of the nonloaded associations, the ORM will load the needed object graph section transparently.

Don't try this at home; you'll soon discover that lazy loading is a quite complex problem to solve! There's an additional inconvenience even if you manage to solve the lazy loading problem: Hibernate no longer takes care of the loaded objects. If the application changes one of those objects, how do you make sure the changes will be propagated to both the database and the index? One last problem with this architecture is that you could end up having two instances of an object representing the same database row, one from Hibernate and one from Lucene, leading to synchronization hell. Which one has the correct information?

1.5   *Summary*

We've shown in this chapter various strategies to provide search functionalities to an application and to help the user on his quest to access information. While categorization and a detailed search screen address some of the needs, the simple search box feature popularized by websites such as Google or Yahoo! has become increasingly important.

Traditional relational database query solutions do not address efficiently (and sometimes not at all) search requirements when it comes to interaction with human demand. Full-text search technologies address those concerns by providing solutions to searching by relevance, searching by approximation, efficiently searching documents matching certain words, and so on.

Full-text search opens a lot of doors that were not accessible by other technologies; it pushes the limits of the user experience by providing a seminatural way of expressing queries. Unfortunately, properly integrating a full-text search engine like Lucene into a classic Java architecture, whether it be SE (Standard Edition) or EE (Enterprise Edition), is not an easy task, and most people have to accept some inconsistency within their programmatic model (from the Java Persistence/Hibernate part and from the Lucene part). The authors believe that these problems are the major reasons for the lack of large-scale adoption of full-text search engines like Lucene by Java applications despite constant pressure by the customers. The price to pay is high enough that project leaders think twice before jumping.

Fortunately, Hibernate Search addresses the three mismatches and makes using Hibernate and Lucene a pleasant experience in which developers can focus on the business value of a search instead of spending most of their time in boring conversions and infrastructure code. This sounds like the perfect time to be introduced to

Hibernate Search! The next chapter will get you started with Hibernate Search in a pragmatic way, from the setup and configuration process to the mapping and query-writing process. While walking through this guide, you'll start to see how Hibernate Search addresses the three mismatches we introduced in this chapter.

Getting started with Hibernate Search

2

In the chapter 1, we discussed difficulties of integrating a full-text search engine such as Apache Lucene into a Java application centered on a domain model and using Hibernate or Java Persistence to persist data. More specifically, we saw three mismatches:

- *Structural mismatch*—How to convert the object domain into the text-only index; how to deal with relations between objects in the index.

- *Synchronization mismatch*—How to keep the database and the index synchronized all the time.
- *Retrieval mismatch*—How to get a seamless integration between the domain model-centric data-retrieval methods and full-text search.

Hibernate Search leverages the Hibernate ORM and Apache Lucene (full-text search engine) technologies to address these mismatches. This chapter will give you an overview of Hibernate Search: how to use it, how to express full-text queries, and how it fits into the Hibernate programmatic model.

Hibernate Search is a project that complements Hibernate Core by providing the ability to do full-text search queries on persistent domain models. Hibernate Core is probably the most famous and most used ORM tool in the Java industry. An ORM lets you express your domain model in a pure object-oriented paradigm, and it persists this model to a relational database transparently for you. Hibernate Core lets you express queries in an object-oriented way through the use of its own portable SQL extension (HQL), an object-oriented criteria API, or a plain native SQL query. Typically, ORMs such as Hibernate Core apply optimization techniques that an SQL hand-coded solution would not: transactional write behind, batch processing, and first- and second-level caching. Hibernate Core is released under an open source license and can be found at http://hibernate.org.

Hibernate Search's full-text technology entirely depends on Apache Lucene. Lucene is a powerful full-text search engine library hosted at the Apache Software Foundation (http://lucene.apache.org/java). It has rapidly become the de facto standard for implementing full-text search solutions in Java. This success comes from several factors:

- It is free and open source.
- It has low-level and very powerful APIs.
- It is agnostic as to the kind of data indexed and searched.
- It has a good record of performance and maturity.
- It has a vibrant community.

All these qualities make Lucene the perfect information-retrieval library for building search solutions. These reasons are why Hibernate Search is built on top of Lucene.

Hibernate Search, which is also released under an open source license, is a bridge that brings Lucene features to the Hibernate world. Hibernate Search hides the low-level and sometimes complex Lucene API usage, applies the necessary options under the hood, and lets you index and retrieve the Hibernate persistent domain model with minimal work. This chapter should give you a good understanding of how Hibernate Search fits into the Hibernate programmatic model and describe how to quickly start and try Hibernate Search.

To demonstrate this integration, we'll start by writing a DVD store application. We won't write the whole application but rather focus on the domain model and the core engine, specifically the search engine.

Our object model will be quite simple and contain an `Item` entity. The `Item` entity represents a DVD. We want to let our users search by some of the `Item` properties. In this chapter, we'll show how to set up Hibernate Search, describe the metadata to make `Item` a full-text searchable entity, index the items stored in the database, and query the system to retrieve the matching DVDs.

2.1   *Requirements: what Hibernate Search needs*

Hibernate Search has been developed with Java 5 and needs to run on the Java Development Kit (JDK) or Java Runtime Environment (JRE) version 5 or above. Aside from this limitation, Hibernate Search runs everywhere Hibernate Core runs, especially in the architecture and environment of your choice. While it's next to impossible to list all the possible environments Hibernate and Hibernate Search run on, we can list a few typical ones:

- Full-featured applications (web based or not) deployed on a Java EE application server
- Simpler web-based applications on a servlet container
- Web-based applications using JBoss Seam
- Swing applications
- So-called lightweight dependency injection frameworks such as Spring Framework, Guice, or Web Beans
- Applications built on Java SE
- Frameworks or platforms that use Hibernate, such as Grails

Hibernate Search integrates well into the Hibernate platform. More specifically, you can use any of the following mapping strategies and APIs while using Hibernate Search:

- Hibernate Core APIs and hbm.xml files
- Hibernate Core APIs and Hibernate Annotations
- Hibernate `EntityManager` APIs and hbm.xml files
- Hibernate `EntityManager` APIs and Hibernate Annotations

In other words, Hibernate Search is agnostic to your choice of mapping metadata (XML or annotations) and integrates with both Hibernate native APIs and Java Persistence APIs.

While Hibernate Search has few restrictions, this chapter has some. The authors expect the reader to understand the basics of Hibernate. The reader must be familiar with the object-manipulation APIs from the Hibernate `Session` or the Java Persistence `EntityManager` as well as the query APIs. She also must be familiar with association mappings and the concept of bidirectional relationships. These requirements are nothing unusual for someone having a few months of experience with Hibernate.

In this book, most examples will use Hibernate Annotations as the mapping metadata. Annotations have some advantages over an XML deployment descriptor:

Metadata is much more compact, and mixing the class structure and the metadata greatly enhances behavior readability. Besides, modern platforms, including the Java platform, are moving away from XML as the preferred choice for code-centric metadata descriptors, which is reason enough for the authors to leave XML alone. Remember, while Hibernate Search uses annotations for its metadata, it works perfectly with hbm.xml-based domain models, and it should be simple to port the examples.

2.2 *Setting up Hibernate Search*

Configuring Hibernate Search is fairly easy because it integrates with the Hibernate Core configuration lifecycle. That being said, we'll go through the steps of adding Hibernate Search in a Hibernate-based application. We'll add the libraries to the classpath and add the configuration properties. But first you need to download Hibernate Search at http://www.hibernate.org or use the JBoss Maven repository (http://repository.jboss.org/maven2/org/hibernate/hibernate-search). It's useful to download the Apache Lucene distribution as well, which is available at http://lucene.apache.org/java/. It contains both documentation and a contribution section containing add-ons that aren't bundled with Hibernate Search. Make sure you use the same Lucene version that Hibernate Search is based on. You can find the correct version in the Hibernate Search distribution in lib/readme.txt.

2.2.1 *Adding libraries to the classpath*

Add Hibernate Search's necessary JARs (Java Archives) into your classpath. Hibernate Search requires three JARs:

- *hibernate-search.jar*—The core API and engine of Hibernate Search
- *lucene-core.jar*—Apache Lucene engine
- *hibernate-commons-annotations.jar*—Some common utilities for the Hibernate project

All three JARs are available in the Hibernate Search distribution, and pulling them from there is the safest way to have a compatible trio. Thus far Hibernate Search has been staying as close as possible to the latest Lucene version to benefit from bug fixes, performance improvements, and new features of the Lucene community.

You can also add the optional support for modular analyzers by adding the following JARs to your classpath:

- solr-common.jar
- solr-core.jar
- lucene-snowball.jar

These JARs (available in the Hibernate Search distribution) are a subset of the Solr distribution and contain analyzers. While optional, we recommend adding these JARs to your classpath because it greatly simplifies the use of analyzers. This feature is available beginning with Hibernate Search 3.1.

NOTE   You can put the full Solr distribution instead of the version provided by Hibernate Search in your classpath if you wish to.

Hibernate Search is not compatible with all versions of Hibernate Core and Hibernate Annotations. It's best to refer to the compatibility matrix available on the Hibernate.org download page. At the time this book was written, the compatibility matrix tells us that:

- Hibernate Search 3.0.*x* is compatible with Hibernate Core 3.2.*x* starting from 3.2.2, Hibernate Annotations 3.3.*x*, and Hibernate EntityManager 3.3.*x*.
- Hibernate Search 3.1.*x* is compatible with Hibernate Core 3.3.*x*, Hibernate Annotations 3.4.*x*, and Hibernate EntityManager 3.4.*x*.

NOTE   You can find dependencies that Hibernate Search has been built on and initially tested on in the Hibernate Search distribution or in the Maven dependency file (POM). Hibernate Search is published to the JBoss Maven repository (http://repository.jboss.org/maven2/org/hibernate/ hibernate-search).

If you use Hibernate Annotations, hibernate-commons-annotations.jar is already present in your classpath.

Adding a JAR to your classpath depends on your deployment environment. It's virtually impossible to describe all likely deployments, but we'll go through a few of them.

In an SE environment, the JAR list is provided to the virtual machine thanks to a command-line argument:

```
# on Windows platforms
java -classpath hibernate-search.jar;lucene-core.jar
    ;hibernate-commons-annotations.jar;solr-core.jar ... my.StartupClass
```

```
# on Unix, Linux and Mac OS X platforms
java -classpath hibernate-search.jar:lucene-core.jar:
    hibernate-commons-annotations.jar:solr-core.jar ... my.StartupClass
```

If you happen to deploy your Hibernate application in a WAR (Web Archive) either deployed in a naked servlet container or a full-fledged Java EE application server, things are a bit simpler; you just need to add the necessary JARs into the lib directory of your WAR.

```
<WAR ROOT>
  WEB-INF
    classes
      [contains your application classes]
    lib
      hibernate-search.jar
      lucene-core.jar
      hibernate-commons-annotations.jar
      solr-core.jar
```

```
      solr-common.jar
      lucene-snowball.jar
      [contains other third party libraries]
...
```

You could also put Hibernate Search-required JARs as a common library in your servlet container or application server. The authors don't recommend such a strategy because it forces all deployed applications to use the same Hibernate Search version. Some support or operation teams tend to dislike such a strategy, and they'll let you know it.

If you deploy your application in an EAR (Enterprise Archive) in a Java EE application server, one of the strategies is to put the third-party libraries in the EAR's lib directory (or in the library-directory value in META-INF/application.xml if you happen to override it).

```
<EAR_ROOT>
  myejbjar1.jar
  mywar.war
  META-INF
     ...
  lib
    hibernate-search.jar
    lucene-core.jar
    hibernate-commons-annotations.jar
    solr-core.jar
    solr-common.jar
    lucene-snowball.jar
    [contains other third party libraries]
...
```

Unfortunately, this solution works only for Java EE 5 application servers and above. If you're stuck with a J2EE application server, you'll need to add a Class-Path entry in each META-INF/MANFEST.MF file of any component that depends on Hibernate Search. Listing 2.1 and listing 2.2 describe how to do it.

Listing 2.1 MANIFEST.MF declaring a dependency on Hibernate Search

```
Manifest-Version: 1.0
Class-Path: lib/hibernate-search.jar lib/lucene-core.jar
  ➥lib/hibernate-commons-annotations.jar lib/solr-core.jar ...
```

Listing 2.2 Structure of the EAR containing Hibernate Search

```
<EAR_ROOT>
  myejbjar1.jar
     META-INF/MANIFEST.MF (declaring the dependency on Hibernate Search)
  mywar.war
  META-INF
     ...
  lib
     hibernate-search.jar
     lucene-core.jar
```

```
hibernate-commons-annotations.jar
solr-core.jar
solr-common.jar
lucene-snowball.jar
[contains other third party libraries]
...
```

The `Class-Path` entry is a space-separated list of JARs or directory URLs relative to where the referencing archive is (in our example, EAR root).

Believe it or not, you just did the hardest part of the configuration! The next step is to tell Hibernate Search where to put the Lucene index structure.

2.2.2   *Providing configuration*

Once Hibernate Search is properly set up in your classpath, the next step is to indicate where the Apache Lucene indexes will be stored. You will place your Hibernate Search configuration in the same location where you placed your Hibernate Core configuration. Fortunately, you do not need another configuration file.

When you use Hibernate Core (possibly with Hibernate Annotations), you can provide the configuration parameters in three ways:

- In a hibernate.cfg.xml file
- In the /hibernate.properties file
- Through the configuration API and specifically `configuration.setProperty(String, String)`

The first solution is the most commonly used. Hibernate Search properties are regular Hibernate properties and fit in these solutions. When you use Hibernate `EntityManager`, the standard way to provide configuration parameters is to use the META-INF/persistence.xml file. Injecting Hibernate Search properties into this file is also supported. This is good news for us, in that there's no need to think about yet another configuration file to package!

What kind of configuration parameters does Hibernate Search need? Not a lot by default. Hibernate Search has been designed with the idea of configuration by exception in mind. This design concept uses the 80 percent-20 percent rule by letting the 80 percent scenarios be the default configuration. Of course, it's always possible to override the default in case we fall into the 20 percent scenarios. The configuration-by-exception principle will be more visible and more useful when we start talking about mapping. Let's look at a concrete example. When using Hibernate Search, you need to tell the library where to find Apache Lucene indexes. By default, Hibernate Search assumes you want to store your indexes in a file directory; this is a good assumption because it provides a good trade-off between performance and index size. However, you'll probably want to define the actual directory where the indexes will be stored. The property name is `hibernate.search.default.indexBase`, so depending on the configuration strategy used, the configuration will be updated as shown in listing 2.3.

Listing 2.3   Hibernate Search configuration

```
#hibernate.properties      ⟵── hibernate.properties file          Define your Hibernate
                                                                    Core properties
#regular Hibernate Core configuration      ⟵──┘
hibernate.dialect org.hibernate.dialect.PostgreSQLDialect
hibernate.connection.datasource jdbc/test              Define Hibernate Search-
                                                        specific properties
#Hibernate Search configuration       ⟵──┘
hibernate.search.default.indexBase /users/application/indexes


<?xml version="1.0" encoding="UTF-8"?>     ⟵── hibernate.cfg.xml file
<!DOCTYPE hibernate-configuration PUBLIC
    "-//Hibernate/Hibernate Configuration DTD 3.0//EN"
    "http://hibernate.sourceforge.net/hibernate-configuration-3.0.dtd">

<!-- hibernate.cfg.xml -->
<hibernate-configuration>
   <session-factory name="dvdstore-catalog">

      <!-- regular Hibernate Core configuration -->
      <property name="hibernate.dialect">
          org.hibernate.dialect.PostgreSQLDialect
      </property>
      <property name="hibernate.connection.datasource">
         jdbc/test
      </property>
                                                    Hibernate Search
      <!-- Hibernate Search configuration -->   ⟵── properties
      <property name="hibernate.search.default.indexBase">
         /users/application/indexes
      </property>
                                        List your entities
      <!-- mapping classes -->   ⟵──┘
      <mapping class="com.manning.dvdstore.model.Item"/>

   </session-factory>
</hibernate-configuration>

                                              META-INF/persistence.xml
<?xml version="1.0" encoding="UTF-8"?>   ⟵──┘
<persistence xmlns="http://java.sun.com/xml/ns/persistence"
           xmlns:xsi="http://www.w3.org/2001/XMLSchema-instance"
           xsi:schemaLocation="http://java.sun.com/xml/ns/persistence
           http://java.sun.com/xml/ns/persistence/persistence_1_0.xsd"
           version="1.0">

   <!-- example of a default persistence.xml -->
   <persistence-unit name="dvdstore-catalog">
      <jta-data-source>jdbc/test</jta-data-source>

      <properties>
         <!-- regular Hibernate Core configuration -->
         <property name="hibernate.dialect"
                   value="org.hibernate.dialect.PostgreSQLDialect"/>

         <!-- Hibernate Search configuration -->
```

```
          <property name="hibernate.search.default.indexBase"
                  value="/users/application/indexes"/>
          </properties>
        </persistence-unit>
      </persistence>
```

Hibernate Search
properties

This is the last time you'll see the XML headers (`doctype` and `schema`) in this book. They should always be there, but for conciseness we'll drop them in future examples.

This is the only configuration property we need to set to get started with Hibernate Search. Even this property is defaulted to `./`, which is the JVM current directory, but the authors think it's more appropriate to explicitly define the target directory.

Another property can be quite useful, especially in test environments: the Lucene directory provider. Hibernate Search stores your indexes in a file directory by default. But it can be quite convenient to store indexes only in memory when doing unit tests, especially if, like the authors, you prefer to use in-memory databases like HSQLDB, H2, or Derby to run your test suite. It makes the tests run faster and limits side effects between tests. We'll discuss this approach in section 5.1.3 and section 9.5.2.

NOTE   IN-MEMORY INDEX AND UNIT TESTING   We'd like to warn you of a classic error we're sure you'll be bitten by that can cost you a few hours until you figure it out. When you run a test on your index, make sure it is on par with the database you're testing on. Classically, unit tests clear the database and add a fresh set of data. Every so often you'll forget to update or clear your file system's Lucene directory. Your results will look confusing, returning duplicate or stale data. One elegant way to avoid that is to use in-memory directories; they're created and destroyed for every test, practically isolating them from one another.

As you can see, configuring Hibernate Search is very simple, and the required parameters are minimal. Well, it's not entirely true—we lied to you. If your system uses Hibernate Annotations 3.3.*x* and beyond, these are truly the only parameters required. But if your system uses Hibernate Core only, a few additional properties are required.

NOTE   HOW DO I KNOW WHETHER TO USE HIBERNATE ANNOTATIONS OR SIMPLY HIBERNATE CORE?   There are three very simple rules:

- If your domain model uses Hibernate Annotations or Java Persistence annotations, you're using Hibernate Annotations.
- If your application uses the Hibernate `EntityManager` API (the Java Persistence API really), you're also using Hibernate Annotations under the cover.
- If you're still unsure, check whether you create a Configuration object or an AnnotationConfiguration object. In the former case, you're using Hibernate Core. In the latter case, you're using Hibernate Annotations.

Why is that? Hibernate Annotations detects Hibernate Search and is able to autowire Hibernate event listeners for you. Unfortunately this is not (yet) the case for Hibernate Core. If you're using only Hibernate Core, you need to add the event listener configuration, as shown in listing 2.4.

Listing 2.4 Enable event listeners if you don't use Hibernate Annotations

```
<hibernate-configuration>
    <session-factory>
        ...
        <event type="post-update">
            <listener
    class="org.hibernate.search.event.FullTextIndexEventListener"/>
        </event>
        <event type="post-insert">
            <listener
    class="org.hibernate.search.event.FullTextIndexEventListener"/>
        </event>
        <event type="post-delete">
            <listener
    class="org.hibernate.search.event.FullTextIndexEventListener"/>
        </event>
        <event type="post-collection-recreate">
            <listener
    class="org.hibernate.search.event.FullTextIndexEventListener"/>
        </event>
        <event type="post-collection-remove">
            <listener
    class="org.hibernate.search.event.FullTextIndexEventListener"/>
        </event>
        <event type="post-collection-update">
            <listener
    class="org.hibernate.search.event.FullTextIndexEventListener"/>
        </event>
    </session-factory>
</hibernate-configuration>
```

Now each time Hibernate Core inserts, updates, or deletes an entity, Hibernate Search will know about it.

NOTE If you use Hibernate Search 3.0.*x*, you need a slightly different configuration. Listing 2.5 describes it.

Listing 2.5 Enable event listeners for Search 3.0 if you don't use Annotations.

```
<hibernate-configuration>
    <session-factory>
        ...
        <event type="post-update">
            <listener
    class="org.hibernate.search.event.FullTextIndexEventListener"/>
        </event>
        <event type="post-insert">
```

```
            <listener
    class="org.hibernate.search.event.FullTextIndexEventListener"/>
        </event>
        <event type="post-delete">
            <listener
    class="org.hibernate.search.event.FullTextIndexEventListener"/>
        </event>
        <event type="post-collection-recreate">        Collection event
            <listener                                   listener differs
    class="org.hibernate.search.event.FullTextIndexCollectionEventListener"/>
        </event>
        <event type="post-collection-remove">
            <listener
    class="org.hibernate.search.event.FullTextIndexCollectionEventListener"/>
        </event>
        <event type="post-collection-update">
            <listener
    class="org.hibernate.search.event.FullTextIndexCollectionEventListener"/>
        </event>
    </session-factory>
</hibernate-configuration>
```

This event listener configuration looks pretty scary, but remember: You don't even need to think about it if you use Hibernate Annotations or Hibernate `EntityManager` 3.3.*x* or above, a good reason to move to these projects!

We'll discuss additional Hibernate Search parameters when the need arises, but what you know right now is more than enough to get started and suits a great many production systems.

2.3   *Mapping the domain model*

Now that Hibernate Search is configured properly, we need to decide which entity and which property will be usable in our full-text searches. Indexing every single entity and every single property doesn't make much sense. Putting aside that such a strategy would waste CPU, index size, and performance, it doesn't make a lot of business sense to be able to search a DVD by its image URL name. Mapping metadata will help define what to index and how: It will describe the conversion between our object-oriented domain object and the string-only flat world of Lucene indexes.

Hibernate Search expresses this mapping metadata through annotations. The choice of annotations was quite natural to the Hibernate Search designers because the metadata is closely related to the Java class structure. Configuration by exception is used extensively to limit the amount of metadata an application developer has to define and maintain.

2.3.1   *Indexing an entity*

Let's go practical now. What's needed to make a standard entity (a mapped plain old Java object [POJO] really) full-text searchable? Let's have a look at listing 2.6.

Listing 2.6   Mapping a persistent POJO

```
package com.manning.hsia.dvdstore.model;

@Entity
@Indexed        ◁──┘ Mark for indexing
public class Item {

    @Id @GeneratedValue        Mark id property shared
    @DocumentId         ◁──    by Core and Search
    private Integer id;
                               Mark for indexing using
    @Field          ◁──────┘   tokenization
    private String title;
                                                              Mark for
    @Field                                                    indexing
    private String description;                               without
                                                              tokenization
    @Field(index=Index.UN_TOKENIZED, store=Store.YES)   ◁──┘
    private String ean;            This property is not
                                   indexed (default)
    private String imageURL;   ◁──
    //public getters and setters
}
```

The first thing to do is to place an @Indexed annotation on the entity that will be searchable through Hibernate Search. In the previous section, you might have noticed that nowhere did we provide a list of indexed entities. Indeed, Hibernate Search gathers the list of indexed entities from the list of persistence entities marked with the @Indexed annotation, saving you the work of doing it manually. The index for the Item entity will be stored in a directory named com.manning.hsia.dvd-store.model.Item in the indexBase directory we configured previously. By default, the index name for a given entity is the fully qualified class name of the entity.

The second (and last) mandatory thing to do is to add a @DocumentId on the entity's identity property. Hibernate Search uses this property to make the link between a database entry and an index entry. Hibernate Search will then know which entry (*document* in the Lucene jargon) to update in the index when an item object is changed. Likewise, when reading results from the index, Hibernate Search will know to which object (or database row) it relates. That's it for the necessary steps: Add @Indexed on the entity, and add @DocumentId on the identifier property. But of course, as it is, it wouldn't be really useful since none of the interesting properties are indexed.

2.3.2   Indexing properties

To index a property, we need to use an @Field annotation. This annotation tells Hibernate Search that the property needs to be indexed in the Lucene document. Each property is indexed in a field that's named after the property name. In our example, the title, description, and ean properties are indexed by Lucene in, respectively, the title, description, and ean fields. While it's possible to change the default Lucene field name of a property, it's considered a bad practice and will make querying more unnatural, as you'll see in the query section of this chapter. imageURL, which is not marked by @Field, won't be indexed in the Lucene document even if Hibernate stores it in the database.

> **NOTE** An object instance mapped by Hibernate roughly corresponds to a table row in the database. An object property is roughly materialized to a table column. To make the same analogy in the Lucene index, an object instance mapped by Hibernate roughly corresponds to a Lucene document, and an object property is roughly materialized to a Lucene field in the document. Now take this analogy with a grain of salt because this one-to-one correspondence isn't always verified. We'll come to these more exotic cases later in this book.

The ean property is indexed slightly differently than the others. While we still use @Field to map it, two new attributes have been defined. The first one, index, specifies how the property value should be indexed. While we have decided to chunk title and description into individual words to be able to search these fields by word (this process is called *tokenization*), the ean property should be treated differently. EAN, which stands for European Article Number, is the article bar code that you can see on just about any product sold nowadays. EAN is a superset of the UPC (Universal Product Code) used in North America. It would be fairly bad for the indexing process to tokenize a unique identifier because it would be impossible to search by it. That's why the index attribute is set to Index.UN_TOKENIZED; the EAN value won't be chunked during the indexing process.

The second particularity of the ean property is that its value will be stored in the Lucene index. By default, Hibernate Search doesn't store values in the index because they're not needed in most cases. As a result, the Lucene index is smaller and faster. In some situations, though, you want to store some properties in the Lucene index, either because the index is read outside of Hibernate Search or because you want to execute a particular type of query—projection—that we'll talk about later in the book. By adding the store attribute to Store.YES in the @Field annotation, you ask Hibernate Search to store the property value in the Lucene index.

The example shows annotations placed on fields. This isn't mandatory; you can place annotations on getters as well. If the annotation is on the getter, Hibernate Search will access the property value through the getter method. Indeed, this is the authors' preferred access strategy. To keep the example as short and readable as possible, this book will show annotations only on fields.

> **NOTE** SHOULD I USE GETTER OR FIELD ACCESS?   There's no performance impact in using one or the other, nor is there any advantage with regard to Hibernate Search. Choosing is more a matter of architectural taste. The authors tend to prefer getter access because it allows an abstraction over the object state. Also, the Java Persistence specification requires accessing data through getters for maximum portability. In any case, consistency is

the rule you should follow. Try to use the same access strategy for both Hibernate Core and Hibernate Search, because it will save you from some unwanted surprises.

We'll now show how to use Hibernate Search on an existing XML-based mapping structure (hbm.xml files).

2.3.3 *What if I don't use Hibernate Annotations?*

The previous example shows the use of Hibernate Search in conjunction with Hibernate Annotations, but the same example would work perfectly with hbm.xml files as well. This is particularly useful if you try to use Hibernate Search on an existing Hibernate Core–based application where the mapping is defined in XML. Have a look at listing 2.7.

Listing 2.7 Mapping a persistent POJO using an hbm.xml file

```
package com.manning.hsia.dvdstore.model;

@Indexed              ◁─────        No Java Persistence
public class Item {                 annotations are
                                    present
    @DocumentId
    private Integer id;

    @Field
    private String title;

    @Field
    private String description;

    @Field(index=Index.UN_TOKENIZED, store=Store.YES)
    private String ean;

    private String imageURL;
    //public getters and setters
}



<hibernate-mapping package="com.manning.hsia.dvdstore.model">
    <class name="Item">              ◁─────        Mapping externalized
        <id name="id">                              in hbm.xml files
            <generator class="native"/>
        </id>
        <property name="title"/>
        <property name="description"/>
        <property name="ean"/>
        <property name="imageURL"/>
    </class>
</hibernate-mapping>
```

It's currently not possible to express the Hibernate Search metadata using an XML descriptor, but it might be added to a future version of the product, depending on user demand.

2.4   *Indexing your data*

We've just shown how the object model will be mapped into the index model, but we haven't addressed when the object model is indexed. Hibernate Search listens to Hibernate Core operations. Every time an entity marked for indexing is persisted, updated, or deleted, Hibernate Search is notified. In other words, every time you persist your domain model to the database, Hibernate Search knows it and can apply the same changes to the index. The index stays synchronized with the database state automatically and transparently for the application. That's good news for us because we don't have anything special to do!

What about existing data? Data already in the database may never be updated, and so Hibernate Search will then never be able to receive a notification from Hibernate Core. Because in most scenarios the index needs to be initially populated with existing and legacy data, Hibernate Search proposes a manual indexing API.

This is our first look at the Hibernate Search API. Hibernate Search extends the Hibernate Core main API to provide access to some of the full-text capabilities. A `FullTextSession` is a subinterface of `Session`. Similarly, a `FullTextEntityManager` is a subinterface of `EntityManager` (see figure 2.1). Those two subinterfaces contain the same methods and especially the one interesting us at the moment: the ability to manually index an object.

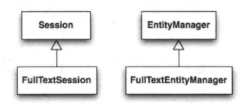

Figure 2.1 `FullTextSession` and `FullTextEntityManager` extend `Session` and `EntityManager`, respectively.

Where can we get an instance of theses interfaces? Internally, the `FullTextEntityManager` and `FullTextSession` implementations are wrappers around an `EntityManager` implementation or a `Session` implementation. Hibernate Search provides a helper class (`org.hibernate.search.jpa.Search`) to retrieve a `FullTextEntityManager` from a Hibernate `EntityManager` as well as a helper class to retrieve a `FullTextSession` from a `Session` (`org.hibernate.search.Search`). Listing 2.8 shows how to use these helper classes.

Listing 2.8   Retrieving a `FullTextSession` or a `FullTextEntityManager`

```
Session session = ...;
FullTextSession fts =
    org.hibernate.search.Search.getFullTextSession(session);      ◁─┐
                                                        Wrap a
                                                        Session
                                                         object

EntityManager em = ...;
FullTextEntityManager ftem =
    org.hibernate.search.jpa.Search.getFullTextEntityManager(em); ◁─┐
                                                        Wrap an
                                                     EntityManager
                                                         object
```

NOTE getFullTextSession and getFullTextEntityManager were named cre-ateFullTextSession and createFullTextEntityManager in Hibernate Search 3.0.

The two full-text APIs have a method named index whose responsibility is to index or reindex an already persistent object. Let's see in listing 2.9 how we would index all the existing items.

Listing 2.9 Manually indexing object instances

```
FullTextEntityManager ftem = Search.getFullTextEntityManager(em);

ftem.getTransaction().begin();

@SuppressWarnings("unchecked")
List<Item> items = em.createQuery("select i from Item i").getResultList();

for (Item item : items) {          Manually index an
    ftem.index(item);    <───────  item instance
}
                                          Index is written at
ftem.getTransaction().commit();   <────── commit time
```

In this piece of code, items is the list of Item objects to index. You'll discover in section 5.4.2 a more efficient solution to massively indexing data, but this one will be good enough for now. The index method takes an item instance and indexes it. The Lucene index will thus contain the necessary information to execute full-text queries matching these items. The initial dataset indexed, subsequent changes, and whether it is item creation, item update, or item deletion will be taken care of by the Hibernate event system. The index and the database stay synchronized.

We now have an up-to-date index ready to be queried, which leads to the next question: How do I query data using Hibernate Search?

2.5 *Querying your data*

Hibernate Search tries to achieve two somewhat contradictory goals:

- Provide a seamless integration with the Hibernate Core API and programmatic model
- Give the full power and flexibility of Lucene, the underlying full-text engine

To achieve the first goal, Hibernate Search's query facility integrates into the Hibernate query API (or the Java Persistence query API if you use the EntityManager). If you know Hibernate Core, the query-manipulation APIs will look very familiar to you; they're the same! The second key point is that Hibernate Search returns Hibernate managed objects out of the persistence context; in more concrete terms it means that the objects retrieved from a full-text query are the same object instances you would have retrieved from an HQL query (had HQL the same full-text capabilities). In particular, you can update those objects, and Hibernate will synchronize any changes to the database. Your objects also benefit from lazy loading association and transparent fetching with no additional work on the application programmer's side.

NOTE   WHAT IS A PERSISTENCE CONTEXT?   While the Hibernate Session is the API that lets you manipulate the object's state and query the database, the persistence context is the list of objects Hibernate is taking care of in the current session lifecycle. Every object loaded, persisted, or reattached by Hibernate will be placed into the persistence context and will be checked for any change at flush time. Why is the persistence context important? Because it's responsible for object unicity while you interact with the session. Persistence contexts guarantee that a given entry in the database is represented as one object and only one per session (that is, per persistence context). While usually misunderstood, this is a key behavior that saves the application programmer a lot of trouble.

To achieve the second goal, Hibernate Search doesn't try to encapsulate how Lucene expresses queries. You can write a plain Lucene query and pass it to Hibernate Search as it is.

Let's walk through the steps to create a query and retrieve the list of matching objects. For Lucene beginners, don't worry; no prerequisite knowledge of Lucene is necessary. We'll walk with you each and every step.

2.5.1 *Building the Lucene query*

The first thing we need to do is determine what query we're willing to execute. In our example, we want to retrieve all items matching a given set of words regardless of whether they are in the `title` properties or the `description` properties. The next step is to write the Lucene query associated with this request. We have a few ways to write a Lucene query. For starters,

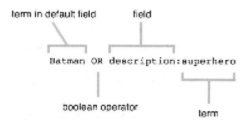

Figure 2.2 Query parser syntax

we'll use the simpler-to-understand query parser solution. Lucene comes bundled with an example of a query parser that takes a string as a parameter and builds the underlying Lucene query from it. The full description of the query syntax is available in any Lucene distribution at docs/queryparsersyntax.html, but let's have a quick look at it. Figure 2.2 describes the components of a query.

A query is composed of terms to look for (words) targeted in a given Lucene document field. The field name is followed by a colon (:) and the term to look for. To query more than one term, Boolean operators such as OR, AND, or NOT (they must be capitalized) can be used between terms. When building a query parser, a default field name is provided. If the term is not preceded by a field name, the default field name applies. When you need to apply some approximation searching to a word (maybe because you don't know the exact spelling), it needs to be followed by a tilde (~). For example:

```
title:hypernate~ OR description:persistence
```

To learn more about the Lucene query syntax, have a look at chapter 7, the Lucene documentation, or the excellent book *Lucene in Action* by Erik Hatcher and Otis Gospodnetič.

How does a field map back to our domain model mapping? Hibernate Search maps each indexed property into a field of the same name (unless you explicitly override the field name). This makes a query quite natural to read from an object-oriented point of view; the property `title` in our `Item` class can be queried by targeting the title field in a Lucene query. Now that we can express our queries, let's see how to build them (listing 2.10).

NOTE You might be afraid that the query syntax is not one your customer is willing or even able to use. The Lucene query parser is provided here to give you a quick start. Most public-faced applications define their own search syntax and build their Lucene queries programmatically. We'll explore this approach later in this book.

Listing 2.10 Building a Lucene query

```
String searchQuery = "title:Batman OR description:Batman";   ◁ ── Query string

QueryParser parser = new QueryParser(                  ◁──────────┐
        "title",                              ◁──── Default     Build a
        new StandardAnalyzer()    ◁──── Analyzer  field        query parser
);                                               used

org.apache.lucene.search.Query luceneQuery;
try {
    luceneQuery = parser.parse(searchQuery);   ◁─── Build Lucene query
}
catch (ParseException e) {
    throw new RuntimeException("Unable to parse query: " + searchQuery, e);
}
```

Once you've expressed the query as a string representation, building a Lucene query with the query parser is a two-step process. The first step is to build a query parser, define the default field targeted in the query, and define the analyzer used during the query building. The default field is used when the targeted fields are not explicit in the query string. It turns out that the authors don't use this feature very often. Next we'll present a more interesting solution. Analyzers are a primary component of Lucene and a key to its flexibility. An analyzer is responsible for breaking sentences into individual words. We'll skip this notion for now and come back to it in greater detail in section 5.2, when you will be more familiar with Hibernate Search and Lucene. The query parser is now ready and can generate Lucene queries out of any syntax-compliant query string. Note that the query hasn't yet been executed.

Lucene provides an improved query parser that allows you to target more than one field at a time automatically. Because Hibernate Search, by default, matches one property to one Lucene field, this query parser turns out to be very useful as a way to finely target which property to search by. Let's see how to use it (see listing 2.11).

Listing 2.11 Using the `MultiFieldQueryParser`

```
String searchQuery = "Batman";
String[] productFields = {"title", "description"}; ◁— Targeted fields

Map<String,Float> boostPerField = new HashMap<String,Float>(2); ◁—┐ Boost
boostPerField.put( "title", (float) 4);                            │ factors
boostPerField.put( "description", (float) 1);                      ┘

QueryParser parser = new MultiFieldQueryParser(  ◁—┐ Build
        productFields,                               │ multifield
        new StandardAnalyzer(),                      │ query parser
        boostPerField                                ┘
);

org.apache.lucene.search.Query luceneQuery;
try {
    luceneQuery = parser.parse(searchQuery);
}
catch (ParseException e) {
    throw new RuntimeException("Unable to parse query: " + searchQuery, e);
}
```

The `MultiFieldQueryParser` allows you to define more than one default field at a time. It becomes very easy to build queries that return all objects matching a given word or set of words in one or more object properties. In our example, the query will try to find *Batman* in either the title or the description field. The `MultiFieldQuery-Parser` also allows you to express the intuitive idea that title is more important than description in the query results. You can assign a different weight (also called *boost factor*) to each targeted field.

2.5.2 *Building the Hibernate Search query*

Our Lucene query is now ready to be executed. The next step is to wrap this query into a Hibernate Search query so that we can live in the full object-oriented paradigm. We already know how to retrieve a `FullTextSession` or `FullTextEntityManager` from a regular `Session` or `EntityManager`. A `FullTextSession` or a `FullTextEntityMan-ager` is the entry point for creating a Hibernate Search query out of a Lucene query (see listing 2.12).

Listing 2.12 Creating a Hibernate Search query

```
FullTextSession ftSession = Search.getFullTextSession(session);

org.hibernate.Query query = ftSession.createFullTextQuery(
        luceneQuery,
        Item.class);  ◁— Return matching Items

query = ftSession.createFullTextQuery(
        luceneQuery);  ◁— Return all matching indexed entities

query = ftSession.createFullTextQuery(
        luceneQuery,
        Item.class,
        Actor.class);  ◁—┐ Return matching
                          │ Items and Actors
```

```
FullTextEntityManager ftEm =
    Search.getFullTextEntityManager(entityManager);

javax.persistence.Query query = ftEm.createFullTextQuery(
        luceneQuery,
        Item.class);
```
Return matching Items

```
javax.persistence.Query query = ftEm.createFullTextQuery(
        luceneQuery);
```
Return all matching indexed entities

```
javax.persistence.Query query = ftEm.createFullTextQuery(
        luceneQuery,
        Item.class,
        Actor.class);
```
Return matching Items and Actors

The query-creation method takes the Lucene query as its first parameter, which isn't really a surprise, but it also optionally takes the class targeted by the query as an additional parameter (see our first example). This method uses a Java 5 feature named varargs. After the mandatory Lucene query parameter, the method can accept any number of Class parameters (from zero to many). If no class is provided, the query will target all entities indexed. If one or more classes are provided, the query will be limited to these classes and their subclasses (Hibernate Search queries are polymorphic, just like Hibernate Query Language [HQL] queries). While most queries target one class, it can be handy in some situations to target more than one entity type and benefit from the unstructured capabilities of Lucene indexes. Note that by restricting the query to a few entity types (and especially one entity type), Hibernate Search can optimize query performance. This should be your preferred choice.

The second interesting point to note is that the query objects are respectively of type org.hibernate.Query or javax.persistence.Query (depending whether you are targeting the Hibernate APIs or the Java Persistence APIs). This is very interesting because it enables a smooth integration with existing Hibernate applications. Anybody familiar with Hibernate or Java Persistence's queries will have no problem executing the query from this point.

2.5.3 Executing a Hibernate Search query

Executing and interacting with a Hibernate Search query is exactly like executing and interacting with an HQL or Java Persistence Query Language (JPA-QL) query simply because they share the same concepts and the same APIs.

Listing 2.13 demonstrates this.

Listing 2.13   Executing a Hibernate Search query

```
//Hibernate Core Query APIs
query.setFirstResult(20).setMaxResults(20);    <— Set pagination
List results = query.list();    <— Execute the query

//Java Persistence Query APIs
query.setFirstResult(20).setMaxResults(20);    <— Set pagination
List results = query.getResultList();    <— Execute the query
```

```
for (Item item : (List<Item>) results) {
    display( "title: " + item.getTitle() + "\nDescription: " +
                item.getDescription() );
}
```

There's no difference here between executing an HQL or JPA-QL query and executing a Hibernate Search query. Specifically, you can use pagination as well as execute the query to return a list, an iterator, or a single result. The behavior and semantic are the same as for the classic queries. Specifically, the returned result is composed of objects from your domain model and not `Documents` from the Lucene API.

The objects returned by the query are part of the Hibernate persistence context. Hibernate will propagate every change made to the returned objects into the database and the index transparently. And, more important, navigating through lazy associations (collections or single-ended associations) is possible transparently, thanks to Hibernate.

While building a query seems like a lot of steps, it's a very easy process. In summary:

1 Build the Lucene query (using one of the query parsers or programmatically).
2 Wrap the Lucene query inside a Hibernate Search query.
3 Optionally set some query properties (such as pagination).
4 Execute the query.

Unfortunately (or fortunately. if you like challenges), queries don't always return what you expect them to return. This could be because indexing didn't happen, or the query you've written doesn't do what you think it should. A tremendously useful tool is available that allows you to have an inside look at the Lucene index and see what queries return. Its name is Luke.

2.6   *Luke: inside look into Lucene indexes*

The most indispensable utility you can have in your arsenal of index troubleshooting tools—in fact it may be the *only* one you need—is Luke. With it you can examine every facet of an index you can imagine. Some of its capabilities are these:

- View individual documents.
- Execute a search and browse the results.
- Selectively delete documents from the index.
- Examine term frequency.

Luke's author is Andrzej Bialecki, and he actively maintains Luke to keep up with the latest Lucene version. Luke is available for download at http://www.getopt.org/luke/, shown in figure 2.3. You can download Luke in several different formats. A Java WebStart JNLP direct download of the most current version is the easiest to retrieve; it's basically automatic. You can also download several .jar file compilations and place them in your classpath any way you want them.

- *lukeall.jar*—Contains Luke, Lucene, Rhino JavaScript, plug-ins, and additional analyzers. This JAR has no external dependencies. Run it with `java -jar luke-all.jar`.

- *lukemin.jar*—A standalone minimal JAR, containing Luke and Lucene. This JAR has no external dependencies either. Run it with `java -jar lukemin.jar`.

- *Individual jars:*
  - luke.jar
  - lucene-core.jar
  - lucene-analyzers.jar
  - lucene-snowball.jar
  - js.jar

Minimum requirements are that at least the core JARs be in your classpath, for example, `java -classpath luke.jar;lucene-core.jar org.getopt.luke.Luke`. Be careful to use the right Luke version for your Lucene version, or Luke might not be able to read the Lucene index schema.

Luke's source code is also available for download from the website shown in figure 2.3 for those of you who want to dig into the real workings of the application.

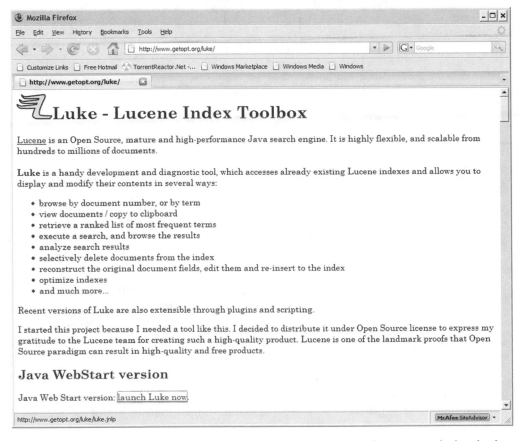

Figure 2.3   Luke's website with download links in various formats along with source code downloads

Let's go on the fifty-cent tour of Luke. We'll start with figure 2.4. The Overview tab is the initial screen when Luke is first started.

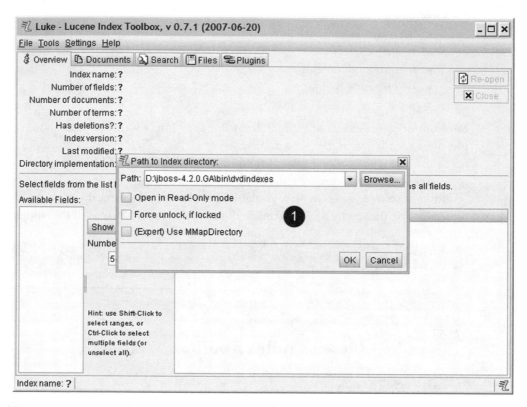

Figure 2.4   Luke's opening screen containing the index path and modes to open it

❶ The Path field contains the operating system path to the index's location and modes you can choose to open the index. A convenient filesystem browser makes navigation easier. Utilizing open modes, you can force *unlock* on an index that may be locked. This could be useful from an administration point of view. Also, you can open the index in read-only mode to prevent making accidental changes. An advanced option allows you to open the index using an `MMapDirectory` instance, which uses nonblocking I/O (NIO) to memory map input files. This mode uses less memory per query term because a new buffer is not allocated per term, which may help applications that use, for example, wildcard queries.

Behind this subwindow you can see the other tabs: Overview, Documents, Search, Files, and Plugins, which are all coming up shortly. Let's move on to the Overview tab. Looking at figure 2.5, you can see a wealth of information in this tab alone.

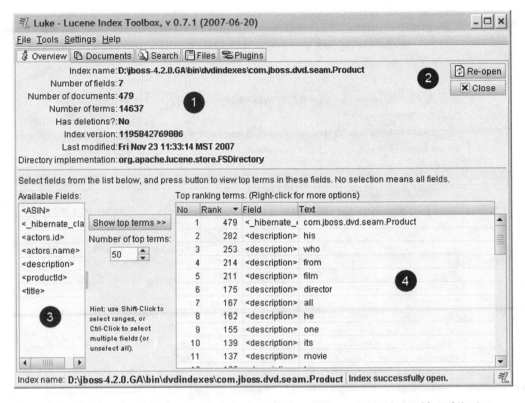

Figure 2.5   The Overview tab showing the index's statistics, fields, and an order ranking of the top terms in the index

❶ The top section is a comprehensive listing of the index's statistics, including last modification date, total number of documents in the index, number of fields, and so on. ❷ is the Re-open button.

NOTE   Documents deleted or updated (a delete followed by an insert in Lucene) are not seen until the index is reopened. When you open an index, you have a snapshot of what was indexed at the time it was opened.

A list of all available fields in the documents is shown at ❸. The field name is the string enclosed in brackets.

❹ is an ordered listing, from the most frequently occurring to the least, of the top terms in the index. From this quadrant of the tab you can do several things. Double-clicking a term transfers you to the Documents tab (we'll talk about that tab next) and automatically inserts the term you double-clicked into the Browse by Term text box. Right-clicking a term in this quadrant gives you several options. Browse Term Docs does the same thing as double-clicking the term: It transfers you to the Documents tab and automatically inserts the term you double-clicked into the Browse by Term text box. Show All Term Docs transfers you to the Search tab (we'll talk about that shortly) and automatically inserts a search based on the Field and Text data in ❸.

Let's move on to the next tab in Luke, the Documents tab. This is shown in figure 2.6.

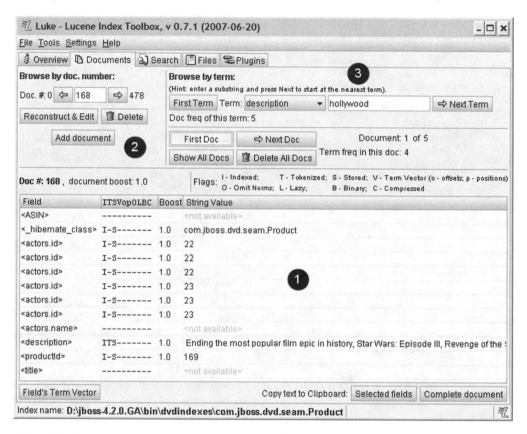

Figure 2.6   The Documents tab, where documents can be stepped through, deleted, and examined

❷ allows you to browse the index's documents by stepping through them one at a time. They are ordered by Lucene's internal document number. You can even add, edit, and delete individual documents by using this quadrant of the tab. The Edit Document screen is shown in figure 2.7. Here you can edit any field in the document. The Stored Original tab will show you the data stored in the index for this document's selected field.

NOTE   If the data is not stored in the index via the Store.YES or Store.COM-PRESS setting, you won't be able to access that data because it's simply not there! You'll see <not available> instead.

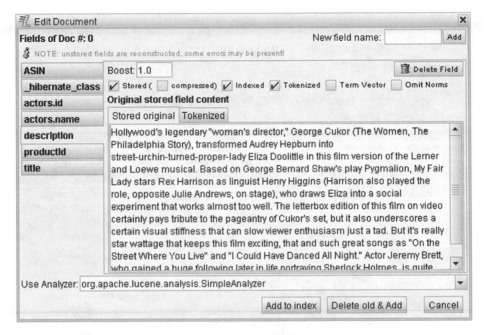

Figure 2.7   The Luke Edit Document screen showing the Stored Original tab

One of the really neat features here is the Tokenized tab. For fields that do store their data in the index, this tab shows the tokenized text based on the analyzer used to index the field.

This is all well and good, but suppose we wanted to browse the index by its terms in term order and not in the order of frequency, as listed in the Documents tab. This is done in the upper-right quadrant ❸ (in figure 2.6) of the tab, Browse by Term, but is not as straightforward as it sounds. Clicking First Term takes you to the first term for that field in the index (alphabetical, numbers first). Of course, Next Term continues forward. Below this button is the document browser. Clicking First Doc takes you to the first document ❶ containing the term in the Browse by Term text box we just talked about. The Show All Docs button takes you to the Search Tab and automatically inserts a search for that field and term in the search window.

NOTE   Be careful with the Delete All Docs button. Be positive about which index you have open before clicking this button. It would be a sad day if you forgot you were looking at the production index!

You may have noticed several terms scattered about this tab like *Doc freq of this term* and *Term freq in this doc*. We'll explain these terms and use them a lot in chapter 12, but for now, don't worry about them. Their meaning will become clear, and they'll mean a lot more then.

We're finally going to discuss the Search tab. This is important because the authors find themselves on this tab the vast majority of time when they're testing the effect of different analyzers, what the stop word effect will be, and the general behavior of a query. Figure 2.8 shows this tab.

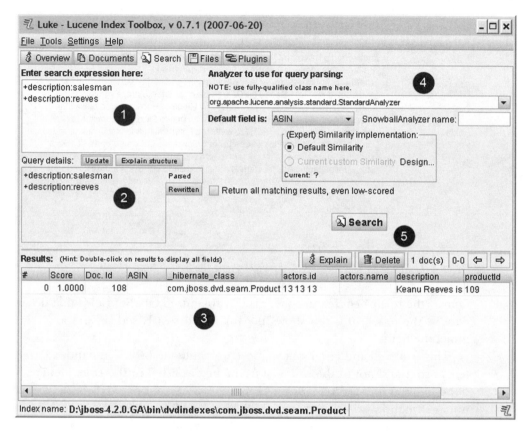

Figure 2.8   The Search tab showing the search window, details, and the results window

❶ is the search window. Here you enter search expressions based on the current index. Searches are expressed utilizing the Lucene query parser syntax. In this example the search is for two terms, both of which must occur in the Description field, and both terms are required (that's what the + signs indicate). A complete discussion of the syntax is given on the Lucene website at http://lucene.apache.org/java/docs/queryparsersyntax.html or in the Lucene documentation available in each distribution. We'll also cover the essential part of this syntax in chapter 7. You must specify the field name of a term (using the `field_name:` syntax) if you wish to query a different field than the one specified in the Default field just under ❹. The uses of the +, -, ~ and other symbols are explained on the website.

After you enter your query in ❶, select the analyzer ❹ to use to parse your query. The default analyzers supported by Luke are:

- StandardAnalyzer
- StopAnalyzer
- WhitespaceAnalyzer
- SimpleAnalyzer

When Luke initializes, it looks in the classpath for any additional analyzers and adds them to the drop-down list. That's how you can test any analyzer that you may have written. All you have to do then is select it from the drop-down list. Then click the Update button between ❶ and ❷, and the parsed query will be shown in the Parsed window ❷. We strongly recommend you get into the habit of doing this because, many times, the analyzer does things a little differently than you think it would. This will save you from heartaches.

The Search button ❺ executes the search displayed in ❷ against the current index and displays the search results in ❸. In this example, a search on the Description field for *salesman* and *reeves* resulted in one matching document, with Lucene ID 108. Double-clicking any matching document will take you back to the Documents tab, with the appropriate information concerning that document being displayed, such as the document number and a vertical listing of the document's fields. Also at ❺ is the Explain button. Clicking this button brings up the Explain window, shown in figure 2.9.

This window shows how the score of a document was calculated against a particular query and what factors were considered. This may not mean much to you now, but when you get into the middle of chapter 12 and we show you exactly what this provides, you'll appreciate it much more. This is especially true if you're one of those who want to modify the way documents are scored.

The next-to-last tab of Luke is the Files tab, shown in figure 2.10. From an administration point of view, this presents a lot of information. First, the Total Index Size value could be important for disk space considerations. Below that is a listing of all the

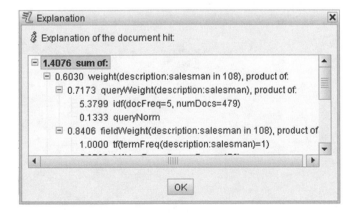

Figure 2.9 The Explain window showing how the document's score was calculated

files associated with the index. There are no right-clicks or double-clicks here. What you see is what you get. This file listing helps with determining whether or not the index needs to be optimized.

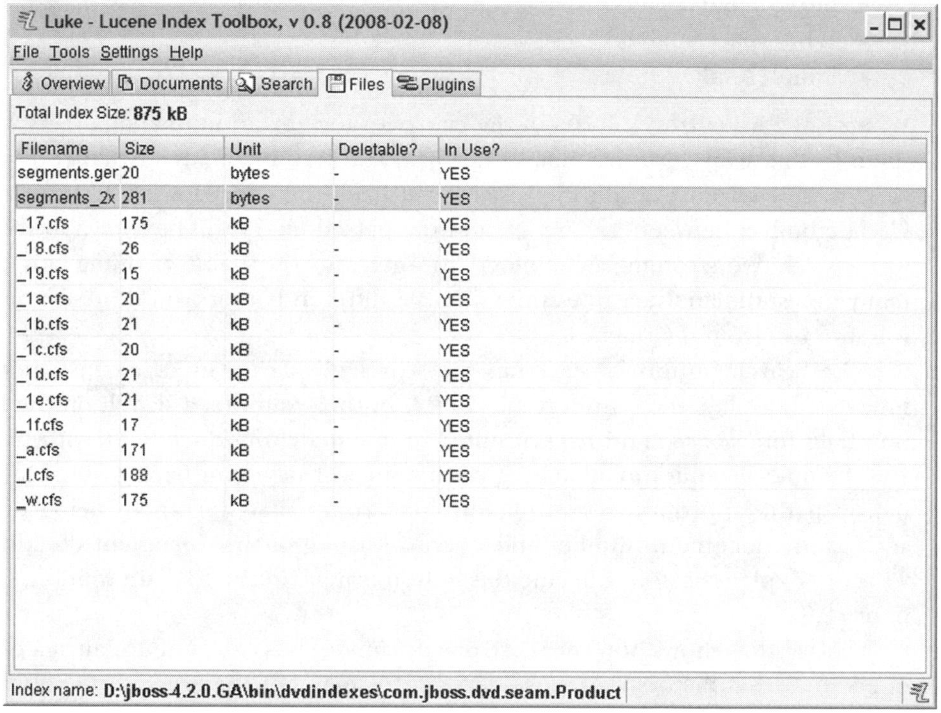

Figure 2.10   This is a listing of all files associated with the currently open index

Remember, the greater the number of segment files (.cfs), the slower searches become, so be sure to optimize. How often you optimize depends on several factors, but this tab will help you determine how often you will need to do it. For more information about optimization, check out section 9.3.

Our last Luke tab is the Plugins tab. This is the developer's tab. Five items on this tab will help you accomplish several things. We're going to show only two of these tabs because they apply more to the discussions we're going to have later in the book. Figure 2.11 shows the Custom Similarity plug-in; this allows you to design and test your own Similarity object which enables you to implement your own document scoring mechanism. You will learn all about this in detail in chapter 12.

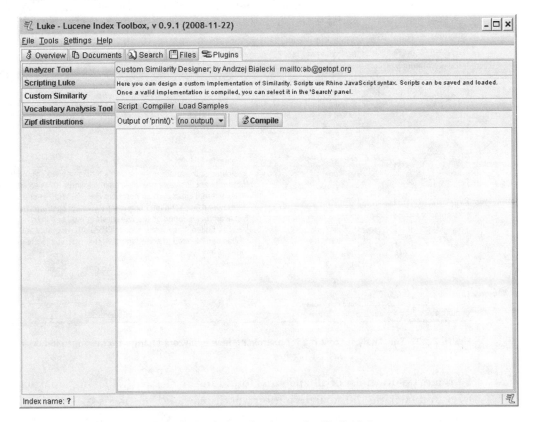

Figure 2.11 The Custom Similarity Designer selection on the Plugins tab

Figure 2.12 shows the Analyzer Tool. This lets you examine exactly how a particular analyzer affects the text that's put into an index.

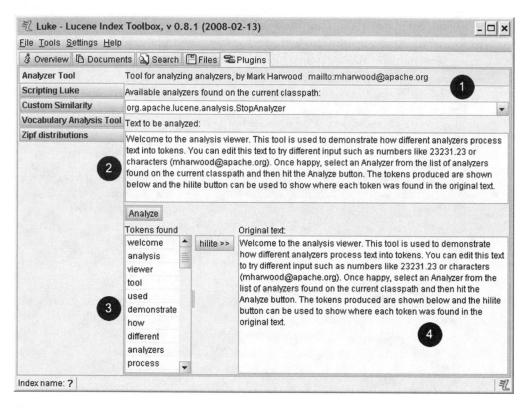

Figure 2.12   The Analyzer Tool tab for examining how analyzers change text put into indexes

❶ is a drop-down list of all analyzers found in the classpath. Picking a particular analyzer and clicking the Analyze button will display a list of tokens ❸ generated by that analyzer from the text you enter in the text window ❷. This makes it quite easy to test an analyzer to see if it generates the tokens you thought it would. Clicking one of the tokens, then clicking the Hilite button will cause that token to be highlighted in the Original Text window ❹.

WARNING   Luke has several known issues when the Java Network Launching Protocol (JNLP) version is used. These are enumerated on the Luke download page. One of these issues is recognizing analyzers on the classpath. When you work with analyzers, the authors recommend that you download one of the standalone Luke versions and work with it.

The best recommendation we can give you for learning how these plug-ins work (and in case you want to write one yourself) is to study Luke's documentation and especially the various plug-ins' source code. Remember, Luke's source code is also available for download from the website.

That's all for Luke right now. Luke is your best friend in the full-text query jungle, so use it!

2.7 Summary

In chapter 1 you saw some of the issues that arise when you try to integrate domain model-centric applications and full-text search technologies (and in particular Lucene). These problems were threefold: a structural mismatch, a synchronization mismatch, and a retrieval mismatch. From what you've seen so far, does Hibernate Search address all these problems?

The first problem we faced was the structural mismatch. The structural mismatch comes in two flavors:

- Convert the rich object-type structure of a domain model into a set of strings.
- Express the relationship between objects at the index level.

Hibernate Search addresses the first problem by allowing you to annotate which property and which entity need to be indexed. From them, and thanks to sensitive defaults, Hibernate Search builds the appropriate Lucene indexes and converts the object model into an indexed model. The fine granularity is a plus because it helps the application developer to precisely define what Lucene needs to process and in which condition. This getting-started guide did not show how Hibernate Search solves the relationship issue, because we have to keep a few subjects for the rest of the book. Don't worry; this problem will be addressed.

The second mismatch involved synchronization: how to keep the database and the index synchronized with each other. Hibernate Search listens to changes executed by Hibernate Core on indexed entities and applies the same operation to the index. That way, the database and index are kept synchronized transparently for the application developer. Hibernate Search also provides explicit indexing APIs, which are very useful for filling the index initially from an existing data set.

The third mismatch was the retrieval mismatch. Hibernate Search provides a match between the Lucene index field names and the property names (out of the box), which helps you to write Lucene queries. The same namespace is used in the object world and the index world. The rest of the Lucene query is entirely up to the application developer. Hibernate Search doesn't hide the underlying Lucene API in order to keep intact all the flexibility of Lucene queries. However, Hibernate Search wraps the Lucene query into a Hibernate query, reusing the Hibernate or Java Persistence APIs to provide a smooth integration into the Hibernate query model. Hibernate Search queries return domain model objects rather than Lucene `Document` instances. Beyond the API alignment, the semantics of the retrieved objects are similar between an HQL query and a full-text query. This makes the migration from one strategy to the other very simple and targeted.

Other than the fundamental mismatches, Hibernate Search doesn't require any specific configuration infrastructure as it integrates into the Hibernate Core configuration scheme and lifecycle. It doesn't require you to list all the indexed entities. We've only started our exploration of Hibernate Search, but you can already feel that this tool focuses on ease of use, has a deep integration with the persistence services, and addresses the mismatch problems of integrating a full-text solution like Lucene into a domain model-centric application.

Hopefully, you want to know more about Hibernate Search and explore more of its functionalities, and there's a lot more to explore. The next chapters of the book are all about making you an expert in Hibernate Search and helping you discover what it can solve for you!

Part 2

Ending structural and synchronization mismatches

In these next three chapters, you will discover how Hibernate Search indexes your objects. Chapter 3 covers the concept of mapping and how to mark an entity and its properties as indexed. Chapter 4, going deeper into the mapping concept, describes how to map relationships between entities and unexpected property types. Chapter 5 tells you where the index information is stored, when and how index operations are performed, and what control you have over them. This chapter also covers the notion of a text analyzer and its relationship to advanced search techniques such as recovering from typos, phonetic approximation, and searching by synonym.

While reading these chapters, you will index your domain model and set up Hibernate Search to answer your searches.

Mapping simple
data structures

This chapter covers

- Index mapping of an entity class and its identity property
- Index mapping of properties (built-in bridge, indexing strategy)
- Using an analyzer

Chapter 2 gave us a very brief introduction to data mapping. This chapter will explain in greater detail each basic mapping structure, the reasoning behind it, and more important, in which situation it is useful. You will learn how to declare an entity as indexable, which properties are indexed in this entity, and what kind of indexing strategy is used. But before that, let's see why mapping is required.

3.1   *Why do we need mapping, again?*

The world in which our primary data structure lives (the object-oriented domain model) has a completely different model than the index structure. Let's talk about a few of the differences highlighted by figure 3.1 and see how those contradictions can be solved.

An object-oriented domain model in Java has a few notable characteristics:

- *It is polymorphic.*   A class can inherit the structure from a superclass.
- *It has a strong type* system.   Each attribute of a class has a type that precisely represents the data. In particular, different data types aren't interchangeable.
- *It has a rich and extensible type system.*   Types can be any of the many built-in types provided by the JRE or a custom one. Specifically, any program can define its own classes.

The Lucene index structure is much more monotonous. An entry is roughly structured as a map (a `Document` in Lucene terminology) containing key value string pairs. Each entry in the Lucene `Document` is called a `Field`, and the key is the `Field` name. Readers familiar with Lucene probably have noticed that this description oversimplifies the actual Lucene model, but it's nevertheless a good first-level approximation. We encourage the curious reader to grab *Lucene in Action* for more information.

Let's highlight some differences with the object model:

- *It is not typed.*   Everything is essentially a string.
- *The type model is not extensible.*   It is not possible to define a custom `Field` type.
- *It is not hierarchical.*   There is no relation between Lucene documents, in particular, no hierarchical relation.
- *It is unstructured.*   Two different documents in the same index can contain different fields.

NOTE   The authors do not imply that the object model is superior to the index model. Both have their respective strengths. In particular, the unstructured nature of the index model provides a great deal of flexibility that's absolutely essential for a multipurpose search engine. As a matter of fact, Hibernate Search heavily depends on the unstructured flexibility provided by Lucene.

Because the two models have conceptual differences in the way they represent data (see figure 3.1), some conversion is necessary when representing the same data in the two models.

Let's explore these differences and see how Hibernate Search reconciles them. We'll deal with three main issues: converting the overall structure, converting types, and defining the fine-grained indexing strategy.

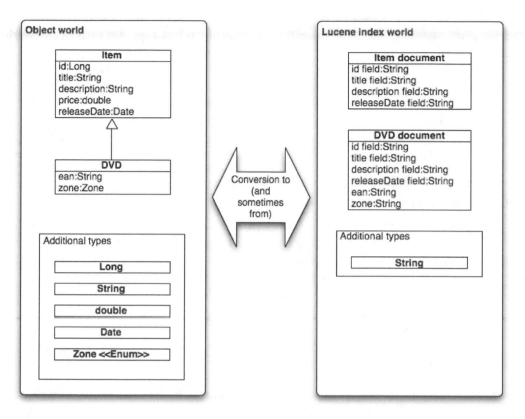

Figure 3.1   Converting the object model (rich type) into the index model (map of strings) leads to several problems.

3.1.1   Converting the structure

The coarse-grained element we want to index is the entity. In the object world, it is represented as a class instance. Hibernate Search represents each class instance as a Lucene Document instance, a Document being the atomic piece of information retrievable by a Lucene search. Queries will then retrieve entities corresponding to the Document instances.

Java classes can be subclassed and, thanks to that, inherit the data structure from their superclass. Unfortunately, Lucene Documents have no notion of subclassing. Even worse, it's impossible to execute queries on correlated Documents because such a notion doesn't exist in Lucene. This isn't a problem in practice, and Hibernate Search maps each subclass instance in its own Document. The Document for a given subclass will contain the data from the subclass attributes as well as the data from all the mapped superclass's attributes. Think of this mapping strategy as a denormalized model. For people familiar with Hibernate's inheritance-mapping strategies, you can see this as equivalent to the table-per-concrete-class mapping strategy.

You now know how Hibernate Search maps the coarse-grained structure of domain models. Let's discuss how each entity attribute is mapped into the Lucene world. Each attribute or property considered to be indexed is mapped as a Lucene field whose default name will be the property name. While the Lucene field name can be overridden, as we will show later, the authors recommend you not do it because the one-to-one mapping between a property name and a field name will make it easier both to write and, more importantly, read Lucene queries.

One-to-one mappings can be made between a property and a field, but how does Hibernate Search convert the Java type into a string—the only type searchable by Lucene?

3.1.2 Converting types

As previously described, the only type Lucene can "speak" is string. Unfortunately (or fortunately, depending on how you see things), in Java, attributes can be of many different types. A URL is treated differently from a date or a number. Numbers are represented by different types depending on what they represent and their range of expectation, from `short` for small integer numbers up to `BigDecimal` for arbitrary-precision decimal numbers.

Hibernate Search needs to convert each possible type into a string representation. For that, Hibernate Search has the notion of *field bridge*. A field bridge is a bridge between the Java type and its representation in the Lucene `Field`, or, to make it simpler, a bridge between a Java object and its string representation.

Hibernate Search comes with a set of built-in field bridges for most of the Java standard types. But it isn't limited to them. In the next chapter we'll explore how you can further extend Hibernate Search support by writing a custom field bridge.

Once a type is converted into a string, the value needs to be indexed.

> **What about null?**
>
> Hibernate Search, by default, doesn't represent null attributes in the index. Lucene doesn't have the notion of null fields; the field is simply not there. Hibernate Search could offer the ability to use a special string as a null marker to still be able to search by "null" values.
>
> But before you jump at the Hibernate Search team's throats, you need to understand why they have not offered this feature so far. Null is not a value per se. Null means that the data is not known (or doesn't make sense). Therefore, searching by null as if it were a value is somewhat odd. The authors are well aware that this is a raging debate, especially among the relational model experts (see http://en.wikipedia.org/wiki/Null_%28SQL%29).
>
> Whenever you feel the need to searching by "null," ask yourself if storing a special marker value in the database would make more sense. If you store a special marker value in the database, a lot of the "null" inconsistencies vanish. It also has the side effect of being queriable in Lucene and Hibernate Search.

3.1.3 Defining the indexing strategy

We've pretty much described how Hibernate Search stores the object structure in the index, but we haven't considered how Lucene should index the data. Lucene offers various strategies on how to index data. Each influences the kind of query that will be available to you. It's important to have a global understanding of these strategies and, of course, to be able to choose among them. We'll discuss those strategies while walking through the Hibernate Search mapping metadata.

Even before thinking about the fine-grained indexing strategies, the first question you should ask is, "Should I index this data?" Or more accurately, "Should I be able to search by this data?" At a coarse-grained level, systematically indexing all your entities makes little sense; only those useful for retrieving information searched by your users should be marked for indexing. This is true as well at the fine-grained level. Not all properties deserve to be indexed. While they could be indexed, and while a query could easily filter them out, you should be aware that excluding them will speed up the following:

- *Indexing time*—Index time is directly correlated to the amount of data to index.
- *Search time*—While the index size doesn't linearly affect the search query time, it has an influence.
- *Some clustering strategies*—The smaller the index is, the faster replication will be.

Fortunately, Hibernate Search makes it intuitive during the mapping to select the relevant part to index.

Enough theory and concepts for now. Since we know why a mapping is needed, let's discover how to map the data structure. The next section will describe how to map the coarse-grained level: an entity.

3.2 Mapping entities

Let's describe the steps required to transform a boring Hibernate entity into a colorful indexed entity. To help us stay concrete, we'll come back to the online store example we started in chapter 2. We want to sell DVDs online; the DVD data structure is represented by a Dvd class.

We'll first explore what makes an entity indexed and what is happening behind the scenes.

3.2.1 Marking an entity as indexed

All Hibernate Search mapping metadata are described through annotations.

NOTE WHY USE ANNOTATIONS?   Hibernate Search metadata is very code-centric and shares a lot of information with the class structure: Annotations are a natural fit and avoid much redundancy compared to other metadata models such as XML. It would be quite simple to add XML deployment descriptor support for Hibernate Search. Nobody has found the time and interest to write this layer (so far), which seems to indicate that the Hibernate Search community doesn't strongly desire this feature.

NOTE All Hibernate Search annotations are contained in the `org.hiber-nate.search.annotations` package.

To mark an entity as indexed by Hibernate Search, place the `@Indexed` annotation on the class, as shown in listing 3.1.

Listing 3.1 An entity is indexed by Hibernate Search when marked @Indexed

```
@Entity
@Indexed          ◁─┐    Mark the entity as
public class Dvd {       @Indexed
    ...
}
```

Much information is inferred, and a lot of work is triggered from this single annotation. When the Hibernate `SessionFactory` bootstraps, Hibernate Search looks for all mapped entities marked as `@Indexed` and processes them. We don't have to explicitly list the indexed entities in a configuration file. This reduces work and limits the risk of mistakes.

The Lucene directory name is also inferred from this annotation. Because we haven't explicitly defined an index name, the default naming convention applies. The index name is the fully qualified class name of the entity, in our example `com.man-ning.hsia.dvdstore.model.Dvd`. You can override this name by using the `name` attribute of `@Indexed` (see Listing 3.2).

Listing 3.2 Overriding an indexed name to refine the targeted Lucene Directory.

```
@Entity
@Indexed(name="Item")  ◁─┐    Index names can
public class Dvd {             be customized
    ...
}
```

The underlying mapping between a Hibernate Search index name and a physical Lucene `Directory` depends entirely on the directory provider (see section 5.1). Let's explore the two most common scenarios: the in-memory directory provider (`RAM-DirectoryProvider`) and the filesystem directory provider (`FSDirectoryProvider`).

Indexes using the `RAMDirectoryProvider` are uniquely identified by their index name for a given `SessionFactory` (`EntityManagerFactory` if you use Java Persistence). Hibernate Search keeps one instance of `RAMDirectoryProvider` per index name and per `SessionFactory` (or `EntityManagerFactory`).

When using `FSDirectoryProvider`, the index name represents the path to the physical filesystem directory. Relative paths are prefixed with the `indexBase` property.

It's perfectly safe to share the same physical Lucene directory among several entities; Hibernate Search partitions the information. If you want to share the same physical Lucene directory across several entities, they need to share the same `@Indexed.name` value (as well as the same `DirectoryProvider` type), like `Dvd` and `Drink` in listing 3.3.

Listing 3.3 Indexed entity sharing the same underlying Lucene `Directory`

```
@Entity
@Indexed(name="Item")        ◁———  The same index name is
public class Dvd {                  shared by both entities
    ...
}

@Entity
@Indexed(name="Item")
public class Drink {
    ...
}
```

The same logical name points to the same physical configuration in Hibernate Search, effectively sharing the index structure.

Should I share the same Lucene directory for all my entities?

Usually this is not necessary.

Sharing the same index will help to optimize queries because Hibernate Search will have to handle fewer file resources at the same time. This is particularly true when the amount of indexed data is low. On the other hand, the query is slightly more complex when an index is shared, because Hibernate Search needs to filter by class type. In addition, when the amount of data starts to grow significantly, splitting the index into several smaller ones will help Lucene to scale; each write lock is applied to a smaller portion of the data, which helps to maintain a good level of scalability. By default, Hibernate Search indexes each entity type in its own index and offers the possibility of using more indexes for the same entity through what is called *index sharding* (see chapter 9).

The gain provided by sharing the directory is usually not significant enough to make a difference. Maintenance might be a stronger criterion, but you can see the glass half full or half empty:

- Having one index per entity helps maintainability and allows incremental rebuild if something goes wrong on an index file.
- Having one single index (arguably) reduces complexity for operation people.

Hibernate Search lets you do what you prefer. The defaults provide good performance most of the time. Make sure you consider ease of development when you make your choice. Everything normalized in a simple and standard way will save you time. The authors generally use the Hibernate Search defaults.

Entity structures can be more complex than the previous example, especially when subclasses are involved.

3.2.2 Subclasses

Hibernate Search, just like Hibernate, is fully polymorphic and lets you map hierarchies of classes as well as express polymorphic queries. In practice, this means that you can write classes and subclasses in your domain model without worrying about Hibernate Search. Back to our store example, our client forgot to tell us that on top of DVDs, the website also has to sell food such as popcorn and drinks such as wine. (I don't know about popcorn, but chilling out with a glass of decent wine in front of a good movie is definitely something I'd be willing to pay for.) We'll refactor our domain model to cope with this new requirement. The website will see `Items` that will be declined in `Dvds`, `Food`, and `Drinks` (see listing 3.4).

Listing 3.4   Mapping a class and its subclass

```
@Entity                           ◁    Superclasses don't
public abstract class Item {           have to be marked
                                       @Indexed
    @Id @GeneratedValue
    @DocumentId
    private Integer id

    @Field                        ◁    Superclasses can
    private String title;              contain indexed
                                       properties
    ...
}
                          Concrete subclasses
@Entity                   are marked @Indexed
@Indexed              ◁
public class Drink extends Item {

    @Field(index=Index.UN_TOKENIZED)
    private boolean alcoholicBeverage;

    ...
}

@Entity
@Indexed
public class Dvd extends Item {

    @Field(index=Index.UN_TOKENIZED)
    private String ean;

    ...
}
```

Hibernate Search will index not only marked properties of a given class but also all marked properties of its superclass. In listing 3.4, the `Drink` entity will be searchable by the following properties:

- `alcoholicBeverage` from `Drink`
- `id` from `Item`
- `title` from `Item`

> **Can I map a view?**
>
> In Hibernate Core, the typical way to map a table view is to map a special entity onto that view. For Hibernate Core, a view is no different from any other regular table. If you cannot materialize the view in your database, you typically use the `@Loader` annotation to describe the SQL query used to load the entity. In both cases, the entity is read-only (and typically marked as `@Immutable`). Any change to the underlying data requires you to reload the entity.
>
> You can index such view entities by marking them as `@Indexed`. Unfortunately, Hibernate Search doesn't know when such an entity changes, because everything happens in the database, and it cannot keep the index updated for you. Use the manual indexing API described in section 5.4 to manually reindex your data efficiently. This is particularly efficient when the data constituting the view doesn't change frequently; in this case, the frequency at which you need to reindex will be reduced.
>
> Note that when using modern JDBC drivers and databases, the difference between a physical database view and a prepared statement is quite minimal, because both are prepared in advance. You can simply map your entity on SQL statements for CRUD (create read update delete) operations without having to use a view.

You might have noticed that the `Item` entity is *not* marked as `@Indexed`. While marking `Item` with `@Indexed` will do no harm, it's not necessary. You should mark entities with `@Indexed` only when:

- You want to be able to search by this entity.
- The entity is of a concrete type (not abstract).

In our system, `Item` is an abstract class and will have no instances of it. If you look back at figure 3.1, you'll see that subclasses are denormalized in the Lucene index: All instances of `Drink` will be indexed in the `org.manning.hsia.dvdstore.model.Drink` index, including the information about its superclass's properties `id` and `title`.

NOTE   Denormalization doesn't prevent you from executing polymorphic queries. As you'll see later in this book, you can search for all `Items` whose `title` contains *valley*. Both the DVD *In the Valley of Elah* and *Napa valley wines* will show up even if `Item` hasn't been marked with `@Indexed`.

Hibernate Search doesn't read metadata annotations from interfaces, but you can, of course, map the implementation class and its properties.

3.2.3   *Mapping the primary key*

The data linking an object instance, a database row, and a Lucene `Document`, besides the entity type, is the identity property (named *primary key* in the database). Hibernate Search requires you to mark the identity property in a given class hierarchy. This property will be stored in the index structure and is one of the properties you'll be able to query by in a full-text query. Have a look at listing 3.5.

Listing 3.5   Mark the `identifier` property as the Lucene `Document` id

```
@Entity
@Indexed
public class Dvd {

    @Id @GeneratedValue                    Mark the id property
    @DocumentId                            with @DocumentId
    private Integer id;

    ...

}
```

Marking a property as the identifier property is as simple as annotating it with @DocumentId. You can use this property in your full-text queries, but be aware that this property is untokenized and stored in the index. Why is that? Hibernate Search needs to find a Lucene Document by its exact entity identifier in order to be able to update its content when the entity instance changes. It also needs to read the identifier value out of the index to retrieve the object from the persistence context. If you need to query the tokenized property, consider using the technique described in section 3.3.4.

NOTE   PRIMARY KEY AND CLASS HIERARCHY   Just like a Hibernate Core entity hierarchy, an indexed class hierarchy can contain only one primary key declaration. If you try to use @DocumentId more than once in a class hierarchy, an exception will be thrown.

Some legacy database models require composite primary keys. At the time when this book was written, Hibernate Search didn't support composite identifiers out of the box. But thanks to the flexible field bridge model, you can work around this limitation. While implementing the actual field bridge is explained in section 4.1.4, we'll take a look at the mapping structure now.

Listing 3.6   Using a composite identifier through a custom `FieldBridge`

```
@Entity
@Indexed
public class Person {                 The property is a
                                      composite identifier    Mark the property as a
    @EmbeddedId                                               document id
    @DocumentId
    @FieldBridge(impl = PersonPKBridge.class)
    private PersonPK id;                                      Convert to something
                                                             chewable by Lucene
    ...

}

@Embeddable
public class PersonPK implements Serializable {

    private String firstName;
    private String lastName;

    ...

}
```

The noticeable element is the `@FieldBridge` annotation. The `PersonPKBridge` class referenced by `@FieldBridge` does the conversion between the composite property and its Lucene index representation (back and forth). This class must implement either `TwoWayFieldBridge` or `TwoWayStringBridge`. We'll show a possible implementation in section 4.1.4.

Marking a nonidentifier property as a document id is not supported by Hibernate Search (and probably has little use).

We're starting to map the object structure into an index structure, but what is the index structure, and how does Hibernate Search physically store the entity into the Lucene index?

3.2.4 Understanding the index structure

Indexing is a complex process, and it sometimes doesn't do what you'd expect it to do. This section will show you the Lucene index structure that Hibernate Search uses. This will help you to dig faster into the index and diagnose what's going wrong. The must-have tool in the Lucene world for diving into the index internals is Luke. If you haven't read the introduction to Luke from section 2.6, we strongly encourage you to do so now.

Let's take the mapping we used in section 3.2.2. We've mapped two entities, `Dvd` and `Drink`, both inheriting from the `Item` superclass. Luke must read the Lucene directory from a filesystem; unfortunately, it's not possible to configure Luke to read in-memory directories. Our project will then use the default `FSDirectoryProvider`, as shown in listing 3.7. Don't forget to set the `indexBase` property.

Listing 3.7 Configuring Hibernate Search to store Lucene indexes on a filesystem

```
<hibernate-configuration>
  <session-factory>

    <property name="hibernate.search.default.directory_provider">
      org.hibernate.search.store.FSDirectoryProvider          Define the
    </property>                                                directory
    <property name="hibernate.search.default.indexBase">       provider
        ./build/indexes          Define the root
    </property>                  directory
    ...

    <mapping class="com.manning.hsia.dvdstore.model.Item"/>
    <mapping class="com.manning.hsia.dvdstore.model.Dvd"/>
    <mapping class="com.manning.hsia.dvdstore.model.Drink"/>
  </session-factory>
</hibernate-configuration>
```

If you look into the ./build/indexes directory (which should be relative to the directory where your Java program started), you'll see two subdirectories:

- com.manning.hsia.dvdstore.model.Drink
- com.manning.hsia.dvdstore.model.Dvd

TIP   If you deploy on JBoss AS, you can use the following `indexBase` value: `../server/[configuration]/data/indexes`. Indexes will be kept next to the hypersonic database content.

Unless you override the index name in `@Indexed`, Hibernate Search creates one index directory per `@Indexed` entity, each index directory name corresponding to the fully qualified class name of the entity class. `Item` doesn't have a Lucene index on its own because the entity isn't marked as `@Indexed`. Using Luke on the `Drink` index and looking at the first document, we see the screen shown in figure 3.2.

Each row represents a Lucene field in the document. Since `Drink` inherits `Item`, we expect to see `title`, `description` (which are denormalized from `Item`), and `alcoholicBeverage`. Note that their values are not stored in the index; the next section will explain why. `id` is the identifier property found in `Item`. Luke confirms to us the indexing strategy required for identifier properties: They are stored, indexed, but not tokenized. All these properties were expected.

`_hibernate_class` was, however, not expected: There is no `_hibernate_class` in `Drink` nor in any of its superclasses. In each document (which represents an entity instance), Hibernate Search stores the entity type (in our case `com.man-ning.hsia.dvdstore.model.Drink`).

Thanks to the identifier property and the entity type in each document, Hibernate Search can:

- Remove the indexed data for a specific entity instance
- Share the same index directory for multiple entity types
- Load an entity from the persistence context from a Lucene query result

In very specific situations, it's quite appropriate to use the `_hibernate_class` property in queries, especially to go beyond what vanilla polymorphism can do. You can reference this special field name in your code by using `DocumentBuilder.CLASS_FIELDNAME`.

You know how to map an entity and that `@Indexed` and `@DocumentId` are the only two mandatory elements. Hibernate Search lets us play nicely with polymorphic domain models and deal with the underlying Lucene index structure.

Doc #: 0 Flags:	I – Indexed; T – Tokenized; S – Stored; V – Term Vector (o – offsets; p – positions) O – Omit Norms; L – Lazy; B – Binary; C – Compressed		
Field	ITSVopOLBC	Norm	String Value
<_hibernate_class>	I-S-------	1.0	com.manning.hsia.dvdstore.model.Drink
<alcoholicBeverage>	----------	--	<not present or not stored>
<description>	----------	--	<not present or not stored>
<id>	I-S-------	1.0	2
<title>	----------	--	<not present or not stored>

Figure 3.2   First document in the `Drink` index showing the `id` property and the special `_hibernate_class` property

All this would be of little use without the ability to index properties. It would be like having a car with no wheel, no seat, no gas pedal, and no cup holder (maybe not that last one): pretty useless. This is the subject of the next section. As a matter of fact, the last few paragraphs already dangerously flirted with the idea of property mapping.

3.3   *Mapping properties*

Some properties in your domain model deserve to be indexed and further searched, but not all of them. Mapping defines which property is selected at a fine-grained level. Mapping properties as indexed is like highlighting parts of a text with a marker: You select which information is relevant for future search requests (see figure 3.3).

Instead of using a marker, you use annotations to mark the properties that need to be indexed. Unlike a regular highlighter, Hibernate Search can guess the type of the annotated property and find the right object-to-string converter. Just as using different highlight colors lets you define different contexts, Hibernate Search annotations let you refine the mapping strategy. Let's explore the various possibilities.

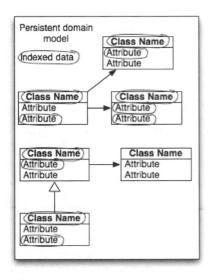

Figure 3.3   Mapping properties is like highlighting the important information.

3.3.1   *Marking a property as indexed*

Hibernate Search can indifferently read the property values from the attribute or from the getter method. When annotations are placed on the attribute, the attribute access is used. When annotations are placed on the getter method, getter access is used. Nothing fancy here! In this book, we refer to properties for either attributes or getters (Java should have had first-class property support from the ground up, but that's another story). Attributes and getters can be of any visibility (from private to public). Choosing one strategy over another is a matter of taste. While the authors tend to prefer the getter access strategy because it properly mimics a true property support, it's more important to keep one consistent access strategy across the board and, if possible, aligned with the Hibernate Core access strategy. Let's explore that in listing 3.8.

To mark a property as indexed, annotate it with @Field.

Listing 3.8   @Field marks a property as indexed.

```
@Entity
@Indexed
public class Item {

    @Id @GeneratedValue
```

```
@DocumentId
private Integer id;                         Title property is indexed
                                            in the title field
@Field
private String title;

@Field
private String description;                 Annotation placed
                                            on field: field
...                                         access is used

@Field
public String getEan() {                    Annotation placed on
    return this.ean;                        getter: getter access
}                                           is used
}
```

In listing 3.8, as you can see, both attribute and getter access are supported. We marked the `title` and `description` fields as well as the `ean` getter. Each property will be added to the Lucene document representing the `Item` instance. The field name will, by default, match the property name. You can override the default Lucene field name by using `@Field.name`. This isn't recommended because the one-to-one matching between the property name and the Lucene field makes writing queries very natural.

It can be handy, however, if you're sharing the index with third-party applications or if you need to map the same property multiple times (see section 3.3.4).

While we know how to mark a property as indexed, how does the actual index operation happen? How is the object data converted into a string structure suitable for Lucene? Bridges are responsible for the conversion between the two worlds.

3.3.2   *Built-in bridges*

A field bridge is the Hibernate Search infrastructure responsible for bridging the object world to the index world. Each property value will be passed to a field bridge, which will add it into the Lucene `Document` representing the entity instance. Bridges convert an object type into a string. Some field bridges also know how to convert the string back into the original object structure (which, you'll see later, is useful for identity properties and projected fields).

The field bridge infrastructure is one of the pillars of Hibernate Search's flexibility, and you can write you own. The set of built-in bridges will be sufficient for most of your indexed properties. Hibernate Search tries to match automatically a built-in bridge from the return type of a property. These rules are described in table 3.1.

This list might evolve over time, so we encourage you to check the Hibernate Search reference documentation for the most up-to-date information. You can find the reference documentation in each Hibernate Search distribution. Most of the time, the result is straightforward: When Hibernate Search recognizes a supported property type, it uses the appropriate field bridge. We need to mention a few points:

- Comparison in Lucene between two property values
- Dates
- The special case of `null`

Table 3.1 Built-in bridges and their associated mapping

Java type	Built-in bridge	Description
String	StringBridge	no-op
short/Short	ShortBridge	Uses `toString()`, not comparable
int/Integer	IntegerBridge	Uses `toString()`, not comparable
long/Long	LongBridge	Uses `toString()`, not comparable
float/Float	FloatBridge	Uses `toString()`, not comparable
double/Double	DoubleBridge	Uses `toString()`, not comparable
BigDecimal	BigDecimalBridge	Uses `toString()`, not comparable
BigInteger	BigIntegerBridge	Uses `toString()`, not comparable
boolean/Boolean	BooleanBridge	String value: "true"/"false"
Class	ClassBridge	Uses `class.getName()`
Enum	EnumBridge	Uses `enum.name()`
URL	UrlBridge	Uses `toString()`
URI	UriBridge	Uses `toString()`
Date	DateBridge	The string representation depends on `@DateBridge`'s `resolution` parameter. Converting `Date` into string and back is not guaranteed to be idempotent.

In Lucene everything is a string. This is particularly true for comparisons. Lucene compares data on two occasions:

- When a Lucene query sorts results by field value rather than by relevance
- When a ranged query is expressed (for example, return products sold between 10 and 20 €)

Because everything is a string in Lucene, comparisons can be a bit surprising at times. For example, the number 2 is higher than 12. This is why numbers are marked as not comparable in table 3.1. We'll find a way to bring back sanity to number comparison in the next chapter when we talk about custom bridges. When using comparisons, always be aware of how the bridge stores data in the index, and remember that it will end up being a string comparison.

Dates are the second topic worth a special mention. Unfortunately, the JDK doesn't have great support for date and time. `java.util.Date` is used to represent everything:

- Date (as in day)
- Time (as in hour and minute)
- Exact period of time (date and time)

The Date object carries all the precision all the time, and only the application knows (sometimes) the context in which Date is used and the expected precision. In the Lucene index, it's not always necessary to store the exact precision all the time. This is particularly true for ranged queries. Lucene's internal implementation of RangeQuery replaces a range restriction by a query of all terms in the index matching this range (for a given field). For example, if we look for dates between 2004 and 2005, and if five elements match this range, the range query will be replaced by a Boolean query matching these five items. The number of matching elements can be quite large if the precision is high, slowing down the query. If your date has a monthly precision, you cannot have more than 12 matching terms for a range encompassing one year; a precision by the minute raises potential matching terms up to 525,600! This problem is also described in section 7.3.4.

Hibernate Search lets you pick the date precision you wish from year to millisecond. The data indexed in Lucene will be up to the precision. When mapping a Date property, you must annotate it with the @DateBridge annotation, as shown in listing 3.9.

Listing 3.9   Mapping a `Date` property

```
@DateBridge( resolution = Resolution.DAY )      ◁─┐  Precision stored in
private Date birthdate;                            │  the index: day

@DateBridge( resolution = Resolution.MINUTE )   ◁─┐  Precision stored in
private Date flightArrival;                        │  the index: minute
```

Dates are stored in the index in absolute format GMT. Depending on the resolution, the format goes from yyyy for year precision up to yyyyMMddHHmmssSSS for millisecond precision. As you can see, comparison between dates is possible with this scheme.

Null is an interesting topic in the persistence field and, to this day, is still debated by experts. Remember we described the meaning of null as either "I don't know the value" or "It is not applicable in this case." For this reason, Hibernate Search does not index null values (see the note "What about null?" in section 3.1.2 for more details). While the authors do not recommend doing so, it's possible to write custom field bridges that store a special queriable marker in lieu of null. At this point you should consider using the same marker in your database as well and avoid the mismatch between your database and the index.

Now that we've reassured you about Hibernate Search taking care of object conversion and have warned you about some of the gotchas, we'll focus on how Lucene indexes this data.

3.3.3   Choosing an indexing strategy

Lucene offers flexibility in how the data is stored and indexed. Depending on the kind of query you want to apply to a given property and on the type of data, one indexing strategy will better fit your needs.

TO TOKENIZE OR NOT TO TOKENIZE

Most of the problems full-text searching aims to address revolve around words:

- Searching for matching words within a sentence
- Finding words matching the same root (*matched* and *matching*, for example)
- Finding words having a similar meaning (for example, *car* and *vehicle*)

To solve these problems, Lucene must identify each word in a document to process it later on. This process is called *tokenizing*. A property that goes through this process is said to be *tokenized*, and each individual word can be queried. This (TOKEN-IZED) is the default operation applied when @Field is used. In listing 3.10, description is tokenized.

Listing 3.10 Indexing a property using the tokenized strategy

```
@Entity
@Indexed
public class Item {
    ...

    @Field                                  A description is
    private String description;    ⊲┘      tokenized
}
```

In some cases the data should be indexed unaltered. Any kind of unique identifier property (and first among them the identifier property matching the database's primary key) should not be tokenized but rather indexed as is. Queries will then be able to target the exact value. Why should unique identifiers remain intact? You certainly don't want identifiers containing spaces, numbers, and case-sensitive data to be scrambled; they would no longer be searchable by their exact value. Dates and numbers might also be a type of data that shouldn't be tokenized. The tokenization process is governed by analyzers, some of which ignore numbers altogether (see section 3.4.1 for more details).

Properties that will be used to sort query results (to sort by property rather than by relevance) must not be tokenized either but must be indexed. You then need to use the UN_TOKENIZED indexing strategy on such properties.

To index a property without using the tokenized process, use the @Field.index property, as shown in listing 3.11.

Listing 3.11 Indexing a property and avoiding the tokenization process

```
@Entity
@Indexed
public class Dvd {
    ...

    @Field(index=Index.UN_TOKENIZED)
    private String ean;          ⊲──  A ean is not tokenized
}
```

The `Index` enum contains two more values: `NO` and `NO_NORMS`.

`NO` can be used to ask Lucene not to index the property. This is useful in case you want to store the value in the Lucene index to allow property projection (see section 11.4) but have no need to search by this particular property. Not indexing the data will save both indexing time and space in the index.

`NO_NORMS` is an advanced feature that you shouldn't use without extra knowledge of Lucene. The `NO_NORMS` option will avoid the tokenization process and avoid storing useful data used to compute the score (the relevance) of a matching document in a query result. While this saves some memory space, it also reduces the feature set.

Indexing is one thing, but you might sometimes need to store the original value in the index for the sake of retrieving it. Hibernate Search lets you do just that.

STORING THE DATA IN THE INDEX

In Lucene, you can index data without storing it in the index. In most cases, the data is retrieved elsewhere, and duplicating the data is unnecessary. By default, Hibernate Search doesn't store the property value in the Lucene index. This is unnecessary because the entities are hydrated from the persistence context (the `Session` or the `EntityManager`). On some occasions, however, it is significantly faster to retrieve the information from the Lucene index itself. Queries retrieving the data from the Lucene index are called *projections* (see chapter 11). Every projected property must be stored in the Lucene index. Storing the value in the index can also be useful if third-party applications access the same Lucene index. To enable data storing, use `@Field.store`, as in listing 3.12.

Listing 3.12   Storing a property value in the index, enabling projection queries

```
@Entity
@Indexed
public class Item {
    ...

    @Field(store=Store.YES)
    private String title;      ◁——— Title value is stored in the index
}
```

Don't store every single property, though. Doing so takes up space in the Lucene index and consumes more input/output, and the field bridges used must obey the `TwoWayFieldBridge` or `TwoWayStringBridge` contract (see section 4.1 for more information).

You can decide to store the value in a compressed manner. This saves some space in the Lucene index at the expense of more CPU consumption at reading and writing time. To store a property in a compressed manner, use the `Store.COMPRESS` value. In listing 3.13, the title is stored as compressed in the index.

Listing 3.13 Storing a property value as compressed in the Lucene index

```
@Entity
@Indexed
public class Item {
    ...
    @Field(store=Store.COMPRESS)        A title value is stored
    private String title;               compressed in the index
}
```

You can also store statistical information about the indexed data.

EXTRACTING STATISTICAL INFORMATION: TERMVECTORS

By default, Lucene stores the necessary information it needs to answer your queries. But your application can look at statistical information on a given field in a given document and extract a few interesting things, for example:

- List of terms (words) used
- Number of occurrences for each term
- Positions in the field (roughly the number of words before a given term)
- Offset in the field (start and end): the position in the string where the term starts and stops

This kind of information can be useful when:

- Doing "more like this" queries
- Highlighting the matching sections

NOTE The term vector feature is available only in Hibernate Search 3.1 and above.

This statistical data isn't stored by default in the Lucene index because it takes space and time to compute. But you can enable it on a per-field basis. Use `@Field.termVector` to choose which data to store:

- `TermVector.NO` (default)—Does not store statistical information
- `TermVector.YES`—Stores terms and their number of occurrences
- `TermVector.WITH_OFFSETS`—Stores terms, their number of occurrences, and the offset information
- `TermVector.WITH_POSITIONS`—Stores terms, their number of occurrences, and the position information
- `TermVector.WITH_POSITION_OFFSETS`—Stores terms, their number of occurrences, and both position and offset information

Listing 3.14 gives a usage example.

Listing 3.14   Storing statistical information for a field

```
@Entity
@Indexed
public class Item {
    ...
                                                    Store occurrence
    @Field(termVector=TermVector.YES)  ←——————     statistics
    private String title;
}
```

Section 12.4.3 gives more information on how to extract and use these statistics. You know a lot about indexing properties now, but we haven't yet shown you how to index the same property multiple times.

3.3.4   *Indexing the same property multiple times*

Indexing the same property multiple times may sound like a waste of time and index space, but it's very handy in specific situations. You've seen that properties used for sorting at query time must not be tokenized because doing so significantly diminishes how you can query given properties. In particular you cannot benefit from the ability to search by word in such properties.

You can work around this limitation by indexing the property multiple times (see listing 3.15).

Listing 3.15   Indexing the same property with different indexing strategies

```
@Entity
@Indexed
public class Item {
    ...                                             Same property
    @Fields({                                       indexed multiple
        @Field(index=Index.TOKENIZED),  ←——————     times
        @Field(name="title_sort", index=Index.UN_TOKENIZED)  ←—┐
    })                                                Use a different
    private String title;                               field name
```

Note that the additional properties must be explicitly named because two fields shouldn't share the same name. Queries will then be able to refer to the additional indexed data by their field name (see title_sort in Listing 3.15).

While mapping entities is like building the skeleton of a body, mapping properties is like adding all the necessary pieces to bring life to it. Mapping properties is directly related to how you'll decide to search your domain model.

Hibernate Search tries to do as much as possible for you through the built-in field bridge infrastructure and makes it as easy as possible thanks to sensible defaults. It also opens the doors for customization, especially as to which indexing strategy should be applied. You'll see in the next chapter how to bring this flexibility to the next level, but before that, let's talk about important concepts in the mapping process and how they'll affect you.

3.4 Refining the mapping

While we covered specific mappings for entities and properties, some mapping descriptors are applicable at both levels. An analyzer takes a text and breaks it into individual words. This isn't as easy as it sounds, and a lot of customized chunk operations can be applied. We'll show you how to choose an analyzer. The second mapping we'll discuss in this section is defining a boost factor to give more weight to one field than another.

3.4.1 Analyzers

Analyzing is the process of taking a text or a sentence and splitting it into several words, which are then indexed by Lucene. As you have seen in section 3.3.3, this analyzing process is triggered on properties marked as TOKENIZED. Analyzers will be described in detail in section 5.2, but we'll show you how to configure an analyzer now because it's part of the mapping process.

In many applications, one global analyzer is good enough. You can define the analyzer you want to use by default through a configuration property, as shown here:

```
hibernate.search.analyzer=org.apache.lucene.analysis.
    standard.StandardAnalyzer
# or
hibernate.search.analyzer=applicationanalyzer
```

hibernate.search.analyzer takes either the fully qualified class name of the analyzer class or the name of an analyzer definition. As you will see in chapter 5, an analyzer definition lets you declare a complex analyzer by name. The StandardAnalyzer class, which should be good for most basic texts in English, is the default value.

It's possible to define different analyzers for different entities. If you need an even finer-grained level, you can define a specific analyzer for a given field. The most local analyzer has priority when choosing the analyzer to use as defined in this list of decreasing analyzer priority:

1 analyzer defined on @Field
2 analyzer defined on a property (attribute or getter)
3 analyzer defined on an entity
4 global analyzer

Listing 3.16 demonstrates these rules.

Listing 3.16 Defining analyzers at different levels of the mapping

```
@Entity
@Indexed
@Analyzer(impl=StandardAnalyzer.class)     ◁——  Default analyzer
                                                 for this class
@AnalyzerDef(name="synonyms", ...)     ◁——  "synonyms"
public class Item {                          analyzer
    ...                                      definition
    @Field
    private String title;
```

```
@Field
@Analyzer(definition="synonyms")        ◁──┐  Use the analyzer
private String description;                    definition

@Fields({
    @Field(name="brand", index=Index.TOKENIZED,
           analyzer=@Analyzer(impl=PhoneticAnalyzer.class)),   ◁──┐
    @Field(name="brand_sort", index=Index.UN_TOKENIZED)
})                                                         Field-level
private String brand;                                      analyzer
```

In listing 3.16, all fields (for example, `title`) of `Item` use `StandardAnalyzer` except:

- The `description` field, which uses the synonyms analyzer
- The `brand` field, which uses a phonetic analyzer

Before you get too excited, let's remember that mixing analyzers should be left to specific cases. In particular, analyzers used to build the query should be compatible with analyzers used to index the queried data; mixing analyzers makes query building more complex. Chapter 7 and specifically section 7.2.3 go into the details of this problem.

The next section describes boost factors. Briefly, boost factors alter the influence a given field has on the relevance of a document. Splitting the different analyzer strategies into two different fields allows us to decide if we want to use the phonetic approach to build the query. For example, we might want to try exact matches before backing up to a phonetic approach if the result list is desperately empty.

Opening possibilities with multiple-field mapping, analyzers, and boost factors

Mixing the ability to index the same property into multiple fields with the use of analyzers provides interesting possibilities. As you'll see later in this book, using analyzers is the key to such features as synonym matching, phonetic approximation, and so on. Using a dedicated field for the approximation strategy will allow the query writer to precisely decide whether or not she wants to benefit from these features and which boost (or weight) she wants to provide to these approaches. The following concrete example demonstrates how a property can be indexed both regularly and by using a phonetic analyzer.

```
@Entity
@Indexed
public class Item {                    Use the
                                       standard
    @Fields({                          analyzer
        @Field(name="title"),      ◁──┘
        @Field(name="title_phonetic",
            analyzer=@Analyzer(impl=PhoneticAnalyzer.class)),   ◁──┐
            boost=@Boost(0.5f)   ◁──┐  Lower field
    })                              influence              Use the
    public title;                                         phonetic
                                                          analyzer
    ...
}
```

If you don't understand all the fuss about analyzers, don't worry; we'll go back to them in detail in 5.2. This chapter showed you how to use an analyzer on a field, on a property, on a class, or globally.

3.4.2 Boost factors

Not all properties and not all entities are equal in the search process. Some have a stronger influence than others. Let's imagine in our store application that a user is looking for the *Band of Brothers* DVD. Finding these words in the title field should push the matching document to a higher priority than finding the same words in the description property.

By default Lucene associates a boost factor of 1.0 to entities and properties. You can override the boost factor to reflect the importance of title over description (see listing 3.17).

Listing 3.17 Using the boost factor to prioritize some properties over others

```
@Entity
@Indexed
public abstract class Item {
    ...
    @Field @Boost(2.0f)        ◁——| Boost
    private String title;              title field

    @Field
    @Analyzer(impl=SynonymsAnalyzer.class)
    private String description;
}
```

The boost factor is a float that can take any value, including lower than 1 if you wish to diminish the impact of a field rather than increase it. The exact influence of the boost factor in the document score is explained in chapter 12.

Can I use negative boost?

As far as the authors know, it's possible to use a negative boost, but you might be surprised by its effects. A *negative boost* means that if a query searches a word contained in a given negatively boosted field, the global document score (or popularity) will diminish if this word is found. Use cases for it do not pop up naturally. You could imagine an entity that stores words in a special property; each of these words not associated with the document should reduce your chances to retrieve the document. This might be used as a way to compensate for the presence of some words that are nonsignificant for the document.

Generally speaking, you shouldn't use negative boosts. If you do, do so only if you understand precisely what you're doing (especially read chapter 12 to understand scoring and section 13.1.2 for an example). If you're looking to exclude words from a query, explicitly exclude them by using – or its programmatic equivalent Boolean-Clause.Occur.MUST_NOT.

You can also boost some entities over others. In our DVD store example, it probably makes sense to return matching DVDs slightly higher in our search results than food items. You can achieve that by boosting the entity, as shown in listing 3.18.

Listing 3.18   Boosting an entity (among others)

```
@Entity
@Indexed
public class DVD {
    ...
}

@Entity
@Indexed
@Boost(.75f)              ←─┤ Reduce the score
public class Drink {         of all Drinks
    ...
}
```

NOTE Rather than promoting or demoting an entity against another, an alternative is to expose the choice to the user by returning the results in different lists. In a DVD store, the main list could return matching DVDs but also propose a small side link to the best-matching actors.

Boost factors are combined; more precisely, they are multiplied by each other. If an entity is boosted by `1.4`, and one of its property is boosted `1.2`, the total boost for the field will be `1.4 * 1.2`. You can boost a specific `@Field` by using `@Field(boost=@Boost(1.2f))`. This is particularly useful when a property is indexed multiple times.

While the authors agree that not all properties and entities are made equal, they also think that defining the priority at indexing time is not the best approach. For example:

- What happens, if after some live testing, you realize that the boost factor should be `1.5` rather than `1.3`?
- What happens if in one use case the optimal boost factor is different than in another use case?

To solve the first problem, you'll have to reindex all your data; the boost factor is defined and stored at indexing time. To solve the second problem, you'll have to give your preference to one use case over another.

Fortunately, Lucene offers tools to work around these problems. You can define boost factors in the query rather than in the index. This essentially delays the boost factor decision until you execute the query. See Section 7.1.6 for more information. While it can make the query writing a bit more tedious, a boost time query is the preferred method of the authors because it gives a lot of flexibility.

3.5 *Summary*

That's it! You now can officially claim that you know how to map all the basic models in Hibernate Search. This was a lot of new information in one chapter, but don't worry. In practice, most of the default values are used, and defining the mapping information comes quite naturally. You should spend most of your time thinking about the data you wish to search by and about the type of query you want to be able to execute. From this knowledge, the mapping description comes naturally.

An attentive reader might have seen that we left some questions about mapping situations unanswered. The next chapter will describe more advanced mapping techniques, some of them at the heart of Hibernate Search's flexibility. If you're still a bit uncomfortable with mappings, or if you think you've had enough mapping information for the day, you can skip the next chapter for now and jump to chapter 5 or even chapter 6. After reading chapters 6 and 7 on how to write a query, you'll understand better the reasons behind the mapping metadata.

Mapping more advanced
data structures

This chapter covers

- Custom bridges
- Mapping relationships

Although Hibernate Search comes with built-in bridges for most useful Java types, they won't cover all your needs. It's not uncommon in an application to need to define specific types. Even if the type you're wanting to index is supported, its string representation generated by Hibernate Search and indexed by Lucene might not be appropriate for the kind of full-text query you're looking for. Generally speaking, what happens when you need to map the unexpected? Hibernate Search has the notion of a *bridge*, which converts the object structure into the Lucene structure. You can extend the supporting types and their behavior by writing your own custom bridge implementation. The first part of this chapter covers this functionality.

NOTE If you're still uncomfortable with the notion of mapping, read chapter 3 again or jump to chapter 5. You can easily come back to this chapter later in your journey. Thanks to chapter 3, you know how to map most of the domain model. For 80 percent of your mapping and even for many applications, this is all you'll need to know. We'll cover more advanced needs in this chapter; the extra 20 percent of mappings require either additional features or more flexibility.

Chapter 3 showed how Hibernate Search maps an entity, its superclasses, and its properties. But it made no mention of another structural mapping problem: relationships. Both in the database model and in the object model, it's possible to create associations between two entities. Databases traditionally employ four types of associations:

- One to one, represented by a type association in Java
- Many to one, represented by a type association in Java
- One to many, represented by a collection or an array in Java
- Many to many, represented by a collection or an array in Java

Lucene provides no built-in association between documents. While this limitation doesn't seem too problematic at first glance, it means that we cannot express correlated queries. *Correlated* queries are queries involving the values of associated object properties. Back to the DVD store example we started in chapter 2, we cannot express the idea of returning all the DVDs whose title contains *mountain* and that feature the artist *ledger*. This is close to a deal breaker. Fortunately, Hibernate Search offers a way to work around this limitation, as you'll see in the second part of this chapter. But let's come back to our first problem, mapping unexpected structures.

4.1 *Mapping the unexpected: custom bridges*

Bridges fulfill the following needs in the Hibernate Search architecture:

- They convert an object instance into a Lucene consumable representation (commonly a string) and add it to a Lucene `Document`.
- They read information from the Lucene `Document` and build back the object representation.

The first operation is mandatory for all bridges and is used every time an entity is created or changed and when its properties have to be indexed. The second operation is optional and is used in two situations, when the bridge is used on:

- An identifier property
- A property stored in the index that aims to be projected in a query

An identifier property needs to be read from the Lucene index and *rehydrated*. This means Hibernate Search needs to be able to build the object representation of the identifier out of the Lucene data. From this rehydrated value, Hibernate Search will be able to retrieve the entity from the persistence context by its id.

Some queries, called *projection queries*, return the property values straight from the index rather than from the Hibernate persistence context. To project a property, its value must be stored in the index, and its bridge must be capable of reconstructing the object representation. Projection queries are described in section 6.5.

Bridges that support the conversion of both the object to Lucene and from Lucene to the object are called *two-way bridges*.

Why not all bridges are two-way bridges

All built-in bridges provided by Hibernate Search are two-way bridges (see table 3.1), but bridges degrading (or losing) information in the process of converting the object instance to a string representation are not uncommon. Because information is lost, building back the object representation is either approximative or simply not possible.

A bridge taking a `Date` object and indexing its year is a typical example. A bridge reading a PDF (represented by an array of bytes) and indexing the content also loses information; all the text structure, style, and metadata are gone.

While listing all the use cases where bridges are useful is quite frankly impossible, some examples will help you get a better grasp on bridges and unleash your imagination. You can:

- Index the text in a PDF represented by an array of bytes; the bridge needs to extract the text from the PDF (see section 13.2.1).
- Index a Microsoft Word document located at a given URL; the bridge needs to access the URL, read the Word document, and extract the text (see section 13.2.2).
- Index the year, month, and day of a `Date` object in separate fields
- Index a `Map` with each entry in a specific Lucene field.
- Combine several properties of an entity and index; the combination results in a single Lucene document field.
- Index numbers in a way to make them comparable; using a padding strategy makes the numbers comparable alphabetically (the only ordering strategy that Lucene understands).

Depending on the bridge complexity and capability, Hibernate Search offers four interfaces that can be implemented. Why so many? The number of interfaces could have been reduced to two, but they would have been too complex for simple cases. Hibernate Search takes away most of the complexity in the simple cases and lets you implement a much simpler interface. If you need extra flexibility, you'll have to pay the price of implementing a more complex interface. But before walking through these scenarios, let's discover how to declare the use of a custom field bridge.

4.1.1   Using a custom bridge

Like any other mapping declaration in Hibernate Search, annotations are the way to use a custom bridge.

The @FieldBridge annotation is placed on a property (field or getter) that needs to be processed by a custom bridge (see listing 4.1). Optional parameters can be passed to the bridge implementation.

Listing 4.1   @FieldBridge declares the use of a custom bridge

```
@Entity
@Indexed
public class Item {
    @Field                            Property marked to
    @FieldBridge(                     use a bridge           Declare the bridge
            impl=PaddedRoundedPriceBridge.class,             implementation
            params= { @Parameter(name="pad", value="3"),
                      @Parameter(name="round", value="5") }
            )
        private double price;         Optionally provide
    ...                               parameters
}
```

When @FieldBridge is present, Hibernate Search uses the explicit bridge rather than relying on the built-in bridge-type inference system. @FieldBridge has an impl parameter that points to the bridge implementation class. You can optionally pass parameters to the bridge implementation. This is quite handy for helping to keep bridge implementations more generic and allowing different configurations for different properties. We'll cover parameters in section 4.1.3.

In listing 4.1, the bridge indexes a number by padding and rounding its value. The application developer can adjust padding and rounding thanks to the bridge parameters.

The @FieldBridge annotation can be added on the identifier property as well (marked by @DocumentId). In this case, the custom field bridge converts the identifier value into a Lucene structure and is able later on to extract the identifier value from the Lucene structure. Identifier values require a two-way bridge.

If you map the same property multiple times, as shown in section 3.3.4, you can still use a custom field bridge. As shown in listing 4.2, the @Field.bridge parameter takes a custom bridge description annotation: @FieldBridge.

Listing 4.2   @FieldBridge can be used in properties indexed multiple times

```
@Entity
@Indexed
public class Item {
    @Fields( {                                          Set @FieldBridge
        @Field(                                         in @Field
            name="price",
            bridge=@FieldBridge(impl=PaddedRoundedPriceFieldBridge.class),
```

```
        @Field( ... ) } )
    private double price;
    ...
}
```

So far, we've seen `@FieldBridge` defining custom bridges on a property or an `@Field`. But it's sometimes useful to work at the entity level rather than on a given property. Here are a few use cases:

- Several properties of an entity need to be combined and the result indexed.
- Some entity metadata deserves to be indexed in the entity `Document`, but this metadata is not stored in the entity itself.
- Generally speaking, the Lucene `Document` that contains the index information of an entity needs to index additional information, and this information is out of the scope of the Entity object.

To solve this class of problems, Hibernate Search supports the notion of a class-level bridge. A class-level bridge is like any other Hibernate Search bridge we've seen so far. The only difference is that the entity instance is passed to the bridge in lieu of a property value. To declare a class bridge, place an `@ClassBridge` annotation on the class, as shown in listing 4.3.

Listing 4.3 Use @ClassBridge to add class-level bridges

```
@Entity
@Indexed
@ClassBridge(          ◁── Mark the use of a
    name="promotion",        class bridge       ◁── Recommended      ◁── Class bridges have
    index=Index.UN_TOKENIZED,                       namespace            properties similar
    impl=ItemPromotionBridge.class )  ◁──                                to @Field
public class Item {                        Class bridge
    ...                                    implementation
}                                          used
```

A class bridge implements the same interface a property bridge does. A class bridge declaration is very similar to an `@Field` declaration except that the class bridge implementation is mandatory because it cannot be inferred from the property type. In particular, a class bridge shares the following `@Field` properties:

- `name`—The Lucene field name. In a class bridge, this name is recommended but might not be followed by the class bridge implementation.
- `store`—The storing strategy used.
- `analyzer`—The analyzer used.
- `index`—The indexing strategy used.
- `termVector`—The term vector strategy used.
- `boost`—The index time boost factor used.

An `@ClassBridge` declaration also needs to provide the `impl` attribute (the class bridge implementation) and optionally provide parameters to the class bridge implementation (by using the `params` attribute).

In listing 4.3, the class bridge adds a promotion field to the Lucene document. The promotion information could, for example, be provided by an external service implementation called by `ItemPromotionBridge`.

More than one class-level bridge can be declared on a given entity. Use `@Class-Bridges` for that purpose.

Since you just learned how to declare property and class bridges, the next step is to see how to implement them. Depending on the complexity and the flexibility you need in your bridge, several solutions are available. The next two sections are dedicated to this subject.

4.1.2 Writing simple custom bridges

Often a bridge is simply a conversion routine from an object representation to a string representation. You might also have to implement the routine to convert the string representation back to the object if the bridge is used on an identifier property or on a property meant to be projected. Let's first discover how to write the simplest bridge: the conversion routine from an object to a string.

ONE-WAY SIMPLE CUSTOM BRIDGES

Hibernate Search offers a simple bridge interface to satisfy such cases: `org.hibernate.search.bridge.StringBridge`.

Let's implement the bridge used in listing 4.1. Listing 4.4 shows both the declaration and the implementation of the field bridge. The bridge implementation is a `StringBridge` that rounds and pads doubles.

Listing 4.4 Declare the use of a bridge and implement it

```
@Entity
@Indexed
public class Item {
    @Field
    @FieldBridge(                                     ❶ Declare bridge
        impl=PaddedRoundedPriceBridge.class           implementation
    )
    private double price;

    ...
}


/**
 * Round a price by range of 5, going to the upper boundaries
 * pad the result with up to 3 non-significant 0
 * Accept double and Double                           Implement
 */                                                   StringBridge
public class PaddedRoundedPriceBridge implements StringBridge {
    public static int PAD = 3;
    public static double ROUND = 5d;
                                                      ❷ Convert property
    public String objectToString(Object value) {         value into String

        if ( value == null ) return null;             Null strings are
                                                   ❸ not indexed
```

```
        if (value instanceof Double) {
            long price = round( (Double) value );
            return pad(price);
        }
        else {
            throw new IllegalArgumentException(
                    PaddedRoundedPriceBridge.class
                    + " used on a non double type: "
                    + value.getClass() );
        }
    }

    private long round(double price) {
        double rounded = Math.floor( price / ROUND ) * ROUND;
        if ( rounded != price ) rounded+= ROUND; //we round up
        return (long) rounded;
    }

    private String pad(long price) {
        String rawLong = Long.toString(price);
        if (rawLong.length() > PAD)
            throw new IllegalArgumentException(
            "Try to pad on a number too big" );
        StringBuilder paddedLong = new StringBuilder();
        for ( int padIndex = rawLong.length() ; padIndex
        < PAD ; padIndex++ ) {
            paddedLong.append( '0' );
        }
        return paddedLong.append( rawLong ).toString();
    }
}
```

4 Raise runtime exceptions on errors

5 Padding implementation

❶ Use the PaddedRoundedPriceBridge to index the price property. ❷ A simple one-way bridge must implement the method objectToString. The value passed is the property value, the price in this example. ❸ Null objects should generally return a null string; the null element is not indexed. ❹ Unexpected inputs should raise a runtime exception. ❺ Padding is an important technique in Lucene to enable a ranged query and sorting on numbers.

The main method to pay attention to is objectToString. This method passes the property value (or the entity instance if the bridge is a class bridge) and expects a string representation in return. Lucene will index this string. While you can do pretty much what you want in the bridge implementation, this example shows a couple of interesting implementation decisions.

Like all built-in bridges, this bridge returns null when a null object is provided. Hibernate Search does not add null string values to the index. Chapter 3 and especially section 3.1.2 explain the reasons behind this decision. While it is recommended to return a null string when a null object is passed, your bridge can go against this rule.

When the bridge receives an unexpected type (in the custom bridge example, any type that is not a double is unexpected), a runtime exception is raised and indexing fails. Once again, a bridge can decide to ignore the issue and degrade nicely, but in most cases the right approach is to raise an alarm to the developer in the form of an exception.

A very useful technique is used in this bridge example: number padding. The only data structure Lucene understands is a string. In particular, comparisons are entirely based on strings. Unfortunately, string comparisons and number comparisons don't play together well. The number 2 is inferior to the number 12, but the string "2" is superior to the string "12". One way to align the number and string comparison is to pad numbers. Padding consists of adding nonsignificant leading zeros; thus, "002" is inferior to "012". The main drawback of this technique is that the number of leading zeros has to be decided upfront. Changing the maximum allowed value would mean reindexing all the elements.

The bridge we've just designed is not sufficient to bridge an identifier property or to bridge properties that need to be projected. The next section describes the extra steps required to make a simple two-way bridge.

TWO-WAY SIMPLE CUSTOM BRIDGES

As indicated by the name, a two-way bridge converts the information back and forth from the object model to the Lucene model. Bridges that degrade information, such as the rounding bridge described in listing 4.4, are not good candidates because there's no way to extract the original information from Lucene. Two-way bridges are necessary when the bridge is used on either:

- An identifier property
- A property meant to be projected (read back from the index)

A two-way bridge that aims to convert an object to and from a string representation implements `org.hibernate.search.bridge.TwoWayStringBridge`. Listing 4.5 shows an implementation.

Listing 4.5   Implementation of a two-way bridge

```
@Entity
@Indexed
public class Item {
    @Field
    @FieldBridge(                        Declare the bridge
        impl=PaddedPriceBridge.class     implementation
    )
    private double price;
...
}

/**
 * pad a price with up to 3 non-significant 0s
 * Accept double and Double                              Implements     ❶
 */                                                 TwoWayStringBridge
public class PaddedPriceBridge implements TwoWayStringBridge {
    public static int PAD = 3;

    public String objectToString(Object value) {
```

```
        if ( value == null ) return null;
        if (value instanceof Double) {
            return pad( (Double) value );
        }
        else {
            throw new
    IllegalArgumentException(PaddedRoundedPriceBridge.class
                    + " used on a non double type: "
                    + value.getClass() );
        }
    }

    public Object stringToObject(String price) {          ❷ Reverse
        return Double.parseDouble(price);                    operation
    }                                                        objectToString

    private String pad(double price) {
        String rawDouble = Double.toString(price);
        int dotIndex = rawDouble.indexOf('.');
        if (dotIndex == -1) dotIndex = rawDouble.length();
        if (dotIndex > PAD)
            throw new IllegalArgumentException(
    ➥"Try to pad on a too big number" );
        StringBuilder paddedLong = new StringBuilder( );
        for ( int padIndex = dotIndex ; padIndex < PAD ; padIndex++ ) {
            paddedLong.append('0');
        }
        return paddedLong.append( rawDouble ).toString();
    }
}
```

❶ A two-way bridge implements `TwoWayStringBridge`. ❷ Two-way string bridges implement the conversion between the string representation stored in the Lucene index and the object representation.

There's nothing spectacular in listing 4.5. The `TwoWayStringBridge` interface includes a `stringToObject` method; the method takes the string value stored in the Lucene index as a parameter and expects the object representation as the return value. In addition to the rules and common practices we've discussed for regular `StringBridges`, `TwoWayStringBridges` should ensure that the object passed as an argument and the result of the operation `bridge.stringToObject( bridge.objectToString( object ) )` are *similar* from a user's point of view. In Java land it usually translates as being equal per the `Object` `equals` operation. If the bridge doesn't follow this rule, it cannot be used for identity properties, and the projected results are likely to surprise your users because the values retrieved would not be the values stored.

While not all one-way bridges can support the two-way contract, the authors encourage you to try to use two-way bridge contracts as much as possible. It's much easier to design a two-way bridge from the ground up than to morph a one-way bridge into a two-way bridge.

You may have noticed in the last two examples that the padding choice is hard-coded into the bridge. It's not possible to reuse the same bridge for numbers larger than 1000. While it was a decent choice for prices in a store that sells DVDs and food, what happens if we start to develop a side business around a home cinema? The padding value more likely should be set to 5. Why not make it a parameter?

4.1.3 Injecting parameters to bridges

You can declare parameters in a bridge declaration. Providing parameters allows the bridge implementation to be more generic. To receive parameters, bridges need to implement the ParameterizedBridge interface. Let's enhance listing 4.4. Listing 4.6 uses parameters injected at declaration time.

Listing 4.6 Inject parameters by implementing `ParameterizedBridge`

```
@Entity @Indexed
public class Item {
    @Field
    @FieldBridge(
            impl=ParameterizedPaddedRoundedPriceBridge.class,
            params= { @Parameter(name="pad", value="3"),
                      @Parameter(name="round", value="5") }       ◁──┐
            )                                               Inject parameters ①
    private double price;
...
}

/**
 * Round a price by range of round, going to
 * the upper boundaries; pad the result with up to pad
 * non-significant 0s.
 * Accept double and Double
 */                                                     ② Implement the
public class ParameterizedPaddedRoundedPriceBridge          appropriate
        implements StringBridge, ParameterizedBridge {  ◁──┘  interface
    private int pad = 6; //9,999,999
    private double round = 1d; //by default round to the next
➥ non decimal amount
                                                   Parameters are injected
    public void setParameterValues(Map parameters) {  ◁──  into setParameterValues

        if ( parameters.containsKey( "pad" ) ) {
            pad =
          ➥Integer.parseInt( (String) parameters.get( "pad" ) );
        }

        if ( parameters.containsKey( "round" ) ) {
            round =
          ➥Double.parseDouble( (String) parameters.get( "round" ) );
        }
    }

    public String objectToString(Object value) {
        if ( value == null ) return null;
        if ( value instanceof Double ) {
            long price = round( (Double) value );
            return pad( price );
```

```
        }
        else {
            throw new
IllegalArgumentException(ParameterizedPaddedRoundedPriceBridge.class
                + " used one a non double type: " +
                    value.getClass() );
        }
    }
    private long round(double price) {
        double rounded = Math.floor( price / round ) * round;
        if ( rounded != price ) rounded+= round; //we round up
        return (long) rounded;
    }

    private
        String pad(long price) { String rawLong = Long.toString(price);
        if ( rawLong.length() > pad )          <—— Use parameters
            throw new IllegalArgumentException( "Try to pad on
            a number too big" );
        StringBuilder paddedLong = new StringBuilder();
        for ( int padIndex = rawLong.length() ; padIndex < pad ;
        padIndex++ )
    {
            paddedLong.append( '0' );
        }
        return paddedLong.append( rawLong ).toString();
    }
}
```

❶ Declare bridge parameters using key/value pairs. ❷ setParameterValues receives a map of parameter names and values.

Parameters are declared when the bridge usage is declared. This set of key/value pair parameter values is passed to bridges implementing ParameterizedBridge.

Parameters are quite convenient because they provide flexibility to bridge implementations. The authors recommend that you define sensible default values for each parameter if possible. Doing so makes the bridge user's life much easier. In listing 4.6, we set the default padding value to be high enough to please most use cases. We also rounded by the unit as decimals are usually not interesting when comparing prices. Of course, any bridge user can override these default values at any time.

What about thread-safety?

Bridges are used in a multithreaded environment. Developers should make sure that bridge methods can be executed concurrently. Because Hibernate Search injects parameters into bridges in a thread-safe way, setParameterValues implementations don't need to guard against concurrency issues.

In general, if you don't change the state of the bridge object after the call to set-ParameterValues, your bridge implementation is safe. Hibernate Search guarantees that the state defined in setParameterValues() is visible to any subsequent bridge method calls.

Not all bridges can cope with the idea of converting the object value into a string. Some bridges need more control and require access to the underlying Lucene API.

4.1.4 *Writing flexible custom bridges*

Some bridges may need to go closer to the metal and have access to the underlying Lucene `Document` object. One fairly common use case involves mapping a property (from the object side) and splitting the information into multiple fields. Let's start with a field bridge that converts from the object world to the index world, one way.

ONE-WAY FLEXIBLE CUSTOM BRIDGES

A marketing study uncovered that our DVD store is visited by a lot of non-English-speaking persons. These persons are interested in rating movies based on voiceover performance. Our object model represents this data as a `Map<String, String>` in `Item`. The map key represents the language used in the voiceover, and the map value represents its user rating. We'd like to be able to do full-text query based on the rating value per language. One approach is to store each language in its own field, as shown in figure 4.1.

To implement such a bridge, you need access to the underlying Lucene `Document` instance. Bridges can access this information when they implement `FieldBridge`. Listing 4.7 shows a possible implementation.

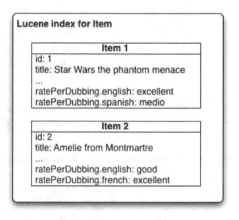

Figure 4.1 We represent each key in the map as a separate field in the Lucene index. For a given instance, a key may or may not be present in the map (and in the index).

Listing 4.7 Use a `FieldBridge` to convert a map into several fields

```
@Entity
@Indexed
public class Item {
    ...

    @Field(store=Store.YES)
    @FieldBridge(impl=MapKeyPerFieldBridge.class)    ◁─┐  Define the bridge
    @CollectionOfElements @MapKey                        implementation
    private Map<String, String> ratePerDubbing =
        new HashMap<String, String>();
}

/**
 * Only Map<String, String> are accepted as value
 * For each key in the map, create a field name.<key> (lowercase) and index
 * its value.
 * For example the map [english:good, french:moyen, spanish:excellente]
```

```
 * will result in the following fields in the index
 * <pre>
 * name.english => good
 * name.french => moyen
 * name.spanish => excellente
 */
public class MapKeyPerFieldBridge implements FieldBridge {

    public void set(String name,
                    Object value,
                    Document document,
                    LuceneOptions luceneOptions) {
        //we expect a Map<String, String> here. checking for Map for
        simplicity
        if (! (value instanceof Map) ) {
            throw new IllegalArgumentException("support limited to
            Map<String, String>");
        }

        @SuppressWarnings("unchecked")
        Map<String, String> map = (Map<String, String>) value;

        for (Map.Entry<String, String> entry : map.entrySet() ) {
            Field field = new Field(
                    name + '.' + entry.getKey().toLowerCase(),
                    entry.getValue().toLowerCase(),
                    luceneOptions.getStore(),
                    luceneOptions.getIndex(),
                    luceneOptions.getTermVector()
            );
            field.setBoost( luceneOptions.getBoost() );
            document.add( field );
        }
    }
}
```

Annotations in the code:
- **①** Implement FieldBridge
- **②** Proposed field name
- **③** Value to index
- **④** Lucene Document instance
- **⑤** Various indexing strategies
- **⑥** Create the new field
- **⑦** Inject boost
- **⑧** Add new field to document

① The `FieldBridge` interface consists of a `set` method that provides access to the underlying Lucene artifacts. **②** The proposed field name is provided by the declaration (and defaults to the property name). It is recommended that you use `name` as the base or prefix to define field names stored in the Lucene `Document`. **③** Provide the value to convert (either the property value for a field bridge or the entity instance for a class bridge). **④** The Lucene `Document` instance represents the entity instance in the index. **⑤** `LuceneOptions` is a holder passed by the declaration to the bridge implementation. It is recommended that you use these options when building Lucene fields. **⑥** The bridge is responsible for creating new field(s). A Lucene Field object takes a name, the string value indexed, and a few indexing configuration parameters in the constructor. We recommend using the `LuceneOptions` values. **⑦** Boost needs to be injected in the boost property. **⑧** Don't forget to add the newly created field into the Lucene document!

The `FieldBridge`'s set method is called when an entity (for a class-level bridge) or a property (for a property-level bridge) is indexed into a Lucene document by

Hibernate Search. One `Document` instance is created per entity instance indexed. All bridges defined on this entity are called, and the same document instance is passed along. The `set` method must be implemented in a thread-safe way so it can be accessed concurrently by Hibernate Search.

NOTE Users of Hibernate Search 3.0 need to implement a slightly different version of the `FieldBridge` interface, in which the `set` method has the following signature:

```
public void set(String name,
        Object value,
        Document document,
        Field.Store store,
        Field.Index index,
        Float boost);
```

The `FieldBridge` interface gives tremendous flexibility to bridge designers because they have access to the native Lucene APIs. This flexibility is particularly valuable for the following use cases:

- Indexing an entity or property in a custom structure that will facilitate future queries (for example, one field per map key).
- Adding metadata into the index for a given entity. A special class bridge is then responsible for adding this information. We could envision adding a promotion flag to some DVDs to push them higher in our query result.

Don't limit your imagination to these examples. We've introduced the `FieldBridge` interface in order to face the unexpected and let you go beyond the standard Hibernate Search capabilities.

The sharp reader has probably noticed that such a bridge cannot be used for identifier properties or projected properties (projected properties extract their value from the Lucene index rather than from the persistence context; see section 6.5). Don't worry; we have a solution for you.

TWO-WAY FLEXIBLE CUSTOM BRIDGES

In the previous chapter, we left a problem unsolved: composite identifiers. Hibernate Search doesn't support composite identifiers out of the box, but you can easily write your own bridge to support such a case. Let's get back to the last chapter's example. A `Person` entity has a composite identity property object comprising both `firstName` and `lastName`. A bridge that's intended to be used on identifier properties needs to fulfill three actions:

- Indexing and storing the property into the Lucene index
- Building the identifier property out of the values stored in a given `Document` instance (it requires a two-way bridge)
- Ensuring that a `Document` can be found and uniquely identified from the identifier property value (through a Lucene query)

Let's see how the bridge solves each of these needs. Listing 4.8 is an example of a composite identifier bridge for a `Person` object. Note that a property marked as `@DocumentId` is stored in the Lucene index. This must be the case in order for two-way bridges to perform their work.

Listing 4.8   Composite identifier bridge for a `Person` object

```
@Entity
@Indexed
public class Person {
    @EmbeddedId @DocumentId Embedded id                     Use the custom
    @FieldBridge(impl=PersonPkBridge.class)   ◁────┘        field bridge
    private PersonPK id;
    ...
}

public class PersonPkBridge implements TwoWayFieldBridge {          ❶ Build composite
                                                                      identifier from
    public Object get(String name, Document document) {   ◁────┘      document
        PersonPK id = new PersonPK();

        Field field = document.getField( name + ".firstName" );
        id.setFirstName( field.stringValue() );

        field = document.getField( name + ".lastName" );
        id.setLastName( field.stringValue() );
        return id;                                     ❷ Create unique
    }                                                     string from
                                                          identifier
    public String objectToString(Object object) {   ◁────┘
        PersonPK id = (PersonPK) object;

        StringBuilder sb = new StringBuilder();
        sb.append( id.getFirstName() )
          .append( " " )
          .append( id.getLastName() );

        return sb.toString();
    }

    public void set(String name,
                    Object value,
                    Document document,
                    LuceneOptions luceneOptions) {
        PersonPK id = (PersonPK) value;
        Store store = luceneOptions.getStore();
        Index index = luceneOptions.getIndex();
        TermVector termVector = luceneOptions.getTermVector();
        Float boost = luceneOptions.getBoost();          ❸ Store each
                                                            subproperty
        //store each property in a unique field            in a field
        Field field = new Field( name + ".firstName",  ◁────┘
                                 id.getFirstName(),
                                 store, index, termVector );
        field.setBoost( boost );
        document.add( field );
```

```
field = new Field( name + ".lastName",
                        id.getLastName(),
                        store, index, termVector );
field.setBoost( boost );
document.add( field );

//store the unique string representation in the named field
field = new Field( name,
                    objectToString( id ),
                    store, index, termVector );
field.setBoost( boost );
document.add( field ); } }
```

❹ Store unique representation in field name

The main goal of a two-way field bridge is to store a property into the index (the set method) and later on to be able to build the property object from the information stored in the index (the get method).

The `get` method reads data from the document in order to build the composite identifier object ❶; each property is stored in a specific field. `objectToString` converts the composite identifier into a unique string representation ❷. Hibernate Search uses this string to find a specific document (through a term query). During indexing, each subproperty is stored in the index in an individual field ❸. These subproperties will be read later on when Hibernate Search builds the composite identifier property by calling `get`. It's preferable to name these fields under the `name` namespace. The unique string representation of the composite identifier is stored in the `name` field ❹. Hibernate Search queries this field (through a term query) to retrieve a document by its identifier value.

The example in listing 4.8 was simplistic; please don't use firstname/lastname as a primary key in a real system. The authors encourage you to always use a surrogate key instead of composite keys.

In the last example, we used . (dot) and the property namespace to build field names. This helps us build Lucene queries that are intuitive to someone familiar with the domain model. Table 4.1 shows how a query looks similar to navigation in an expression language.

`set`, `get`, and `objectToString` must be thread-safe because a bridge is shared by many concurrent calls.

Table 4.1 Queries are similar to object navigation in an expression language when Lucene field names are named after the root namespace followed by a dot (.) followed by the property name.

Object navigation	Lucent query
`item.getRatePerDubbing().` ⮕`get( "french" ).` ⮕`equals( "moyen" );`	`ratePerDubbing.french:moyen`
`person.getId().` ⮕`getLastName().` ⮕`equals( "Griffin" );`	`id.lastName:Griffin`

On top of the rules we've just discussed, a two-way bridge targeted at supporting identifier properties must follow two additional rules:

- `objectToString` must generate a unique string representation of the identifier. Hibernate Search will search this string in the field named after the `name` parameter in the `set` method. This query retrieves the document from its entity's identifier property.
- The `set` method must add a field named name (a parameter of the method `set`), which indexes the `objectToString` value untokenized. A Lucene term query will be used to retrieve a document by its identifier.

You've just discovered the most flexible way to convert an object structure to a Lucene index and are now ready to face the Wild, Wild West of domain models.

Custom bridges are the most popular extension point of Hibernate Search. While in most situations you won't need to use custom bridges, they'll soon become an essential tool for mapping exotic domain models. You might feel right now that this puts too much power in your hands, that you don't need such flexibility (and in a lot of cases you'll be right), but after reading chapters 6 and 7 on queries, you'll need to bend the index structure to suit your needs in order to make the most of your full-text queries. Bridges will be there for you.

4.2   *Mapping relationships between entities*

Until now, we have quite elegantly avoided talking about a very important aspect of domain models: relationships. Without relationships, you simply could not express queries involving more than one entity; you could not search for all authors whose name is Bernard (property `Author.name`) and who live in Atlanta (property `Author.address.city`). It's important to preserve in one way or another the concept of relationship in the index structure.

4.2.1   *Querying on associations and full-text searching*

Deep inside both the relational model and the object model lies the idea of relationship (or association) between entities. Both models allow you to navigate from one entity to an associated entity. Because associations are a native part of the model, it's possible to express queries that apply restrictions on associated objects. We'll call such queries *correlated* queries.

Unfortunately in Lucene, queries on related documents cannot be expressed; the notion of relationship between documents has not been built into Lucene. Figure 4.2 shows the different concepts as they are represented in the object model, the relational model, and the index model.

The main consequence for us is that we cannot express correlated queries. The reasoning behind Lucene's choice is interesting. Lucene is not a database; it is an index. Indexes typically sacrifice normalization, data precision, and query expressive-

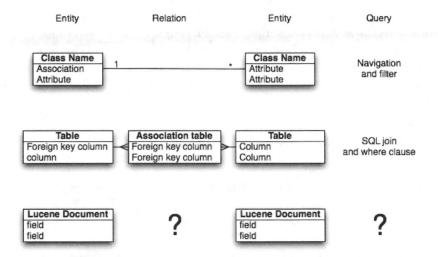

Figure 4.2 Expressing queries on related objects in the object, relational, and index worlds

ness for performance. This is what we're asking them to do. Lucene, which is essentially an index technology, follows this rule.

Hibernate Search works around this problem by denormalizing associations.

Since a Lucene query takes only a single document into consideration to evaluate its relevance and has no notion of a document join or association, contrary to the object and relational models, Hibernate Search indexes the object graph into a single document. In figure 4.3, you can see that when the item entity is indexed, its associated director and actors are indexed in the same document.

Each of the association's entity properties is indexed in the association's namespace. In our example, the director's name is indexed in director.name, which is exactly how we'd express a navigation to the director's name of a given item in an expression language or in HQL.

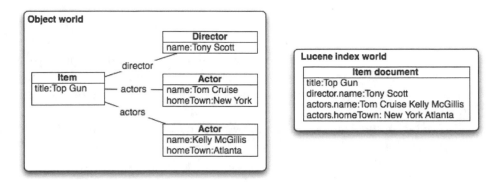

Figure 4.3 Hibernate Search denormalizes associations to make them queryable. The information in an object graph is rendered in a flat form in a single Lucene document.

It's worth noting that collections are flattened during the denormalization process. In our example this means that the names of all actors associated with a given item are stored and indexed in a single field, `actors.name`. What are the consequences? In theory, it limits some of the query's expressibility. In practice, this should not affect you too much. With this model, it's possible to express queries such as returning the items where:

- Both Cruise and McGillis are in the movie.
- One of the actors is either Cruise or McGillis.
- Cruise is in the movie but not McGillis.

You won't be able to express queries involving a correlation between two properties of a given entity in a collection. Let's imagine that `Actor` has a `homeTown` property. You won't be able to express a query like `"return items where one of the actors is Tom and his hometown is Atlanta"`.

The reason is that the whole collection of data is seen as a single element. Don't give up, though. It's often possible to either:

- Turn the query upside down by targeting `actor` as the root entity, then collecting the matching items.
- Use a query filter to refine an initial query (see chapter 8).

I tried but cannot find a way around the collection limits

Sometimes you'll end up at a dead-end. No matter how hard you try, you won't be able to express the query in Lucene. Good advice here is to step back and see if an HQL query could do the job. Full-text searching is like a new toy in the beginning. You'll be tempted to use it more than necessary. Always remember that you can go back to plain HQL or work in a three-step process: Apply part of the query (the discriminant part) in Lucene, collect the matching identifiers, and run an HQL query that restricts by these identifiers and some other criteria.

It would be quite disastrous to index the entire object graph every time a root object is indexed. The index would be quite big, indexing would be long, and the index would be polluted with tons of not–so-useful information. Just like property indexing, Hibernate Search uses an opt-in approach: In the mapping you decide which associated object or collection needs to be indexed based on the type of queries you need to perform.

The rest of the chapter will show how to map associations. We'll start with a simple case: embedded objects.

4.2.2   *Indexing embedded objects*

Embedded objects in Java Persistence (they're called components in Hibernate) are objects whose lifecycle entirely depends on the owning entity. When the owning entity is deleted, the embedded object is deleted as well.

Let go back to our DVD store example. A DVD is rated. Rating has several dimensions: scenario, soundtrack, picture, and of course an overall rating. A rating doesn't make sense without a DVD, so we'll model it as an embedded object. To index the associated `Rating` object, simply place `@IndexedEmbedded` on the association and mark the `Rating` properties for indexing. The name `@IndexedEmbedded` is derived from the operation performed; we embed the indexing information in the main document. Listing 4.9 describes how to declare an object as embedded in the index.

Listing 4.9   Using `@IndexedEmbedded` objects in the same Lucene document

```
@Embeddable                                                        Mark
public class Rating {                                              properties
    @Field(index=Index.UN_TOKENIZED) private Integer overall;   ◁─ for indexing
    @Field(index=Index.UN_TOKENIZED) private Integer scenario;
    @Field(index=Index.UN_TOKENIZED) private Integer soundtrack;
    @Field(index=Index.UN_TOKENIZED) private Integer picture;
    ...
}

@Entity
@Indexed
public class Item {
    @IndexedEmbedded private Rating rating;   ◁─┐  Add new field to Mark the
    ...                                        ❶ association for indexing
}
```

When Hibernate Search finds an `@IndexedEmbedded` annotation on rating ❶, it processes the `Rating` properties and indexes each property marked with an `@Field` annotation (or an `@IndexedEmbedded` annotation). It also executes each class-level bridge present on the `Rating` object. There's a small difference: Each field name in the Lucene index is prefixed with the name of the association and a dot, `rating.` in our example. The Lucene document contains `rating.overall`, `rating.scenario`, `rating.soundtrack`, and `rating.picture`. This approach makes queries smell like regular object property navigations.

If the association isn't marked with `@IndexedEmbedded`, it's ignored.

Sometimes the field prefix generated by Hibernate Search doesn't match your expectations because you're mapping to an existing index, or your index-naming conventions are different, or your taste is different. The `prefix` attribute lets you control the prefix used to index properties of the associated objects. Note that in listing 4.10 queries need to target `rate_overall` rather than `rating.overall`. The dot is part of the default prefix and disappears when overridden.

Listing 4.10   Override the @IndexEmbedded default naming convention

```
@Embeddable
public class Rating {
    @Field(index=Index.UN_TOKENIZED) private int overall;
    @Field(index=Index.UN_TOKENIZED) private int scenario;
    @Field(index=Index.UN_TOKENIZED) private int soundtrack;
    @Field(index=Index.UN_TOKENIZED) private int picture;
    ...
}

@Entity                                          Association prefix ❶
@Indexed                                             is overridden
public class Item {
    @IndexedEmbedded(prefix="rate_") private Rating rating;   ◁
    ...
}
```

@IndexEmbedded ❶ marks the association as embedded. The Lucene document contains rate_overall, rate_scenario, rate_soundtrack, and rate_picture.

Some developers like to work with interfaces rather than implementations to provide so-called abstraction. While the authors don't understand the reasoning for domain model objects, Hibernate Search lets you use this code style. Imagine that Rating is an interface and the implementation is RatingImpl. If you use the same mapping as shown in listing 4.9, Hibernate Search complains about Rating not being a mapped entity. @IndexEmbedded.targetElement (as shown in listing 4.11) forces Hibernate Search to use a specific class instead of the returned type.

Listing 4.11   Use an interface in an annotation marked for @IndexEmbedded

```
@Embeddable
public class RatingImpl {
    @Field(index=Index.UN_TOKENIZED) private int overall;
    @Field(index=Index.UN_TOKENIZED) private int scenario;
    @Field(index=Index.UN_TOKENIZED) private int soundtrack;
    @Field(index=Index.UN_TOKENIZED) private int picture;
    ...
}

@Entity
@Indexed
public class Item {                                    ❶ Define
    @IndexedEmbedded(targetElement=RatingImpl.class)  ◁    target class
    private Rating rating;
    ...
}
```

@IndexedEmbedded ❶ marks the association as embedded. RatingImpl is used in lieu of Rating to find the index mapping.

So far we've shown you simple value associations, and you may wonder if they work for collections. Absolutely! The same annotation is used to mark a collection as embedded in the index document. Each embedded object in the collection is indexed. As discussed in section 4.2.1, the same Lucene field contains all the collection element values for a given property. Listing 4.12 describes how to mark a collection as indexed.

Listing 4.12 Mark a collection as embedded in the indexed document

```
@Embeddable
public class Country {
    @Field private String name;
    ...
}

@Entity
@Indexed
@ClassBridge(name="promotion", index=Index.UN_TOKENIZED,
  impl=ItemPromotionBridge.class )
public class Item {                      Collection of elements
    @CollectionOfElements                embedded in the document
    @IndexedEmbedded      ◁──────┘
    private Collection<Country> distributedIn = new ArrayList<Country>();
     ...
}
```

All collections supported by Hibernate are supported by Hibernate Search:

- `java.util.Collection`
- `java.util.Set`
- `java.util.SortedSet`
- `java.util.List`
- `java.util.Map`
- `java.util.SortedMap`
- arrays of objects

Note that the index part of indexed collections (`List` and `Map`) and arrays is not indexed in the document. If you need to index the index (or key), consider using a custom bridge, as explained in section 4.1.4.

Don't abuse `@IndexedEmbedded`. Just like for `@Field`, you must think about the queries your users need to perform and mark associations for indexing only if you need to. Be particularly careful about collections. Indexing time can be much longer than usual if the collection size is significant, because Hibernate Search needs to walk through each element and index the information. This becomes even worse if elements in the indexed collection themselves contain a collection marked as `@Indexed-Embedded`. Not only will indexing time be longer, but the index size will increase because more data is indexed.

You've now mastered indexing embedded objects and collections of embedded objects. The next section brings us to the problem of indexing associations between entities. We'll also discuss how to limit the amount of association indexing in a cascade and thus define a graph depth boundary for embedded associations. While this limitation can be applied to and is sometimes useful for collections of embedded objects, it's much more common when associations between entities are indexed.

4.2.3   Indexing associated objects

When it comes to associations between entities, things are a bit more complicated compared to the associations with embedded objects we just described. At first sight, associations with embedded objects and associations with entities seem quite similar, and, indeed, they are in many ways. The big difference lies in the lifecycle. Embedded objects' lifecycles are entirely dependent on their owning entity and cannot be referenced by other entities. This is all good and fine for Hibernate Search because when the embedded object is updated, Hibernate Core will raise an event claiming that the owning entity is updated. Hibernate Search has only to update the Lucene document for this entity.

This isn't as easy in associations between entities. Remember that using @Indexed-Embedded is essentially a way to denormalize your data and embed the information of two or more entities into a single Lucene document. When an associated entity is updated, Hibernate Search needs to know which other entities this entity is associated with in order to update their Lucene documents. Otherwise the denormalized data will be desynchronized (see figure 4.4).

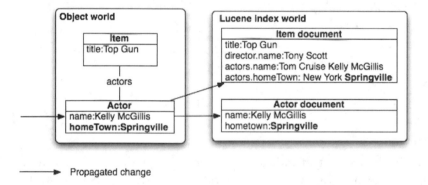

Figure 4.4   When a change is made to an associated entity, Hibernate Search must
update all the documents in which the entity is embedded.

Let's take Figure 4.4 as our working example. When `actor` is updated, Hibernate Search needs to update the items related to `actor`. One strategy would be to update all the items in our inventory to make sure everything is up to date. Of course this solution doesn't fly very far because it would mean loading all the items from the database and reindexing them. Instead, Hibernate Search requires us to make the association bidirectional (if it isn't already) and mark the association pointing back to the parent entity with `@ContainedIn`. Listing 4.13 shows an example of `@ContainedIn` usage.

Listing 4.13   Relations between entities should be bidirectional

```
@Entity @Indexed
public class Item {
    @ManyToMany
```

```
        @IndexedEmbedded                          Embed actors
        private Set<Actor> actors;                when indexing

        @ManyToOne
        @IndexedEmbedded                          Embed director
        private Director director;                when indexing
        ...
    }

Entity @Indexed
public class Actor {
    @Field private String name;

    @ManyToMany(mappedBy="actors")        ❶ actor is contained
    @ContainedIn                             in item index
    private Set<Item> items;
    ...
    }

@Entity @Indexed
public class Director {
    @Id @GeneratedValue @DocumentId private Integer id;
    @Field private String name;

    @OneToMany(mappedBy="director")           director is contained
    @ContainedIn                              in item index
    private Set<Item> items;
    ...
    }
```

@ContainedIn ❶ is paired with an @IndexedEmbedded annotation on the other side of the relationship. @ContainedIn can be placed on both collections and single-value associations whether or not the association is the owning side of the bidirectional relationship. When Hibernate Search finds a change in an entity having an @ContainedIn association (director in our example), it marks the associated entity instance(s) as changed (items contained in director.items in our example). One or more Lucene document updates will then be triggered.

Some people are confused by @IndexedEmbedded and @ContainedIn. They don't know which side needs to be marked as @IndexedEmbedded to enable the query they want. Think about it this way: @IndexedEmbedded is the property you can navigate to in your queries; @ContainedBy is not.

NOTE Sometimes, it's inconvenient to have to make a relationship bidirectional to please Hibernate Search. If the associated entity never changes in your system (immutable entity), you don't have to add @ContainedIn. Since no changes will happen behind Hibernate Search's back, your index will be kept synchronized.

If the associated entity changes, but you cannot afford a bidirectional relationship, it's always possible to trigger a manual reindexing of the owning entity (see section 5.4). Taking listing 4.13 as an example, you could decide to manually reindex all the item entities every night. Or you could keep track of the actor changes and cherry-pick the item entities that need to be reindexed using an HQL query.

It's not uncommon to have *nested associations*: embedded entities containing embedded relationships. We can even imagine these embedded relationships pointing to other entities that have embedded relationships and so on. You should avoid embedding too much information in a single Lucene document because indexing takes longer and the index directory grows bigger. A Lucene document should contain only the necessary bits of information to express planned queries. This poses the question of how to stop embedding associations and at which level to stop.

By default, Hibernate Search stops embedding associations in a given object's graph branch when the same class has already been processed. Figure 4.5 describes the default strategy. Hibernate Search raises an exception in this situation to prevent infinite loops created by circular relationships.

The default behavior won't always match your needs:

- It's common to have a class associated with itself that needs to be indexed (parent-child relationships from the same class are a good example).
- Entities that are both embedded and root indexed could lead to deep indexed object graphs. For example, the Actor entity is embedded in the Item entity but is also indexed separately because we'd like to be able to search for actors specifically.

@IndexedEmbedded allows you to control the depth at which association embedding stops. By default, the depth is not limited, and the method described in figure 4.5 applies. A depth limit is defined per association; it's the maximum amount of embedding allowed in the branch started by the association (including the current association). Figure 4.6 is a revised version using an explicit depth limit.

In figure 4.6, each association is either marked with an explicit depth or left at the default depth (infinite). The upper branch shows that from entity A, Hibernate Search is allowed to embed only two associations in depth for that branch. B is then included. The association between B and C indicates that the depth from this association cannot be higher than three. The association from C to B is not embedded because the maximum number of jumps allowed by the association from A to B was

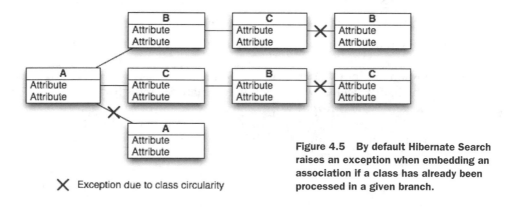

✕ Exception due to class circularity

Figure 4.5 By default Hibernate Search raises an exception when embedding an association if a class has already been processed in a given branch.

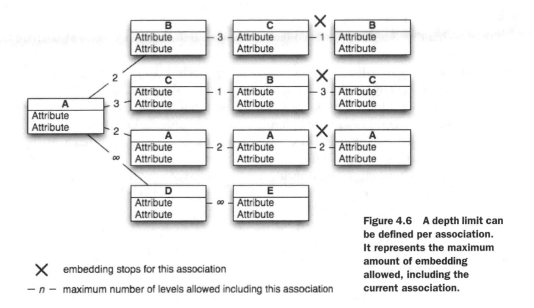

X   embedding stops for this association

— *n* —   maximum number of levels allowed including this association

Figure 4.6   **A depth limit can be defined per association. It represents the maximum amount of embedding allowed, including the current association.**

two (one jump from A to B and one jump from B to C). The third branch shows how to limit the depth in a branch involving circular references. The last branch, using an infinite depth, shows the default resolution explained by figure 4.5. Infinite depth (or undefined depth), which is the default if you don't set a depth, will stop right before the same class is encountered for the second time (to avoid circularity issues).

The `depth` attribute in `@IndexedEmbedded` (see listing 4.14) is the place to define the maximum depth for a given association.

Listing 4.14   The maximum depth is defined by `@IndexedEmbedded.depth`

```
@Entity @Indexed
public class Item {
    @ManyToMany                              Limit the depth
    @IndexedEmbedded(depth=4)    ◁⎯┘
    private Set<Actor> actors;

    @ManyToOne                               Limit the depth
    @IndexedEmbedded(depth=1)    ◁⎯┘
    private Director director;
    ...
}
```

One last warning: Embedding too many associations is a bad practice. To convince you, remember that Hibernate Search needs to read the data for all the associated entities. This could load a big object graph if too many associations are marked `@IndexedEmbedded`.

4.3 Summary

In chapters 3 and 4, you have learned how to define the mapping Hibernate Search uses to transparently convert domain models into index models. Chapter 4 specifically showed you advanced strategies for mapping object graphs and, generally speaking, for mapping any unforeseen object structure, thanks to the flexible bridge model.

This was a lot of information, sometimes even boring (we know this crossed your mind). The good news is that all this tedious learning is about to pay off in the following chapters! Chapter 5 will explain how indexing happens, what you should care about, and, more important, what you should not care about. The next part of the book, part 3, will dive into queries and how to make the most of a full-text search.

Indexing: where, how, what, and when

Indexing is the action of preparing data so Lucene can answer your full-text queries in an efficient way. The index should be as close as possible to your real data changes and not lag behind. Why does Lucene need to prepare data? In order to answer full-text queries efficiently, Lucene needs to store some efficient representation of the data. Since most full-text search queries revolve around the idea of words, the index is organized per word. For each word, the index structure stores the list of documents and fields matching a given word as well as some statistical information. Section 1.3.1 gave us an idea of the index structure kept by Lucene.

Lucene's job is to build this magic structure and enable its superpowers, right? True, but it needs a little help from you:

- You need to store the index structure.
- You need to decide which of the features you require and which data preparation Lucene will do for you.
- You need to ask Lucene to index your information.

The index structure in Lucene must be stored somewhere. The two main storage solutions are in a file directory and in memory. We'll cover how to ask Hibernate Search to use each of these strategies.

The key feature of full-text search solutions comes from their ability to split a text into individual words and process these individual words in a way that will enhance the query capabilities. In Lucene jargon, this processing is called *analyzing*. Analyzers are a superpower framework: You can choose which analyzer to use or write one to set your own magic tricks. We'll describe a few of the analyzers Lucene provides and how to configure them.

In a pure Lucene usage you need to feed Lucene the data you want to search. Some part of your program must read the data, transform the data into an indexable format (we showed how to do that in chapters 3 and 4), and ask Lucene to index it. This isn't an easy task, and some difficulties arise along the way:

- Gathering data (and if possible only the data that changes) can be long and painful.
- The index process in Lucene has to follow specific rules.

Indexing in Lucene requires you to know how things work. Here are some gotchas you need to overcome:

- You cannot run more than one indexing process per Lucene index.
- Indexing a lot of data in one shot is faster than indexing documents one by one.
- You must determine how often you need to index your data—right away, once per hour, or once a day.
- After several change operations, a Lucene index needs to be optimized (defragmented).

Problems add up quickly. The first problem becomes particularly tricky when you need to put a clustered architecture in place. Soon you'll start implementing some helper classes around Lucene to cope with your situation, and you'll have to make up your mind about all those problems.

Fortunately, Hibernate Search takes the indexing responsibility off your shoulders and makes the whole process transparent for you and your application. Because a transparent process doesn't fit everybody's architecture, Hibernate Search also lets you index entities manually. We'll cover all that in the last part of this chapter.

But let's first answer the question of where to store the index structure.

5.1 *DirectoryProvider: storing the index*

Lucene stores its index structure in a `Directory`. A `Directory` is an abstract concept that can be materialized in different storage structures. Lucene provides a filesystem `Directory` as well as a RAM (in-memory) `Directory` out of the box. This is an extensible system, and you can find various implementations on the internet, including clustered cache directories, a Berkeley database backend, and a JDBC backend.

Hibernate Search integrates with the two default backends provided by Lucene. The integration is handled by a directory provider. Before diving into the configuration details for each backend, let's examine how a Lucene directory is associated with an entity.

5.1.1 *Defining a directory provider for an entity*

As you've seen in section 3.2.1, an entity is marked as indexed thanks to `@Indexed`. The default index name is the fully qualified class name of the entity class, but you can override this name by using the `index` attribute.

All details concerning a given index are configured through configuration properties. As you've seen in chapter 2 (section 2.2.2), you can provide properties to Hibernate Search through the following:

- hibernate.properties file
- hibernate.cfg.xml file if you use Hibernate Core
- persistence.xml file if you use Hibernate `EntityManager`
- Programmatic API (for example, `Configuration.setProperty`)

Each index can have specific key value properties defined in the configuration. To define the type of directory provider for an index, use the `directory_provider` suffix, as demonstrated in Listing 5.1.

Listing 5.1   Setting the directory provider for a specific index

```
hibernate.search.com.manning.hsia.dvdstore.model.Item.directory_provider
➥ org.hibernate.search.store.FSDirectoryProvider
```

The property name structure is composed of `hibernate.search`, followed by the index name (the entity's fully qualified class name by default), followed by the configuration suffix. In almost all applications, all indexes will share the same directory provider type. Hibernate Search provides some form of configuration inheritance. All indexes will share properties from the default pool unless a setting is explicitly overridden. Use the `default` key in lieu of the index name to define global values inherited by indexes unless overridden.

In listing 5.2, all indexes share the same directory provider definition, thanks to the `hibernate.search.default` context, except `Item`, which overrides the `directory_provider` value.

> **Listing 5.2   All indexes except `Item` use the filesystem directory provider**
>
> ```
> hibernate.search.default.directory_provider
> ➥org.hibernate.search.store.FSDirectoryProvider
> hibernate.search.com.manning.hsia.dvdstore.model.Item.directory_provider
> ➥org.hibernate.search.store.RAMDirectoryProvider
> ```

This mechanism drastically reduces the number of lines of configuration you need to write and is not limited to the `directory_provider` property. Any property available to a directory provider will be shared as well. Use this opportunity to reduce the configuration settings.

If you use sharded indexes (that is, an index split into several small indexes), the configuration might change a bit. Read section 9.4.1 for more information on this topic.

Now that you know how to configure the directory provider for an index (or for a set of indexes), let's check the available opportunities.

5.1.2   Using a filesystem directory provider

The default and most useful storage for a Lucene directory is a filesystem (if possible, a local filesystem). Such a model is efficient for several reasons:

- The index can be huge, and most of the index structure will remain in the filesystem (as opposed to in memory).
- Local filesystems are now fast enough to accommodate Lucene's read operations efficiently.
- Lucene caches information in memory to avoid unnecessary reads to the filesystem. This caching is done at the `IndexReader` level, and Hibernate Search benefits from it by reusing `IndexReader` instances as much as possible.
- A filesystem is the most used and tested solution in Lucene deployments.
- The index is persistent, and it can easily be backed up and replicated.
- You can navigate into the index internals thanks to Luke (see section 2.6).

The filesystem storage is the default choice in Hibernate Search: If you don't specify the `directory_provider` property, `org.hibernate.search.store.FSDirectoryProvider` is used.

Where does Hibernate Search store the index directory? It tries to be as smart and intuitive as possible and define names automatically out of the box, but it also lets you override different part of the directory-naming strategy:

- `indexBase` is the property suffix that describes the root directory containing the index directories. The default value is the current directory (which is usually where your virtual machine has been launched).
- `indexName` is the property suffix that describes the index directory name; the full path is defined by `indexBase` plus `indexName`. The default value for `indexName` is the index name (which itself defaults to the fully qualified class name of the indexed entity); `indexName` is rarely used in Hibernate Search deployments.

While Hibernate Search lets you define your filesystem index directory in a lot of funky ways, the authors recommend that you define a single root directory (using `hibernate.search.default.indexBase`) where all index directories are stored and let the default strategy play its role from here. You'll have a better understanding of what's going on, and maintenance will be much easier. Listing 5.3 is an example of a directory structure where indexes follow Hibernate Search's conventions.

Listing 5.3 The recommended approach to defining a filesystem index directory

```
# Configuration
hibernate.search.default.indexBase /User/production/indexes        ◄─┐
                                                   The only property to set is
                                                  indexBase, the root directory
# File directory structure
/Users
   /Production                               Each index directory will be
      /indexes                               under indexBase and named
         /com.manning.hsia.dvdstore.model.Item   ◄─  from its index
         /com.manning.hsia.dvdstore.model.Actor
```

If possible, use a local filesystem or a storage area network (SAN) filesystem. Regular network filesystems (NFS) tend to be problematic for Lucene. Lucene needs to acquire a global pessimistic lock when it updates an index. The default locking strategy represents the lock as a file. Due to some caching strategies in place in most network filesystems, the lock file cannot always be read appropriately. If you absolutely must use a network filesystem, the authors recommend that you check the Lucene resources available on the subject. The Lucene team is making a lot of progress in this area.

While a filesystem is the mainstream way of storing indexes, another interesting strategy is to store the index in memory.

5.1.3 *Using an in-memory directory provider*

It's possible to define a Lucene index as stored in memory. Of course, as soon as the application shuts down (more precisely as soon as the Hibernate `SessionFactory` or `EntityManagerFactory` is closed), the index data goes away. It is nevertheless quite useful in several situations.

The primary situation is unit testing. Unit testing has spread across the development community. The general idea is to test individual functionalities or subsystems independently from each other. Speed is a primary concern. If a test suite is too long, people have the tendency to not launch it and commit the code hoping for the best (ah, humans!). Unit test purists test individual classes independently from each other and are horrified when two subsystems are tested together. Let's discuss what we, the authors, think is a slightly more pragmatic approach.

Thanks to in-memory databases such as HSQLDB, H2, or Derby, and thanks to the abstraction provided by Hibernate, it's possible to test a system all the way down to the database from a fresh data set in a matter of seconds or milliseconds (as opposed to minutes when a remote database is used). Hibernate Search lets you embrace this fast approach to test Lucene indexes. Unit tests using both in-memory databases and in-memory indexes can initiate quickly the data set before each test. The test then verifies the application behavior in a well-defined environment that's cleaned between each test. While it's possible to do the same with a regular database and a filesystem–based index, the in-memory version makes the unit test suite run much faster, because it avoids unnecessary network or filesystem input/output. You can find more information on unit testing and in-memory approaches in section 9.5.2.

If you followed the recommendation we gave you in the previous section (define a default `directory_provider`), you can easily switch from an in-memory provider in your unit tests to a filesystem–based directory provider in production (or in your dedicated test environment). Listing 5.4 shows two different configurations, depending on the targeted environment (test or production).

Listing 5.4 Two configurations, depending on test or production environment

```
# Test Configuration
hibernate.search.default.directory_provider
➥org.hibernate.search.store.RAMDirectoryProvider

# Production configuration
hibernate.search.default.indexBase /User/production/indexes
hibernate.search.default.directory_provider
➥org.hibernate.search.store.FSDirectoryProvider
```

The in-memory directory provider is `org.hibernate.search.store.RAMDirectoryProvider`.

In-memory indexes can also be used when the index is to be built quickly and retained temporarily. These temporary indexes can be useful when some offline operations require fast searching for the duration of the batch process; the index is built in-memory, used, then discarded. If the index needs to be made persistent, Lucene allows you to persist an in-memory index in a filesystem at any moment.

Be careful not to index too much data when using an in-memory index. It may sound quite obvious, but the index size cannot go beyond the size of your memory or `OutOfMemoryException` will become your worst nightmare. Speaking of nightmares, so far we've left out the problems arising in a clustered environment.

5.1.4 *Directory providers and clusters*

You've seen that network filesystems have problems with hosting Lucene directories. Can clusters work? Clustering Lucene indexes is problematic also because changing a Lucene index requires a global pessimistic lock.

NOTE GLOBAL PESSIMISTIC LOCK—GLOBAL TO WHAT? When we refer to global pessimistic locks, the global attribute is applied to all the players willing to update a given Lucene index in a cluster of nodes. However, this lock is not global to all directories in which your entities are indexed. One global lock per Lucene `Directory` is present.

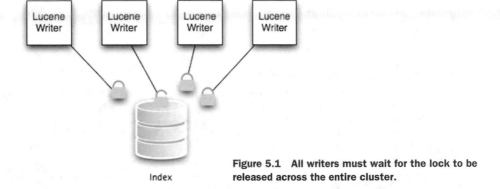

Index

Figure 5.1   All writers must wait for the lock to be released across the entire cluster.

This global pessimistic lock limits the cluster scalability. As shown in figure 5.1, all nodes willing to write must wait for the current writer to release the lock.

To avoid the scalability problem, Hibernate Search provides a recommended architecture to cluster a Lucene-based full-text indexing system. As shown in figure 5.2, one master node is solely responsible for updating the Lucene index while nonwriters (the slaves) execute full-text queries on a local copy of the index. On a regular basis, each slave updates incrementally its local version from the published master version.

This architecture has interesting advantages:

- It doesn't suffer the scalability problems we just described that are caused by the global pessimistic lock (the lock is solely shared by the master).
- Full-text searches don't suffer from remote input/output latency because they're executed on a local index copy.

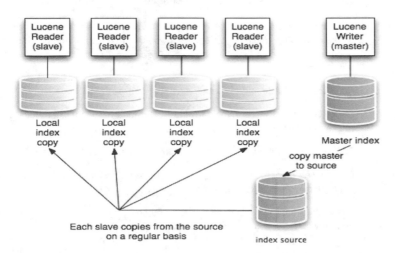

Figure 5.2   One master is responsible for all writing operations. Each reader (slave) copies the index from the master on a regular basis.

You might wonder how Hibernate Search ensures that only the master node updates the index. Slaves delegate the work to the master. We won't describe the magic potion here. You can read more on this subject in section 5.3.3 and in chapter 10.

> **What about in-memory clusters?**
>
> Hibernate Search uses filesystem-based directories and copies them to the various slaves. Why not use a distributed in-memory approach?
>
> This is absolutely possible! Several providers such as JBoss Cache, Terracotta, and GigaSpace offer solutions for using an in-memory distributed Lucene Directory. The global pessimistic lock problem remains: This lock must be shared across the cluster when index changes happen. The second factor you need to take into account is the index size. Most of the time, the index doesn't fit in memory. To work around this problem, these solutions use some kind of garbage-collection mechanism that releases bits of the index. When a released bit is needed back, it's requested across the network. You must compare the local filesystem input/output performance with the network performance. We'll discuss in-memory cluster models in chapter 10.

Let's see how to configure the directory providers for such an architecture. As in section 5.1.2, the master and the slave directory provider work on a filesystem–based local copy of the index. The same properties are used to configure the directory (indexBase, indexName). In addition, the master node pushes a stable version of the index to a common source directory. This directory will be polled regularly by the slaves. Table 5.1 lists the properties available for master directory providers.

Table 5.1   Configuration of the master node directory provider

Property name	Description
directory_provider	org.hibernate.search.store.FSMasterDirectoryProvider Directory provider implementation. While you can use a different implementation in unconventional scenarios, FSMasterDirectoryProvider is the recommended provider.
indexBase	Root directory of the index directory working copy.
indexName	Directory name of the working copy index. Defaults to the index name. This value is used in conjunction with indexBase.
sourceBase	Root directory of the index directory source. Typically a shared filesystem.
source	Directory name of the source index. Defaults to the index name. This value is used in conjunction with sourceBase.
refresh	The working copy index is copied to the source every refresh seconds. The default value is one hour (3600 seconds).

The slave nodes copy the index stored in the source directory into their working copy on a regular basis. The source directory is the shared content between master and slaves. This directory is generally placed in a shared filesystem. Table 5.2 lists the properties available for slave directory providers.

Table 5.2   Configuration of the slave node directory provider

Property name	Description
directory_provider	org.hibernate.search.store.FSSlaveDirectoryProvider Directory provider implementation. While you can use a different implementation in unconventional scenarios, FSSlaveDirectoryProvider is the recommended provider.
indexBase	Root directory of the index directory working copy.
indexName	Directory name of the working copy index. Defaults to the index name. This value is used in conjunction with indexBase.
sourceBase	Root directory of the index directory source. Typically a shared filesystem.
source	Directory name of the source index. Defaults to the index name. This value is used in conjunction with sourceBase.
refresh	The source index directory is copied to the working directory every refresh seconds. The default value is one hour (3600 seconds).

Usually you'll simply need to configure directory_provider, indexBase, and sourceBase (as shown in listing 5.5) and let the default values finish the work for you.

Listing 5.5   Configure indexBase and sourceBase for all indexes

```
# Master configuration

hibernate.search.default.directory_provider
➥ org.hibernate.search.store.FSMasterDirectoryProvider

# refresh every half hour
hibernate.search.default.refresh 1800

# master working directory location
hibernate.search.default.indexBase /Users/prod/lucenedirs

# source directory location where the master is copied to
hibernate.search.default.sourceBase
➥ /mnt/sourcevolume/lucenedirs

# Slave configuration

hibernate.search.default.directory_provider
➥ org.hibernate.search.store.FSSlaveDirectoryProvider

# refresh every half hour
hibernate.search.default.refresh 1800

# slave working directory location
hibernate.search.default.indexBase /Users/prod/lucenedirs
```

```
# source directory location where the master is copied to
hibernate.search.default.sourceBase
➥ /mnt/sourcevolume/lucenedirs
```

In this example, both master and slave share the index content in /mnt/sourcevolume/lucenedirs. sourceBase is identical in both configurations and points to the same physical storage. The refresh period is also identical. While it's not necessary to make these settings the same, it's usually a good practice unless you have specific reasons not to.

The truth and nothing but the truth?

The copy operations are slightly more complex than depicted previously. It would be dangerous to copy the value of one index directory into another one while the index is in use. The source directory contains two versions of the index: the active version, from which slaves copy the information, and the passive version, into which the master copies the new version. Hibernate Search copies the master to the shared source when no operations are at stake. A future version of Hibernate Search will probably use the Lucene snapshot feature to copy indexes while indexing operations are still running.

Slaves copy the index from the active source. Copies are done asynchronously from the main operations. When the copy is finished, the newly copied directory becomes the active directory. Don't worry; everything is taken care of for you by Hibernate Search.

An index can be quite big. Copying the entire index all the time would be quite inefficient. Hibernate Search tries to do a better job and copies only the incremental changes. You can think of it as a poor version of rsync. A file is copied only if it has changed since the last copy. The first time you copy the index or when a huge Lucene optimization has been executed, the copy will be total and slower. The subsequent copies will be lighter and thus faster.

We know you may need to implement custom directory providers to accommodate particular situations. Hibernate Search is flexible and lets you use your own implementation and logic.

5.1.5   *Writing you own directory provider*

There may be a time when the Hibernate Search built-in directory providers are insufficient for your needs. It might be because you need to tweak things a bit, because you have written a custom Lucene Directory, or because you want to reuse a JBoss Cache, Terracotta, or GigaSpace Lucene directory. Hibernate Search lets you write your own custom DirectoryProvider. The DirectoryProvider implementation benefits from the same configuration infrastructure available for built-in directory providers. The list of properties matching the current index name is passed to the initialize method. The property names are unqualified: Default properties or index-specific properties are merged and passed to the `initialize` method.

Writing a `DirectoryProvider` might require some knowledge of Lucene. An example of a directory provider is in section 11.3.

Once you know where your index structure will go, the questions in your agenda are, what happens during indexing? Can you influence it? Can you tweak it? We'll cover this in the next section.

5.2 Analyzers: doors to flexibility

Analyzers are one of those things in Lucene that people tend to "leave for later." Some people even tend to see them as some dark magic and haunted artifacts. While we cannot deny some dark magic things happen in some analyzers, they're not that complex. And they are indeed very useful and definitely worth the effort to learn about them. Some of them are fascinating in that they reflect the complexity of our languages. Before diving into the dark magic, let's see what an analyzer does.

5.2.1 What's the job of an analyzer?

Analyzers are basically responsible for taking text as input, breaking it into individual words (called *tokens* in Lucene terminology), and optionally applying some operations on the tokens. We'll call these operations *filters*, but they do more than filter in the common sense of the word: A filter operation can alter the stream of tokens as it pleases. Said otherwise, it can remove, change, and add words.

Once the filter centrifuge is finished, Lucene uses the list of words (a stream really). Each word is indexed, along with statistical information.

TOKENIZING: SPLITTING TEXT INTO WORDS

The first step of an analyzer is to take a stream of characters (text in human terminology) and return a stream of tokens (a list of words in human terminology).

This looks like a piece of cake: We take the text and split it each time we find a space, a dot, or a comma (basically at every nonletter or number character), and we're good! This approach might work most of the time in classic Latin-based languages, but we'll reach some harder problems pretty fast:

- *Hyphenation*   A dash is not always a word separator, especially in texts extracted from newspapers (because of thin columns).
- *URLs, acronyms, and other particular groupings*   A dot is not a word separator.
- *Elision (in languages like French, Dutch, Italian, Portuguese, and Spanish)*   The last vowel of a word might be suppressed when the following word starts with a vowel. An apostrophe separates the two words: *l'avion* (the plane) should be considered as two words (literally *le avion*). Sometimes an apostrophe should be considered as a single word: *aujourd'hui* (today). In case you didn't know, every rule of French grammar has an exception (except this one, maybe).

If we start to consider non-Latin languages, things get even worse. Some languages don't even have a clear notion of words. Chinese and Japanese, for example, do not separate words with a space. As a matter of fact, traditional Chinese does not have a word to designate the idea of *word* as an identifiable graphical unit.

Since when is a word a word?

The idea of words is not as old as you might think. The grammar experts of ancient Greece and Rome didn't manage to clearly define the notion of words, and continuous script was the norm. Continuous script consisted of not having any space between words: thisisanexampleofcontinuousscriptwhilereadableitsquitehardtofindinformationquicklyinsuchaflow. Continuous scripting was good enough at that time because most reading was done aloud.

The idea of adding word breaks was driven by the need for quick reference searching, by the need to read in a foreign language in the Middle Ages (reading in Latin, which was no longer the common language, was quite difficult in continuous script), and by the need to move away from reading aloud.

For more information, you can read *Space between Words: The Origins of Silent Reading*, by Paul Saenger.

Depending on the targeted language, a tokenizer algorithm might be more accurate than another type of algorithm.

FILTERING: OPTIMIZING THE INDEXING CONTENT

Assuming we have a stream of tokens from a text, some additional operations can (or even should) be applied. Some words are so common that it would be best not to index them. They should literally be filtered out. In most cases, accentuation and case are not discriminant in searching and should be removed before indexing. Filters can add, modify, or remove any token in the token stream to optimize the final content indexed by Lucene. You could think of filters as a bunch of interceptors, each one handling a specific operation on the token stream.

WHERE TO FIND ALL THESE ANALYZERS AND HOW TO USE THEM

Lucene comes bundled with some basic analyzers, tokenizers, and filters. The contribution part of Lucene (which you can find in the Lucene distribution) provides many additional analyzers, tokenizers, and filters. Finally, Apache Solr comes with a nice analyzer configuration framework that Hibernate Search reuses. Make sure to add solr-core.jar and solr-common.jar to your classpath. You can find these JARs in the Hibernate Search distribution, in the Solr distribution, or in a Maven repository (such as the JBoss repository at http://repository.jboss.org/maven2). The authors recommend using the JARs provided in the Hibernate Search distribution to avoid any version conflict.

TIP   If you use `@AnalyzerDef`, you must add solr-core.jar and solr-common.jar to your classpath.

We'll explore some of these resources in the rest of this section, but don't hesitate to browse the Lucene and Solr source code and documentation.

Once you've found the analyzer, tokenizer, or filter of your dreams, you can apply it globally, per entity, or per property, as shown in section 3.4.1. However, we haven't shown how to specify an analyzer definition and its associated tokenizer and filters. All this can be defined using the @AnalyzerDef or @AnalyzerDefs annotation. Listing 5.6 gives us an example. An analyzer definition (@AnalyzerDef) makes it very easy to assemble tokenizers and filters; it lets you declare a TokenizerFactory and a list of TokenFilterFactorys adapted to your needs.

> **Listing 5.6   An analyzer definition can be used anywhere in the domain model**

```
@Entity @Indexed                              Analyzer
@AnalyzerDef(                                  definition
    name="applicationanalyzer",    ◁───┘       name        Tokenizer factory
    tokenizer =
        @TokenizerDef(factory = StandardTokenizerFactory.class),   ◁───
    filters = {
    @TokenFilterDef(factory=LowerCaseFilterFactory.class),    ◁───┐
        @TokenFilterDef(factory = StopFilterFactory.class,        │ Filter
            params = {                                              factory
                @Parameter(name="words",   ◁───┐
                           value=              │ Parameters passed to
➡ "com/manning/hsia/dvdstore/stopwords.txt"), │ the filter factory
                @Parameter(name="ignoreCase", value="true")
            } )
} )
} )                                           Use a predefined
@Analyzer(definition="applicationanalyzer")   ◁───┘ analyzer
public class Item {
    ...
}
```

An analyzer definition is referenced by a name. An analyzer definition can be referenced by name on any @Analyzer.definition or even the global analyzer definition (defined by hibernate.search.analyzer), regardless of where it has been defined (in the same or different class). Each analyzer definition receives a TokenizerFactory described by @TokenizerDef and a list of TokenFilterFactorys described by @Token-FilterDef. Each TokenizerFactory or TokenFilterFactory can receive a set of parameters (a key/value pair) passed thanks to the @Parameter annotation. This sounds a bit theoretical right now, but don't worry. The next few sections give practical examples.

Solr comes bundled with a huge variety of factories, most of them building and configuring tokenizers and filters from the Lucene distribution. If you don't find the factory for a given tokenizer or filter class, don't hesitate to implement your own; it's as simple as implementing org.apache.solr.analysis.TokenizerFactory for a tokenizer or org.apache.solr.analysis.TokenFilterFactory for a filter. Finally, if you have a specific tokenizer or filter requirement, you can implement your own. This is a fairly advanced topic that we won't cover in this book. The authors recommend that you study the source code of existing implementations and read *Lucene in Action* from Manning.

A couple of analyzers, tokenizers, and filters fulfill essential services, so you must be aware of them. We'll discuss these in the next section.

5.2.2   *Must-have analyzers*

The most useful and basic analyzer you should be aware of is `StandardAnalyzer`: This is the default analyzer in Hibernate Search, and it does a decent job for a number of European languages even though it's primarily targeted at English. This analyzer is composed of the following:

- `StandardTokenizer`
- `StandardFilter`
- `LowerCaseFilter`
- `StopFilter`

`StandardTokenizer` should support most needs for English (and most European language) texts. It splits words at punctuation characters and removes punctuation marks with a couple of exception rules (see the Javadoc for more information). You can use the `StandardTokenizer` through the `StandardTokenizerFactory` provided by the Solr integration.

The `StandardFilter` removes apostrophes and removes dots in acronyms. Solr provides a `StandardFilterFactory` that you can use in an analyzer definition to use the `StandardFilter`.

The `LowerCaseFilter` changes all characters to lowercase. Solr provides a `Lower-CaseFilterFactory`. If you plan to index Russian or Greek, be sure to check the language-specific analyzer in the Lucene `contrib` package at `org.apache.lucene.analysis`. Russian and Greek need a specific lowercase filter (because of their special alphabets).

The `StopFilter` eliminates some commonly used words. Words very common in a language (like *a*, *the*, and *is* in English) are usually not relevant to the search and dilute the results. They are sometimes called noise words and are usually filtered out. By default, `StopFilter` will remove commonly used English words, but you can pass a specific stop word file, which contains one word per line. You can also ask the stop filter to ignore case, but we recommend that you apply a true `LowerCaseFilter` before using `StopFilter`. Listing 5.7 is an example of an analyzer using `StopFilter`.

Listing 5.7   A `StopFilter` uses a stop list file and ignores case

```
@AnalyzerDef(
    name="applicationanalyzer",
    tokenizer =
        @TokenizerDef(factory = StandardTokenizerFactory.class ),
    filters = {
```

```
...,
@TokenFilterDef(factory = StopFilterFactory.class,        ◁─┐  Stop word
    params = {                                                 factory
        @Parameter(name="words",
                    value=
    "com/maning/hsia/dvdstore/stopwords.txt"),        ◁─┐  File containing
                                                           stop words
            @Parameter(name="ignoreCase", value="true")  ◁──  Purposely
        } )                                                    ignore case
} )
```

TIP If you don't specify a list of stop words, Lucene uses its own predefined list that's suited to the English language. The list is *a, an, and, are, as, at, be, but, by, for, if, in, into, is, it, no, not, of, on, or, such, that, the, their, then, there, these, they, this, to, was, will,* and *with.*

Even if you plan to index texts in English, take a deep look at this list. None of these words will be present in the Lucene index. If you plan to index numerous documents discussing countries and their differences, *of* in *Republic of China* might be useful. Start with the list provided by Lucene and adjust it to your needs.

Remember that applying filters normalizes the data and is an essential process. The filtered words (token) will be indexed as is by Lucene. If you don't apply the lowercase filter, for example, your search will be case sensitive.

Listing 5.8 shows the analyzer definition corresponding to the use of Standard-Analyzer.

Listing 5.8 Analyzer definition equivalent to `StandardAnalyzer`

```
@AnalyzerDef(name="standardanalyzer",
    tokenizer =
        @TokenizerDef(factory = StandardTokenizerFactory.class ),
    filters = {
        @TokenFilterDef(factory = StandardFilterFactory.class),
        @TokenFilterDef(factory = LowerCaseFilterFactory.class),
        @TokenFilterDef(factory = StopFilterFactory.class) } )
```

NOTE Filters in `@AnalyzerDef` annotations are applied in their declared order. In listing 5.8, `StandardFilter` is applied before `LowerCaseFilter`, which is applied before `StopFilter`.

This is a lot of theory! Let's take a sentence and see what happens step by step when the standard analyzer is used. Listing 5.9 walks us through the process.

Listing 5.9 A sentence processed step by step by the standard analyzer

```
#original sentence
During this lovely day, the waiter told me: Look, a plane!    ❶ Tokenize the
                                                                  sentence
#after the StandardTokenizer
During|this|lovely|day|the|waiter|told|me|Look|a|plane|    ◁   ❷ Filter
                                                               apostrophe
#after StandardFilterFactory                                   and so on
During|this|lovely|day|the|waiter|told|me|Look|a|plane|    ◁
```

```
#after LowerCaseFilter
during|this|lovely|day|the|waiter|told|me|look|a|plane|
```
3 **Lowercase words**

```
#after StopFilter
during|lovely|day|waiter|told|me|look|plane|
```
4 **Remove stop words**

We first split the phrase into individual tokens **1**. The next step is silent for our particular sentence **2**. Then all cases are removed, **3** then noise words are identified and removed **4**.

If you want to index accented content such as texts in Spanish or French, a filter is available to replace accented letters by their nonaccented equivalent. Use `ISOLatin1AccentFilterFactory` to enable this filter.

These will be the most useful tools for you on a daily basis. If you target non-English languages, we encourage you to go to Lucene Contrib and check the source code of your target language analyzer. You'll learn some interesting information there. For example, the French package contains an `ElisionFilter`.

The basic analyzers, tokenizers, and filters work well for lots of projects. But in some cases, you'll need better and more appropriate solutions:

- Approximative search
- Phonetic search
- Search by synonyms
- Search by word family

Let's explore some of the coolest features of Lucene!

5.2.3 *Indexing to cope with approximative search*

One way to cope with typos or wrong orthography (either in the indexed text or in the query provided by the user) is to make use of `FuzzyQuery`. This system doesn't require any special processing at indexing time. It computes the Levenshtein distance (edit distance) and takes this value into account when retrieving matching documents. All the work is done when the query is executed. We'll discuss fuzzy searching in more detail in sections 7.1.4 and 7.3.5.

Another strategy consists of preparing the index structure to best serve an approximation query. In most cases, a typo or wrong orthography alters a word in one or two places. Part of the word, however, is correct. The user might have the beginning, the end, or the middle of the word right. The *n*-gram algorithm is based on this idea.

An *n*-gram is a sequence of *n* consecutive characters in a word. The list of trigrams (3-grams) for the word *hibernate* is *hib, ibe, ber, ern, nat,* and *ate* (see figure 5.3). Instead of indexing the whole word, an *n*-gram tokenizer or filter will index each available *n*-gram for a given word. When the query is built, the same process is applied to the query terms.

Let's imagine a query where a user is looking for *ybernat*. The query will look like ybe OR ber OR ern OR nat. Some of the *n*-grams match the Hibernate *n*-grams, and the matching document will be picked up. The more *n*-grams an element matches, the

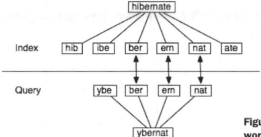

Figure 5.3 Applying an *n*-gram filter to the words helps you find approximate matches.

higher the ranking will be. The higher *n* is, the better the precision is (that is, there will be few false positives) but the less likely multiple typos will be recoverable.

The Contrib part of Lucene contains an `NGramTokenFilter`. Solr has the corresponding `NGramFilterFactory`. This factory accepts two parameters: `minGramSize` and `maxGramSize`. The filter will build all *n*-grams where *n* varies from `minGramSize` to `maxGramSize`. Setting `minGramSize` and `maxGramSize` to 3 is a good default.

5.2.4 *Searching by phonetic approximation*

An alternative technique to the approximation problem, besides using a fuzzy query or *n*-grams as discussed in the previous section, is to use a phonetic approach. Despite the widespread reliance on the internet, text messaging, and other text media, we still live in a world where oral communication is an important part of our life.

A couple of algorithms reduce a word to its phonetic equivalent. When two words are phonetically equivalent (same phonetic reduction), they're likely to be the same word separated by a few typos.

Most phonetic algorithms are based on phonetic rules that eliminate nondiscriminant letters and encode the remaining ones. The most elaborate of these algorithms use contextual information before reducing a letter to a sound. Unfortunately, most of them are focused on the English language.

When you add Solr analyzers (provided in the Hibernate Search distribution) and Apache Commons Codec (in version 1.3 at the time this book was written; available at http://www.apache.org) to your class path, Hibernate Search provides access to four algorithms:

- *Soundex*—The most widely known and one of the oldest phonetic algorithm for English texts.
- *RefinedSoundex*—A variation of Soundex more focused on spell checking.
- *Metaphone*—Provides a variable-length phonetic representation of a word. This algorithm was developed by Lawrence Philips to fix deficiencies in Soundex. It uses a larger set of rules than Soundex.
- *DoubleMetaphone*—An enhancement of the Metaphone algorithm developed by Lawrence Philips. This algorithm handles more irregularities, including those in such languages as English, German, Greek, French, and Chinese.

Let's imagine you listen to the radio in your car and hear about this fantastic DVD based on a novel by Victor Hugo. How do you spell this damn French word? It must be *Lay Meeserable* from what the speaker said. Close, but not quite. The proper title is *Les Misérables*. By using the DoubleMetaphone algorithm, both interpretations are reduced to "LS MSRP." Be sure to apply the same algorithm on both the indexed and the query terms. These algorithms are very useful in conjunction with a fuzzy search (which computes the distance or similarity between two strings.) The index contains the phonetic reduction of the words and enables phonetic-based searches.

TIP   Index properties make use of approximation analyzers in dedicated fields. The flexibility of the queries you will be able to write will be greatly enhanced (see section 5.2.7).

Listing 5.10 shows the use of the `PhoneticFilterFactory` to do a phonetic reduction of the indexed tokens.

Listing 5.10   Using a filter to do phonetic reduction of indexed tokens

```
@AnalyzerDef(name="phonetic",                            Enable the      ❶
    tokenizer =                                       phonetic filter
        @TokenizerDef(factory = StandardTokenizerFactory.class ),
    filters = {
        @TokenFilterDef(factory = StandardFilterFactory.class),
        @TokenFilterDef(factory = StopFilterFactory.class,
            params = @Parameter(name="words", value="stopwords.txt") ),
        @TokenFilterDef(factory = PhoneticFilterFactory.class,
            params = {
                @Parameter(name="encoder", value="DoubleMetaphone"),
                @Parameter(name="inject", value="false")
            } )                          Don't inject the  ❸    Define the
} )                                       original word          encoder
                                                                strategy  ❷
```

The phonetic filter is activated ❶ (make sure you add solr-core.jar, solr-common.jar, and commons-codec.jar to your classpath). By defining the encoding parameter ❷, you can select the appropriate phonetic algorithm from `Soundex`, `RefinedSoundex`, `Metaphone`, and `DoubleMetaphone`. The `inject` parameter ❸ (defaults to true) specifies whether to add the original token value and the phonetic reduction or simply the phonetic reduction (as shown in the example) to the token stream. The authors recommend that you set this parameter to false and index the nonphonetic word in a different field. While this takes more time when indexing, it also provides more flexibility at query time.

Which algorithm should you chose? There is no definitive answer; the best solution is to test each algorithm on your data set and check the pertinence of the results. Don't forget to involve your users in the test; their feedback will be invaluable for building a set of test data.

5.2.5 Searching by synonyms

Several approaches to searching by synonyms are possible; one of them is to anticipate the problem at indexing time. Instead of simply indexing a word, you index the word as well as all its synonyms in Lucene (see figure 5.4). A query using any of the synonyms will then match the document. Lucene acts as if someone had put in every possible synonym each time a given word is present in a phrase.

Figure 5.4 A word is indexed with all its synonyms. A filter adds all the synonyms to the stream of tokens.

A slightly different approach is to replace a given word by its reference synonym; all synonyms share the same reference word (see figure 5.5). By applying the same operation in the query, Lucene will be able to find all synonyms as if they were a single word.

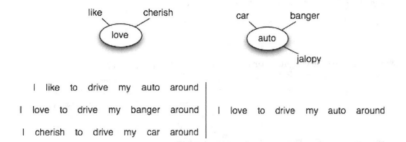

Figure 5.5 A word is replaced by its reference synonym at both index time and query time.

Hibernate Search lets you use either of these strategies.

NOTE The first strategy (adding all the synonyms to the index) involves only index time changes. You should take care to not apply the same analyzer at query time. This analyzer breaks the golden rule, which is to always apply the same analyzer at index and query time (see section 7.2.4 for more information).

Be aware that the second strategy can affect the scoring of your results (the Solr documentation on `SynonymFilterFactory` has some information about the impacts of such a choice).

You could use a generic synonym dictionary as input, but a lot of synonym rules are business tainted. You'll probably enhance the accuracy of your search engine if you build a synonym dictionary specific to your domain and business.

Synonym processing is available as a filter. `SynonymFilterFactory` accepts three parameters:

- ignoreCase—Ignore case when processing the tokens. The default is false.
- expand—If true, replace a token with several tokens (one for each synonym) in the token stream. If false, replace a token with its primary synonym. The default is true.
- synonyms—The resource name of the synonym file (for example, com/acme/synonyms.txt).

The synonym file format is best explained by the Solr reference documentation itself. Listing 5.11 is a small excerpt of this documentation.

Listing 5.11   Synonym file format as understood by the Solr filter

```
# blank lines and lines starting with pound are comments.

#Explicit mappings match any token sequence on the LHS of "=>"
#and replace with all alternatives on the RHS. These types of mappings
#ignore the expand parameter in the schema.
#Examples:
i-pod, i pod => ipod,
sea biscuit, sea biscit => seabiscuit

#Equivalent synonyms may be separated with commas and give
#no explicit mapping. In this case the mapping behavior will
#be taken from the expand parameter in the schema. This allows
#the same synonym file to be used in different synonym handling strategies.
#Examples:
ipod, i-pod, i pod
foozball , foosball
universe , cosmos

# If expand==true, "ipod, i-pod, i pod" is equivalent to the explicit mapping:
ipod, i-pod, i pod => ipod, i-pod, i pod
# If expand==false, "ipod, i-pod, i pod" is equivalent to the explicit
   mapping:
ipod, i-pod, i pod => ipod

#multiple synonym mapping entries are merged.
foo => foo bar
foo => baz
#is equivalent to
foo => foo bar, baz
```

Check the complete Solr documentation for more information.

While synonyms do merge words with different meanings, this technique does not do an efficient job at considering *persist* and *persistent*, for example, which are words from the same root.

5.2.6   *Searching by words from the same root*

If we were performing a query for the term *craftsmen*, would we also want documents returned that contained terms like *crafted, craftier, craftily, crafts, craft,* or *crafty*? More than likely we would, but based on what we've discussed so far, this would not happen. That's where *stemmers* come in handy.

A little bit of history

While the Porter stemming algorithm is the best-known stemming algorithm in the Lucene community thanks to the widespread usage of the Snowball language written by Dr. Porter, it isn't the first. The first-published stemming algorithm was the Lovins stemming algorithm by Julie Beth Lovins in 1968. See http://snowball.tartarus.org/algorithms/lovins/stemmer.html for some additional information.

The Google search engine started using stemming technology in 2003.

In 1979, Martin Porter designed an algorithm for reducing words to their root by removing their suffixes. This became known as the Porter stemming algorithm. The Porter stemming algorithm website is http://tartarus.org/~martin/PorterStemmer/index.html, and it has a link to the original algorithm paper along with links to the algorithm written in 22 programming languages, including Java, Perl, Ruby, C#, and even ERLANG.

In the first phase, rules are applied as in table 5.3.

Remember that these rules are applied in sequence. That's why the SS rule is applied before the S rule. If the rules were not applied in that order, the S rule could change things in a way that we would not want it to. The application of later rules deals with the length of the word to ensure that the matching portion is indeed a suffix and not so much a part of the word that it would lose its meaning if the supposed suffix were removed. For example, take the words *abatement* and *cement*. If we remove the suffix *ment* from them, we're left with *abate* and *ce*. Clearly, *cement* has lost its meaning and would not be stemmed.

The Lucene project has links to the Snowball stemming language, also developed by Porter. It's named in honor of the early (circa 1960s) string-manipulation programming language SNOBOL and is located at http://snowball.tartarus.org. Snowball is not just for the English language. The website has discussions of the algorithm in more than 15 languages, and it would be good for you to get involved if your native language is not listed there. Also, in the Contribution section, Lucene includes classes that perform the stemming functions along with a precompiled .jar file that can easily

Table 5.3   The first rule set in the sequential process of stemming a word

Rule					Example
SSES	->	SS	Caresses	->	Caress
IES	->	I	Ponies	->	Poni
SS	->	SS	Caress	->	Caress
S	->		Cats	->	Cat

be added to your application library. The JAR is located at lucene_install_directory/ contrib/snowball/lucene-snowball-*.jar. A `SnowballPorterFilterFactory` is available in Solr.

Let's see how to use the stemmer analyzer (listing 5.12).

Listing 5.12 Configure the Snowball filter for English

```
@Entity @Indexed
@AnalyzerDef(
    name="englishSnowball",
    tokenizer =
        @TokenizerDef(factory = StandardTokenizerFactory.class ),
    filters = {
        @TokenFilterDef(factory=StandardFilterFactory.class),
        @TokenFilterDef(factory=LowerCaseFilterFactory.class),
        @TokenFilterDef(factory = StopFilterFactory.class,
            params = @Parameter(name="words",
                                value="com/manning/hsia/dvdstore
                        ⇨ /stopwords.txt") ),
        @TokenFilterDef(                                        ❶ Use the
            factory = SnowballPorterFilterFactory.class,  ◁──┘   Snowball filter
            params = @Parameter(name="language",
                                value="English") )  ◁──┐
} )                                                   ❷ Define the
public class Item {                                     language
    @Fields( {
        @Field(name="title"),
        @Field(name="title_stemmer",
            analyzer=@Analyzer(definition="englishSnowball"))  ◁──┐
    })                                              title_stemmer uses │
    private String title;                           the Snowball filter │
    ...
}
```

Hibernate Search uses the `SnowballPorterFilterFactory` ❶ when indexing. It defines the language targeted ❷ (Danish, Dutch, English, Finnish, French, German, German2, Italian, Kp, Lovins (the first published stemming algorithm), Norwegian, Porter (original implementation of the Porter Stemming algorithm), Portuguese, Russian, Spanish, or Swedish). The default is English.

Listing 5.13 is an example of how to employ the Snowball analyzer to stem words during both the index build phase and the query phase. Don't focus here on how to write a query; we'll come to it in chapters 6 and 7.

Listing 5.13 Results of stemming both index and query terms

```
//ensure stemming works accordingly
public String checkStemmingIndex() {
    FullTextSession ftSession = SessionHolder.getFullTextSession();
    try {
        SearchFactory searchFactory = ftSession.getSearchFactory();
        Analyzer entityScopedAnalyzer =
            searchFactory.getAnalyzer(Item.class);
```

```
QueryParser parser =
   new QueryParser("id", entityScopedAnalyzer );        ◄──┘  ❶ Use Item
                                                                  analyzer
   //search on the exact field     ◄──┘  Build Lucene query
   Query query = parser.parse("title:saving");
                                                              Search the
   if ( ! "title:saving".equals( query.toString() ) ) {  ◄──┘ exact word
       return "searching the exact field should not alter the query";
   }
                                                          Return
                                                          matching
   org.hibernate.search.FullTextQuery hibQuery =          results
       ftSession.createFullTextQuery(query, Item.class);  ◄──┘
   @SuppressWarnings("unchecked")
   List<Item> results = hibQuery.list();

   //we find a single matching result
   int exactResultSize = results.size();
   if ( exactResultSize != 1 ) {
       return "exact match should only return 1 result";   Search same
   }                                                        word on the
   query = parser.parse("title_stemmer:saving");    ◄──┘   stemmed field

   if ( ! "title_stemmer:save".equals( query.toString() ) ) {  ◄──
       return "searching the stemmer field should search the stem";
   }                                                   Search the stem
   //return matching results                         version of each word ❷
   hibQuery = ftSession.createFullTextQuery(query);
   results = hibQuery.list();                        More matching
                                                     results are
   if ( results.size() <= exactResultSize ) {   ◄──┘ found
       return "stemming should return more matches";
   }
   return null; //no error
}
catch (ParseException e) {
   throw new SearchException(e);
}
}
```

When using the entity scoped analyzer provided by the Hibernate Search Session-Factory, ❶ the same analyzer will be used both at index time and search time, generating the same tokens. When searching the field using the englishSnowball analyzer, the query is rewritten by Lucene to search the stemmed version of each word (matching the token stored in the index) ❷.

Be sure to use the same analyzer during indexing and in preparing your queries because the terms need to be reduced in the same way. In listing 5.13, checkStemmingIndex() returns null; more results are returned when the stemmer analyzer is used.

TIP   To use the same analyzer at indexing and querying time, retrieve it from
        fullTextSession.getSearchFactory().getAnalyzer(Targeted-
        Entity.class). See Section 7.2.

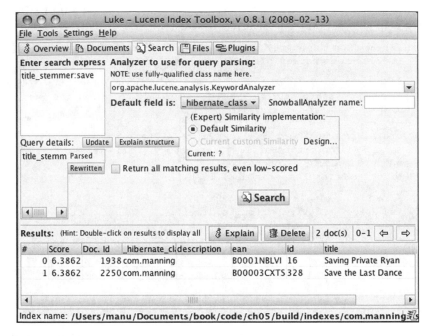

Figure 5.6   Luke is used to examine the index created from *saving* and *save* and shows that the index contains only one term, save.

Figure 5.6 shows Luke examining the generated index. Notice that even though we indexed two different words (*saving, save*), the index of the `title_stemmer` field contains only one term, *save*.

When you are playing the wizard with analyzers, always keep an eye on Luke. This will save you a lot of time.

What about relevance?

How does this stemming process affect relevance? After all, we've reduced the number of terms indexed, as shown in figure 5.6, which should lead to an increase in search efficiency. At the same time we've reduced query terms to their lowest common denominator, which will result in more hits.

As it turns out, stemming as opposed to using a nonstemmed system is looked at as a Recall enhancer. Stemming causes the number of both retrieved and relevant documents to increase, but the retrieved count increases at a higher rate than the relevant count. If you examine the relevance equations in chapter 12 (sections 12.34 and 12.35), you'll see that Precision suffers as the number of retrieved documents (the Precision denominator) increases. At the same time, Recall increases since the count of retrieved documents (the Recall denominator) increases faster than the total number of relevant documents (the Recall numerator).

If you don't understand this right now, it's not an issue; you will as soon as you read chapter 12.

That's just about as deep into the stemming process as we wish to go. We hope you enjoyed diving into the tricky little details of languages as much as we did. But when should you apply all those techniques?

5.2.7 Choosing a technique

Should you use all these techniques? All at once? No. Hibernate Search provides easy access to these tools. Some of them are competing in the same space (*n*-gram, phonetic approximation). Check what's best for your search engine by building fast prototypes. Don't forget that the more complex an analyzer, the longer indexing will take. Sometimes the simplest solutions do marvels.

The authors recommend that you use approximation analyzers in dedicated fields. For example, listing 5.14 uses the classic analyzer as a default to index a property and uses the *n*-gram analyzer on a secondary field to index the same property.

Listing 5.14 Using approximation analyzers in dedicated fields

```
@Fields({
    @Field(index=Index.TOKENIZED),
    @Field(name="title_ngram",
           index=Index.TOKENIZED,
           analyzer=@Analyzer(definition="ngramanalyzer")
})
private String title;
```

The interesting part of this approach is the ability to do searches in layers, expanding the approximation level each time. The search engine applies different sets of rules ranging from very strict to very loose in layers. If the search is specific enough, the strict search will find sufficient information; if the search terms are somewhat fuzzy, a query using the approximation fields will provide better results. The search engine can execute the strict query first, and if more data is required, it can execute a second query using approximation techniques, and so on. Once the search engine has retrieved enough information, it bypasses the next layers (see section 6.4.3 for more information). Remember that a Lucene query is quite cheap. Running several Lucene queries per user query is perfectly acceptable.

We've answered the question of how to index. Isn't it marvelous to see the Lucene flexibility in action and how it copes with the complexity of our language(s)? As we promised, analyzers are not that difficult to use and open a lot of possibilities. Of course, analyzing means nothing if you don't know when to index your data and which part of your data needs indexing.

5.3 Transparent indexing

One of the main burdens of using naked Lucene is trying to decide which data has changed and needs reindexing and when to index the changing data. Keeping track of the changed data set is a problem in itself, but indexing this data efficiently is arguably a bigger challenge that traditionally requires writing infrastructure code on top of Lucene.

Thankfully, Hibernate Search does all this hard work for you.

5.3.1 *Capturing which data has changed*

Hibernate Search has the ability to capture every change made by Hibernate Core. When an entity is created, updated, or deleted, or when a collection is changed, Hibernate Search determines which index documents need to be either created or deleted.

> **NOTE**   A LUCENE DOCUMENT IS READ-ONLY   While a Lucene index (a collection of documents) can be updated, each individual document (representing an entity entry) is read-only. When a change is made on an entity, the Lucene document must be deleted and a new document created. In this book, *updating* a document should be understood as deleting and creating a document.

Capturing changes becomes a cross-cutting concern for the application. All changes applied in the following ways are captured:

- Through an explicit Hibernate `Session` or `EntityManager` call (`persist`, `remove`, `merge`, and so on).
- By cascading on an object graph
- On the domain model and processed at flush time by Hibernate

How can we enable automatic change tracking?

If you use Hibernate Annotations or Hibernate EntityManager (versions 3.3.1 or above), Hibernate Search transparently plugs in the necessary event listeners. Nothing is required in the configuration.

> **NOTE**   A bug covering change tracking for collections has been solved in Hibernate Search 3.0.1 and Hibernate Core 3.2.6. Be sure to use at least these versions.

If you use Hibernate Core without Hibernate Annotations, a few extra steps are required. The event listeners are not transparently registered for you, and you'll need to add some properties in your hibernate.cfg.xml file. Listing 5.15 shows such a configuration file.

Listing 5.15   Hibernate Core without Hibernate Annotations requires extra steps

```
<hibernate-configuration>
    <session-factory>
        ...
        <event type="post-update">
            <listener
    class="org.hibernate.search.event.FullTextIndexEventListener"/>
        </event>
```

```
        <event type="post-insert">
            <listener
    class="org.hibernate.search.event.FullTextIndexEventListener"/>
        </event>
        <event type="post-delete">
            <listener
    class="org.hibernate.search.event.FullTextIndexEventListener"/>
        </event>

        <event type="post-collection-recreate">
            <listener
    class="org.hibernate.search.event.FullTextIndexEventListener"/>
        </event>
         <event type="post-collection-remove">
            <listener
    class="org.hibernate.search.event.FullTextIndexEventListener"/>
        </event>
        <event type="post-collection-update">
            <listener
    class="org.hibernate.search.event.FullTextIndexEventListener"/>
        </event>
    </session-factory>
</hibernate-configuration>
```

WARNING If you use the old Hibernate Search 3.0.*x*, check listing 2.5 in section 2.2.2 because the configuration is slightly different. The collection-related events work only on Hibernate Core 3.2.6 and above.

That's it! While we encourage you to use Hibernate Annotations, the extra steps required to use plain Hibernate Core are fairly minimal.

Hibernate Search knows all about the changes that need to be applied to the Lucene indexes thanks to the event listeners. But when does it apply them? And how? This is what we will discover now.

5.3.2 *Indexing the changed data*

Hibernate Search is notified when a change needs to be made to the index. One possible strategy would have been to apply each change right away. This strategy unfortunately suffers from two main drawbacks:

- Performance
- ACID

Applying changes one at a time is fairly inefficient in Lucene: You need to open the index file(s), apply the changes, flush the changes to the disk, and close the file(s). However, Lucene is pretty efficient at applying updates in batch.

The second problem is related to your application workflow. To understand this, let's step back a little and examine how ORMs work. An ORM does not execute an update as soon as your entity changes. That would be fairly inefficient. Instead, it tries to delay as long as possible the database updates. If everything goes well, all the database changes are applied right before the database commit. Applying changes is called *flushing*. Flushing can happen anytime before commit, in order to keep the results of queries consistent.

Let's imagine for a moment that Hibernate Search indexes changes as soon as they're flushed. If the transaction is rolled back, no changes will eventually be persisted to the database but they will to the index. Nobody wants to have stale data in the query results. We need a solution.

When a flush triggers a change to an indexed entity or collection, Hibernate Search adds the change to a queue. This queue is scoped by transaction. During the commit operation, whether it is triggered explicitly by the application or implicitly through declarative transaction demarcation, Hibernate Search processes the queue and applies the changes to the index. The sequence of events is shown in figure 5.7.

This process has the following benefits:

- Changes on the index are not applied until the transaction is committed (and the database persists the changes).
- All changes are applied at the same time in the indexes.

When a transaction is rolled back, the queue is simply discarded without being processed. Not only do the database and the index stay synchronized, but minimal work is performed until the transaction is committed.

In most scenarios, your transaction changes will span more than one entity type. If you use the default Hibernate Search configuration, changes will span more than one index. By indexing changes when a commit happens rather than when a change happens, you reduce the amount of input/output necessary for Lucene and the time a Lucene index is locked, increasing scalability.

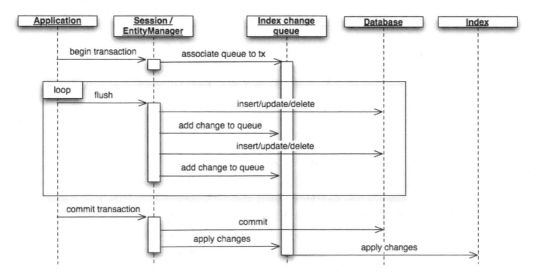

Figure 5.7 Hibernate Search queues all changes applied to the database during a flush. During the commit operation, the queue is processed and the index is updated.

Are changes made in the indexes transactional?

While changes to a Lucene index can be made transactional, Lucene is not an XA resource. If we step back and look at the resources involved in the transaction, we have:

- The database
- Several Lucene indexes (one per entity type by default

Hibernate Search doesn't try very hard to make Lucene look like an XA resource and apply a two-phase commit (2PC) protocol. Several reasons have driven this choice.

Hibernate Search in its design treats the database as the central container of information. The Lucene indexes are considered more like convenient data structures that enhance the user experience. As a matter of fact, indexes can be entirely rebuilt from the database. Ensuring transactional integrity for such data structures is not critical.

Lucene and Hibernate Search will enhance the user experience. It would be bad for the user's business to grind to a halt if the indexing operations fail. Let's look at an example. A website has an order process that registers a customer and an order. Do we want the order to fail because the indexing process has failed? Or is it preferable to get the order into the system and deal with the indexing issue later on? In a pure 2PC system, if one resource fails, all resources abort; if Lucene fails to index, the database aborts the transaction.

The final argument in favor of a loose transactional approach is to allow the indexing process to be applied asynchronously (either at a different time or on a different server). The next section discusses the benefits of indexing asynchronism and how it could be made recoverable.

In brief, Hibernate Search does not make Lucene index XA resources, and this was done on purpose.

People familiar with Hibernate and Seam know the pattern called conversation. A *conversation* is a series of request-response cycles in which the user ends up with a set of changes atomically applied to the database. One example is a wizard screen, but nowadays with the use of AJAX, a lot of operations are conversational in nature. Keeping a database transaction open during several request-response cycles is usually not an option, especially when the user decides to go get coffee between two request-response cycles!

A common solution to work around this problem is to keep a Hibernate session open for the duration of the conversation and set the flush mode to manual. In manual mode, the session keeps all the object changes without applying them to the database. The last request-response cycle flushes all changes to the database and atomically commits. Seam goes even further by letting you describe conversations declaratively and does the hard work for you.

How does Hibernate Search play in the conversation model? Very well indeed. Because the Hibernate session delays all changes, Hibernate Search is not even notified until the last flush operation. From your point of view, Hibernate Search participates in the conversation.

Some people apply database changes outside a transaction, usually for obscure, unjustified, ideological reasons. In this situation, Hibernate Search applies changes to the index right away because it doesn't have a context to attach the change queue to. You should always use database transactions, even for read-only operations; contrary to popular belief, using a transaction for a series of read-only operations may be faster than not using an explicit transaction depending on the database engine. Without explicit transactions, the database has to create one implicit transaction for each read-only operation.

One additional benefit of queuing changes per transaction is that the list of changes can be applied in an asynchronous way, even by another server. We'll explore this topic in the next section.

5.3.3   *Choosing the right backend*

In the previous section, we did not describe what happens when Hibernate Search applies the changes to the Lucene index. Multiple scenarios are possible.

The most straightforward solution and the default in Hibernate Search consists of indexing the changes using Lucene. Lucene directly applies the changes to the involved index(es) when the commit operation happens. Once indexing is done, the commit operation is considered complete. The commit operation can be triggered explicitly by calling the `commit` method from the `Session` or the `EntityManager` if a JDBC transaction is used (see figure 5.8). It can also be triggered transparently in a container-managed transaction environment such as EJB, JBoss, Seam, or Spring.

This solution is sufficient for most cases and ensures that the index is synchronously up to date with the database.

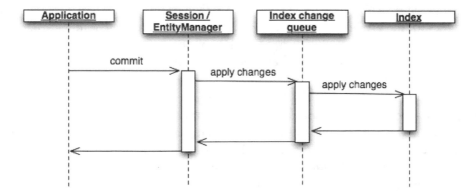

Figure 5.8   By default, Hibernate Search applies changes to the index during the commit operation in a synchronous way.

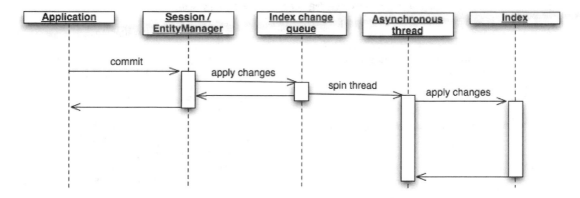

Figure 5.9 **Hibernate Search applies changes to the index asynchronously in a different thread to provide faster response time.**

A second strategy is possible. In lieu of executing the indexing operations synchronously during commit, a separate thread is spun. The indexing work is delegated to the thread. Figure 5.9 shows the chain of events.

This approach minimizes the user response time; the price (in time) spent on indexing and waiting for input/outputs is not directly paid by the user. It also gracefully absorbs heavy writing periods.

Updating a Lucene index requires a pessimistic lock, which essentially prevents any other updates from occurring during this period. Applying the changes asynchronously helps smooth the impact of heavy change periods. Hibernate Search lets you enable asynchronous mode and define the maximum number of threads spun. You configure these setting though the properties described in table 5.4.

Defining the buffer queue size is best done through performance testing. The queue should be high enough to absorb most of your processing peaks but should not consume too much memory. When the buffer size is reached, subsequent indexing operations are done in the `commit` method synchronously. This provides a feedback loop to your architecture.

Resource control is a trade-off problem. Should a server accept as many requests as possible at the risk of replying to these requests in an unreasonable amount of time? Or should the server decline the requests it cannot handle to keep a decent quality of service on the accepted ones? Regardless of your answers, limiting the buffer size will provide the necessary feedback to take action, because the rest of your architecture will be aware of the indexing overhead.

Don't worry too much, and don't envision doom scenarios right away. Lucene is a high-performance library that's known to handle massive charges for well-known websites. Don't optimize prematurely. Run performance benchmarks, and check the reactions of your architecture. The limiting factor is likely to be elsewhere.

Table 5.4   Enabling asynchronous indexing is done through properties.

Property	Description
`hibernate.worker.execution`	`sync` or `async`: `sync` will index changes during the commit operation synchronously. `async` will delegate the work to a dedicated thread. Default is `sync`.
`hibernate.worker.thread_pool.size`	Define the number of threads available in the pool for index purposes. Default is `1`.
	Unless different transactions are likely to operate on different indexes, using a pool larger than 1 will have no significant effect.
`hibernate.worker.buffer_queue.max`	Amount of indexing work queued for processing by the thread pool. This is essentially the buffer size. Default is `infinite`.
	Defining a limit is recommended to avoid stacking up unfinished work and potentially experiencing `OutOfMemoryException` problems.
	If the queue limit is reached, the indexing work is processed in the caller's thread (which will likely wait for the directory lock).

The strategies we've seen so far could be summarized as these:

- Drop the pen, do the work right away, and call back when the work is done.
- Continue working on the initial task, keep the additional work in mind, and do it in parallel.

In both cases, the virtual machine (VM) is still responsible for the work. Finishing the task right away or saving it for later doesn't make any difference to the total amount of work the VM has to do. There's an even better approach: delegate! Why not ask someone else you trust to do the work?

Hibernate Search can delegate the indexing work to another server. Instead of processing the change queue right away or spinning a thread to process the change queue in parallel, Hibernate Search can send the change queue (essentially the work to be done) to another virtual machine. The default implementation uses Java Message Service (JMS). The change queue is sent to a JMS queue. Another instance of Hibernate Search listens to and processes the JMS queue; this instance is often referred to as the *master*. The chain of events on the slave is shown in figure 5.10.

Delegating the work has several advantages:

- No resources (time, CPU, IO) are consumed by the VM that processes the main operations (serving web requests, applying the database changes).
- The VM processing the main operations is not impacted by the Lucene global pessimistic lock; the inherent scalability issue of the Lucene design is not propagated to the rest of the application.

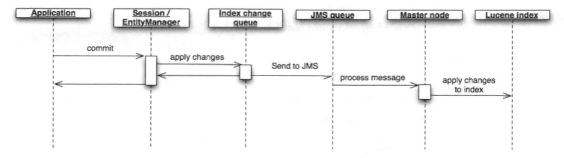

Figure 5.10 Hibernate Search sends the information to run the indexing work to a JMS queue.

- The risk of OutOfMemoryException that asynchronous mode suffers from is no longer present.
- This system can be clustered naturally.

This approach has a lot of benefits. However, as in real life, when you delegate, you like to receive the work done at some point (unless you delegate to your trash bin). Changes processed by the master need to be propagated to the other Hibernate Search instances. We previously described one solution for this in this chapter. Section 5.1.4 offers a way to share a Lucene directory across a cluster without suffering from Lucene's global lock scalability difficulties.

As in many configuration strategies in Hibernate Search, enabling JMS mode is a matter of adding a few configuration properties:

1 Enable the JMS backend:

```
hibernate.worker.backend jms
```

2 (Optional) Define the Java Naming Directory Interface (JNDI) configuration properties in your Hibernate configuration file using the hibernate.worker.jndi.* prefix or place them in a jndi.properties file.

 If you run in an application server where the JMS connection factory and queue are bound, you won't need to configure JNDI. Otherwise you might need to add a jndi.properties file containing something similar to this:

```
java.naming.factory.initial=org.jnp.interfaces.NamingContextFactory
java.naming.provider.url=localhost:1099
java.naming.factory.url.pkgs=org.jboss.naming:org.jnp.interfaces
```

Alternatively, if the JNDI properties shouldn't be shared, you can use the Hibernate Search properties and add them to your Hibernate configuration file, like this:

```
hibernate.search.worker.jndi.class=
  org.jnp.interfaces.NamingContextFactory
hibernate.search.worker.jndi.url=localhost:1099
hibernate.search.worker.jndi.java.naming.factory.url.pkgs=
  org.jboss.naming:org.jnp.interfaces
```

The configuration values described are typical for JBoss AS. Refer to your application server configuration for more information.

3 Define the JNDI name of JMS connection factory (`/ConnectionFactory` in JBoss AS):

```
hibernate.worker.jms.connection_factory /ConnectionFactory
```

4 Define the JNDI name of the JMS queue. The JMS queue will receive the Hibernate Search change queues as individual messages.

```
hibernate.worker.jms.queue queue/hibernatesearch
```

A typical configuration file will contain the properties described in listing 5.16.

Listing 5.16   Typical configuration properties to enable the JMS backend

```
hibernate.worker.backend jms
hibernate.worker.jms.connection_factory /ConnectionFactory
hibernate.worker.jms.queue queue/hibernatesearch
```

Chapter 10 gives you a better picture of clustered environments and how JMS, the distributed `DirectoryProvider`, and Hibernate Search work together to cluster your search architecture.

Hibernate Search provides several alternatives to the seasoned architectures. You can adjust the search indexing operations to the application's needs. But what if this is not enough—can we go further? Are we limited to the "genuine" Hibernate Search architectures? Not at all; Hibernate Search is agnostic to the architecture and offers lots of extension points.

5.3.4   *Extension points: beyond the proposed architectures*

Hibernate Search has a pluggable architecture that allows you to change when and how indexing happens. To understand what can be changed, let's dive into some of the architecture's details and see how it works. Figure 5.11 shows the relationships between the architecture's components.

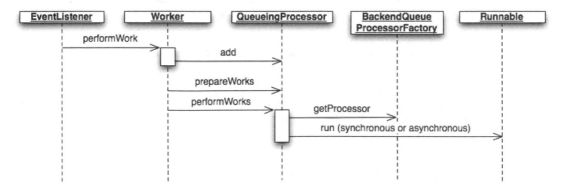

Figure 5.11   Sequence of operations from an entity change to its propagation

The three main systems at play are:

- Worker—Responsible for receiving all entity changes, queueing them by context, and deciding when a context starts and finishes.
- QueueingProcessor—Responsible for piling up changes in a given context, preparing the work for Lucene, and triggering the work either synchronously or asynchronously.
- BackEndQueueProcessorFactory—Responsible for providing a Runnable instance that will perform the list of Lucene changes.

NOTE The APIs described here are semipublic. Although they haven't changed since the first Hibernate Search's final General Availability (GA) release, they might evolve over time in Hibernate Search if such a need arises. The Hibernate Search project policy guarantees it won't break these APIs inside a given microrelease; for example, all 3.1.x releases will remain compatible.

Let's have a closer look at each element.

WORKER: DEFINING THE CONTEXT

By default Hibernate Search keeps track of entity changes per transaction. The piece of code responsible for collecting the changes and sorting them per transaction is the TransactionalWorker.

The Worker is responsible for keeping track of changes per context and for deciding when a context starts and stops. Upon a context stop, the Worker implementation should perform (usually delegate) the work accumulated in the context. In the default implementation, when a transaction commits, the Worker prepares the work (essentially converts the entity changes into Lucene changes) and performs it.

A Worker implementation must be thread-safe because it is shared for a given SearchFactory; a SearchFactory has the same lifecycle as a SessionFactory or an EntityManagerFactory.

Although the transactional context makes the most sense for a variety of reasons (because of the definition of transactions and the way ORMs behave), one can envision a context piling up all concurrent changes and flushing them based on the number of changes or even a context lifecycle driven by application events.

Overriding the default context implementation is done through a configuration property, as shown in listing 5.17. All properties starting with the prefix hibernate.search.worker. are passed to the Worker implementation at initialization time.

Listing 5.17 Define a custom Worker implementation

```
org.hibernate.search.worker.scope my.custom.applicationtriggered.WorkerImpl
org.hibernate.search.worker.triggers_before_run 5
```

Most likely you won't need to create a custom Worker implementation. The transaction-scoped approach is the most appropriate.

As the work is collected, it needs to be kept by context. Once the context ends, the queue of entity changes must be prepared and processed. This is the role of the QueueingProcessor.

QUEUEINGPROCESSOR: CONVERTING AN ENTITY CHANGE INTO A LUCENE CHANGE

A QueueingProcessor keeps together entity changes for a given context. It fulfills three functions:

- Queues all the entity changes for a given context
- Converts entity changes into Lucene changes
- Passes the queue of Lucene changes to the BackendQueueProcessorFactory

The process that converts entity change notifications into a list of Lucene Documents to either delete or add to the indexes involves several actions:

- Eliminating duplicate change notifications
- Applying the relevant field bridges for a given entity
- Processing the associations marked as embedded
- Determining associated entities containing the processed entities

All this is done by the prepareWorks method; this method is solely responsible for converting the object to its index representation.

The QueueingProcessor then passes the Lucene change queue to the BackendQueueProcessorFactory either synchronously or asynchronously depending on the settings (see section 5.3.3 for more information). Note that you cannot override the default implementation. The preparation code is very specific and subtle, so the need for a custom implementation is unlikely. If you have this need, bring it up to the Hibernate Search developers at hibernate-dev@lists.jboss.org.

BACKENDQUEUEPROCESSORFACTORY: GETTING IT OUT OF HIBERNATE SEARCH'S WAY

Now that we have a list of Lucene index changes to apply, we need to apply them. The most obvious solution is to fire up Lucene and delegate the work to the library. This is essentially what LuceneBackendQueueProcessor does. The work isn't as easy as it sounds, because you need to acquire locks to various Lucene indexes in a way that prevents deadlocks and should take care of Hibernate Search sharding strategies (see section 9.4). It's unlikely that you'll need to adjust this implementation.

More surprisingly, LuceneBackendQueueProcessor isn't the only implementation Hibernate Search provides. Another implementation named JMSBackendQueueProcessorFactory sends the Lucene change list to a JMS queue instead of processing it locally. You've already started to see some of the benefits of JMS as a distributed model in section 5.3.3, and you'll see more in chapter 10.

Some people, for one reason or another, want to use a different communication layer than JMS (probably because of the myth that JMS is heavyweight). Implementing a custom BackendQueueProcessorFactory is the perfect solution for that. A BackendQueueProcessorFactory is responsible for returning a Runtime instance that, when executed, will push the Lucene change list out of Hibernate Search's responsibility (either by applying the changes or by delegating the changes to another instance).

Defining the `BackendQueueProcessorFactory` implementation to use is one property away (see listing 5.18 for an example). Like the `Worker` implementations, all the properties prefixed with `hibernate.search.worker` are passed to the `Backend-QueueProcessorFactory` at initialization time.

```
org.hibernate.search.worker.backend
➥ my.custom.JGroupsBackendQueueProcessorFactory
org.hibernate.search.worker.use_multicast true
```

The fully qualified class name of the factory is defined in `org.hibernate.search.worker.backend`.

This section is in no way comprehensive, but it should give you a good idea of Hibernate Search's flexibility and the pieces you can customize. Remember, these APIs are semipublic. Don't blame us if you need to tweak them a bit between two major Hibernate Search releases.

You probably have noticed that this section is almost free of Java code. No, the authors have not become lazy. We warned you in the title of this section. Hibernate Search takes care of all the indexing bookkeeping for your applications. As soon as Hibernate Core makes a change, Hibernate Search propagates the change to Lucene *transparently*.

But what can you do if you need to index your data manually? What about the existing data set lying in the database? Should you really wait for an update before Hibernate Search wakes up and indexes the data? The next section will answer these questions.

5.4　*Indexing:when transparency is not enough*

While transparent indexing is easy and covers most cases, you'll find situations where your application wants Hibernate Search to explicitly index entities. Transparent indexing happens when Hibernate Core applies a change to an entity (add, update, or delete), but at times you'll want to index when no change happens. The initial indexing of an existing database is the most obvious and prominent use case, but it isn't the only one, as you'll see later in this section.

Hibernate Search provides a way to directly ask for manual indexing as part of its core API.

5.4.1　*Manual indexing APIs*

When Hibernate Search receives a change event from Hibernate Core, it triggers either the object indexing to the Lucene index or the object removal from the Lucene index. Those two primitive operations are available in the `FullTextSession` and `FullTextEntityManager` APIs:

- `index(Object entity)`—Index or reindex an entity managed by the session without triggering any database change.

- `purge(Class entityType, Serializable id)`—Remove from the Lucene index an entity with the given identifier without removing the entity from the database.
- `purgeAll(Class entityType)`—Remove from the Lucene index all entities of a given type (and all its subclasses) without removing them from the database.

Listing 5.19 shows how to index all objects of a given type. Don't copy this example because it suffers a major flaw (see section 5.4.2 for more information). But it should be good enough if you're indexing a handful of objects.

Listing 5.19 Indexing all objects manually (the naïve approach)

```
tx = session.beginTransaction();

//read the data from the database
Query query = session.createCriteria(Item.class);    ❶ Retrieve entities to
List<Object> items = query.list();                        be indexed

for (Object item : items) {          ❷ Mark them for
    session.index( item );              indexing
}
                                     ❸ Indexing work performed at
tx.commit();                            commit time
```

The objects to be indexed need to be managed by the session ❶. Objects to be manually indexed are added ❷. The Lucene index is updated during commit (synchronously or asynchronously) ❸.

Manually indexing an object is done by passing it to the `index` method. The entity must be managed (that is, attached to the session). Typically the list of objects will be loaded by id or through a query before being passed to the `FullTextSession` (or `FullTextEntityManager`) index method. Another strategy is to reattach the entity instance by calling `lock`, `saveOrUpdate`, or `merge`.

WARNING Don't forget that `merge` doesn't attach the object but returns a managed copy of the object. The returned value is the one to index.

```
Object managedCopy = session.merge( detachedEntity );
session.index( managedcopy );
```

Don't use listing 5.19 to initially index all entities from the database; you'll most likely suffer from `OutOfMemoryException`. We'll discuss a better technique in a bit.

The second main operation (listing 5.20) consists of removing an obsolete entity from the index without removing the entity from the database.

Listing 5.20 Removing objects from the Lucene index

```
tx = session.beginTransaction();

for (Integer id : ids) {             ❶ Mark an entity
    session.purge(Item.class, id);      for purge
}
                                     ❷ Actual purge happens
tx.commit();                            at commit time
```

Removing an entity from the index does not require the entity instance. ❶ The entity type and id are sufficient. Changes are applied at commit time ❷ (synchronously or asynchronously).

This operation does not require the entity instance; the entity type and its id are used.

Sometimes, especially when you want to completely reindex your data (or when running unit tests), you need to remove all information about a given entity type from the index. The purgeAll operation does just that. Listing 5.21 demonstrates how to use the API.

> **Listing 5.21 Removing all entities for a given type from the index**
>
> ```
> tx = session.beginTransaction()            ❶ Remove all index
>                                               data for Item
> session.purgeAll( Item.class );    ◁──┘              ❷ Actual removal happens
>                                                         at commit time
> tx.commit();                       ◁──────────────┘
> ```

Remove all entities of type Item from the index ❶ (including the subclasses of Item if any). Changes are applied at commit time ❷ (synchronously or asynchronously).

All information about the given entity type and its subclasses will be removed from the index. Note that it will not erase the Lucene directory but will remove elements from it.

After doing massive indexing or purging, it's a good idea to trigger an optimize operation. Optimizing the index is very similar to defragmenting a disk. See section 9.3 for more details.

We recommended that you apply indexing and purging operations in a transaction. If you don't, Hibernate Search will need to apply changes one by one to the Lucene indexes, which will be suboptimal to say the least.

Earlier in this section, we hinted that indexing a lot of information could lead to OutOfMemoryExceptions. Let's discuss why and, more important, how to avoid that (this is an "in Action" book, after all).

5.4.2 Initially indexing a data set

We now have a nice new search engine for our DVD store website and are ready to kick some butts in the retail market—almost. We have a huge legacy database that knows all about our DVD catalog, and we need to initially index this catalog. We know that when we add, change, or remove a DVD from the catalog, Hibernate Search takes care of keeping the index up to date. But what about the existing data?

We'll use the manual indexing APIs we just discovered, but the naïve approach described in listing 5.19 won't work. This approach consists of loading all the DVDs and indexing them. Unfortunately (or on the contrary fortunately) for us, the number of DVDs is large enough to exceed the VM memory available. We need to read entities by batch, index them, and remove them from memory before processing the next batch. An even better approach would be to read entities as a stream, then process them. As shown in listing 5.22, Hibernate Search offers a solution.

Listing 5.22   Index entities without suffering from `OutOfMemoryException`

```
session.setFlushMode(FlushMode.MANUAL);        1  Disable flush operations
session.setCacheMode(CacheMode.IGNORE);
                                                  Disable 2nd-level
tx = session.beginTransaction();               2  cache operations

//read the data from the database
//Scrollable results will avoid loading too many objects in memory
ScrollableResults results = session.createCriteria( Item.class )
        .scroll( ScrollMode.FORWARD_ONLY );       Ensure forward only
                                               3  result set
int index = 0;
while( results.next() ) {
    index++;                                   4  Index entities
    session.index( results.get(0) );
    if (index % BATCH_SIZE == 0) {                Apply changes to
        session.flushToIndexes();              5  the index
        session.clear();        Clear the session,
    }                           releasing memory
}
                        Apply the remaining
tx.commit();            index changes
```

1 Prevent Hibernate Core from doing unnecessary flush operatons. **2** Prevent Hibernate Core from interacting with the second-level cache. Since a lot of entities are expected to be processed, using a second-level cache would be unproductive. **3** Use a forward-only scroll to ensure the JDBC driver does not cache the previously processed rows. **4** Apply indexing to the current entity. **5** On every `BATCH_SIZE` operation, apply index changes, freeing the index queue, and clear the session to free up memory

By using a forward-only scrollable result set and by clearing the session every *n*th operation, we ensure that memory doesn't leak. Well, almost. Remember that Hibernate Search doesn't apply the change in the index until commit; rather it keeps track of the changes and consumes memory. This defeats the whole purpose of using `clear`. To work around this problem, Hibernate Search lets you call `flushToIndexes()`. On the method call, all index changes are executed (to the backend). By releasing the index change queue and clearing the session, you ensure that the memory consumption stays under control.

NOTE   If you use Hibernate 3.0.*x*, `flushToIndexes()` isn't available. Instead, you can define a batch size that limits the number of operations queued before being applied to Lucene. Check listing 5.23 to see how this property is configured. Make sure this value equals the batch size in your loop.

Listing 5.23   Define the entity job queue batch size (Hibernate Search 3.0)

```
# the batch size must equal the loop size in your indexing code
hibernate.search.worker.batch_size 1000
```

Use the same algorithm described in listing 5.22 and simply remove the call to `flushToIndexes()`.

This solution is inferior and more error prone for these reasons:

- Batch size in the configuration and in the code must be the same.
- This limit is applied to all transactions regardless of the use of the manual indexing.

This is a very good reason to upgrade to the latest version!

If you follow this pattern, you'll likely ensure fast enough indexing time without risking `OutOfMemoryException`.

Indexing all my data is still really slow What's going on?

It's hard to give numbers because they vary so much depending on these factors:

- Size of the data to index
- Input/output disk performance
- Database performance
- Network performance
- Size of the index directories

Nevertheless, if you think Hibernate Search is way too slow to index your data, something is wrong. Let's explore some of the things that could go wrong:

- The indexing code doesn't follow the strategy described in listing 5.22; using a scrollable result set, avoiding interaction with the second-level cache, and clearing the session on a regular basis are critical.
- `flushToIndexes()` is not called before `clear()`; the memory is not released.
- Hibernate does multiple queries when indexing an object (enable SQL logging to see what's going on behind the scene).

Remember that associations embedded in the index and associations marked as `@ContainedIn` must be loaded and traversed by Hibernate Search. If your initial query doesn't load these associations, Hibernate Search will hit the database to request them, and you'll essentially face the infamous *n*+1 queries problem. You have several possible solutions:

- Write a query that loads the traversed graph in one shot.
- Make use of the passive fetching strategies offered by Hibernate Core (subselect and entity/collection batch size).
- Use both techniques.

If you're ranting about the number of associations that need to be loaded, chances are you didn't follow our advice from chapter 4. Make sure to use `@IndexedEmbedded` and `@ContainedBy` if you really need to query the association. That's okay; the next time you'll pay more attention. ;o)

This is a first-aid kit for improving performance. Make sure to read section 9.1 for more information on indexing optimization.

This is the primary, and in a lot of applications the only, use case for using a manual indexing API. But the manual indexing API can be useful in a couple of other situations. Let's explore some of them.

5.4.3   *Disabling transparent indexing: taking control*

In traditional Lucene applications, one of the indexing strategies consists of indexing the data once a day in one big batch operation (see figure 5.12). This is a legitimate approach because it solves some of the problems encountered in Lucene:

- There's no locking issue, because the batch process is the only one in control.
- Indexing in a batch operation is the best approach with Lucene performance-wise.
- It does not affect front-end production servers.

There are drawbacks associated with such a strategy:

- Queries can return stale data (up to one day old).
- Contrary to the standard Hibernate Search approach, the database needs to be hit again when reindexing occurs because the data has to be loaded. This puts more pressure on the database.

Hibernate Search lets you simulate such a mode by disabling the event model. When it is off, changes made by Hibernate Core are not monitored by Hibernate Search, but you can still use the manual indexing APIs. In such a system, the batch indexing process would read the database and use the manual indexing APIs to update a Lucene directory. The updated Lucene directory would then be pushed one way or another to the front end (copy, rsync, shared directory, and so on).

To disable event processing in Hibernate Search, use the `hibernate.search.indexing_strategy` property:

```
hibernate.search.indexing_strategy manual
```

WARNING   Even if the events are not processed, the event listeners must still be present for Hibernate Search to work. If you use Hibernate Annotations, you'll have no problem because the event listener registration is done transparently for you. But if you use Hibernate Core, you must be sure to keep the event listeners in the configuration (see section 5.3.1 for more information).

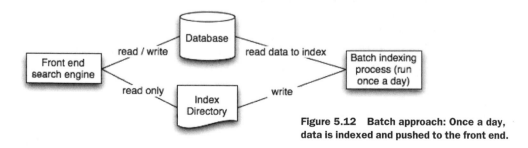

Figure 5.12   Batch approach: Once a day, data is indexed and pushed to the front end.

If you think this approach fits your application model better, don't run too fast. You can mix the Hibernate Search event model and still index data in a dedicated server once a day. By using the clustered JMS mode, Hibernate Search sends all domain model modifications to a queue. The Message-Driven Bean reading the JMS queue can process it once a day rather than as soon as the message arrives (see figure 5.13). Alternatively, messages can be processed as they arrive (which will smooth the workload on the dedicated server), but the updated indexes can be copied once a day rather than once per hour.

Keeping the event model has its benefits:

- It's fairly lightweight for the front end because it doesn't apply indexing.
- The batch-indexing process doesn't have to figure out which part of the data set needs reindexing.
- The batch indexing process doesn't have to read the data from the database, and the database workload is reduced.

One of the drawbacks is that the same entity might be updated several times between two runs of the batch process. It will uselessly be indexed multiple times. There are no functional consequences for the index, just some spare cycles lost.

The second use case we'll discuss involves third-party applications. Sometimes your application is not the only one updating the data you're relying on. This is quite problematic in a transparent event-based model because Hibernate Search won't be notified of these changes by default. The manual indexing API can be used in several ways to work around this problem.

You can disable the event model and manually update or recreate your indexes on a regular basis. The batch process is then responsible for reindexing the part of the data set that changed or the entire data set if the indexing time is acceptable.

Another solution that might require more work on your side is to open a public API in the application that's to be notified of an external change. Let's say your core application is in Java, but part of it is done in Ruby. You can easily expose a URL or a service that your Ruby application will call when it changes an entity. When receiving

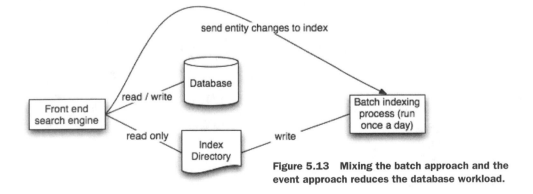

Figure 5.13 Mixing the batch approach and the event approach reduces the database workload.

an event (the entity type and its primary key), your application invokes the manual indexing API and keeps the index up to date (see figure 5.14).

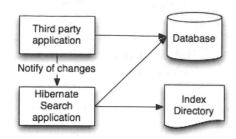

Try to stay as much as possible in the transparent indexing model, but don't panic if you cannot. Hibernate Search has the necessary APIs to palliate when the event model doesn't catch up with all the necessary changes.

Figure 5.14   A third-party application that modifies the same data set can notify the Hibernate Search application of any change.

5.5   *Summary*

This chapter covered the missing pieces of how indexing is done in Hibernate Search. Where chapters 3 and 4 covered the mapping between the object model and the index model, chapter 5 focused on the infrastructure needs of the indexing process:

- Where to store the index information and how to customize that with `DirectoryProviders`.
- How to properly normalize the text to be indexed and add new search features such as synonyms and phonetic search.
- How to not worry about indexing because Hibernate Search uses the Hibernate Core event model to list all the required changes and apply them in an optimized way.
- How to take control of the indexing process if the application requires it.

All this hard work would be useless in and by itself. But everything is now in place to write mind-blowing full-text search queries. While the book goes into great detail about mapping and the Hibernate Search indexing architecture, you'll care little about it in your day-to-day work. And that's the intention: Hibernate Search takes care of the hard infrastructure work to free you to build fine-tuned queries specific to your business rules. The next part of the book is all about that.

Part 3

Taming the
retrieval mismatch

Now you are ready to tackle how to write full-text queries and retrieve information. Chapter 6 describes how to efficiently retrieve matching entities from a Hibernate Search query and how this query model is integrated with Hibernate Core. Chapter 7 covers what you need to know about Lucene in order to create and build the right queries for your needs. Chapter 8 introduces you to the notion of query filtering and describes how to declaratively apply cross-cutting restrictions on your searches.

Querying with
Hibernate Search

6

This chapter covers

- Creating and executing a Hibernate Search query
- Using pagination
- Using projection
- Converting results in a different structure (ResultTransformer)
- Defining a fetching strategy

Hibernate Search queries are the key component shielding your application from the mismatches between the index model and the domain model and helping you to migrate queries from SQL, HQL, or Criteria to full-text queries easily. Building a full-text query with Hibernate Search consists of two steps:

1 Build a Lucene query to express the full-text search (either through the query parser or the programmatic API).
2 Build a Hibernate Search query that wraps the Lucene query.

But first you need to understand why we need this wrapper around Lucene queries.

6.1   *Understanding the query paradigm*

You may wonder why we'd use Hibernate Search to execute our query rather than plain Lucene. After all, chapters 3, 4, and 5 showed how Hibernate Search helps us index data in a regular Lucene index. Let's imagine that we use plain Lucene to find our data and explore the problems we'd face.

6.1.1   *The burdens of using Lucene by hand*

You need to build the Lucene query to match your needs. While this step requires you to interact with the Lucene query API (either the query parser or the programmatic query APIs), this isn't a problem in practice. You need to be aware of the Lucene features you want to use, such as fuzzy search, boost factors, and so on. Because Hibernate Search defines Lucene fields with the same name as their respective object properties by default, understanding a query and its target is fairly easy. The query `title:hibernate description:search author.firstname:emmanuel` targeting book objects is fairly straightforward to understand when you're familiar with the object model. If you need to refresh your memory on how to map properties into fields, look at chapter 3. Chapter 7 explains in great detail how to build the Lucene query.

Once the query is built, you need to execute it. If you don't use Hibernate Search, you have to follow these steps:

1 Open the Lucene directory (or directories) involved.
2 Build one or several `IndexReaders` and an `IndexSearcher` on top of them.
3 Call the appropriate execution method from `IndexSearcher`.

To keep Lucene as efficient as possible, you should reuse the same `IndexSearcher` or `IndexReader`. Lucene works best after the searcher has warmed up. You'll need to keep the searcher around for as long as you can, but not too long; a searcher doesn't see the changes made after it is opened. Almost every Lucene user has to write some kind of resource management framework around the raw Lucene APIs. When you use Hibernate Search, these optimizations are done for you under the cover.

Back to our plain Lucene approach. Once the query is executed and the list of matching `Documents` is returned, you need to convert them into objects of your domain model. Several solutions are possible: You could "rehydrate" them from the field values stored in the Lucene index, or you could use a Hibernate `Session` to load them and retrieve Hibernate managed objects. The first approach may seem interesting, but it has some problems in the long run. As we have seen in section 1.4.3, these hydrated objects don't have their associations lazily loaded and transparently accessible. Changes made to these objects will not be propagated to the database and the index unless you take some sort of manual action. The second approach (using Hibernate Core to load the objects) doesn't suffer from these drawbacks, but it needs to be done in an efficient way. Loading objects one by one won't work very well!

Alternatively, you could decide to not convert the Lucene results into objects and use the native Lucene APIs. This is a legitimate choice but requires changes to your overall application. In lieu of manipulating (managed) objects from your domain model all the way up to your presentation layer, you'll need to deal with native Lucene API objects and play by their lifecycle. This could mean a significant API and programmatic shift in your application, and you'd lose the benefits of object-oriented design, such as type-safety and strong typing. Hibernate Search relieves you of this burden.

As you've just seen, working manually with Lucene to execute the query and process the elements has some challenges. This chapter will show you how Hibernate Search makes this process much simpler for the application developer.

6.1.2 Query mimicry

Ideally, creating and invoking a full-text query should be no different than creating and invoking an HQL query. The APIs and the process should be similar enough for the application developer to feel at home. This is exactly the goal Hibernate Search tries to achieve. Queries run by Hibernate Search are similar to queries created in HQL, JPA-QL, or the Criteria API (Hibernate Criteria query API) in many ways:

- Returned objects are Hibernate managed objects.
- The query API is similar.
- The query semantic is also similar.

Objects returned by a Hibernate Search full-text query are regular Hibernate managed objects attached to a persistence context. You can:

- Navigate from them and benefit from the transparent lazy-loading mechanism.
- Change the state of these objects; the change will be propagated to the database (and the index).

As a matter of fact, a JPA-QL query and a full-text query that retrieve the same set of objects will return the same object instances (in a given Hibernate Session or Java Persistence EntityManager). Listing 6.1 shows the mimicry in action. Queries returning the same objects will benefit from the persistence context unicity regardless of the query mechanism.

Listing 6.1 Mimicry in action

```
Item itemFromGet = (Item) session.get( Item.class, id );        ◁── Look up an
                                                                     object
Criteria criteriaQuery = session.createCriteria( Item.class )
                         .add( Restrictions.idEq( id ) );
Item itemFromCriteria = (Item) criteriaQuery.uniqueResult();    ◁──

TermQuery termQuery = new TermQuery( new Term( "id", id.toString() ) );
Item itemFromFullText = (Item) session                          Load through
     .createFullTextQuery( termQuery, Item.class )              the Criteria API
     .uniqueResult();            ◁──────────── Load through a full-
                                               text query
assert itemFromGet == itemFromCriteria;
assert itemFromCriteria == itemFromFullText;   ◁──  All object references
                                                    are the same
assert itemFromGet == itemFromFullText;
```

Since objects returned by a full-text search are retrieved from the persistence context, interacting with them in the rest of the application is completely transparent. They are treated as any object retrieved by Hibernate (HQL, Criteria query, lookup, or full-text).

Hibernate Search pushes the similarity even further by sharing the same query interface as the other Hibernate query facilities. The object returned by the full-text query build method (`FullTextSession.createFullTextQuery()`) implements either `org.hibernate.Query` or `javax.persistence.Query`. Once the query object is created, using it is exactly the same as using a traditional HQL query (execution, pagination, and so on).

Now that you're aware of the semantics, let's see how Hibernate Search converts a Lucene query into Hibernate objects.

6.1.3   *Getting domain objects from a Lucene query*

Let's assume that you have a Lucene Query object ready to be executed (see chapter 7 for more information). Instead of manually opening a Lucene Index Reader object and calling the search method, you pass the raw Lucene Query object to Hibernate Search. Hibernate Search applies its magic sauce to the Lucene query: Some ingredients are put in before execution, but most after. The query execution logic is displayed in figure 6.1.

Hibernate Search prepares the Lucene query before its execution:

1 It determines the Lucene `Directory`s and opens the correct `IndexReaders` based on the targeted classes (generally, Hibernate Search will reuse `IndexReader` instances instead of physically opening them for each query).

2 It sets the optional sort criteria (sorting is described in section 6.7).

3 It applies the optional declarative filters (chapter 8 covers this topic).

The Lucene query is then executed. At this stage, by executing the Lucene query and without having to load any object or document, we know the total number of objects matching the query.

In the next step, Hibernate Search reads the necessary matching Lucene `Documents`. Depending on the execution choice (`list()`, `iterate()`, `scroll()`) and the

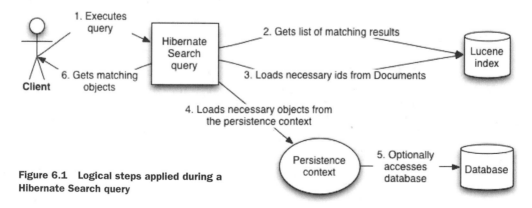

Figure 6.1   Logical steps applied during a Hibernate Search query

use of pagination, the number of elements read can be drastically reduced (and performance improved). As you will see in section 6.4, using pagination limits is recommended from both a performance and a business point of view.

Hibernate Search extracts the class and identifier from each `Document`. These two pieces of information will be necessary to load the object corresponding to the `Document` from the persistence context. If the query uses projection (see section 6.5), this operation also reads projected properties from the index.

Hibernate Search loads the necessary entity instances based on their class and identifier using the Hibernate `Session`, the persistence context. Various techniques are used to minimize the number of database queries. The retrieved objects are returned in the same order as the Lucene `Documents` (usually ordered by relevance) and passed to the application as a `List`, `Iterator`, or `ScrollableResults` as an `org.hibernate.Query` or `javax.persistence.Query` would do for an HQL query. Hibernate Core provides these objects from the persistence context; lazy loading, transparent navigation, and transparent object management (any change to the object is propagated to the database and the index) are granted.

Isn't hydrating objects from the Hibernate Session much slower than from Lucene?

Retrieving documents matching a Lucene query consists of two steps:

1. Read the index files to find the matching documents and order them by relevance (if you use Lucene's sort capability, this becomes slightly more complicated but is in essence similar).
2. Load the stored fields for each accessed `Document`.

`Document` fields are stored in a different set of files than the index information. Loading a `Document` is essentially leading to a random file access.

Looking up a row from a database by id and retrieving the columns is not fundamentally different from the second step in Lucene.

The performance difference between the two techniques more likely depends on additional factors, such as:

- Input/output performance differences between Lucene (usually disk access and random file access) and the database (usually network access)
- Availability of the data in the database cache

On top of the raw performance of each operation, don't forget that Hibernate caches objects in the persistence context (and if set up, in the second-level cache), which in some situations eliminates database round-trips.

Beyond performance, the level of features available to objects loaded from the persistence context (lazy loading, managed objects, unicity, and so on) negates the performance consideration most of the time. Hibernate Search also provides a projection mode that lets you bypass the persistence context if needed. We'll describe this mode in greater detail in section 6.5.

Hibernate Search queries have one additional benefit. If the index is slightly out of date compared to the database, some documents can point to objects that are no longer present in the database. Index desynchronization can come from the small replication delay occurring in a cluster when asynchronous replication is used (see chapter 10) or because some third-party applications have updated the database and the change has not yet been reflected. Hibernate Search transparently removes those orphaned documents from the results, and this inconsistency is hidden to the application.

Enough theory for now; let's see how to build a Hibernate Search query!

6.2   *Building a Hibernate Search query*

A Hibernate Search query is essentially a smart wrapper around a Lucene query. The first step for an application developer is to write the Lucene query that will retrieve the necessary objects. We'll cover this vast topic in chapter 7. The next step is to build a Hibernate Search query.

Like most operations specific to Hibernate Search, creating a full-text query is done through the `FullTextSession` or `FullTextEntityManager` API.

6.2.1   *Building a FullTextSession or a FullTextEntityManager*

Hibernate Search queries are created from a `FullTextSession` object, just like a Hibernate HQL query is created from a `Session` object. `FullTextSession` is an interface that subclasses `org.hibernate.Session`. It is quite transparent to replace `Session` references by `FullTextSession` references in a code base. The `FullTextSession` implementation is a wrapper around a `Session` object, which can be built using the `org.hibernate.search.Search.getFullTextSession` method, as shown in listing 6.2.

Listing 6.2   Creating a `FullTextSession` or `FullTextEntityManager`

```
//with the Hibernate Core
Session session = sessionFactory.openSession();        ←──┐  Retrieve a session

FullTextSession ftSession =
    org.hibernate.search.Search.getFullTextSession( session );   ←─┐
                                                         Wrap a session in a
...                                                      FullTextSession  ❶
session.close();


//with Java Persistence
//in an application managed environment
EntityManager entityManager = entityManagerFactory.createEntityManager();  ←┐
FullTextEntityManager ftEntityManager =
      org.hibernate.search.jpa.Search.getFullTextEntityManager(
    entityManager );  ←─┐                                        Retrieve an
...            Wrap an EntityManager in                          entityManager
entityManager.close();  ❷  a FullTextEntityManager

//in a container managed environment
```

③ Get an EntityManager injected

```
@PersistenceContext private EntityManager em;    ◄──┐

public List<Item> findItems(String query) {
    FullTextEntityManager ftEm =           ◄──┐
        org.hibernate.search.jpa.Search.getFullTextEntityManager( em );
    ...
}
```

Wrap an EntityManager in a FullTextEntityManager

① A full-text session is created out of a regular Hibernate `Session`. **②** A full-text entity manager is created out of a regular Hibernate `EntityManager` object. **③** When using a managed entity manager, there's no need to close it even when it is wrapped by Hibernate Search.

Developers using Hibernate `EntityManager` simply wrap their `EntityManager` objects with `FullTextEntityManager` by using the `org.hibernate.search.jpa.Search.getFullTextEntityManager` method (note the `jpa` package).

NOTE `getFullTextSession` and `getFullTextEntityManager` were named `createFullTextSession` and `createFullTextEntityManager` in Hibernate Search 3.0.1 and previous versions.

A `FullTextSession` is a simple wrapper around a `Session` object; it holds no state in and by itself. In particular, calling `close()` on `FullTextSession` is equivalent to calling `close()` on the underlying `Session` object. Don't call `close()` on both objects!

Generally speaking, the session opening and closing should be left to an application framework such as EJB 3.0, Spring, or JBoss Seam. By relieving developers from managing the session as a resource, these frameworks reduce the amount of potential bugs. In such an environment, simply wrap the `Session` object or the `EntityManager` object into its full-text version, and forget about its lifecycle management.

On the JBoss Seam website, seamframework.org, you can read the following statement: "Seam is a powerful open source development platform for building rich internet applications in Java. Seam integrates technologies such as ... into a unified full-stack solution, complete with sophisticated tooling."

Good news for Hibernate Search users: Seam also integrates with Hibernate Search. `FullTextSession` or `FullTextEntityManager` instances are directly injected by Seam. Listing 6.3 shows how to use it.

Listing 6.3 Injecting `FullTextSession` or `FullTextEntityManager`

```
//with native Hibernate
@In FullTextSession session;                    ◄──┐
public List<Item> findItems(String query) {
    //work with the full-text session
}

//in a Java Persistence environment
@In FullTextEntityManager entityManager;        ◄──┐

public List<Item> findItems(String query) {
```

The FullTextSession object is injected

The FullTextEntityManager object is injected

```
}    . . .    ◁──┐  Work with the
                 └  FullTextEntityManager instance
```

In JBoss Seam, you no longer need to use the Search wrapping methods. This makes the code slightly more natural.

We now have access to the right API. Let's create a Hibernate Search query.

6.2.2 *Creating a FullTextQuery*

A Hibernate Search query is a wrapper around a Lucene query exposed as a standard Hibernate or Java Persistence query object. If you use a FullTextSession object, an org.hibernate.Query object is returned by the createFullTextQuery() method. If you use a FullTextEntityManager object, a javax.persistence.Query object is returned by the createFullTextQuery() method. This is particularly interesting when migrating traditional SQL/HQL-based queries to full-text queries. While the creation of the query changes, subsequent manipulations (settings, execution, and so on) do not.

NOTE   All subsequent code examples in this chapter make use of a simple yet powerful framework to deal with Session or EntityManager. It also transparently opens and closes transactions. This framework shields the example codes from plumbing code and makes them more readable. This framework wraps every public method around an invocation interceptor (SessionInvocationHandler). Before the public method is executed, a Session or EntityManager is opened, and a transaction is started. The Session or EntityManager is stored in a thread local variable (and available to the public method). The public method is executed. After the method execution, the transaction is committed (or rolled back if something goes wrong), and the Session or EntityManager is closed. This logic is described in listing 6.4.

Listing 6.4   Interceptor-based framework

```
public class SessionInvocationHandler implements InvocationHandler {

    private SessionFactory factory;
    private Object delegate;

    public SessionInvocationHandler(Object delegate,
                               ➥SessionFactory factory) {
        this.factory = factory;
        this.delegate = delegate;
    }

    public Object invoke(Object proxy, Method method, Object[] args)
            throws Throwable {

        FullTextSession session =
          Search.getFullTextSession(
          factory.openSession()       ◁──┐  Create a full-text
        );                              ❶ session object           ❷ Store it in
                                                                      a thread
        SessionHolder.setFullTextSession( session );  ◁──┘            local
```

```
                         Transaction tx = null;
                         Object result;
                         try {                                      3  Start the
                             tx = session.beginTransaction();   ⟵┐     transaction
                             result = method.invoke( delegate, args );  ⟵┐ Execute the
                             tx.commit();                               4  method
                         }
                         catch (HibernateException e) {
                             rollbackIfNeeded( tx );   ⟵┐
                             throw e;                    │  Roll back in case
                         }                                  of exception
                         catch (SearchException e) {
                             rollbackIfNeeded( tx );
                             throw e;
                         }                              5  Always close
                         finally {                         and free
                             session.close();   ⟵┘
                             SessionHolder.setFullTextSession( null );
                         }
                         return result;
                     }

                     private void rollbackIfNeeded(org.hibernate.Transaction tx) {
                         if ( tx != null && tx.isActive() ) {
                             tx.rollback();
                         }
                     }
                 }
```

We first open a Session and wrap it around a FullTextSession ❶. This session is stored in a thread local variable ❷. Each method call ❹ is wrapped in a transaction ❸. As good citizens, we always free resources and clear the thread local variable ❺.

This framework is quite primitive and aims at reproducing the kind of transaction and resource management you can find in an EJB 3.0 container or in a Spring or JBoss Seam container. Remember that every example runs inside a transaction.

If you're interested in this framework and how it uses dynamic proxies, have a look at the test cases provided in the book's example source files.

As a Hibernate Core or Hibernate EntityManager user, you already know how to execute and use these APIs. Listing 6.5 shows you how to create such full-text queries.

Listing 6.5 Creating a FullTextQuery object

```
private org.apache.lucene.search.Query buildLuceneQuery(   ⟵┐ Create a
        String words,                                        ❶ Lucene query
        Class<?> searchedEntity) {       ❷  Get the most
    Analyzer analyzer;                   ⟵  appropriate
    if (searchedEntity == null) {            analyzer
        analyzer = getDefaultAnalyzer();   ⟵┐ Get the
    }                                          default analyzer
    else {
```

```
        analyzer = SessionHolder
                .getFullTextSession()
                .getSearchFactory()
                .getAnalyzer( searchedEntity );   ⟵   Get the entity
    }                                                   scoped analyzer

    QueryParser parser = new QueryParser( "title", analyzer );
    org.apache.lucene.search.Query luceneQuery = null;
    try {
        luceneQuery = parser.parse( words );
    }
    catch (org.apache.lucene.queryParser.ParseException e) {
        throw new IllegalArgumentException(
            "Unable to parse search entry into a Lucene query", e );
    }
    return luceneQuery;
}


//Hibernate Core APIs
public List findByTitle(String words) {
    FullTextSession ftSession =                      ❸  Get the
        SessionHolder.getFullTextSession();   ⟵         FullTextSession

    org.apache.lucene.search.Query luceneQuery =
buildLuceneQuery( words, null );
                                                     ❹  Create the full-
    org.hibernate.Query query =                         text query
        ftSession.createFullTextQuery( luceneQuery );   ⟵
    @SuppressWarnings("unchecked")
    List<Item> results = query.list();   ⟵  Execute it
    return results;
}


//Java Persistence APIs
public List findByTitle(String words) {
    FullTextEntityManager ftEntityManager =
  ➥EntityManagerHolder.getFullTextEntityManager();

    org.apache.lucene.search.Query luceneQuery =
        buildLuceneQuery( words, null );

    javax.persistence.Query query =
        ftEntityManager.createFullTextQuery( luceneQuery );   ⟵
                                                                  Create the
    return query.list();   ⟵  Execute it                          full-text
}                                                              ❹  query
```

❶ The Lucene query describes the full-text query: Search the words in the title property. ❷ When the target type of the query is known, it's more appropriate to use the
entity-specific analyzer (see listing 5.13). ❸ Retrieve the Session object initialized by
the interceptor framework. ❹ org.hibernate.Query is built from a Lucene query
when Hibernate Core APIs are used. ❺ javax.persistence.Query is built from a
Lucene query when Hibernate EntityManager APIs are used.

Building the Lucene query is not the focus of this chapter, but listing 6.5 shows a Lucene query built using a Lucene query parser targeting the title field. Building the Hibernate Search full-text query is straightforward and consists of calling `create-FullTextQuery` and passing the Lucene query.

EXCEPTIONS When errors occur, Hibernate Search raises `SearchException`. This exception is a runtime exception and is used for all Hibernate Search errors: mapping errors, configuration errors, engine execution errors, and usage errors.

We lied to you in this section. The `createFullTextQuery` methods return more than the standard `Query` interfaces. The query objects returned actually implement a subinterface of `org.hibernate.Query` and `javax.persistence.Query`: respectively `org.hibernate.search.FullTextQuery` and `org.hibernate.search.jpa.FullText-Query`. These interfaces are useful when accessing some specific Hibernate Search features. Don't bother with this technical detail. You'll naturally use the full-text version of this interface when the need arises.

The attentive reader may have noticed that nowhere do we state which entity type the query is supposed to return. We'll do so now.

6.2.3 *Limiting the types of matching entities*

A Lucene query doesn't target specific `Document` types simply because Lucene doesn't have any notion of document type. Unless stated otherwise, Hibernate Search queries target all types and are applied to all indexed entities. Hibernate Search makes sure to apply the query on all the Lucene indexes and retrieve the matching results regardless of the entity type. The set of objects returned by a Hibernate Search query can be a mix of any of the indexed entities.

This tremendous flexibility is essentially due to Lucene. In SQL the schema is highly structured, and query clauses target columns of specific tables. In Lucene, queries targeting fields (by name) can be applied to any index because indexes are totally unstructured. Take the following Lucene query: `title:batman`. Any entity type having an index property named `title` will be considered, regardless of the type of entity it represents.

This flexibility is very useful in some situations, but in most use cases an application expects to retrieve matching results of a particular entity type. Our DVD store example needs to retrieve matching DVDs and display them. Retrieving `Actor` objects is not acceptable because our display logic only copes with `Dvd` objects: a `Class-CastException` is likely to happen somewhere.

Hibernate Search lets you restrict the entity types returned by a query. Let's implement this restriction in the DVD store application in listing 6.6.

Listing 6.6   Restrict full-text results to Item objects

```
public List<Item> findItemByTitle(String words) {
    FullTextSession ftSession = SessionHolder.getFullTextSession();
    org.apache.lucene.search.Query luceneQuery =
        buildLuceneQuery( words, Item.class );

    org.hibernate.Query query = ftSession.createFullTextQuery(
        luceneQuery,
        Item.class );          ⟵───┐   List entities to
    return query.list();            │   restrict by
}
```

As you can see in listing 6.6, we return a list of `Items` rather than a generic list of results. You can return multiple entity types. The class parameter in `createFullText-Query` is a vararg (a feature introduced in Java 5) and accepts a list of classes. `ftSession.createFullTextQuery(luceneQuery, Item.class, Actor.class);` returns matching results of type `Item` and `Actor`. The same API is available on `org.hibernate.search.jpa.FullTextQuery`.

Should a query return multiple types?

It's quite common for a search engine to return matching results classified by type. The online DVD store could return the list of matching `Items` as well as the lists of matching `Actors` and `Categorys` and display them in separated visual buckets to emphasize the difference to the users. Let's imagine a query that requests `Steve McQueen`. Our user interface expects to display the matching DVD, the matching actors, and the (unlikely) categories matching in three separate lists.

Two strategies are possible:

- Execute one full-text query returning the matching `Item`, `Actor`, and `Category` elements, and separate them into three lists in the application code.
- Execute three separate queries, each targeting one of the element types; the elements are already separated for the application.

The first approach has one main benefit. The score (relative relevance of one element compared to another) is computed homogeneously for all types and can be compared. This might provide a more useful classification and help the application decide whether or not to display a given type depending on its score.

However, the authors advise using the second approach. Executing three different queries has several advantages:

- Executing the Lucene query is very efficient and cheap. Running it three times won't have a significant impact on response time.
- The application code is more type-safe, cleaner, and easier to read. This argument should be your main concern.

> **Should a query return multiple types?** *(continued)*
>
> - Pagination can be handled per targeted types. While we're ready to display 20 DVDs, we want to display only the best three categories and the best three actors.
>
> The final decision is up to you. The authors have found the second approach easier to deal with and the performance drawback not significant enough to be a bother.

Like Hibernate Core, Hibernate Search is fully polymorphic. The list of filtered classes includes classes listed in the `createFullTextQuery` call and all their indexed subclasses. In listing 6.6, Hibernate Search returns `Item` classes and all its subclasses (`Dvd`, `Pizza`, `Wine`, assuming these three classes are subclasses of `Item`). If you need to specifically target matching `Pizza` and ignore the other types, use this class instead of `Item` when you create the full-text query.

> **Can I return matching elements of a given class excluding one subclass?**
>
> This is possible, but it doesn't make a lot of sense from an object-oriented point of view. If you face such a need in your system, chances are that your domain model has been incorrectly designed and that you've overused inheritance.
>
> To return all `Item`s excluding `Pizza`, create the full-text query listing all the subclasses allowed:
>
> ```
> fullTextEntityManager.createFullTextQuery(luceneQuery, Dvd.class, Wine.class);
> ```
>
> An alternative approach is to use the special field Hibernate Search stores in the index to restrict the Lucene query: `DocumentBuilder.CLASS_FIELDNAME`. Lucene queries are explained in chapter 7, but you should have little trouble understanding the meaning of listing 6.7.

> **Listing 6.7 Filter out a class at the Lucene query level**
>
> ```
> private org.apache.lucene.search.BooleanQuery addExclusionClause(
>     org.apache.lucene.search.Query userQuery) {
>
>     org.apache.lucene.search.Query filterQuery = new TermQuery(
>         new Term( DocumentBuilder.CLASS_FIELDNAME,
>             Pizza.class.getName() )          ◁── ❶ Create the filtering term
>     );
>     org.apache.lucene.search.BooleanQuery luceneQuery = new
>         BooleanQuery();
>                                                       ❷ Join the user query
>     luceneQuery.add(userQuery, Occur.MUST);   ◁──┘
>     luceneQuery.add(filterQuery, Occur.MUST_NOT);   ◁── ❸ Exclude the filtering term
>
>     return luceneQuery;
> ```

Can I return matching elements of a given class excluding one subclass?
(continued)

```
    }

    fullTextEntityManager.createFullTextQuery(
            addExclusionClause( userQuery ), Item.class );
```

1 Create a term query matching the class to filter using the Hibernate Search special field. **2** Add the Lucene query created by the user and mark it as mandatory. **3** Exclude the filter clause explicitly from the results.

The first approach is preferable, because:

- It is much easier to read
- Hibernate Search can potentially reduce the number of indexes to run the query on.

It's good practice to limit the returned result types and explicitly list them. Hibernate Search can optimize the interaction with Lucene by limiting the number of indexes loaded. Beyond the optimization, the application code tends to be cleaner because it's more aware of the potential returned types. In most cases, it's the root entity in a class hierarchy (Item in the DVD store example).

Hibernate Search loads objects from the persistence context as efficiently as possible. Strategies vary depending on a number of factors:

- How the query is executed (list(), iterate(), or scroll())
- Whether or not projection is used (see section 6.5)
- Some characteristics of your identifier
- Whether or not the fetching strategy is overridden
- Potential additional factors

Depending on these factors, Hibernate Search loads objects using one of the following strategies:

- Create one or more SQL queries that load the matching objects by their identifier.
- Lazily load the objects by looking at them in the persistence context using EntityManager.getReference() or Session.load() and subsequently force the object initialization.

The first strategy is almost always the fastest approach and requires no intervention on your part. This is the solution Hibernate Search uses most of the time. However, in some situations, the second approach is necessary. The second approach works best if a batch size is defined at the object level; rather than using *n* queries to initialize *n* objects, Hibernate Search will trigger (n/batch size) queries. It's a good idea to define a batch size for all your indexed objects, as shown in listing 6.8. What's the best value for batch size? A value equal or superior to the pagination value used in your query. The pagination value is simply the number of objects your query will retrieve. We'll explain how to control pagination in section 6.4

Listing 6.8 Define batch size through annotation

```
@Entity
@Indexed                    1  Reduce database
@BatchSize(20)       ⟵┐        round-trips
public class Item {
    ...
}
```

Simply place an `@BatchSize` ❶ annotation on your entity.

NOTE   Depending on the static fetching strategies of your object graph defined in the Hibernate or Java Persistence mapping, subsequent queries might be triggered. This typically happens when you choose a select or subselect association loading instead of a join. You typically face this problem in Hibernate when you look up objects by identifier. In this situation, you need to adjust some mappings. For additional information on how to handle these situations, we highly recommend *Java Persistence with Hibernate* by Christian Bauer and Gavin King and published by Manning. An alternative approach is to refine the fetching strategy for this particular full-text query; this solution is described in section 6.8.

You might be a bit frustrated and wonder in which situations Hibernate Search uses the query approach versus the lazy object loading approach. Hibernate Search has improved and is still improving at a constant pace in this area. If we were to detail the various cases, it would likely be obsolete by the time this book is published.

After creating a full-text query and making sure it will run reasonably fast, the next step is to execute the query and finally get what we're searching for.

6.3   *Executing the full-text query*

People familiar with the Java Persistence query API or the Hibernate query API will be at ease when it comes to executing the query. The same methods are available, and they have the same semantics:

- `list()` or `getResultList()`
- `uniqueResult()` or `getSingleResult()`
- `iterate()`
- `scroll()`

Each approach has different characteristics, and its efficiency depends on the situation. Let's explore some of the underlying details for each of these strategies to better understand when to use each one.

6.3.1 Returning a list of results

The most used and useful API returns a `List` containing all matching objects. Listing 6.9 shows this in action.

Listing 6.9 Retrieving results as a `List`

```
//using Hibernate Core
public List<String> displayAllByMatchingTitle(String words) {

    FullTextSession ftSession = SessionHolder.getFullTextSession();
    org.apache.lucene.search.Query luceneQuery =
      buildLuceneQuery( words, Item.class );

    org.hibernate.Query query = ftSession
      .createFullTextQuery( luceneQuery, Item.class );

    @SuppressWarnings("unchecked")
    List<Item> items = query.list();

    List<String> results = new ArrayList<String>();
    for (Item item : items) {
      StringBuilder itemInString = new StringBuilder( "Item " )
        .append( "(" ).append( item.getEan() ).append( ")" )
        .append( " " ).append( item.getTitle() );
      results.add( itemInString.toString() );
    }
    return results;
}

//using Hibernate EntityManager
public List<String> displayAllByMatchingTitle(String words) {

FullTextEntityManager ftEntityManager =
EntityManagerHolder.getFullTextEntityManager();
    org.apache.lucene.search.Query luceneQuery =
        buildLuceneQuery( words, Item.class );

    javax.persistence.Query query =
        ftEntityManager.createFullTextQuery( luceneQuery, Item.class );

    @SuppressWarnings("unchecked")
    List<Item> items = query.getResultList();

    List<String> results = new ArrayList<String>();
    for (Item item : items) {
      StringBuilder itemInString = new StringBuilder( "Item " )
        .append( "(" ).append( item.getEan() ).append( ")" )
        .append( " " ).append( item.getTitle() );
      results.add( itemInString.toString() );
    }
    return results;
}
```

❶ Return a list of items

❷ Return a list of items

❶ Use the Hibernate `list()` method: All matching objects are loaded eagerly. ❷ Use the Hibernate `getResultList()` method: All matching objects are loaded eagerly.

All object identifiers are extracted from the Lucene index. All objects are loaded and added to the list in the order retrieved by Lucene. This is important because it respects ordering the user requests. This strategy is particularly efficient when you expect to use all objects returned by a query. Hibernate Search usually manages to load all necessary objects in a minimal number of SQL queries.

If your application needs only a subset of the matching objects, Hibernate Search allows pagination, as you will see in section 6.4. In some situations, most of the objects are already present in the persistence context or in the second-level cache. In these situations an iterator is more efficient.

6.3.2 Returning an iterator on the results

While Java Persistence does not offer this option, Hibernate provides the ability to return an iterator on the matching results, and so does Hibernate Search. Listing 6.10 shows the use of an iterator with the assumption that most objects will be found in the persistence context or the second-level cache. Retrieving results through an iterator is optimal when objects can be found in the persistence context or the second-level cache.

Listing 6.10 Retrieving results through an iterator

```java
public List<String> displayAllByMatchingTitleUsingCache(String words) {
    FullTextSession ftSession = SessionHolder.getFullTextSession();
    org.apache.lucene.search.Query luceneQuery =
      buildLuceneQuery( words, Item.class );

    org.hibernate.Query query = ftSession
      .createFullTextQuery( luceneQuery, Item.class );

    @SuppressWarnings("unchecked")
    Iterator<Item> items = query.iterate();            ❶ Retrieve an
                                                           iterator on items
    List<String> results = new ArrayList<String>();    ❷ Load object from
    while ( items.hasNext() ) {                             the persistence
        Item item = items.next();                          context
        StringBuilder itemInString = new StringBuilder( "Item " )
            .append( "(" ).append( item.getEan() ).append( ")" )
            .append( " " ).append( item.getTitle() );
        results.add( itemInString.toString() );
    }
    return results;
}
```

❶ Read the necessary information from Lucene and return an `Iterator`. ❷ On `next()`, the current object is loaded from the persistence context.

All object identifiers are extracted from the Lucene index, but objects are not loaded until they are accessed (more precisely until `iterator.next()` is called). This approach is very efficient if the objects loaded are already present in the persistence context or the second-level cache. The number of database round-trips is limited to the number of times an object is neither in the persistence context nor in the second-level cache. This solution will work very poorly if most objects have to be loaded from the database, because we'll face the infamous *n*+1 loading issue. Like `list()`, `iterate()` returns objects in the same order in which Lucene provides matching `Documents`.

All object identifiers are loaded eagerly during `Iterator` creation to free Lucene resources right away. While you can use pagination to mitigate the problem and limit the load, loading all matching documents from Lucene might not be the perfect approach for your problem. An alternative solution involves the `Scrollable-Results` API.

6.3.3   *Returning a scrollable result set*

A third querying approach involves using the Hibernate `ScrollableResults` API. The `ScrollableResults` API offers these advantages over the iterator API:

- Both objects and Lucene `Documents` are loaded on demand, reducing the memory usage and latency.
- The navigation API is much richer, allowing navigation back and forth as well as letting you seek a particular result.

Hibernate Search's implementation minimizes resource consumption because Lucene `Documents` and objects are lazily loaded. It is best suited for when the application needs to navigate through part of the result set. Listing 6.11 shows how to use the scroll API. Results are returned in the order in which `Documents` are returned by Lucene. This method displays results starting from the middle of the result list up to *n* elements.

Listing 6.11   Scrolling through part of the results minimizes resource consumption.

```
public List<String> displayMediumResultsByMatchingTitle(String words, int n)
  {
    FullTextSession ftSession = SessionHolder.getFullTextSession();
    org.apache.lucene.search.Query luceneQuery =
      buildLuceneQuery( words, Item.class );

    FullTextQuery query = ftSession
      .createFullTextQuery( luceneQuery, Item.class );     ❶ Define fetch size

    query.setFetchSize(n);
    ScrollableResults items = query.scroll();              ❷ Retrieve
                                                             ScrollableResults
    List<String> results = new ArrayList<String>();
    try {
      items.beforeFirst();         ❸ Go to the first position

      int mediumIndexJump = query.getResultSize() / 2;     Jump to the
       items.scroll( mediumIndexJump );    Jump to a       position before
                                           ❹ specific position   the medium
      int index = 0;                                            element
      while ( index < n ) {
```

```
if ( items.next() ) {              5  Load the next element
   Item item = (Item) items.get()[0];   6  Read the object

   if ( item != null ) {
      StringBuilder itemInString = new StringBuilder( "Item " )
         .append( "(" ).append( item.getEan() ).append( ")" )
         .append( " " ).append( item.getTitle() );
      results.add( itemInString.toString() );
      index++;
   }
   else {
      //mismatch between the index and the database   <---    7  Ignore null
   }                                                            entries
}
else {
   break;
}
}
}
finally {
   items.close();    <---
}                      8  Close resources
return results;
}
```

1 Elements will be preloaded by batch of fetch size. **2** Execute the query; no object and no Lucene document are loaded at that point. **3** Set the cursor before the first position. **4** Move forward `mediumIndexJump` elements to reach the medium element. **5** Move to the next element and return true if within it. **6** Load the Lucene `Document` and the object (up to the next fetch size elements) and return an array of objects containing the entity instance. **7** Elements could be null when a mismatch exists between the index and the database. **8** Close the Lucene resources associated with this `ScrollableResults` in a `finally` block.

As listing 6.11 shows, you need to close the `ScrollableResults` object after you're finished with it. Not following this rule will lead to Lucene reader leaks. A good approach is to use a `try finally` structure, closing the ScrollableResults in the `finally` block.

Internally, the `ScrollableResults` implementation loads the Lucene `Documents` and persistence context objects when they're requested. To increase efficiency, it's possible to use a cache where elements are preloaded. The cache size is define by the `setFetchSize()` method. You should keep the fetch size and the object batch size (`@BatchSize`) at the same value. This is useful when Hibernate Search cannot use the query approach strategy. To load *n* objects in a row, Hibernate Search would trigger (*n*/*fetch size*) SQL queries.

NOTE   Contrary to the other execution methods (list(), iterate(), and unique()), scroll() doesn't try to shield the application from objects found in the index but no longer available in the database. When such a situation occurs, the scroll method returns null instead of the object. While this is a fairly uncommon case, the code should make sure the returned objects are not null.

One of the common use cases for scroll() is to walk through all the results and apply some operations even when the results are too big to fit in memory. As shown in listing 6.12 you need to clear the session on a regular basis to avoid generating an OutOfMemoryException. Make sure to call flush() and flushToIndexes() before clearing the session to propagate any object changes.

flush()'s job is to synchronize the persistence context changes to the database. By not calling flush(), you'd lose all object changes the minute you call clear() and you would not see the change events propagated to Hibernate Search. Make sure to call flush() before flushToIndexes() if changes have occurred in the persistence context.

When you call flushToIndexes(), you apply all necessary changes to the Lucene indexes and free the Hibernate Search work queue and memory.

When indexing an entity, Hibernate Search sometimes needs to initialize a lazy property or association; this cannot be done if the object is detached (for example, after calling clear()).

Listing 6.12   Use `scroll` to navigate through a large matching result set

```
public void applyBatchChange(String words) {

    FullTextSession ftSession = SessionHolder.getFullTextSession();
    org.apache.lucene.search.Query luceneQuery =
        buildLuceneQuery( words, Item.class );

    FullTextQuery query = ftSession
        .createFullTextQuery( luceneQuery, Item.class );

    query.setFetchSize(FETCH_SIZE);          ◁──┐   ❶ Define fetch size as
                                                      (window size)/N
    ScrollableResults items = query.scroll();

    log( "Results changed: " + query.getResultSize() );
    try {
        items.beforeFirst();
        int index = 0;
        while( items.next() ) {
            Item item = (Item) items.get()[0];
            index++;
            if ( item != null ) {                ❷ Update item
                applyChange( item );   ◁──┘
            }
            if ( index % WINDOW_SIZE == 0 ) {  ◁──  ❸ Clear memory
              ftSession.flush();    ◁──┐             every window size
                                        Flush changes to
                                        the database
```

```
                ftSession.flushToIndexes();                        Flush changes
                ftSession.clear();                              4  to the index
            }
        }
    }
    finally {
        items.close();
    }
}
```

4 Flush changes to the index

5 Clear memory

1 Align fetch size and the window size so that window size is a multiple of fetch size to maximize performance. **2** Apply some changes to the objects. **3** Flush and clear after the last of the groups of elements in the window have been processed and before triggering a new preloading. **4** In addition to calling Hibernate `flush()`, call `flush-ToIndexes()`. **5** Release memory by clearing.

Note that the scrollable fetch size is aligned to the window's size to minimize the number of database round-trips. In practice, window size has to be a multiple of fetch size. Make sure to flush and clear right before the next scrollable `get()` operation triggers the fetching. The `get()` call in the first loop iteration will load `WINDOW_SIZE` objects. After the `WINDOW_SIZE` interations in the loop, `flush` and `clear` are executed, and the next `get()` call will load the next batch of objects.

What's a good window size?

You should choose the window size carefully to avoid generating an `OutOfMemoryEx-ception`. Aside from that, the bigger the window, the better. You can also adjust fetch size to minimize the number of database round-trips. While 100 for fetch size and 1000 for window size is a safe bet, your mileage may vary depending on the complexity of your object graph. We highly recommend you test your code in a production environment to determine the ideal value.

Of course, if you don't modify the objects, calling `flush()` and `flushToIndexes()` isn't necessary; use only `clear()`.

If you know which object window to look for in advance (for example, from the 10th to the 19th matching results) and if the number fits easily in memory, using pagination and `list()` is more suited.

While the previous example shows how to walk through all the results, it's interesting sometimes to retrieve exactly one result.

6.3.4 *Returning a single result*

If you know the query is expected to return a single element, and if returning more than one element is considered an error, you can use the `uniqueResult` (in Hibernate) or `getSingleResult` (in Java Persistence) method. An interesting use case is to implement a feature similar to the I'm Feeling Lucky™ button in the Google search

engine. This feature returns only the first matching element of a full-text query. Listing 6.13 shows an implementation of this feature.

Listing 6.13   Implement the lucky feature: Return the first matching object

```
//Hibernate Core
public String displayIMFeelingLuckyByMatchingTitle(String words) {

    FullTextSession ftSession = SessionHolder.getFullTextSession();
    org.apache.lucene.search.Query luceneQuery =
        buildLuceneQuery( words, Item.class );

    org.hibernate.Query query = ftSession
        .createFullTextQuery( luceneQuery, Item.class );

    Item item = (Item) query                            ❶ Use pagination to
        .setFirstResult(0).setMaxResults(1)                return one result
        .uniqueResult();                    ❷ Return one element

    StringBuilder itemInString = new StringBuilder( "Item " );
    if ( item == null ) {
        itemInString.append( "not found" );
    }
    else {
        itemInString.append( "(" ).append( item.getEan() ).append( ")" )
            .append( " " ).append( item.getTitle() );
    }
    return itemInString.toString();
}

//java Persistence
public String displayIMFeelingLuckyByMatchingTitle(String words) {

    FullTextEntityManager ftEntityManager =
        EntityManagerHolder.getFullTextEntityManager();
    org.apache.lucene.search.Query luceneQuery =
        buildLuceneQuery( words, Item.class );

    javax.persistence.Query query =
        ftEntityManager.createFullTextQuery( luceneQuery, Item.class );

    Query hSearchQuery = query
            .setFirstResult( 0 ).setMaxResults( 1 );

    Item item;
    try {                                          ❸ Return one
        item = (Item) hSearchQuery.getSingleResult();     element
    }
    catch (NoResultException e) {       Guard against no
        item = null;                    element found
    }

    StringBuilder itemInString = new StringBuilder( "Item " );
    if ( item == null ) {
        itemInString.append( "not found" );
    }
    else {
        itemInString.append( "(" ).append( item.getEan() ).append( ")" )
```

```
          .append( " " ).append( item.getTitle() );
     }
     return itemInString.toString();
  }
```

❶ Use pagination to return the first matching element: the lucky one. **❷** `uniqueResult()` returns either `null` or the unique object (if more than one object is returned, an exception is raised). **❸** `getSingleResult()` returns the unique object or a `NoResultException` if no object is found.

WARNING The semantics of `org.hibernate.Query.uniqueResult()` and `javax.persistence.Query.getSingleResult()` are different. The former returns `null` if no object is found; the latter raises a `NoResult-Exception`.

We've shown various ways to retrieve information depending on what needs to be done with it. Regardless of the approach you choose, we suggest using pagination as a solution to improve performance.

6.4 *Paginating through results and finding the total*

Pagination is the idea of retrieving a subset of the total matching results by defining the first element to retrieve and the total number of elements to retrieve. It has several technical advantages. It reduces the following:

- Lucene index work (CPU usage and input/output)
- Database work
- Network traffic between the database and the application server
- The application's CPU and memory usage
- Response time

The throughput of your application will consequently increase.

Surprisingly pagination also provides advantages to your user and application. Realistically a user cannot browse through 100,000 results, so we could limit the total number of results to the first 100 elements. Because results are ordered by relevance, chances are that the user will find information in the first few matching results. If the user is unlucky, however, he'll probably change his query after browsing the first few dozen results or simply give up. Why is that? Your user will see (or feel) a decrease of usefulness in the result list (because the results are ordered by decreasing relevance). These are typical search patterns that you could expect; the following story is more interesting.

Google did a user survey and, fairly unanimously, users were asking for more results per page. Google conducted a test and returned 30 results per page rather than the traditional 10. The revenue and traffic dropped by 20 percent. Why were customers who said they wanted more results per page now acting as if they didn't like it? It turns out that people are very sensitive to time. Nobody likes to wait for a search result, and people have little patience. Amazon did a similar experiment. It artificially delayed the result page rendering in increments of 100 milliseconds and found that even small delays would result in a significant drop in revenue.

There are several ways to speed up performance, and pagination is one of them. Of course, depending on the target user and the type of data, the pagination window needs to be adjusted.

Users have no pity

There's nothing worse for a user than to rely on a search engine and fail to receive an answer (well, maybe there are worse things, but you get the point). A key influence on user happiness is to have the search engine tuned to maximize the relevance of the results, especially the first few results.

One way to achieve that is to study the kind of queries users enter and the kind of results they expect. From there, you can adjust the properties you search into, their boost factors and the kind of Lucene queries you use (fuzzy, range, and so on; see chapter 7 for more information).

Let's explore the pagination API.

6.4.1 Using pagination

The same pagination API used by HQL queries is used in full-text queries. You've already seen this API in listing 6.13 while implementing the I'm Feeling Lucky™ feature. Listing 6.14 shows a more traditional use of pagination to display partial results.

Listing 6.14 Using pagination on a full-text query

```
//Hibernate Core
public List<String> displayAllByMatchingTitle(
    String words,
    int pageNumber,
    int window) {

    FullTextSession ftSession = SessionHolder.getFullTextSession();
    org.apache.lucene.search.Query luceneQuery =
        buildLuceneQuery( words, Item.class );

    org.hibernate.Query query = ftSession.createFullTextQuery(
        luceneQuery, Item.class );

    @SuppressWarnings("unchecked")
    List<Item> items = query                                    ❶ Set first result
            .setFirstResult( (pageNumber - 1) * window )           from the page

            .setMaxResults( window )
            .list();                          ❷ Set number of results
    List<String> results = new ArrayList<String>();
    for (Item item : items) {
        StringBuilder itemInString = new StringBuilder( "Item " )
            .append( "(" ).append( item.getEan() ).append( ")" )
```

```
                .append( " " ).append( item.getTitle() );
            results.add( itemInString.toString() );
        }
        return results;
    }

    //Java Persistence
    public List<String> displayAllByMatchingTitle(String words, int pageNumber,
    ➡int window) {

        FullTextEntityManager ftEntityManager =
            EntityManagerHolder.getFullTextEntityManager();
        org.apache.lucene.search.Query luceneQuery =
            buildLuceneQuery( words, Item.class );

        javax.persistence.Query query =
            ftEntityManager.createFullTextQuery( luceneQuery, Item.class );

        @SuppressWarnings("unchecked")
        List<Item> items = query
                .setFirstResult( (pageNumber - 1) * window )   ◁─┐  Set pagination
                .setMaxResults( window )                          │  according to
                .getResultList();                              ❸ │  the window
        List<String> results = new ArrayList<String>();
        for (Item item : items) {
            StringBuilder itemInString = new StringBuilder( "Item " )
                .append( "(" ).append( item.getEan() )
                .append( ")" ) .append( " " ).append( item.getTitle() );
            results.add( itemInString.toString() );
        }
        return results;
    }
```

❶ Set the first element returned starting from index 0 (the first page starts at 0, the second at window 1, and so on). ❷ Set the maximum number of results returned. ❸ The same API is available from Java Persistence.

Pagination limits the number of Lucene documents loaded as well as the number of objects hydrated. Because executing a Lucene query is quite cheap, you should execute the query a second time when a user wishes to see the next page rather than keeping the results around.

TIP   maxResults represents the maximum number of results returned and is usually the total number of results returned. However, if firstResult is close to the end of the list (less than maxResults away from the last index), the total number of results is lower than maxResults. If firstResult is beyond the end of the list, no result is returned. Make sure your pagination client code is aware of this behavior.

One of the traditional problems with pagination in SQL lies in the fact that you cannot find the total number of matching results unless a second query (select count(*) from ...) is performed.

6.4.2   *Retrieving the total number of results*

Full-text queries are completely different from SQL queries, and the total number of results is accessible without the extra SQL query cost. Hibernate Search exposes this information in the FullTextQuery API (see listing 6.15).

Listing 6.15   Using the total number of results to adjust a query

```
//Hibernate Core
public int displayResultSizeByMatchingTitle(String words) {

    FullTextSession ftSession = SessionHolder.getFullTextSession();
    org.apache.lucene.search.Query luceneQuery =
        buildLuceneQuery( words, Item.class );
    FullTextQuery query = ftSession.createFullTextQuery(
        luceneQuery, Item.class );

    return query.getResultSize();        ⬅──  ❶ Number of matching
}                                                results (cheap)
public ResultHolder displayResultsAndTotalByMatchingTitle(
        String words,
        int pageNumber,
        int window) {

    FullTextSession ftSession = SessionHolder.getFullTextSession();
    org.apache.lucene.search.Query luceneQuery =
        buildLuceneQuery( words, Item.class );

    FullTextQuery query = ftSession.createFullTextQuery(
        luceneQuery, Item.class );

    @SuppressWarnings("unchecked")
    List<String> results = query
            .setFirstResult( (pageNumber - 1) * window )
            .setMaxResults( window )        ❷ Return
            .list();           ⬅─────┘        matching results       ❸ Return total
    int resultSize = query.getResultSize();   ⬅──────────────┘          number of
                                                                        results
    ResultHolder holder = new ResultHolder( results, resultSize );
    return holder;
}

public class ResultHolder {
    private final List<String> results;
    private final int resultSize;

    public ResultHolder(List<String> results, int resultSize) {
        super();
        this.results = Collections.unmodifiableList( results );
        this.resultSize = resultSize;
    }

    public List<String> getResults() {
        return results;
    }
    public int getResultSize() {
        return resultSize;
```

```
        }
    }

    //Java Persistence
    public int displayResultSizeByMatchingTitle(String words) {

        FullTextEntityManager ftEntityManager =
            EntityManagerHolder.getFullTextEntityManager();
        org.apache.lucene.search.Query luceneQuery =
            buildLuceneQuery( words, Item.class );

        FullTextQuery query = ftEntityManager.createFullTextQuery(
            luceneQuery, Item.class );
        return query.getResultSize();
    }
```

4 **Number of matching results (cheap)**

1 `FullTextQuery.getResultSize()` executes the Lucene query without loading objects or Lucene `Documents`. **2** When `list()` is executed, the result size is computed and available. **3** Subsequent `getResultSize()` calls no longer trigger a query. **4** Java Persistence's `FullTextQuery` also contains the `getResultSize()` method.

If you call only `FullTextQuery.getResultSize()`, the Lucene query is executed, but no Lucene document is accessed and no object is loaded from the persistence context. The result is not influenced by pagination. This is a very powerful and efficient tool for building a multistage search engine, and we'll cover it next.

TIP If you want both the total number of results and the (paginated) list of results, call `list()`, `scroll()`, `iterate()`, and `getResultList()` before calling `getResultSize()` on the same query object. This uses one Lucene query instead of two.

This feature can be used beyond displaying the total number of results to your user. Let's explore an interesting example.

6.4.3   *Multistage search engine*

A multistage search engine executes one query per stage. Subsequent stages remove restrictions on the user query or increase the targeted elements. Figure 6.2 illustrates the process of a multistage search engine.

For each stage in the search engine, `getResultSize()` is executed on the Full-TextQuery object. If the number of results doesn't match expectations, the next stage is processed. If the next stage meets the requirements, `list()` is executed on the `FullTextQuery` object, and the results are returned. Each stage executes a broader query to gather additional results.

Now that we've selected the appropriate amount of results to display to the user, we need to decide what to display. Sometimes loading the whole object (graph) to display two simple properties is overkill. Projection is helpful in such situations.

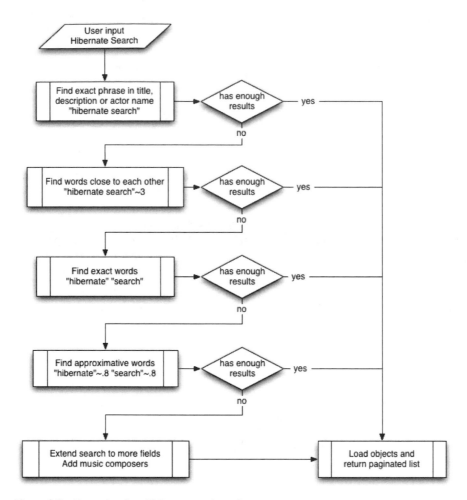

Figure 6.2   Example of multistage search engine

6.5   *Projection properties and metadata*

In Hibernate Core, a *projection query* is a query that returns some properties rather than the full managed object. Properties are projected to the result set. Projection queries are exactly the same in Hibernate Search. They are a way to retrieve some properties rather than the full managed object, the principal difference being that the data is retrieved from the Lucene index rather than from the database.

If, after using pagination, you find that returning the hydrated object is still too slow for your needs, projection might give you what you expect performance-wise. But projecting a property requires some advance preparation. Because the value is extracted from the index and pushed to the query results, projected properties must be stored, and their associated field bridges must be two-way. All built-in bridges provided by Hibernate Search are two-way: They convert the data back and forth between the object model and the index (see section 4.1).

TIP   Storing properties increases the index size and might slow down queries overall. Be sure to select and store only properties you expect to project.

Unlike with SQL, full-text queries do not have a `select` clause; `fullTextQuery.set-Projection()` describes the properties to project for a given query (see listing 6.16). Properties must be stored in the index and have a two-way bridge. If no property is projected and defined through `setProjection()`, regular managed objects are returned.

Listing 6.16 Projecting specific properties

```
@Entity
@Indexed
@Table(name="PRODUCTS")
@Inheritance(strategy=InheritanceType.JOINED)
public class Item {

  @Id
  @GeneratedValue
  @DocumentId
  @Column(name="PROD_ID")
  private Integer id;

  @Field(index=Index.TOKENIZED, store=Store.YES)     ◄─┐
  @Column(name="TITLE")                                 │
  @NotNull                                              │   ❶ Property is
  @Length(max=100)                                      │      stored in index
  private String title;                                 │
                                                        │
  @Field(index=Index.UN_TOKENIZED, store=Store.YES)  ◄─┘
  @Column(name="ASIN")
  @Length(max=16)
  private String ean;
}

public List<ItemView> displayProjectionByMatchingTitle(String words) {

    FullTextSession ftSession = SessionHolder.getFullTextSession();
    org.apache.lucene.search.Query luceneQuery =
        buildLuceneQuery( words, Item.class );

    FullTextQuery query = ftSession.createFullTextQuery(
        luceneQuery, Item.class );

    List<Object[]> results = query            ❷ Set the projected
            .setProjection( "ean", "title" )  ◄─┘   properties
            .list();

    List<ItemView> endResults = new ArrayList<ItemView>( results.size() );
    for (Object[] line : results) {
        endResults.add(
            new ItemView(                  ◄──   Build object from
                (String) line[0],          ❸     projection array
                (String) line[1]
            )
        );
```

```
    }
    return endResults;
    }
```

Projected properties must be stored in the index and use a two-way bridge (all built-in bridges are two-way) ❶. Contrary to nonprojected queries that return objects, each returned element is an array of objects ❸. Each entry in the array corresponds to the projected property defined by `fullTextQuery.setProjection()` ❷ in the same index position. If a property is not present for a given result, its index is set to `null`. The same API is also available on `org.hibernate.search.jpa.FullTextQuery`.

Projection is also the preferred mechanism to provide metadata associated with the matching Lucene document. The following special fields are available:

- `FullTextQuery.THIS`—Returns the managed object.
- `FullTextQuery.DOCUMENT`—Returns the Lucene Document object.
- `FullTextQuery.SCORE`—Returns the document score for the given search.
- `FullTextQuery.ID`—Returns the object identifier.
- `FullTextQuery.DOCUMENT_ID`—Returns the Lucene `Document` id.
- `FullTextQuery.OBJECT_Class`—Returns the object class
- `FullTextQuery.EXPLANATION`—Returns the Lucene Explanation object for this document.

`THIS` returns the object that would have been returned had projection not been used. It is useful for retrieving metadata along with the managed object. This operation will retrieve information from the persistence context. Listing 6.16 is an example of such a usage.

`DOCUMENT` returns the plain Lucene Document object. This is particularly useful when using some Lucene-specific features not (yet) integrated into the Hibernate Search ecosystem.

`SCORE` returns the relative importance of a document compared to the other documents for that particular query. A score can only compare documents within the same query. Let me say it for the third time: Comparing the score of documents from different queries makes no sense. Score is nevertheless a very useful feature because it emphasizes the relative importance of two documents. Your search engine might purposely decide to ignore all documents whose score is one-tenth that of the most relevant document in order to emphasize quality over quantity. For a long discussion of score, please refer to chapter 12.

`ID` returns the object identifier, its primary key in the database, whereas `DOCUMENT_ID` returns the internal Lucene `Document` identifier. `DOCUMENT_ID` is quite useful for interacting with some of the native Lucene APIs.

WARNING A Lucene document id is not stable over time. The optimize operation among others can redefine a document id.

OBJECT_CLASS does return the object type. EXPLANATION returns the Lucene Explana-tion object for this document and this query. An Explanation object explains why a given document has been picked up by a query. This is very useful when some results are puzzling. Be careful, because building an Explanation object is as expensive as executing the query: For each result, significant work is performed. Project this field if you're sure the number of results is limited (or if you have time). Otherwise, use FullTextQuery.explain(). See listing 6.17 for more information.

Let's have a look at a projection using some of these metadata fields (listing 6.17).

Listing 6.17　Projecting metadata fields

```
public List<ItemView> displayProjectionAndMetadataByMatchingTitle(String
➥words) {

    FullTextSession ftSession = SessionHolder.getFullTextSession();
    org.apache.lucene.search.Query luceneQuery =
        buildLuceneQuery( words, Item.class );

    FullTextQuery query = ftSession.createFullTextQuery(
        luceneQuery, Item.class );

    @SuppressWarnings("unchecked")
    List<Object[]> results = query
            .setProjection(
                "ean",
                "title",                              ❶ Project the
                FullTextQuery.SCORE)   ◄──┐             document score
            .list();

    List<ItemView> endResults = new ArrayList<ItemView>( results.size() );
    for (Object[] line : results) {
        ItemView itemView = new ItemView(
                (String) line[0],
                (String) line[1],        ❷ Retrieve the
                (Float) line[2] );   ◄──┐  document score
        endResults.add( itemView );
    }
    return endResults;
}
```

❶ Metadata is projected along with regular properties using their constant placehold-ers. ❷ Score is available at the expected position.

Some might complain that playing with Object[] as a returned element is not the easiest thing on earth. As a matter of fact, in listing 6.16 we convert the Object[] into an ItemView object manually. Hibernate Search allows you to transform the structure before returning it by the query.

6.6　*Manipulating the result structure*

One common use case for projection is to display two or three fields of the matching results and expose them as view objects. A view object is a read-only object used to convey data from the backend layer to the frontend layer for display. Typically, the view object structure is different from the raw domain model structure (some aggregation or preparation is performed on fields, and so on).

Hibernate Search queries let you transform the projection's `Object[]` structure into the structure of your choice by providing a `ResultTransformer` API. This API has two methods; the most interesting one is `transformTuple`, which takes the `Object[]` and returns the structure of your choice. Listing 6.18 demonstrates a `ResultTransformer` returning a `Map<String, Object>` containing the property name projected as a key and the property value as a value. A `ResultTransformer` instance can be set on a `FullTextQuery` (based on the Hibernate Core or Java Persistence API).

Listing 6.18 ResultTransformer converting `Object[]` into a `Map<String,`

```
public class ProjectionToMapResultTransformer implements ResultTransformer {

    public Object transformTuple(          Method called
        Object[] tuple,                  ❶  for each result
        String[] aliases) {

        Map result = new HashMap( tuple.length );
        for (int i = 0; i < tuple.length; i++) {
            String key = aliases[i];
            if ( key != null ) {
                result.put( key, tuple[i] );
            }
        }
        return result;
    }

    public List transformList(List collection) {
        return collection;
    }
}

List<Map<String, Object>> results = fullTextQuery
            .setProjection( "ean", "title" )
            .setResultTransformer(           ❷  Attach the result
                                                transformer
                new ProjectionToMapResultTransformer()
            )
            .list();
```

❶ `transformTuple()` takes the `Object[]` returned by a regular projection query and the associated aliases and returns the data in a different structure. ❶ The `Query` instance is configured with the `ResultTransformer` object.

Two `ResultTransformer` objects that are quite useful are provided by Hibernate out of the box:

- `AliasToBeanResultTransformer`
- `AliasToBeanConstructorResultTranformer`

The first one injects projected properties into the setter of the same name (or the field of the same name). The second one injects projected properties through a specific constructor. See listing 6.19.

Listing 6.19   Using AliasToBeanResultTransformer to populate a view object

```
public class ItemView {              ❶ Projected property
    private String ean;                matches the attribute
    private String title;

    public String getEan() {
        return ean;
    }
    public String getTitle() {
        return title;
    }

    public float getScore() {
        return score;
    }
}

public List<ItemView>
    displayProjectionUsingResultTransformerByMatchingTitle(String words) {

    FullTextSession ftSession = SessionHolder.getFullTextSession();
    org.apache.lucene.search.Query luceneQuery =
        buildLuceneQuery( words, Item.class );

    FullTextQuery query = ftSession.createFullTextQuery(
        luceneQuery, Item.class );

    @SuppressWarnings("unchecked")
    List<ItemView> results = query
            .setProjection( "ean", "title" )       ❷ Attach the result
            .setResultTransformer(                    transformer
                new AliasToBeanResultTransformer( ItemView.class )
            )
            .list();
    return results;
}
```

❶ Field names (or setters) match the property names projected; the projected values are stored in their respective field or getter in `ItemView`. ❷ The `ResultTransformer` instance is passed to the query; the query now returns a `List<ItemView>`.

WARNING   Objects built by a `ResultTransformer` are not managed by the persistence context.

Hibernate provides additional `ResultTransformers` that can be found in the `org.hibernate.transform` package, but this interface is meant to be implemented by applications to fit their needs. Don't limit yourself to the list of built-in ones.

We've just shown how to adjust the object-retrieval process and especially how to retrieve a custom structure from a projection query. Stepping back, it would be nice to customize the order in which objects are returned to us. Read on.

6.7   *Sorting results*

By default, objects returned by a full-text query are provided by descending score: The most relevant object is returned first. While this will satisfy your needs in most cases, returning objects ordered by one or several properties is sometimes more pertinent for your user. You can do that with Hibernate Search.

Sort is applied to the Lucene query (on the value stored in Lucene fields) rather than to the database query. To order using a database query, Hibernate Search would need to read and extract the identifiers for all matching documents (potentially millions!) and create an SQL query from them. This would be very inefficient in most cases.

Hibernate Search delegates the sort operation to Lucene. Fields used for the sort have one restriction: They must use either one of these two indexing strategies: `Index.UN_TOKENIZED` or `Index.NO_NORMS`. Remember, you can map the same object property multiple times: once to build a sortable field, once to build a searchable field (see section 3.3.4). More than once you will index a field specifically for sorting, even if you're not interested in searching by it.

Sort is described by a Lucene `Sort` object, which contains the list of fields to sort by, each field sort being represented by a `SortField` object. Let's look at a simple example in listing 6.20. Each field must be indexed but not tokenized.

Listing 6.20   Sorting results by a set of fields

```
@Entity
@Indexed
public class Item {

    @Id @GeneratedValue
    @DocumentId
    private Integer id;

    @Fields(
            {@Field(index=Index.TOKENIZED, store=Store.YES),
             @Field(name="title_sort",
                    index=Index.UN_TOKENIZED),          ◁──┐   Properties untokenized
            })                                          ❶  can be sorted
    @NotNull @Length(max=100)
    private String title;

    @Field
    @Length(max=5000)
    private String description;

    @Field(index=Index.UN_TOKENIZED, store=Store.YES)@Length(max=16)   ◁──┐
    private String ean;                            Properties untokenized
    ...                                               can be sorted ❷
}

public List<String> displayAllByMatchingTitleOrderedBy(String words, OrderBy
    orderBy) {

    org.apache.lucene.search.Query luceneQuery =
        buildLuceneQuery( words, Item.class );
```

```
FullTextSession ftSession = SessionHolder.getFullTextSession();

FullTextQuery query = ftSession.createFullTextQuery(
    luceneQuery, Item.class );

Sort sort = null;
switch (orderBy) {                        Sort by
                                          ean
case EAN:
    SortField sortField =                               3   Build a SortField
new SortField( "ean", SortField.STRING );
    sort = new Sort( sortField );
    break;                                      4   Wrap it in a Sort
                             Sort by title,
case TITLE_THEN_EAN:         then by ean             5   Multiple sort
    SortField[] sortFields = new SortField[2];              fields are possible
    sortFields[0] = new SortField( "title_sort", SortField.STRING );
    sortFields[1] = new SortField( "ean", SortField.STRING );
    sort = new Sort( sortFields );
    break;

default:
    assert sort == null : "Unknown OrderBy." + orderBy;
}                                    6   Assign Sort to
                                         the query
query.setSort( sort );

@SuppressWarnings("unchecked")
List<Item> items = query.list();

List<String> results = new ArrayList<String>();
for (Item item : items) {
    StringBuilder itemInString = new StringBuilder( "Item " )
        .append( item.getTitle() )
        .append( " (" ).append( item.getEan() ).append( ")" );
    results.add( itemInString.toString() );
}
return results;
}
```

❶ A sortable version of `title` is indexed in `title_sort` in the field `UN_TOKENIZED`. ❷ `ean` is already sortable. ❸ A `SortField` object takes the field name and the sort style. ❹ `Sort` receives the `SortField` objects; the order in which they are provided to `Sort` is significant. ❺ You can sort by multiple fields. You can sort by `title_sort`, and for identical `title_sort` values you can sort by `ean`. ❻ `Sort` is associated with the `FullTextQuery` object.

The sort algorithm differs slightly depending on the property type. Each `SortField` can define its type. The available types are:

- `SortField.INT`—Integer comparator
- `SortField.LONG`—Long comparator
- `SortField.FLOAT`—Float comparator
- `SortField.DOUBLE`—Double comparator
- `SortField.STRING`—String comparator
- `SortField.CUSTOM`—Custom comparator

WARNING   Lucene supports `SortField.AUTO`, which determines the type based on the first result. The authors recommend against using it because it can have unintended consequences. What if the first result looks like an int but turns out to be a long or a String?

Sorting by field is not free. In order to sort data, Lucene needs to load and keep the field ordering. Lucene uses some tricks to keep ordering for numeric values efficient in terms of memory usage. String and custom field sorting cannot benefit from these optimizations. Make sure you test sort on a real dataset and measure memory consumption.

Beyond field-based sorting, Lucene allows you to sort by score (descending) and by Lucene document id (ascending), using respectively the following special `Sort-Field` instances:

- `SortField.FIELD_SCORE`—Sort documents by their score (highest score first).
- `SortField.FIELD_DOC`—Sort documents by Lucene document id (lowest first).

Listing 6.21 extends listing 6.20 by supporting sorting by title and score and makes use of these special fields.

Listing 6.21   Sorting results using field types and score

```
case TITLE_THEN_SCORE:          ◁⏋  Sort by title and for
{                                   equal titles by EAN

    SortField[] sortFields = new SortField[2];
    sortFields[0] = new SortField( "title_sort", SortField.STRING )

    sortFields[1] = SortField.FIELD_SCORE;   ◁⏋  Sort by score
    sort = new Sort( sortFields );            ❶ after title
    break;

}
```

❶ `SortField` holds two constants, `FIELD_SCORE` and `FIELD_DOC`, that can be used to sort respectively by score and document id.

If you want to know more about sorting in Lucene, we highly recommend *Lucene in Action,* published by Manning. This book has a comprehensive and dedicated section on the subject. The `Sort` Javadoc is of great help as well.

You now have the knowledge required to retrieve the objects you want, sorted in the order of your choice, but we haven't yet described what part of the object graph is loaded and how.

6.8   *Overriding fetching strategy*

By default, Hibernate Search uses the standard fetching strategy defined in your mapping. Associations won't be loaded when they're marked as lazy. When an association is marked as eager, the fetching strategy defined in your mapping is used (join, subselect, select). In some cases, your application code will want to navigate through associations marked as lazy in an efficient manner.

You can override the fetching strategy used to load objects from the persistence context in a full-text query. This is critical for avoiding both of the following:

- `LazyInitializationException`; for example, during the rendering view
- Any performance issue; for example, facing the famous *n+1* problem

If you know the application needs to navigate through a certain object path, it's more efficient to load the graph up front. You define the fetching strategy in Hibernate Search by passing to the `FullTextQuery` object a Hibernate Core Criteria query (see listing 6.22).

Listing 6.22 Use a Criteria query to define the fetching strategy.

```
public List<String> displayItemAndDistributorByMatchingTitle(String words) {

    org.apache.lucene.search.Query luceneQuery =
        buildLuceneQuery( words, Item.class );
    FullTextSession ftSession = SessionHolder.getFullTextSession();

    FullTextQuery query = ftSession.createFullTextQuery(
        luceneQuery, Item.class );
                                        Create criteria on   ❶
                                         targeted entity           Set fetching  ❷
    Criteria fetchingStrategy =                                      profile
        ftSession.createCriteria( Item.class )       ◁─┘
                .setFetchMode( "distributor", FetchMode.JOIN );  ◁─┘
    query.setCriteriaQuery( fetchingStrategy );   ◁─┐
                                                     Set criteria on
    @SuppressWarnings("unchecked")                ❸ full-text query
    List<Item> items = query.list();

    List<String> results = new ArrayList<String>();
    for (Item item : items) {
        StringBuilder itemInString = new StringBuilder( "Item " )
            .append( "(" ).append( item.getEan() ).append( ")" )
            .append( " " ).append( item.getTitle() )
            .append( " - " ).append(
➥item.getDistributor().getName() );          ◁─┐
        results.add( itemInString.toString() );  ❹  Use preloaded
    }                                               associations
    return results;
}
```

❶ The Criteria query must be based on the same entity type used to filter the full-text query. ❷ Fetching strategies can be overridden, but no restriction should be added to the Criteria query. ❸ The Criteria query is passed to the `FullTextQuery` object and will be used to load objects (instead of the regular fetch strategy based on the static mapping). ❹ Access to `distributor` does not trigger a second query because it has been loaded previously.

Only a subset of the Criteria API capabilities is available. Be sure to target a single entity type in `createFullTextQuery` when overriding the fetching strategy through a Criteria API. The Criteria query must target this entity type and not apply any restrictions; only fetching operators are allowed. `FulltextQuery.setCriteriaQuery` is available when using the Java Persistence APIs of Hibernate Search, but be aware that

Criteria is still a pure Hibernate Core API and requires a Session object to be built. You can access the Session object underneath a Hibernate EntityManager instance by using the getDelegate() method: Session session = (Session) entityManager.getDelegate();. When Java Persistence supports a Criteria-like API, Hibernate Search will likely migrate to it.

WARNING   Be sure to use the same entity type for both the Criteria instance and the full-text query targeted entity. Hibernate Search raises an exception otherwise.

Some people are tempted to use additional restrictions on the Criteria query injected into a Hibernate Search query. After all, it would mean restricting the query further by some additional SQL clauses on top of the Lucene restrictions. This approach has two major problems: Pagination is no longer respected, and the total number of results is incorrect.

Pagination is applied to the Lucene query before loading any object and does not take into account that objects will be filtered out by the Criteria/SQL restriction. After pagination is applied, if an object cannot be loaded for a given document (because it cannot be found by the loading query), it is ignored and not returned in the results. The list of results seen through pagination is like a gigantic piece of Gruyere: It has lots of holes, making it practically unusable.

Likewise, the total number of results is built from the total number of matching Lucene documents and cannot account for the SQL-based filtering.

Some Lucene results will puzzle you. Fortunately, there are ways to understand what's going on.

6.9   *Understanding query results*

You know very well that a computer does what we ask it to do, not what we think we are asking it to do. Likewise, some search results will really surprise you. Fortunately, Hibernate Search and Lucene give you tools to answer the following questions:

- Why is this object in the result list?
- Why is this result higher than another result?

Lucene can generate an Explanation object, which describes how the score has been computed for a given document (object) in a given query. Remember, the score is entirely dependent on the query. Using this object is considered a fairly expert technique by the Lucene community and is not especially user friendly. But it can be an invaluable tool when you have to understand what's going on. The Explanation object roughly describes which term matches and in which Lucene field, and for each term it gives the associated score.

You can have access to this information in three ways.

In the search screen of Luke, you can navigate through the list of matching documents. For a given document, you can click the Explain button, which will expose a text version of the `Explanation` object. This approach is useful when you test your Lucene queries.

From a given `FullTextQuery` instance, you can call the `explain` method, passing the document id of the object for which you want the explanation. Document ids can be retrieved by using a projection (see section 6.5 for more details). Listing 6.23 shows how to use the API.

Listing 6.23 Retrieve the Explanation object for a given document id

```
public Explanation explainFirstMatchingItem(String words) {
    FullTextSession ftSession = SessionHolder.getFullTextSession();
    org.apache.lucene.search.Query luceneQuery =
        buildLuceneQuery( words, Item.class );

    FullTextQuery query = ftSession.createFullTextQuery(
        luceneQuery, Item.class );

    @SuppressWarnings("unchecked")
    Object[] result = (Object[]) query
                        .setProjection(
                            FullTextQuery.DOCUMENT_ID,        ◁──┐ Retrieve the
                            FullTextQuery.THIS)                   │ document id
                        .setMaxResults( 1 )
                        .uniqueResult();
    return query.explain( (Integer) result[0] );  ◁──┐ Explain a given
}                                                     │ document
```

Finally, you can ask Hibernate Search to project the `Explanation` object for all matching documents by using `query.setProjection(FullTextQuery.EXPLANATION);`. This approach is not recommended unless you know that the number of matching documents is limited (by using pagination, for example). Building an Explanation object is as expensive as executing the Lucene query.

By reading chapter 12, you'll have a much better understanding of the Explanation object. We use it extensively to explain how a score is computed. You can also check *Lucene in Action*, which has a nice section on the subject.

6.10   *Summary*

This chapter taught you how to write Hibernate Search queries. These queries are totally integrated into the Hibernate Core or Java Persistence programmatic logic in the following ways:

- The same query APIs are used.
- Objects returned by full-text queries are regular Hibernate managed objects, allowing transparent navigation through lazy loaded associations and state synchronization between the object and the database (and the Lucene index).

You now have a good understanding of what is happening when a Hibernate Search query is executed. The Lucene query is executed first, then pagination is applied, and the necessary objects are loaded from the persistence context as efficiently as possible based on their relative Documents returned by Lucene. You've seen ways to execute queries and their use cases, and you've seen how to use pagination and the total number of results to increase both performance and user feedback in the search engine. We also explored projection, a feature that allows us to return a couple of properties rather than a full managed object and how, thanks to ResultResolvers, we can transform the returned objects to match application needs. Finally, we explored how to sort data by fields rather than by relevance and how to customize the fetching strategy of matching objects to increase application performance.

You know how, from a full-text question, to retrieve matching objects in a way that suits your application without a paradigm shift compared to traditional HQL queries. In chapter 7 you'll discover how to express this full-text question by writing the adequate Lucene query.

Writing a Lucene query

7

This chapter covers

- Parsing and the `QueryParser` syntax
- The `QueryParser` and user-friendly query entry
- Tokenization and analyzers
- Lucene's base `Query` classes

You've purchased something online. Maybe it's a book or clothing from a department store with an online presence. Your order is a week overdue, so you go back to the website to check its status, but you've misplaced the order number. You call the contact number and are told, "I'm sorry, I can only look up your order if you can give me your Order ID." Oh-oh, does this sound familiar?

These all-or-nothing database-style searches are quickly being overtaken by the search techniques we discuss in this book. These much more flexible methods can query for a document where the title contains *Wright Brothers* and the body contains *bicycle*. Just about any way you can think of searching for something can be converted into a data query.

Information indexing is a standard, rigid process, but querying that gathered information can be performed in myriad ways. This process and the building of these queries is the subject of this chapter.

We'll begin by studying the `QueryParser`, how it parses expressions and allows for user-friendly queries and the syntax it generates from our queries. Understanding this syntax is important when you run into problems. What could possibly be wrong if you query for a person's last name such as Smith-Jones and obtain no results when you're positive the name exists in the index?

Then we'll move on to a discussion of analyzers and how they extract and manipulate queries. Finally, we'll look at the types of queries that are provided out of the box and how to use and manipulate them for our needs.

Parsing an expression is the process of analyzing a sequence of tokens—in Lucene's case, words—and transforming them into some predefined data structure suitable for later processing. Lucene contains the class `org.apache.lucene.queryParser.Query-Parser` which performs this function through its `parse(String query)` method.

The output of this method can be anything from a single-term expression to a complicated phrase depending on the complexity of the query. Before we get into parsing too deeply, it's important to understand the syntax that the parser generates in these phrases. This will help you understand why things turn out the way they do and point out what changes may be necessary.

The next section introduces the query parser syntax. For a full discussion of it refer to the document located at *lucene_install_directory*/docs/queryparsersyntax.html. Also remember that Manning's *Lucene in Action* is an excellent additional reference for the various discussions in this chapter.

7.1   *Understanding Lucene's query syntax*

Let's face it. Queries can be as simple as a single word and as complicated as a multi-word, nested Boolean expression with a range query added on, and so on, up to the limits of your imagination. A semi-mathematical style of notation can make things a little easier to understand, and that's what Lucene uses. A small set of special characters can convey a lot of information accurately.

Understanding the query syntax is of the utmost importance if you're going to troubleshoot a query that didn't produce expected results. Is the problem in the index or the query? You don't want to waste time barking up the wrong tree.

Our old friend Luke, introduced in chapter 2, is excellent for showing exactly how your entered query will be parsed into a Lucene-usable expression and is an outstanding troubleshooting tool for use with query parsing. We'll be utilizing it here to demonstrate parsing, and we recommend you use it often when developing so you have a minimum of surprises.

7.1.1   *Boolean queries—this and that but not those*

Lucene and Hibernate Search support the use of the Boolean operators AND, OR, and NOT. The equivalent shorthand notation for these is + for AND, – for NOT, and no symbol for OR. If you use the *word syntax*, the operators *must* be in uppercase. Table 7.1 contains some examples.

Figure 7.1 shows Luke's interpretation of the equivalent of the first query from table 7.1 (the AND query).

Table 7.1   A comparison of Boolean word syntax and shorthand syntax

Word syntax	Shorthand syntax
a AND b	+a +b
a OR b	a b
a NOT b	+a –b

Notice three things here (if you haven't looked at the Luke explanation in chapter 2 yet, this would be a good time to do so). First, we didn't have to enter the field name for the *titanic* term because the default field is set to title and that's the field we're looking in for that term. Second, after we clicked Update, the *title* field-name was inserted for us. Third, because we used the AND Boolean operator in the query, meaning both terms are required for the query to be successful, the + sign was prepended to both terms.

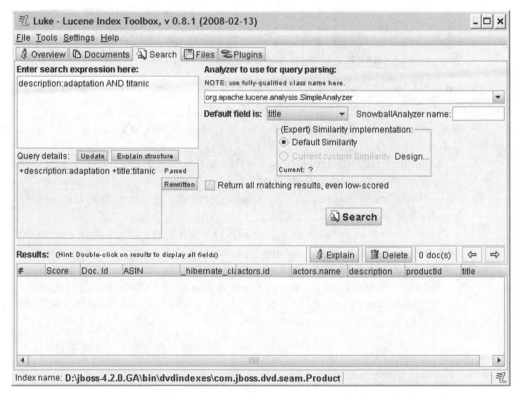

Figure 7.1   Luke's equivalent interpretation of the first query from table 7.1 (a AND b)

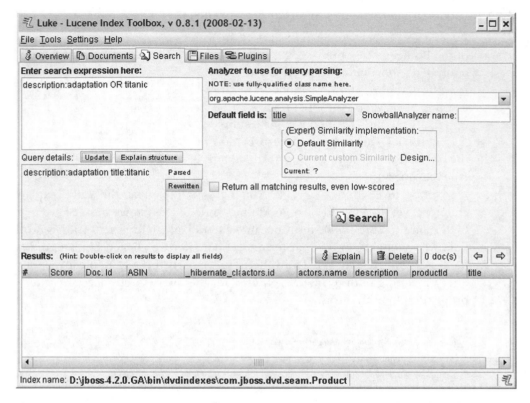

Figure 7.2   Luke's equivalent interpretation of the second query from table 7.1 (a OR b)

The second query from table 7.1 (the OR query) is shown in figure 7.2, again utilizing Luke.

The only real difference between this and figure 7.1 is that the + signs have been removed from the parsed query. This means that either the *adaptation* term *or* the *titanic* term must be present for the query to be successful, but neither term is required.

The – (NOT) operator can sometimes get you in trouble if you aren't careful. Let's assume we're querying a customer name field for the name *Evans – Sutherland*. Figure 7.3 shows how Luke interprets this query.

Surprise! What is this - (minus) sign doing here? The – (dash) was interpreted as the NOT Boolean operator. This could cause trouble because it has absolutely nothing to do with what we were looking for.

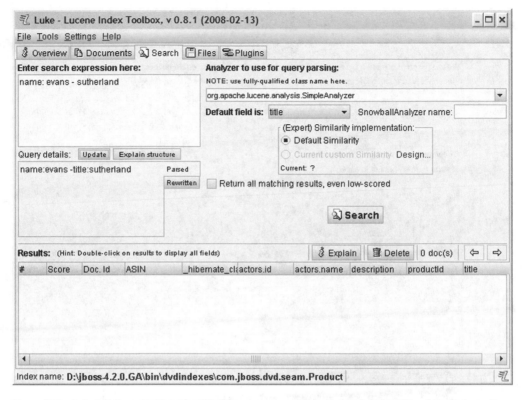

Figure 7.3 **Luke's interpretation of a query for** *evans – sutherland* **showing that the - (dash) doesn't always behave as you'd expect and can sometimes be misinterpreted as the** – (NOT) **operator.**

How do we get around this problem with – (dash and not minus)? All *special characters* must be *escaped* by using the \ character. Let's try this in Luke and see what happens. Figure 7.4 shows our escaped – (dash) and the result of our search.

Our search expression now has the escaped special character as \, and it was parsed correctly as title:evans title:Sutherland. We'll talk about programmatically fixing this problem shortly and explain how to accomplish this escaping in section 7.3.1. A complete list of the characters considered special characters is given there as well.

NOTE　We cannot emphasize enough that analyzers greatly affect how the query string is interpreted. Depending on the analyzer chosen, the – (dash) may be completely removed from the query.

The next query type is the WildcardQuery, which uses two special characters in different ways to allow searching for many combinations of characters easily.

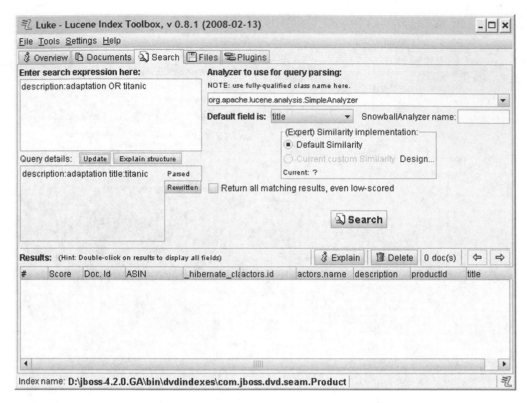

Figure 7.4   Escaping the special character to prevent it from interfering with our query

7.1.2   Wildcard queries

Lucene contains two characters that are considered *wildcards*. What are wildcards? Wildcards match any characters in an index entry. Two special characters are used to represent them: the ? (question mark) and the * (asterisk). The ? represents any single character in a query. For example,

> ?atch matches batch or match or catch

The single-character wildcard ? can be used more than once in a query. For example,

> t??t matches test, text, and toot

The * character matches any one or more characters. For example,

> came* matches camera or cameron or camel or cameo

The QueryParser class has a setter method setAllowLeadingWildcard(Boolean allowLeadingWildcard) that turns on the ability to utilize leading wildcards in queries.

WARNING   The authors recommend against using leading wildcards in queries unless they are *absolutely* necessary. Even then, we recommend you rethink your application logic. Leading wildcards can cause almost geometric performance degradation with index size—the larger the index size, the more degradation there is. Be careful, and test and quantify everything!

An additional query type that comes from the `WildcardQuery` is the `PrefixQuery`. When a term ends in the * wildcard character, such as a query for `titan*`, it's automatically converted to a `PrefixQuery`. This is done for you by the `QueryParser`, which will automatically rearrange terms into various query types as it sees fit.

Next up is the `PhraseQuery`. With this query type you can search for multiple terms in a specified order or degree of closeness.

7.1.3 Phrase queries

You're not limited to querying specific terms in Lucene. A `PhraseQuery`, also known as a *proximity search*, allows a query with more than one term in the same field. You can do this in two ways. One way is a literal search, which places the terms inside a set of quotation marks in the order you want them queried. For example,

```
name: "portsmouth england"
```

This queries for the two terms *portsmouth* and *england* as stated, in that order and next to one another.

A second way is known as a *proximity query,* which uses the ~ (tilde) character to express a *slop* factor. This slop factor expresses how far apart the terms in the phrase can be from one another and still be returned as a result to the query. For example,

```
name: "titanic iceberg"~5
```

This query states that if the terms *titanic* and *iceberg* are within five words of one another, it is a query match.

Let's revisit figure 7.3. In that figure the query was `"evans - sutherland"`, with spaces on both sides of the dash, resulting in a term search of `-title:Sutherland` (a NOT query). Now look at figure 7.5. If the spaces are removed, the query is parsed to the phrase query `"evans sutherland"`. The query parser no longer sees the – as a NOT. The analyzer has removed the - sign in this case and treated the entered terms as a phrase query.

One more point: If the query had been `"evans_sutherland"`, the query would again be parsed to `"evans sutherland"` The analyzer would again remove the _ in this case and treat the entered terms as a phrase query. We're going to say it again. We hope you realize that it's *extremely important* to understand exactly what's going on when parsing and what effect the chosen analyzer has on your data. Not knowing exactly what you have to work with makes it difficult to solve problems.

Is it possible to query with terms that the user just happened to misspell and still find relevant results? Yes, it is, when you use a `FuzzyQuery`. This is the topic of the next section, and those of you who may have been wondering what this *fuzzy* phenomenon is all about will find this an interesting discussion.

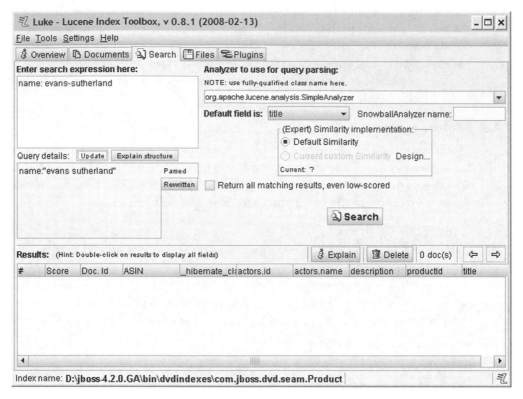

Figure 7.5   The – (dash) with no spaces between it and the surrounding words is interpreted as a phrase query.

7.1.4   *Fuzzy queries—similar terms (even misspellings)*

In looks only, a *fuzzy query* is similar to the proximity query we've discussed. It utilizes the ~ (tilde) character, and it's followed by a numeric value, but that's where the similarity ends. Here's an example of a fuzzy query:

```
name: portsmouth~0.8
```

The only visible difference between this query and the proximity query that's plainly noticeable is the use of a float value after the ~ (tilde) character. In fuzzy queries this value can range between 0.0 and 1.0, and it's known as the minimumSimilarity. Its meaning will become clear in a minute.

Fuzzy queries make use of what is called the *Levenshtein distance*. This distance is defined as the minimum number of operations needed to transform one string into the other. An excellent discussion of this algorithm is *Levenshtein Distance, in Three Flavors* by Michael Gilleland, located at http://www.merriampark.com/ld.htm#FLAVORS. This website also contains the source code for the algorithm in three languages: Java, C++, and Visual Basic.

Here's an example. The Levenshtein distance between *kitten* and *sitting* is 3, since three edits change one into the other, and there's no way to do so with fewer than three edits:

1 kitten→ sitten (substitution of *s* for *k*)
2 sitten → sittin (substitution of *i* for *e*)
3 sittin → sitting (insert *g* at the end)

While the Levenshtein distance uses an integer to represent the number of necessary edits, Lucene's fuzzy query specifies *how similar two terms must be* for them to satisfy the query criteria of a match. In other words, a minimumSimilarity of 1.0 means the same thing as an exact term match, and as its value decreases toward 0.0, the more edits are allowed to see if a match occurs. Be advised that as you decrease the value of the minimumSimilarity, you drastically increase the number of query matches, and on first glance some of the results may not seem to be related to the query at all (and they probably are not).

The authors have found that a minimumSimilarity value (the float value after the tilde (~)) ranging from 0.70 to 0.80 gave decent results when used in our queries, but, as always, this depends on the application. You'll have to experiment with this one until you're satisfied.

An alternative approach to fuzzy-style queries was detailed in sections 5.2.3 and 5.2.4. There we used *n*-gram queries and Soundex-type queries. You should experiment with both of these along with fuzzy queries to determine which is a best fit for your particular application.

Our next QueryParser syntax example is the RangeQuery. We'll discuss one of the problems with RangeQuerys resulting from the fact that all Lucene fields are string values.

7.1.5 *Range queries—from x TO y*

Range queries are those types of queries that allow you to search for results *between* two values. Two types of brackets and the keyword TO (must be uppercase) are used to specify a query of this type. Here's an example:

```
dateEntered: [20080112 TO 20080201]
```

Hibernate Search dates

When you index an object in Hibernate Search and that object contains a Date property, you have the ability to specify the minimum resolution to use when storing the date. In this example you'd specify @DateBridge(resolution=Resolution.DAY).

This query is looking for all index documents where the value in the dateEntered field is between 12 January 2008 and 1 February 2008. The use of square brackets here causes the date boundaries to be included in the query. If you wanted the boundary dates to be excluded from the query, you'd use { } (curly brackets). You cannot have one of each. That is, you cannot have one square bracket and one curly bracket in the same query. If you try it, you'll generate an exception. Querying for dateEntered: [20080112 TO 20080201} generates this exception:

```
org.apache.lucene.queryParser.ParseException: Cannot parse '[20061201 TO
    20010101}': Encountered "<EOF>" at line 1, column 22. Was expecting:
    "]" ...
```

Range queries are not limited to dates. Strings can be used also. For example,

```
lastname: [shutt TO weatbrook]
```

This queries for all last names between *shutt* and *weatbrook*, inclusive, as a lexico-graphic range.

Range queries on numeric values have additional problems. All field values in Lucene are strings; string representations of numeric values of different length appear in a different order than you would at first expect. For example, 10 comes before 2 because the strings are looked at character by character and not by value. One additional processing step, called *padding*, is necessary to get the strings to the same length. That is, the 2 would be changed to 02. That way 02 comes before 10. We'll talk about this more in a later section of this chapter and show you how to accomplish it utilizing a Hibernate Search bridge as we did in section 4.1.1.

The last syntax topic is how to utilize a boost factor. This rearranges results so that certain specified characteristics bring some results closer to the top of the returned documents than they would be if they didn't have these characteristics.

7.1.6 *Giving preference with boost*

It is sometimes desirable to rearrange the order in which results are returned. Results are returned in scoring order, which means that the closer a result matches a query, the higher its score; therefore it returns closer to the top of the results.

You can manipulate this position somewhat by applying a *boost* factor to some characteristic of the query. A boost factor is denoted by the ^ (caret) symbol followed by a multiplying factor. For example, suppose we want to query on two fields: title and description. We want to search title for *titanic* and description for *spielberg*, but we want the title field matches to be twice as important in the final results. Here's how to accomplish this:

```
title:titanic^2    description:spielberg
```

This causes the score for the title term to be multiplied by a boost factor of 2 so that results matching title:titanic will be more relevant, and therefore higher in the results, than those matching just description:spielberg.

By default, the boost factor is 1. Although the boost factor must be positive, it can be less than 1 (for example, 0.2). A less-than-1 boost factor causes matching results to

> ### Hibernate Search Boost
>
> Boost is supported at both the class level and the field level. For example, either or both of the following are allowed:
>
> ```
> @Entity
> @Boost(2.0F)
> public class Essay {
> …
> @Field(index=Index.TOKENIZED, store=Store.YES)
> @Boost(2.5f)
> public String getSummary() {
> ```

be pushed farther down in the results. We discuss this in greater detail in section 13.1.2. Also, a negative boost factor can be applied programmatically. Refer to the sidebar in section 3.4.2.

Now that you have a grasp of the syntax of the QueryParser, our last topic of discussion is controlling exactly how our query syntax is executed. When multiple query types are involved, the order of execution becomes critical.

7.1.7 Grouping queries with parentheses

Lucene allows the order of execution of queries to be modified to allow finer control of how we want our query to be executed. Also, it allows expressions to be grouped not only to improve the readability of the query expression but also to perform multiple operations on one field without having to enter a lot of expressions. The following two sections show how to use parentheses to accomplish this.

CONTROLLING THE ORDER OF EXECUTION

If you remember your math foundations, the solution to an equation can be completely changed by the use of parentheses. Take the following equation, for example:

```
3 * 2 + 5 = 11
```

If we change the order of calculations, the answer is different:

```
3 * ( 2 + 5 ) = 21
```

Parentheses can change the order of evaluation with queries also. Let's use the following two pieces of data as our index contents:

"From The Terminator to Titanic, you can always rely on writer-director James Cameron"

"In The Terminator the future is determined by the past"

Now look at the following two queries executed on this data.

```
Terminator AND future OR Cameron
Terminator AND (future OR Cameron)
```

Since the first query has no parentheses, the order of execution is from left to right. *Terminator* is ANDed with *future* to find the second index value; then this is ORed with *Cameron,* which has no additional effect since the second result doesn't contain *Cameron.* The second index value is the final result.

When we execute the second query, because parentheses are present, the order of query execution has been changed. First, *future* is ORed with *Cameron,* yielding both index values as the result. Then these values are ANDed with *Terminator,* making the final result equal to both index values.

GROUPING EXPRESSIONS

Parentheses are also used to group expressions not only to reduce the amount of typing that you have to do but also to improve query readability. Look at the following query:

```
+contents:terminator actor:hanks actor:jones -contents:titanic
```

This query is not impossible to figure out, but is this not much more readable?

```
contents:(+terminator -titanic) actor:(hanks jones)
```

Parentheses can be utilized as needed to group terms immediately following the field name and separator : (colon). By the way, have you figured out what we're querying for with this expression? This query is asking for all index entries where the contents field contains *terminator* AND not *titanic* AND the actor field contains *hanks* OR *jones.* That's enough about syntax. Hopefully these examples have demonstrated what parentheses can do for you.

Be sure to read the API documentation for the few query types that we didn't cover here.

Before we move on to the topic of tokenization and analyzers, let's look at the QueryParser class itself. This class translates a user-entered query and translates it into the syntax that we've talked about up to this point.

7.1.8   *Getting to know the standard QueryParser and ad hoc queries*

Ad hoc queries are the "user-friendly" queries of Lucene. Users enter one or more terms to query an index, and they receive their answer back. From their point of view, that's all that happens. As we know, much more is involved than that. Let's take a look at the QueryParser class and the important parts of its API.

NOTE   The QueryParser class is the backbone of ad hoc query generation. This is the class that converts the user-entered query terms into a Query that contains the syntax that the search engine is expecting.

The QueryParser class itself is generated by the Java parser/scanner generator JavaCC (Java Compiler Compiler™). The grammar file QueryParser.jj, used to generate the class, is included in Lucene's source code, should you wish to examine it.

The most important method in its API is parse(String). This method takes a query string and returns an org.apache.lucene.search.Query built from it. The query string is all of the different symbols that we have covered up to this point in the chapter: +, -, *, ^, and all the others. For those of you familiar with Backus-Naur notation, the official definition of the query string is

```
Query  ::= ( Clause )*
   Clause ::= ["+", "-"] [<TERM> ":"] ( <TERM> | "(" Query ")" )
```

If you're not familiar with this notation, don't worry. Stick to the syntax we've shown to this point, and you'll not have a problem. Let's work some examples of the parse method with varied query strings and discuss a few of the other API methods that you may come in contact with. The example parsings are given in listing 7.1.

Listing 7.1 Several examples of query strings and their equivalent parsed queries

```
public class TestQueryParserQueryGeneration
{
  public void testQueryParser() throws Exception {

    String queryString = "The Story of the Day";
    QueryParser parser =
      new QueryParser("title",                        Build query
                 new StandardAnalyzer());             for title field
    Query query = parser.parse(queryString);
    assert query.toString().equals(                   Generated query for
 "title:story title:day");                            StandardAnalyzer

    queryString = "The Story of the Day";
    parser = new QueryParser("title",                 Use
                 new SimpleAnalyzer());               SimpleAnalyzer
    query = parser.parse(queryString);
    assert query.toString().equals(                            Generated
 "title:the title:story title:of title:the title:day");       query

    queryString = "Story*";                    Build wildcard
    parser =                                   (Prefix) query
      new QueryParser("title", new StandardAnalyzer());
    query = parser.parse(queryString);                 As expected,
    assert query.toString().equals("title:story*");    nothing changed

    queryString = "Story~0.8 Judgement";               Create compound
    parser =                                           query with
      new QueryParser("title", new StandardAnalyzer());  FuzzyQuery
    parser.setDefaultOperator(QueryParser.
      Operator.AND);                                   Set default
    query = parser.parse(queryString);                 ❶ operator to AND
    assert query.toString().equals(
 "+title:story~0.8 +title:judgement");      Require both
  }                                          terms now
}
```

Additional API methods you may need to become familiar with are:

- `static String escape(String s)`   Returns a string where those characters that `QueryParser` expects to be escaped are escaped by a preceding \. We discuss this in greater detail in section 7.3.1.
- `setAllowLeadingWildcard(boolean allowLeadingWildcard)`   False by default; set this to true to allow leading wildcard characters. The authors gave a warning about allowing this and the problems it may cause in section 7.1.2.
- `void setDefaultOperator(QueryParser.Operator op)`   The default mode is `QueryParser.Operator.OR`, with which terms without any modifiers (+ -) are considered optional. This can be set to `QueryParser.Operator.AND`, which causes terms without any modifiers (+ -) to be required. Examine ❶ in listing 7.1.

WARNING   The `QueryParser` class is not thread-safe! It's your responsibility to ensure that when multiple threads access it, they behave themselves. It has a drawback as well. The `QueryParser` cannot reproduce the syntax of all the query types available with the Lucene/Hibernate Search API. Examples of this problem are the many different types of `SpanQuerys`, which can query in many different ways. An example is finding all documents where the phrase "white star" is near the phrase "Portsmouth, England." Boolean `ANDed` `PhraseQueries` can approximate this, but they have no concept of *nearness*.

So how does a pile of unorganized information start to become an organized searchable index? That's our next focus of attention. Let's start by reviewing some of the topics that were introduced in chapters 3 and 4, so that these idioms are fresh in your mind.

7.2   *Tokenization and fields*

A *document unit* (this is not the `Document` class of Lucene) is the initial piece of information that we wish to enter into an index. It could be the text of a book, a summary of a book, a paragraph, or even a sentence—in short, any information that is index capable and searchable for our purposes. Our first step is to assemble these document units; after assembling them, we'll place each unit into a field or property.

7.2.1   *Fields/properties*

A field (Lucene) or property (Hibernate Search) is the basic *container* from which documents are composed. Fields hold the tokens/terms that are queried against. A field name followed by a colon followed by a term makes up a basic query, for example, `description:adaptation`. This is exactly what we were looking at with Luke in the first few figures of this chapter, so this should be a review of what we talked about then. Figure 7.6 shows Luke with this query.

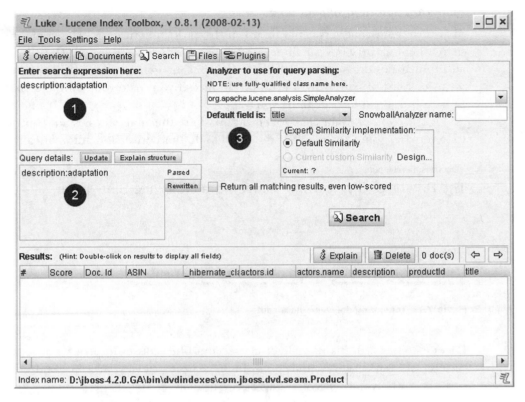

Figure 7.6 Luke querying the description field for the term *adaptation*

In figure 7.6 **1** is the query we entered. After we clicked the Update button, our query was parsed and shown **2**. This is the most basic type of query, one term on one field, so there are no surprises here. Notice **3** the default field is set to title. This required us to enter the field name of the field we were querying. If the default field had been set to description, then the field name and colon would not have been necessary.

Once we have our fields/properties assembled, we need to put them through a process called *tokenization*.

7.2.2 *Tokenization*

Tokenizing is the task of chopping a document unit into pieces, called *tokens*, perhaps at the same time throwing away certain characters such as punctuation marks. We can even throw away whole words. These words are known as *stop words* and are common words that are unlikely to help determine the relevance of a document against a query. Words such as *the, an, or, but,* and so on are often defined as stop words but do not necessarily have to be. Although the usage is not strictly correct in the information-retrieval world, for our purposes *term* and *word* are synonymous, and we'll use these two idioms interchangeably.

Analyzers perform the act of tokenizing a document unit. Let's look at them next.

7.2.3   *Analyzers and their impact on queries*

As you've seen, analyzers generate tokens from document units. They perform more than tokenization. They can filter out the stop words we mentioned. They can convert all input to lowercase, filter all numeric input, or generate the stems of the query terms or a list of synonyms, and so on. In fact, if you write your own analyzer, it can process input text into anything you want.

Figure 7.7 is an example of tokenization where the analyzer does not convert terms to lowercase. Some analyzers are designed to do this conversion automatically.

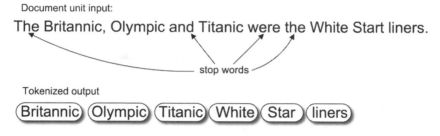

Figure 7.7   Tokenizing document unit input

Lucene comes with many analyzer classes and filter classes to process input text in a variety of ways as an index is built. These classes are contained in the `org.apache.lucene.analysis` package. An analyzer that is used quite often is the `StandardAnalyzer` in the `org.apache.lucene.analysis.standard` package. Recently, this analyzer has been significantly improved speedwise.

Hibernate Search also supports the Apache Solr analyzers. Solr is an open source enterprise search server based on Lucene; the project home page is located at http://lucene.apache.org/solr/. The Solr analyzer jar apache-solr-analyzer.jar contains an incredibly varied selection of filters that can be utilized in the manner explained in section 5.3.2.

We want to take a minute here and discuss analyzers and the care you should take when working with them. That's the topic of our next section.

7.2.4   *Using analyzers during indexing*

In section 5.3 we covered analyzers and filters in detail. After reading this section you should be able to chain filters and attach them to analyzers in such a way that you can accomplish just about any kind of analysis. Look back at section 5.3.2 specifically to review how easy it is to chain filters utilizing the `@Analyzer` and `@AnalyzerDefs` annotations. You should keep some things in mind when applying analyzers during indexing and searching.

Oddities of analyzers: breaking the golden rule

In section 3.5 we saw that one of the synonym filter strategies involved copying all synonyms in the token stream instead of only the initial word. This strategy means that a query no longer has to care about synonyms: if either one of the synonyms is present in the query, the document will match. In this particular case, this filter should not be applied to the query. It would simply make the query less efficient and less accurate.

To work around this problem, follow these simple steps:

1 Declare an `@AnalyzerDef` similar to the `@AnalyzerDef` used to index the field containing synonyms, but remove the `SynonymFilter`. This will ensure tokens are processed in the same way except for the synonym's expansion. Let's name this analyzer definition *query-synonyms*.

2 Retrieve the analyzer from Hibernate Search defined for a specific entity: `searchFactory.getAnalyzer(ScopedEntity.class)`.

3 Retrieve the query-synonyms analyzer from Hibernate Search by name: `searchFactory.getAnalyzer("query-synonyms")`.

4 Create a Lucene `PerFieldAnalyzerWrapper` analyzer, passing the scoped analyzer in the constructor and adding the query-synonyms analyzer on the field containing the synonyms.

Here's a code snippet showing this process:

```
@AnalyzerDefs({
    @AnalyzerDef(name="synonyms",
            tokenizer = @TokenizerDef(factory =
                            StandardTokenizerFactory.class ),
            filters = { @TokenFilterDef(factory =
                            StandardFilterFactory.class),
                    @TokenFilterDef(factory =
                        StopFilterFactory.class,
                        params = @Parameter(name="words",
                                    value="stopwords.txt") ),
                @TokenFilterDef(factory =
                    SynonymFilterFactory.class,
                    // expand all synonyms in the token stream
                        params = @Parameter(name="expand",
                                        value="true") )
                }
    ),

    @AnalyzerDef(name="query-synonyms",
        tokenizer = @TokenizerDef(factory =
            StandardTokenizerFactory.class ),
        filters = { @TokenFilterDef(factory =
            StandardFilterFactory.class),
                // synonym filter is removed
```

Oddities of analyzers: breaking the golden rule *(continued)*

```
                @TokenFilterDef(factory = StopFilterFactory.class,
                        params = @Parameter(name="words",
                                value="stopwords.txt") )
            }
        )
    })
    public class ScopedEntity {
        @Fields( {@Field(name="field3"),
            @Field(name="field3-synonyms",
                analyzer=@Analyzer(definition="synonyms"))}})
        private String field3;
        ...
    }

    Analyzer scopedEntityAnalyzer =
        searchFactory.getAnalyzer(ScopedEntity.class);
    Analyzer querySynonymsAnalyzer = searchFactory.getAnalyzer("query-
            synonyms")
    PerFieldAnalyzerWrapper queryAnalyzer = new
            PerFieldAnalyzerWrapper(scopedEntityAnalyzer );

    queryAnalyzer.addAnalyzer("field3-synonyms", querySynonymsAnalyzer);
```

You can use the PerFieldAnalyzerWrapper instance to build your query. All default analyzers will be used except for the specific synonym field, which will use query-synonyms.

Let's take a more detailed look at the `@Analyzer` annotation described in section 3.4.1.

When Hibernate Search indexes data, it allows you to place analyzers at three different points in your code. The `@Analyzer` annotation states:

```
@Target( { ElementType.TYPE, ElementType.FIELD, ElementType.METHOD} )
```

For this discussion we're concerned with the first two items, TYPE and FIELD (METHOD would simply apply to a getter method of a field). You can place an analyzer on an individual field of an entity (`ElementType.FIELD`). This implies that different analyzers can easily be placed on different fields of the same entity. You can also assign an analyzer to an entity, in which case the analyzer applies to all fields (except those that specify an analyzer at the field level). The `ScopedEntity` class in listing 7.2 demonstrates this.

Listing 7.2   Applying different analyzers to an entity and a field in the same entity

```
@Entity
@Indexed                                          Apply the analyzer
@Analyzer(impl = StandardAnalyzer.class)   ◁──┐   to the entity
public class ScopedEntity {
```

```
@Id
@GeneratedValue
@DocumentId
private Integer id;

@Field(index = Index.TOKENIZED, store = Store.YES)
private String field1;

@Field(index = Index.TOKENIZED, store = Store.YES)
@Analyzer(impl = WhitespaceAnalyzer.class)          ◁─────┐
private String field2;
...
```

**Override the
entity analyzer
for this field**

This allows for an extremely high degree of flexibility while building your indexes. The one thing the authors want to emphasize, though, is that *when you query an index that was built with a specific analyzer, unless you really know what you're doing, you should employ the identical analyzer when querying.* This guarantees that expectations concerning the data you're querying are valid and there will be no surprises. This gremlin really rears it ugly head in the case of punctuation. Read the Javadoc of the `org.apache.lucene.analysis.standard.StandardTokenizer` class for an example of exactly what this tokenizer does. It could cause you problems if you're not aware that it was employed to index the data you're querying.

How do we get around this problem? As of this writing, with Lucene you're out of luck. Either you have to know which analyzer was used to create the index via documentation, or the index creator could store the analyzer class type somehow, somewhere, so that it can be retrieved and reused. Hibernate Search, on the other hand, allows you to retrieve at query time which analyzer was employed at index time.

We'll get to how Hibernate Search does this in just a minute, but first we want demonstrate how to manually apply an analyzer to a query. You never know when this will come in handy.

7.2.5 *Manually applying an analyzer to a query*

Some query types allow the application of an analyzer out of the box. At the same time, many more queries don't allow it. This section demonstrates how to apply an analyzer to a query by taking a query string and manually applying a `StandardAnalyzer` analyzer to it. This enables you to apply whatever analyzers you wish to a multifield query and combine them into a `BooleanQuery` query. Listing 7.3 shows how to do this.

Listing 7.3   Manually applying an analyzer to a query

```
public class TestManualAnalyzer {
    public void testManualAnalyzer() throws Exception {       ◁──┐ Build query
                                                                 │ from this string
        String search = "The Little Pony";                    ◁──┘

        Reader reader = new StringReader(search);         ◁─┐ Generate a
                                                            │ reader for the
        Analyzer analyzer = new StandardAnalyzer();       ❶ Analyzer stream
```

```
        TokenStream stream =
          analyzer.tokenStream("title", reader);    ◁──   Instantiate a
                                                      2   TokenStream
        Token token = new Token();

        token = stream.next(token);    ◁───  3  Grab the first token

        BooleanQuery query = new BooleanQuery();
        while (token != null) {
          if (token.termLength() != 0) {

            String term = new String(token.termBuffer(),          Create a term
                           0,                                  4   from the token
                           token.termLength());
            //add it to the query by creating a TermQuery
            query.add(new TermQuery(new Term("title", term)),    5   Build a
            ⇒BooleanClause.Occur.SHOULD);    ◁──────────             TermQuery
          }
          token = stream.next(token);    ◁──┐
        }                                      Grab the next
        assert query.toString().equals(   6  token and loop
            ⇒"title:little title:pony"):    ◁──┐
            ⇒"incorrect query generated";         Assert the
      }                                       7  generated query
    }
```

Because analyzers need input in the form of a Reader, we create one ❶ for our input string. With this reader we can generate a TokenStream ❷ and retrieve the first token from it ❸. We create the first term by creating a copy of the contents of the term buffer ❹. This way we can safely reuse the token. With this term we create a new Term-Query and add it to the BooleanQuery as the first clause ❺.

We've jumped the gun a little at ❺ by programmatically creating an instance of a BooleanQuery before we discussed it. If you have a problem understanding it, hang in there because we talk about that in the next section. We're sure you'll understand it by the end of that section.

We then get the next token and loop until the token stream is exhausted ❻; ❼ asserts that the query equals "title:little title:pony".

Now for what we talked about at the end of section 7.2.4, the fact that Hibernate Search allows you to retrieve at query time which analyzer was employed at index time.

When you use separate analyzers per field to build an index, Hibernate Search provides a ScopedAnalyzer. The org.hibernate.search.util.ScopedAnalyzer class keeps track of all the analyzers specified in an entity and allows you to recall them as needed. An analyzer specified on all entities through the configuration specification is known as a *global analyzer*. In the event no explicit analyzer exists for a particular field, the global analyzer is returned.

The next section contains an example of the ScopedAnalyzer and a discussion of when to use it and when not to.

7.2.6 *Using multiple analyzers in the same query*

Once we retrieve the analyzers that were used to build the query, how do we employ them so that they can be applied to their individual fields as needed during a query? If you use the QueryParser to build your query—and that is a big if—the ScopedAnalyzer class will automatically apply the specified analyzer to its matching field. Everything will be taken care of without the need for any intervention on your part.

If you chose not to use the query parser, you're on your own, sort of. The Scoped-Analyzer class is your friend in this case.

Why did we say, "sort of"? Because you must manually implement the appropriate analyzer on your query. Listing 7.4 gives an example utilizing the ScopedEntity class from listing 7.2.

SearchTestCase

Listing 7.4, along with almost all of the tests in chapters 11, 12, and 13 and the remaining tests in this chapter, inherit from the SearchTestCase class. This class provides several utility methods used in the tests. SearchTestCase also inherits from HsiATestCase, and this class also provides several methods such as buildSessionFactory and configure.

The individual test classes will override the methods in these two superclasses as needed to perform the tests.

Listing 7.4 Applying individual analyzers

```
public class TestAnalyzerWrapper extends SearchTestCase {
  @Test
  public void testScopedAnalyzer() throws Exception {
    FullTextSession session =
      Search.getFullTextSession( openSession() );
    Transaction tx = session.beginTransaction();

    buildIndex(session, tx);

    try {
      SearchFactory searchFactory =
        session.getSearchFactory();

      FullTextQuery hibQuery =
        buildQuery(searchFactory, "field2", session);
      List<ScopedEntity> results = hibQuery.list();

      assert result.size() == 0:          ❶ Zero results after
      "incorrect result count";             field2 search

      assert hibQuery.toString().equals(
        "FullTextQueryImpl(+field2:TEST)"):  ❷ First generated
        "incorrect query";                     query string

      hibQuery = buildQuery(searchFactory, "field1", session);
```

```
    results = hibQuery.list();                Two results after
                                          ❸ fieldl search
    assert result.size() == 0:
    "incorrect result count";

    assert hibQuery.toString().equals(
      "FullTextQueryImpl(+field1:TEST)"):    ❹ Second generated
      "incorrect query";                          query string

      for (Object element :
        session.createQuery("from "
          + ScopedEntity.class.getName()).list())
        session.delete(element);
      tx.commit();
  }
  finally {
    session.close();
  }
}

private FullTextQuery buildQuery(SearchFactory factory,
String field, FullTextSession session) throws IOException {

    Reader reader = new StringReader("TEST");

    TokenStream stream =
      factory.getAnalyzer( ScopedEntity.class )    ❺ TokenStream from
        .tokenStream( field, reader);                  ScopedAnalyzer
    BooleanQuery bq = new BooleanQuery();

    Token token = new Token();         ❻ Get the first token
    token = stream.next( token );

    while (token != null) {
      if ( token.termLength() != 0) {
        String term =
          new String( token.termBuffer(),    ❼ Extract the term
            0,
            token.termLength() );

        bq.add( new TermQuery( new Term(field, term)),    ❽ Add the term to
          BooleanClause.Occur.MUST );                        the BooleanQuery
      }
      token = stream.next( token );        Loop for the
    }                                  ❾ next token
    return session.createFullTextQuery(bq,
ScopedEntity.class);               Return the
}                                ❿ complete query

private void buildIndex() {
  tx = session.beginTransaction();

  ScopedEntity entity = new ScopedEntity();
  entity.setField1("test field1");
  entity.setField2("test field2");
  session.save(entity);

  entity = new ScopedEntity();
  entity.setField1("test field3");
  entity.setField2("test field4");
```

```
    session.save(entity);

    tx.commit();
  }
}
```

The results of our first query ❶ of TEST on field2 returned zero results. Looking at ❷ we see that the generated query string was +field2:TEST. According to listing 7.2 the ScopedAnalyzer should have applied a WhitespaceAnalyzer to the field during indexing and during the query. The WhitespaceAnalyzer does not pass its tokens through a LowercaseFilter, so the query of TEST would have remained uppercase and therefore would not have found any results. That is exactly what happened; so far, so good.

Now the second query ❸ illustrates that the query returned two results for the query string +field1:test ❹. The query in this case was lowercased. Examining listing 7.2 again we see that no explicit analyzer was applied to the field1 field. Therefore, the ScopedAnalyzer would have applied the global analyzer, which is by definition the StandardAnalyzer. This analyzer *does* lowercase its tokens, so ScopedAnalyzer works exactly as we expected. It applied a WhitespaceAnalyzer to field2 and a Standard-Analyzer to field1.

Let's examine how the query was built. A TokenStream is obtained from the Scoped-Analyzer ❺. Since the name of the field being analyzed is passed as a parameter, it allows the ScopedAnalyzer to determine the appropriate context and return the appropriate analyzer. The first token is retrieved from the stream at ❻. We use the next(Token token) method in lieu of the next() method because it is faster. Read the Javadoc for the org.apache.lucene.analysis.TokenStream.next(Token result).

We extract the term from the token via the char[] buffer in the token ❼ and copy it to a new string, so it's safe to reuse the token. We start building the query ❽ and loop for more tokens ❾. Once the tokens are exhausted, we return the completed query ❿.

As you can see, this requires a fair amount of additional programming, but it guarantees that the analyzer used at query time is the same as the one used at index time. For a thorough treatment of the ScopedAnalyzer API, we recommend that you spend some time examining the testScopedAnalyzerAPI unit test in org.hibernate.search.test.analyzer.AnalyzerTest.

Next we're going to talk about programmatic custom query generation. This is the real power of full-text searching. The sky is basically the limit here. You can clean up user queries before they ever make it to your application's search engine. You can split queries in any manner you wish across any number of fields. In short, use your imagination.

We're going to discuss the API version of the queries. When we arrive at the BooleanQuery you'll finally see how to put these many different types together to form custom queries exactly as you want them.

7.3   *Building custom queries programmatically*

It's not always necessary to use a query parser to generate a query. You can instantiate a particular type of query and work directly with it. This is usually how search engines with deep business logic do it, especially when they want to hide search complexity from the general user. To see the plethora of queries available for your use, look at the Javadoc for the `org.apache.lucene.search.Query` class and examine its high number of subclasses. Be sure to read the individual queries' documentation, because they all have different requirements in some form or other.

In the following sections we're going to examine several different types of queries and see them in action. They are:

- `TermQuery`
- `PhraseQuery`
- `WildcardQuery`
- `PrefixQuery`
- `FuzzyQuery`
- `RangeQuery`
- `BooleanQuery`

Along the way we'll clean up some of the loose ends left over from previous code examples that we told you to wait for until we got to this part of the chapter. We'll start with the simplest and arguably the most common of these, the `TermQuery`. But first let's look at a troubleshooting aid that can save you a lot of time.

7.3.1   *Using Query.toString()*

When we were using Luke, we received instant gratification on exactly how the query parser interpreted our query when we clicked the Update button. How can we do this while we're developing our applications, and can this help us improve them over time?

The `Query` interface specifies two `toString` methods.

- `String toString()` This outputs the query in the same format as the examples we discussed in section 7.1. We use this in log entries as a troubleshooting aid.
- `abstract String toString(String field)` This outputs the query in the same way as the previous method except that `field` is considered the default and is omitted from the result. This is similar to the search expression we entered in figure 7.1.

NOTE   In all of the following sections of this chapter, the examples will have a call to the `Query.toSting()` method to illustrate how the query was parsed and what's being sent to the Lucene engine.

An additional use of the `toString` methods is to help with data mining from your log files. The output of these methods in addition to a count per unit time of entries and time-of-day data can tell you a lot about what's going on in your application and what your users are looking for.

7.3.2 *Searching a single field for a single term: TermQuery*

The basic building block of queries is the term query. One of the first operations carried out by any class that extends the `Query` class is to reduce a given query to the simplest form possible via the `rewrite` method. The vast majority of queries can almost always be broken down into one or more series of term queries utilizing the `QueryParser` syntax you learned throughout section 7.1. For example, a `PrefixQuery` will be rewritten into a `BooleanQuery` that consists of `TermQuerys`. We'll show this happening in the section on the `PrefixQuery`, which comes along shortly.

We used the `TermQuery` in listing 7.3, but we'll take the time to explain it a little further here. Let's look at an example of a basic `TermQuery` in listing 7.5.

Listing 7.5 Utilizing a `TermQuery` to search for "salesman"

```
public class TestTermQuery extends SearchTestCase {
  String[] descs = new String[]{"he hits the road
➥as a traveling salesman",
    "he's not a computer salesman",
    "a traveling salesman touting the wave of the future",
    "transforms into an aggressive, high-risk salesman",
    "a once-successful salesman"};

  @Test
  public void testTermQuery() throws Exception {
    FullTextSession session =
      Search.getFullTextSession( openSession() );
    Transaction tx = session.beginTransaction();

    try
    {
      buildIndex(session, tx);
      String userInput = "salesman";

      tx = session.beginTransaction();
      Term term = new Term("description", userInput);      ❶ Create a Term
                                                              to search for
      TermQuery query = new TermQuery(term);           ❷ Generate a TermQuery
                                                          from the Term
      System.out.println(query.toString());

      org.hibernate.search.FullTextQuery hibQuery =
        session.createFullTextQuery(query, Dvd.class);
      List<Dvd> results = hibQuery.list();

      assert results.size() == 5 : "incorrect hit count";
      assert results.get(0).getDescription()
        .equals("he's not a computer salesman");

      for (Dvd dvd : results) {
        System.out.println(dvd.getDescription());
      }

      for (Object element : session.createQuery("from " +
➥Dvd.class.getName()).list()) session.delete(element);
      tx.commit();
    }
```

```
  finally {
    session.close();
  }

  private void buildIndex(FullTextSession session, Transaction tx) {
    for (int x = 0; x < descs.length; x++) {
      Dvd dvd = new Dvd();
      dvd.setDescription(descs[x]);
      dvd.setId(x);
      session.save(dvd);
    }
    tx.commit();
    session.clear();
  }
}
```

description:salesman   ➌ **Generated**
                           ⟵┘ **query syntax**

```
he's not a computer salesman
a once-successful salesman
he hits the road as a traveling salesman
a traveling salesman touting the wave of the future
transforms into an aggressive, high-risk salesman
```

Notice that we've introduced a new class in addition to `TermQuery`. The `Term` class ➊ takes a field name and a string to search for. It is then passed to the `TermQuery` constructor ➋ to create the query.

This example should illustrate why most queries are reduced to sets of `TermQuery`s. After all, queries are nothing more than a series of single terms. The generated query syntax is shown at ➌.

Before we cover the use of several of the individual query-generation classes, let's discuss an important topic that can help with anticipating the text users enter in queries. This important topic is utilizing *regular expressions* to make sure that what users enter as a query is really what they intended to enter.

SPECIAL CHARACTERS

With applications there's no way to anticipate what a user will enter as the text of a query. Toward the end of section 7.1.1 we discussed the problem with the – (dash) character being misinterpreted as a Boolean `NOT` operator. You cannot expect the users of your application to know and understand that they will have to escape dashes with a backslash (that just won't happen). Well, surprise, it is not just the – character you will have to consider escaping.

Lucene uses several *special characters* to go about normal everyday tasks, and, as we've shown in section 7.1.1, these could be misinterpreted if they were used as is in queries. Table 7.2 shows a list of those characters.

How can we escape these special characters in our application when we have no control over how users enter their query strings? Listing 7.6 is one example of how to accomplish this. Feel free to use this code as you see fit in your applications. If you're running a Java version earlier than 1.5, the `QueryParser` class supplies a method that accomplishes the same results: `public static String escape(String s)`.

Table 7.2 Special characters and their interpretation

Special character	Where it is used	Special character	Where it is used
+	shorthand for AND	[	inclusive lower bound
–	shorthand for NOT	]	inclusive upper bound
&&	additional shorthand for AND	^	term boost
||	additional shorthand for OR	"	phrase query delimiter
!	additional shorthand for NOT	~	proximity query slop factor fuzzy query minimumumSimilarity
( )	grouping parentheses	*	multicharacter wildcard
{	exclusive lower bound	?	single-character wildcard
}	exclusive upper bound	:	fieldname/term delimiter
		\	escape character

Listing 7.6 Programmatically escaping special characters from user-entered queries

```
private static final String[] SPECIALS =           Define the
  new String[]{                                    special
    "+", "-", "&&", "||", "!", "(", ")", "{", "}",  1  characters
    "[", "]", "^", "\"", "~", "*", "?", ":", "\\"
};

protected String escapeSpecials(String clientQuery)
{
  String regexOr = "";
  for (String special : SPECIALS)
  {
    regexOr += (special
      .equals(SPECIALS[0]) ? "" : "|") + "\\"      Build the
        + special.substring(0, 1);                  2  regex string
  }
  clientQuery = clientQuery
    .replaceAll("(?<!\\\\)(" + regexOr + ")",       Substitute escaped
               "\\\\$1");                            3  characters for specials
  return clientQuery.trim();
}
```

We start ① by defining the special characters in a String array. In the loop at ② we build our regular expression. In this case the expression string is

\+|\-|\&|\||\!|\(|\)|\{|\}|\[|\]|\^|\"|\~|*|\?|\:|\\

As you'd expect, this is each of the special characters preceded by the escape character \ and separated from the next special character by the | (OR) character. The meat of the code is ③. The String.replaceAll() java method steps through the client-Query string and replaces any of the special characters it finds with that special character preceded by \. With a `clientQuery` of `"comment: first : line"`, the result would be `"comment: first \: line"`.

The regex expression

For those of you who really want to know how the regular expression works and are not quite sure, it uses *negative look behind* on each of the characters in the `client-Query`. This look behind examines each character and rejects any that are already preceded by a \ character and continues to the next character. If the character is not already preceded by a \ and it matches any of the expressions in the `regexOr` string, the expression is substituted for the character, so `:` becomes `\:`.

Now let's examine how to query across several fields.

7.3.3   *MultiFieldQueryParser queries more than one field*

The `QueryParser` class was designed to perform ad hoc queries on a single field, but what do you do if what the user entered is supposed to query across more than one field? For example, your application could have several drop-down boxes where the user selects field names and query types for each of these, or your application hides this complexity from your user and targets, transparently, several fields, choosing different boost levels (weight) for each. That's where the `MultiFieldQueryParser` class comes in. It was custom-made for just such a situation.

`MultiFieldQueryParser` is a subclass of `QueryParser` and as such it inherits its methods. This means that it also has the factory methods necessary to generate the many different types of queries that were listed in the previous section. Moreover, it has additional `static parse` methods that are the heart and soul of the class. They are:

- `static parse(String[] queries, String[] fields, Analyzer analyzer)`
- `static Query parse(String[] queries, String[] fields, BooleanClause.Occur[] flags, Analyzer analyzer)`
- `static Query parse(String query, String[] fields, BooleanClause.Occur[] flags, Analyzer analyzer)`

It's important that you understand the differences between these methods because they look similar but behave differently.

The first parse method accepts an array of query strings and an array of fields plus an analyzer. These arrays function as parallel arrays. That is, query[0] applies to field[0], query[1] applies to field[1], and so on up to query[n] applying to field[n]. When this static method is called to generate a query, all of these queries are limited to being `OR`ed together. This is rather restrictive. What if we wanted to utilize the parser to `AND` or maybe even `NOT` a query in the same set of queries? That's where the other two parse methods come in.

The second parse method accepts the query and field arrays just like the first one did, but it also accepts another array of type `BooleanClause.Occur` that determines whether queries are ANDed, Ored, or NOTed. Therefore, all bases are covered with the addition of this third array. Section 7.3.6 will have an example of these `Boolean-Clause.Occur` types.

The third and final parse method is almost exactly like the second one except that, since it has only one query instead of an array of them, that query is applied across all the fields specified in the array of field names.

Figure 7.8 shows an admittedly simplistic screen that could be used to gather the description and title terms that are utilized in listing 7.4. This should give you a frame of reference as to what we're trying to demonstrate in the listing.

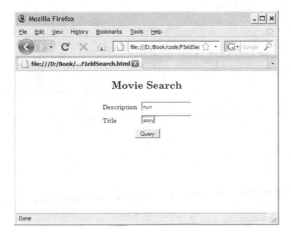

Figure 7.8 The example screen that could possibly gather the data given in listing 7.4

An example of the `MultiFieldQueryParser` class in listing 7.7 demonstrates the first listed parse method.

Listing 7.7 Utilizing the `MultiFieldQueryParser` class

```
public class TestMultiField extends SearchTestCase {
  String[] titles = new String[]{"The Nun's Story",
    "Toy Story", "The Philadelphia Story", "Toy Story 2",
    "Ever After - A Cinderella Story",
    "Dodgeball - A True Underdog Story",
    "The Miracle Maker - The Story of Jesus",
    "Films of Faith Collection", "Dragonfly"};
  String[] descs = new String[]{"", "", "", "", "", "", "",
    "Fred Zinneman's epic The Nun's Story",
    "Belief gets us there explains nun Linda Hunt"};

  @Test
  public void testMultiFieldQueryParser() throws Exception {
    FullTextSession session =
      Search.getFullTextSession(openSession());
    Transaction tx = session.beginTransaction();
```

```
      try {
        buildIndex(session, tx);      String query0 = "nun";
        String query1 = "story";
        String field0 = "description";
        String field1 = "title";

        String[] fields = new String[]{field0, field1};
        String[] queries = new String[]{query0, query1};
        tx = session.beginTransaction();

        Query query = MultiFieldQueryParser.parse(queries,
                fields, new StopAnalyzer());
        System.out.println(query.toString());

        org.hibernate.search.FullTextQuery hibQuery =
          session.createFullTextQuery(query, Dvd.class);
        List<Dvd> results = hibQuery.list();

        assert results.size() == 9:
          "incorrect hit count";
        assert results.get(0).getTitle()
          .equals("Films of Faith Collection");

        for (Dvd dvd : results) {
          System.out.println(dvd.getTitle());
        }

        for (Object element : session.createQuery("from " +
            Dvd.class.getName()).list())
          ssession.delete(element);
        tx.commit();
      }
      finally {
        session.close();
      }
    }

  private void buildIndex(FullTextSession session, Transaction tx) {
    for (int x = 0; x < titles.length; x++) {
      Dvd dvd = new Dvd();
      dvd.setTitle(titles[x]);
      dvd.setDescription(descs[x]);
      dvd.setId(x);
      session.save(dvd);
    }

    tx.commit();
    session.clear();
  }
}

description:nun title:story

Films of Faith Collection
Dragonfly
Toy Story
The Philadelphia Story
Toy Story 2
The Nun's Story
```

1 Generate the queries and fields

2 Call the static parse method

3 Generated query syntax

```
Ever After - A Cinderella Story
Dodgeball - A True Underdog Story
The Miracle Maker - The Story of Jesus
```

We start ❶ by creating our field and query strings and generating arrays of these values. At ❷ we call the static parse method and pass the arrays. This is why we're limited to the queries being ORed together. We cannot call the setDefaultOperator method using this format. The generated query syntax is shown at ❸.

The next-simplest query type is PhraseQuery. We look at that in the following section.

7.3.4 Searching words by proximity: PhraseQuery

Phrase queries, also known as *proximity searches,* consist of multiple terms surrounded by quotation marks. They are known as proximity searches because this type of search allows for intervening terms between the entered search terms. The number of intervening terms, or *edit distance,* is controlled by what is called the *slop* factor. The higher the slop factor, the more terms can appear between the search terms.

By default, the slop factor is set to 0, meaning that terms in the index must appear exactly as entered. As an example, if we were searching for a two-term phrase and didn't change the slop factor, any results must match the two entered terms exactly in their entered order. But if we didn't care in which order they appeared in the result, the slop factor must be at least 2, since each word must change position in the search.

Let's look at an example PhraseQuery in action. First we'll use an exact match query, then we'll increase the slop factor to see what effect it has on the results. The exact match PhraseQuery is shown in listing 7.8.

Listing 7.8 Querying for an exact match `PhraseQuery`

```
public class TestPhraseQuery extends SearchTestCase {
    String[] descs = new String[]{"he hits the road as a
    traveling salesman", "Star Trek The Next Generation",
        "the fifth season of star trek", "to Star Trek fans
    everywhere the stellar second season",
        "a once-successful salesman"};

    @Test
    public void testPhraseQuery() throws Exception {
        FullTextSession session = Search.getFullTextSession(openSession());
        Transaction tx = session.beginTransaction();

        try {
            buildIndex(session, tx);                      ❶ Query in
            String userInput = "star trek";                  lowercase
            StringTokenizer st =                          ❷ Split user input
                new StringTokenizer(userInput, " ");         into distinct terms

            tx = session.beginTransaction();
            PhraseQuery query = new PhraseQuery();
            while (st.hasMoreTokens()) {                  ❸ Generate the
                query.add(new Term("description",            PhraseQuery
                            st.nextToken()));
            }
```

```
        System.out.println(query.toString());

        org.hibernate.search.FullTextQuery hibQuery =
            session.createFullTextQuery(query, Dvd.class);
        List<Dvd> results = hibQuery.list();

        assert results.size() == 3: "incorrect hit count";
        assert results.get(0).getDescription()
          .equals("Star Trek The Next Generation");

        for (Dvd dvd : results) {
          System.out.println(dvd.getDescription());
        }

        for (Object element : session.createQuery("from " +
    Dvd.class.getName()).list()) session.delete(element);
        tx.commit();
      }
      finally {
        session.close();
      }
    }

    private void buildIndex(FullTextSession session,
                    Transaction tx) {
      for (int x = 0; x < descs.length; x++) {
        Dvd dvd = new Dvd();
        dvd.setDescription(descs[x]);
        dvd.setId(x);
        session.save(dvd);
      }
      tx.commit();
      session.clear();
    }
  }
```

④ **Check the first description**

⑤ **Generated query syntax**

```
description:"star trek"

Star Trek The Next Generation
the fifth season of star trek
to Star Trek fans everywhere the stellar second season
```

Since the user has entered a string of terms, we must break them up into individual terms ② by utilizing a StringTokenizer. The PhraseQuery is built by adding each of the entered words one at a time ③ as new Terms. Why did we convert the description field to lowercase before we made the assertion at ④? Remember that our index was created utilizing the StandardAnalyzer, which converts all searchable tokens to lowercase before they are indexed. Since the tokens are not passed through an analyzer before being added to the PhraseQuery, we are responsible for not only converting the assertion to lowercase but also converting the original search string at ①.

NOTE   Three query types are not passed through analyzers. These are WildcardQuery, PrefixQuery, and PhraseQuery.

The generated query syntax is shown at ⑤.

Now let's do the same query except we'll add the word *season* to the query and set a slop factor of 0.4f to see what we get back as results. This query is shown in listing 7.9.

Listing 7.9 Querying with a `PhraseQuery` utilizing a slop factor of 4

```
public class TestPhraseQueryWthSlop extends SearchTestCase {
  String[] descs = new String[]{"he hits the road as a traveling salesman"
         , "Star Trek The Next Generation",
      "the fifth season of star trek", "to Star Trek fans everywhere
   the stellar second season",
      "a once-successful salesman"};

  @Test
  public void testSloppyPhraseQuery() throws Exception {
    FullTextSession session = Search.getFullTextSession(openSession());
    Transaction tx = session.beginTransaction();

    try {
      buildIndex(session, tx);
      String userInput = "star trek season";          ◁─┐ ❶ Write query in
      StringTokenizer st =                                     lowercase
        new StringTokenizer(userInput, " ");

      tx = session.beginTransaction();
      PhraseQuery query = new PhraseQuery();
      while (st.hasMoreTokens()) {
        query.add(new Term("description", st.nextToken()));
      }                       ❷ Set slop factor to 4
      query.setSlop(4f);     ◁─┘
      System.out.println(query.toString());

      org.hibernate.search.FullTextQuery hibQuery =
        session.createFullTextQuery(query, Dvd.class);
      List<Dvd> results = hibQuery.list();

      assert results.size() == 2: "incorrect hit count";
      assert results.get(0).getDescription()
        .equals("the fifth season of star trek");   ◁─  Results are now
                                                     ❸ not contiguous
      for (Dvd dvd : results) {
        System.out.println(dvd.getDescription());
      }

      for (Object element : session.createQuery("from " +
   Dvd.class.getName()).list()) session.delete(element);
      tx.commit();
    }
    finally {
      session.close();
    }
  }

  private void buildIndex(FullTextSession session, Transaction tx) {
    for (int x = 0; x < descs.length; x++) {
      Dvd dvd = new Dvd();
      dvd.setDescription(descs[x]);
      dvd.setId(x);
```

```
        session.save(dvd);
    }
    tx.commit();
    session.clear();
  }
}
```

description:"star trek season"~4   ◄─┐   ❹ **Generated**
                                              query syntax

```
the fifth season of star trek
to Star Trek fans everywhere the stellar second season
```

At ❶ we add the third term, *season*, to our query and increase the slop factor to 4 at ❷. Decreasing the slop factor makes things more strict and results in a lower number of results returned until eventually no results are returned at all. We have to break up the assertions ❸ into individual term assertions because there's no guarantee now that the query terms will be contiguous in the results. ❹ shows the generated query syntax.

We examine the next two queries, PrefixQuery and WildcardQuery, together because they're quite similar.

7.3.5   *Searching for more: WildcardQuery, PrefixQuery*

The PrefixQuery and WildcardQuery are very closely related. In fact the sole difference between the two query types is that a WildcardQuery can have the wildcards * and ? anywhere in the query terms, while a PrefixQuery ends with the wildcard character *.

WARNING Several of Lucene's query types, including WildcardQuery and PrefixQuery, can generate an exception that is not intuitive to new users. This is the org.apache.lucene.search.BooleanQuery.TooManyClauses exception. It's caused by many of the query types eventually being converted to BooleanQuerys. By default a BooleanQuery allows 1024 clauses and, if this number is exceeded, as it can easily be with wildcards, the exception is generated. You can increase the default value by calling the static method BooleanQuery.setMaxClauseCount(int maxClauseCount). As a side effect, this will increase memory usage somewhat. RangeQuerys are also susceptible to this problem, but Hibernate Search takes care of it. Look at section 8.2.2 for a discussion and solution to this problem.

Let's look first at an example of a WildcardQuery in listing 7.10 and follow that by examining a PrefixQuery.

> **Listing 7.10   A WildcardQuery searching for the term "st*or?"**

```
public class TestWildcards extends SearchTestCase {
  private static final String FIELD_NAME = "title";
  String[] titles = new String[]{"The Ice Storm",
    "The Nun's Story", "Toy Story",
```

```
            "The Philadelphia Story",
            "Toy Story 2", "Ever After - A Cinderella Story",
            "Dodgeball - A True Underdog Story",
            "The Miracle Maker - The Story of Jesus"};


      @Test
      public void testWildcardQuery() throws Exception {
         FullTextSession session = Search.getFullTextSession(openSession());
         Transaction tx = session.beginTransaction();

         try {
            buildIndex(session, tx);      String userInput = "s*or?";

            tx = ssession.beginTransaction();
            WildcardQuery query =
               new WildcardQuery(new Term("title",
                              userInput));
            System.out.println(query.toString());

            org.hibernate.search.FullTextQuery hibQuery =
               session.createFullTextQuery(query, Dvd.class);
            List<Dvd> results = hibQuery.list();

            assert results.size() == 8: "incorrect hit count";

            for (Dvd dvd : results) {
               assert (dvd.getTitle().indexOf("Story") >= 0
                  || dvd.getTitle().indexOf("Storm") >= 0);
               System.out.println(dvd.getTitle());
            }

            for (Object element : session.createQuery("from " +
         Dvd.class.getName()).list()) session.delete(element);
            tx.commit();
         }
         finally {
            session.close();
         }
      }

      private void buildIndex(FullTextSession session, Transaction tx) {
         for (int x = 0; x < titles.length; x++) {
            Dvd dvd = new Dvd();
            dvd.setTitle(titles[x]);
            dvd.setId(x);
            session.save(dvd);
         }
         tx.commit();
         session.clear();
      }
   }
title:st*or?

The Ice Storm
Toy Story
The Philadelphia Story
Toy Story 2
The Nun's Story
```

1 Instantiating a WildcardQuery

2 Iterate through the results

3 The generated query syntax

4 The list of found titles

```
Ever After - A Cinderella Story
Dodgeball - A True Underdog Story
The Miracle Maker - The Story of Jesus
```

We instantiate a `WildcardQuery` at ❶, and after querying we iterate through the result list. We know that either *Story* or *Storm* will be in the result list, so we can test for those ❷. The generated query syntax is shown at ❸, and the list of found titles is given at ❹.

Next, the `PrefixQuery` is shown in listing 7.11.

Listing 7.11   A `PrefixQuery` searching for the term "sea"

```java
public class TestPrefixQuery extends SearchTestCase {
    String[] titles = new String[]{"Sleepless in Seattle",
        "Moonlighting - Seasons 1 & 2",
        "Song of the Sea",
        "he's not a computer salesman",
        "Friends - The Complete Tenth Season"};

    @Test
    public void testPrefixQuery() throws Exception {
        FullTextSession session = Search.getFullTextSession(openSession());
        Transaction tx = session.beginTransaction();
        buildIndex(session, tx);

        String userInput = "sea";

        tx = session.beginTransaction();
        PrefixQuery query =
            new PrefixQuery(new Term("title", userInput));    ◁─┐  ❶ Instantiate a
        System.out.println(query.toString());                       PrefixQuery

        org.hibernate.search.FullTextQuery hibQuery =
            session.createFullTextQuery(query, Dvd.class);
        List<Dvd> results = hibQuery.list();

        assert results.size() == 4: "incorrect hit count";    ❷ Iterate through
        for (Dvd dvd : results) {                          ◁─┘   the results
            assertTrue(dvd.getTitle().indexOf("Sea") >= 0);
            System.out.println(dvd.getDescription());
        }

        for (Object element : session.createQuery("from " +
    ➥Dvd.class.getName()).list()) session.delete(element);
        tx.commit();
        session.close();
    }

    private void buildIndex(FullTextSession session, Transaction tx) {
        for (int x = 0; x < titles.length; x++) {
            Dvd dvd = new Dvd();
            dvd.setTitle(titles[x]);
            dvd.setId(x);
            session.save(dvd);
        }
        tx.commit();
        session.clear();
    }
```

```
}
title:sea*
Sleepless in Seattle
Moonlighting – Seasons 1 & 2
Song of the Sea
Friends - The Complete Tenth Season
```

③ Examining the query syntax

④ Printing the results

We instantiate a `PrefixQuery` at ❶, and after querying we iterate through the result list. We know that *Sea* will be in every part of the result list, so we can test for it ❷. The generated query syntax is shown at ❸, and the list of found titles is given at ❹.

Did you notice that, unlike the `WildcardQuery`, which contained the wildcard characters where we or the user wanted them, the `PrefixQuery` does not require the * (asterisk) in the query? You can see, though, that it inserted one for us at ❸.

The `FuzzyQuery` is next, and we'll also demonstrate a coding tip to enumerate terms automatically generated by the query.

7.3.6 *When we're not sure: FuzzyQuery*

First we'll look at a typical fuzzy query in listing 7.12, then we'll show you something that you've probably been wondering about since our discussion of fuzzy queries in section 7.1.4. Is it possible to examine the list of terms that the `FuzzyQuery` generates and uses to search the index for matches?

Listing 7.12 FuzzyQuery search for "title" with a minimumSimilarity of 0.4f

```
public class TestFuzzyQuery extends SearchTestCase {
    String[] titles = new String[]{"Titan A.E.",
        "Little Women", "Little Shop of Horrors",
        "The Green Mile", "Somewhere in Time"};

    @Test
    public void testFuzzyQuery() throws Exception {
        FullTextSession session = Search.getFullTextSession(openSession());
        Transaction tx = session.beginTransaction();

        buildIndex(session, tx);      String userInput = "title";

        tx = session.beginTransaction();
        FuzzyQuery query =
            new FuzzyQuery(new Term("title", userInput),          ❶ Instantiate a
          0.4f);                                                      FuzzyQuery
        System.out.println(query.toString());

        org.hibernate.search.FullTextQuery hibQuery =
            session.createFullTextQuery(query, Dvd.class);
        List<Dvd> results = hibQuery.list();

        assert results.size() == 5: "incorrect hit count";
        assert results.get(0).getTitle().equals("Titan A.E.");

        for (Dvd dvd : results) {
            System.out.println(dvd.getTitle());
        }

        for (Object element : session.createQuery("from " +
```

```
➥Dvd.class.getName()).list()) session.delete(element);
    tx.commit();
    session.close();
  }

  private void buildIndex(FullTextSession session, Transaction tx) {
    for (int x = 0; x < titles.length; x++) {
      Dvd dvd = new Dvd();
      dvd.setTitle(titles[x]);
      dvd.setId(x);
      session.save(dvd);
    }
    tx.commit();
    session.clear();
  }
}
title:title~0.4
```

2 **Generating the query syntax**

```
Titan A.E.
Little Women
The Green Mile
Somewhere in Time
Little Shop of Horrors
```

3 **Printing the results**

First, we instantiate a FuzzyQuery **1** with a very loose minimumSimilarity value of 0.4. Remember, the lower the value, the less strict the matching rules are. By default the minimumSimilarity value is set to 0.5. The generated query syntax is shown at **2**, and the list of fuzzy results is given at **3**. We'll revisit this list shortly.

WARNING Be aware that setting the minimumSimilarity to too low a value can result in responses that don't seem to fit what the query intended. For, example reducing it to 0.3f (and having a much larger result set) would cause the number of results to increase dramatically, and some of the results would have very little to do with what we're looking for. You'll have to experiment with this to determine the optimal value for your applications.

So, *is* it possible to examine the actual search term list generated by a FuzzyQuery? Yes, but it will take extra work to do it. We need to utilize the FuzzyTermEnum class to generate an enumeration of terms. From there it's a simple iteration through the list. Listing 7.13 shows our use of the FuzzyTermEnum class.

Listing 7.13   Enumerating a FuzzyQuery term list with FuzzyTermEnum

```
public class TestFuzzyTermEnum extends SearchTestCase {
  String[] titles = new String[]{"Titan A.E.", "Little Women",
                    "Little Shop of Horrors",
                    "The Green Mile",
                    "Somewhere in Time"};

  @Test
  public void testFuzzyQueryEnum() throws Exception {
    FullTextSession session =
```

```
        Search.getFullTextSession(openSession());
      Transaction tx = session.beginTransaction();
      try {
        buildIndex(session, tx);
        String userInput = "title";

        tx = session.beginTransaction();
        FuzzyTermEnum termEnum =                              ❶ Instantiate
          new FuzzyTermEnum(getReader(session),                 MyFuzzyQuery
            new Term("title", userInput), 0.4f);

        System.out.println(termEnum.term().text());       ⟵
                                                              ❷ Retrieve a
        while (termEnum.next()) {                               FuzzyTermEnum
          System.out.println(termEnum.term().text());
        }

        for (Object element : session.createQuery("from " +
    Dvd.class.getName()).list()) session.delete(element);
        tx.commit();
      }                                                    ❸ Get the first Term
      finally {
        if (termEnum != null) {
          termEnum.close();      ⟵
        }                        ❹ Iterate the
        session.close();            remaining Terms
      }
    }

    private void buildIndex(FullTextSession session, Transaction tx) {
      for (int x = 0; x < titles.length; x++) {
        Dvd dvd = new Dvd();
        dvd.setTitle(titles[x]);
        dvd.setId(x);
        session.save(dvd);
      }
      tx.commit();
      session.clear();
    }

    private IndexReader getReader(FullTextSession session) {
      SearchFactory searchFactory = session.getSearchFactory();
      DirectoryProvider provider =
        searchFactory.getDirectoryProviders(Dvd.class)[0];
      ReaderProvider readerProvider = searchFactory.getReaderProvider();
      return readerProvider.openReader(provider);
    }
  }

title:title~0.4

little     ⟵
mile        ❺  Close the
time           enumeration
titan
```

We start by instantiating a `FuzzyTermEnum` ❶ and setting the `minimumSimilarity` to the same value as the query in listing 7.12. Next we get the first term by calling the termEnum.term().text() method ❷. We need to do this or we'll miss the first term. The remaining terms are retrieved by iterating through the enumeration ❸. Finally, we close ❹ the enumeration to release all resources. The list of search terms used by the FuzzyQuery is shown at ❺. Compare this list with the generated search result list at ❸ of listing 7.12. We think now you'll understand why the results of listing 7.12 are the way they are.

NOTE In addition to the FuzzyTermEnum class, Lucene includes two other enumerator classes that you can utilize in a similar manner. These are the RegexTermEnum class, which will list search terms generated by regular expression queries, and the WildcardTermEnum class, which will list search terms generated by WildcardQuerys. In short, any subclass of the MultiTermQuery class has the getEnum(reader) method.

The RangeQuery is an excellent way to query dates. It can also be used to search numeric ranges and even string ranges. In the next section we look at querying numeric ranges because there's an inherent problem that needs to be taken care of.

7.3.7   *Searching in between: RangeQuery*

In our discussion of range queries in section 7.1.5 we discussed the fact that searching numeric values has problems not shared by date or normal text searches. This is because Lucene stores all data as strings. String representations of numeric values of different length appear in a different order than you'd at first expect; 10 comes before 2, for example, because the strings are looked at character by character and not by value.

To help demonstrate this problem the RangeQuery-related listings utilize a simple class, Num, that consists of a string that holds a number and an int Id.

Listing 7.14 exposes the ordering problem.

> **Listing 7.14   Demonstrating the RangeQuery numeric value ordering problem**

```
public class TestBadRangeQuery extends SearchTestCase {
  private static final String FIELD_NAME = "number";
  int[] numbers = new int[]{1, 2, 3, 4, 5, 6, 7, 8, 9, 10};      ⟵   Our int array
                                                                 ❶  of test data
  @Test
  public void testNumericRangeQuery() throws Exception {
    FullTextSession session = Search.getFullTextSession(openSession());
    Transaction tx = session.beginTransaction();

    buildIndex(1000, session, tx);

    try {
      buildIndex();
      Term lower = new Term("number", "1");      ❷  The range
      Term upper = new Term("number", "3");         boundaries 1 TO 3

      tx = session.beginTransaction();
      RangeQuery query = new RangeQuery(lower, upper, true);      ⟵
      System.out.println(query.toString());
                                                      A RangeQuery with
                                                      inclusive terms  ❸
```

```
        org.hibernate.search.FullTextQuery hibQuery =
            session.createFullTextQuery(query, Num.class);
        List<Num> results = hibQuery.list();

        List<String> numbers = new ArrayList<String>();
        for (Num num : results) {
            numbers.add(num.getNumber() + "");
            System.out.println(num.getNumber());
        }

        assert results.size() == 4:                    4  The four results
            "incorrect return count";
        assert numbers.contains("10");

        for (Object element : session.createQuery("from "
      + Num.class.getName()).list()) session.delete(element);
        tx.commit();
      }
      finally {
        session.close();
      }
    }

    private void buildIndex(int indexStart, FullTextSession session,
                    Transaction tx) {
      for (int x = 1; x < numbers.length + 1; x++) {
        Num num = new Num();
        num.setId(x);
        num.setNumber(numbers[x - 1]);
        session.save(num);   ◁           Save as a string to
      }                             5    build index
      tx.commit();
      session.clear();
    }
}

number:[1 TO 3]
1
2                       6  Result contains 10
3
10
```

We declare our integer data first ❶, then specify the upper and lower bounds of our search ❷. When the index is created, we convert the `int` data to strings ❺. Our `RangeQuery` with these bounds (`true` means inclusive) is instantiated ❸. After the search is performed, our assertions show ❹ four results and not the expected three. This is due to 10 being included in the results, as we explained previously. The result contents are printed at ❻.

   How do we fix this problem? It will be necessary to make the strings equal in character length so that when they are compared character by character, 02 is less than 10 and the proper sequence is maintained. This will be necessary when both building the index and querying it. How do we get these strings to the same length? We *pad* them with leading zeros. A custom bridge class that accepts numeric values and returns padded string representations of the numbers is all we need. Listing 7.15 shows the utility class named `PadNumbers`.

Listing 7.15   A custom bridge class used to pad numerics during indexing and querying

```
public class PadNumberBridge
    implements StringBridge {
    private final int PAD = 5;

    public String objectToString(Object value) {
        if (value == null ) return null;
        int num = 0;
        if (value instanceof Integer) {
            num = (Integer) value;
        }
        else {
            throw new IllegalArgumentException( "PadNumberBridge.class " +
➥ "received a non-int type " + value.getClass());
        }
        return pad(num);
    }

    private String pad(int num) {
        String rawInt = Integer.toString(num);
        if (rawInt.length() > PAD)
            throw new IllegalArgumentException(
                " integer too large to pad");                    Pad ints with
        StringBuilder paddedInt = new StringBuilder(PAD);        preceding zeros
        for (int padIndex = rawInt.length();
            padIndex < PAD; padIndex++)
            paddedInt.append("0");
        return paddedInt.append( rawInt ).toString();
    }
}
```

`PadNumberBridge` utilizes a `StringBuilder` and a simple loop to prepend the correct number of zeros to bring all numbers to a uniform length. For example, 213 would become 00213. Any `PAD` number length can be used here; just be certain that you use enough zeros to support your largest numeric value. This example could obviously be improved upon by not hardcoding the `PAD` value and possibly passing in the value as a parameter. This class would then be required to extend `ParameterizedBridge`. Refer to section 4.1.3 if necessary.

Listing 7.16 shows `PadNumbers` at work. It utilizes a `PaddedNum` class that differs from the `Num` class only in its declaration of the custom bridge on the number field.

Listing 7.16   Fixing the problem in listing 7.15 using numeric padding

```
public class TestGoodRangeQuery extends SearchTestCase {

    private static final int INDEX_START = 1000;
    int[] numbers = new int[]{1, 2, 3, 4, 5, 6, 7, 8, 9, 10};

    @Test
    public void testNumericRangeQuery() throws Exception {
```

```
    FullTextSession session = Search.getFullTextSession(openSession());
    Transaction tx = session.beginTransaction();

  try {
    buildIndex(session, tx);

    PadNumberBridge brd = new PadNumberBridge();
    Term lower =
      new Term("number",
        brd.objectToString(1));              ❶ Pad the query terms
    Term upper =
      new Term("number",
        brd.objectToString(3));

    tx = session.beginTransaction();
    RangeQuery query = new RangeQuery(lower, upper, true);
    System.out.println(query.toString());

    org.hibernate.search.FullTextQuery hibQuery =
        session.createFullTextQuery(query, PaddedNum.class);
    List<PaddedNum> results = hibQuery.list();

    List<PaddedNum> numbers = new ArrayList<PaddedNum>();
    for (PaddedNum num : results) {
      numbers.add(num);
      System.out.println(num.getNumber());
    }
    assert results.size() == 3:
      "incorrect return count";            ❷ Result with 10 no
    assert !numbers.contains("10");           longer present

    for (Object element : session.createQuery("from "
      + PaddedNum.class.getName()).list())
      session.delete(element);
    tx.commit();
  }
  finally {
    session.close();
  }
}

private void buildIndex(FullTextSession session, Transaction tx) {
  for (int x = INDEX_START;
      x < numbers.length + INDEX_START;
      x++) {
    PaddedNum num = new PaddedNum();
    num.setId(x);
    num.setNumber(numbers[x - INDEX_START]);
    session.save(num);
  }
  tx.commit();              ❸ Bridge called on
  session.clear();             these numbers
 }
}

number:[00001 TO 00003]
1
2                    ❹ Results
3                      demonstrating
                       padding
```

Since we know that numeric values must be padded both when building the index and when querying, we pad the query data at ❶; when the built objects are committed, the bridge will perform ❸ the padding operation. Our assertions at ❷ show that we now have exactly what we wanted. We have only three result values and 10 is no longer in the results, which are printed at ❹ along with the query string.

> **NOTE** If you find yourself manually building RangeQuerys often, the authors recommend that you take a look at the ConstantScoreRangeQuery class. The reasons for this are explained in the RangeQuery Javadoc. One of these reasons is speed. The authors have found in tests that the ConstantScoreRangeQuery is an order of magnitude faster than the standard RangeQuery. RangeQuerys built by the QueryParser are automatically constructed as ConstantScoreRangeQuerys.

Our last query type is the BooleanQuery. The examples given will demonstrate to you how to utilize it to pull everything together.

7.3.8   *A little of everything: BooleanQuery*

Querying on various combinations of more than one term or more than one type of query is the domain of the BooleanQuery. This allows you the freedom to combine the terms with the AND, OR, and NOT operators we discussed earlier. This does not mean that you're limited to utilizing multiple single-term queries as search parameters. You can use *any* of the other types of queries supported by Lucene as inputs for Boolean queries. For example, we could have a combination of a PhraseQuery ANDed with a FuzzyQuery and the result of this combination NOTed with a TermQuery. It is even possible to have nested BooleanQuerys. That is, any of these types of queries could actually be another BooleanQuery consisting of other query types. Any combination is possible.

> **NOTE** Earlier in this chapter we discussed the QueryParser and the queries it can generate. Remember that these generated queries can also be part of a complicated BooleanQuery. As we said, the sky is the limit with BooleanQuerys (along with the TooManyClausesException).

To demonstrate how to manipulate the BooleanQuery, we will simplify things and stick to the use of TermQuerys in our example in listing 7.18. Please note that it's a simple matter of replacing any TermQuery with the query type of your choice and making any necessary changes for that type of query.

Let's assume that your application provides three entry points for user query terms. The first entry point is for the major query term. The second entry point is for an optional term to look for, and the third entry point is an optional term that must be excluded from the results. From this description you can see that we have one required term and two possible optional terms, one of which can exclude results. Listing 7.17 shows that BooleanQuerys are not always exactly as you think they should be; execution order is paramount.

```java
public class TestBooleanQuery extends SearchTestCase {
  private FullTextSession s;
  private Transaction tx;

  private static final String FIELD_NAME = "title";
  String[] titles = new String[]{"The Nun's Story",
    "Toy Story", "The Philadelphia Story",
    "Toy Story 2", "Ever After - A Cinderella Story",
    "Dodgeball - A True Underdog Story",
    "The Miracle Maker - The Story of Jesus",
    "The Office - Season One",
    "Gargoyles - Season Two, Vol. 1"};

  public void testBooleanQuery1() throws Exception {
    FullTextSession session = Search.getFullTextSession(openSession());
    Transaction tx = session.beginTransaction();
    try {
      buildIndex();

      String required = "season";
      String optional = "story";
      String omitted = "complete";

      Term requiredTerm = new Term("title", required);
      Term optionalTerm = new Term("title", optional);
      Term omittedTerm = new Term("title", omitted);

      tx = session.beginTransaction();

      BooleanClause requiredClause =
      new BooleanClause(new TermQuery(requiredTerm),           ❶ Create a
                BooleanClause.Occur.MUST);                        BooleanClause

      BooleanQuery query = new BooleanQuery();                ❷ Add the clause
      query.add(requiredClause);                                to the query
      query.add(new TermQuery(optionalTerm),
            BooleanClause.Occur.SHOULD);
      query.add(new TermQuery(omittedTerm),                  ❸ Add the
            BooleanClause.Occur.MUST_NOT);                      TermQuerys
      System.out.println(query.toString());

      org.hibernate.search.FullTextQuery hibQuery =
        session.createFullTextQuery(query, Dvd.class);
      List<Dvd> results = hibQuery.list();

      assert results.size() == 2: "incorrect hit count";
      assert results.get(0).getTitle()
        .equals("The Office - Season One");
      for (Dvd dvd : results) {
        System.out.println(dvd.getTitle());
      }

      for (Object element : session.createQuery("from " +
   Dvd.class.getName()).list()) session.delete(element);
    }
    finally {
    tx.commit();
```

```
            session.close();
        }
    }

    private void buildIndex(FullTextSession session, Transaction tx) {
        for (int x = 0; x < titles.length; x++) {
            Dvd dvd = new Dvd();
            dvd.setTitle(titles[x]);
            dvd.setId(x);
            session.save(dvd);
        }
        tx.commit();
        session.clear();
    }
}
+title:season title:story -title:complete
```

❹ **Generated query syntax**

```
The Office - Season One
Gargoyles - Season Two, Vol. 1
```

A `BooleanQuery` can be created in different ways, and this example demonstrates a couple of them. At ❶ we create a `BooleanClause` and add it to the query ❷. Next we create two `TermQuerys` and add them ❸. From this you can see how any query type could easily be added.

Hopefully, you immediately noticed the `Boolean.Occur` terms in the `Boolean-Clause` and the `query.add()` statements. The possible selections for this enumeration are shown in table 7.3.

Table 7.3   The three `Boolean.Occur` options and their meanings

Occur operators	Meaning
`Boolean.Occur.MUST`	Clauses or queries with this operator must appear in the matching documents.
`Boolean.Occur.MUST_NOT`	Clauses or queries with this operator must not appear in the matching documents. **NOTE**: If a `BooleanQuery` contains a `MUST_NOT` clause at least one `MUST` or `SHOULD` clause is also required. It's not possible to search for queries that consist of only a `MUST_NOT` clause. However, it is possible to simulate the effect of this by creating a `BooleanQuery` consisting of your `MUST_NOT` clause and another clause consisting of a `MatchAllDocsQuery`. This results in all documents being returned *except* those you excluded with your `MUST_NOT` clause. Obviously, you can easily generate variations of this.
`Boolean.Occur.SHOULD`	Clauses or queries with this operator should appear in the matching documents. **NOTE**: If a `BooleanQuery` has no `MUST` clauses, one or more `SHOULD` clauses that must match a document for the `BooleanQuery` to generate results are also required.

Let's take a closer look at the generated query syntax ❹ and compare it with the results of the query. These results may not have been exactly what some of you were expecting. A strict interpretation of the syntax would be "the results must have *season* or *story* and not *complete*." If that's the case, where are the results with *story*? None of them appeared. The key to this is the `Boolean.Occur.MUST` operator applied to *season*. The way this query was written, the MUST effectively *overrides* the SHOULD. If a document does not have the *season* term, which is required, then no result will be generated for it, canceling the effect of the SHOULD.

What you may have been expecting was a disjunction query (OR) of *season* and *story*. To accomplish this, change the `Boolean.Occur.MUST` to SHOULD when you create the `BooleanClause` at ❶. The syntax and results would then be:

```
title:season title:story -title:complete

The Office - Season One
Gargoyles - Season Two, Vol. 1
Toy Story
The Philadelphia Story
Toy Story 2
The Nun's Story
Ever After - A Cinderella Story
Dodgeball - A True Underdog Story
The Miracle Maker - The Story of Jesus
```

Now, *story* is included in the results. Perhaps this is what you were originally expecting. The point here is, *be careful* how you construct your query. Check it, and make sure it's really what you wanted.

One last topic before we close this chapter is the programmatic use of boost to adjust document scoring.

7.3.9 Using the boost APIs

We discussed utilizing a boost factor in section 7.1.6. Boost can also be managed programmatically in several places of the API. Listing 7.18 illustrates how Hibernate Search defines an @Boost annotation.

Listing 7.18 The definition of Hibernate Search's @Boost annotation

```
@Retention( RetentionPolicy.RUNTIME )
@Target( {ElementType.TYPE,          ❶ Define on field, getter
        ElementType.METHOD,            method, or class
        ElementType.FIELD} )
@Documented
public @interface Boost {            ❷ Define as a
  float value();                       float value
}
```

❶ defines a boost value as able to be attached to any of a FIELD, METHOD, or TYPE class, and it is defined as a float value ❷.

An example of a properly annotated Hibernate Search entity with a boost factor set on the entity itself and one of the getter methods is shown here:

```
@Entity
@Indexed
@Boost (1.5f)
@Analyzer(impl = Test1Analyzer.class)
public class MyEntity {
  @Id
  @GeneratedValue
  @DocumentId
  private Integer id;

  @Boost(1.2f)
  private String entity;

  @Field(index = Index.TOKENIZED store = Store.YES, boost = 2.0f)
  public String getEntity() {
...
```

The order of precedence for these boost factors is the field/method boost followed by the entity boost. The resulting boost for the getEntity method in the example above would be the product of the @Boost value from the field and the @Field value, or 2.4f.

In addition to utilizing the @Boost annotation on different parts of an entity, Hibernate Search has a boost factor available in the @ClassBridge annotation, which is designated as follows:

```
@Entity
@Indexed
@ClassBridge(name="branchnetwork",
         index=Index.TOKENIZED,
         store=Store.YES,
         boost=@Boost(2.0f),
         impl = CatFieldsClassBridge.class,
         params = @Parameter( name="sepChar", value=" " ) )
public class Department {
  private int id;
  private String network;
  private String branchHead;
  private String branch;
...
```

Lucene provides several ways to apply boost factors to various elements from fieldable objects to documents to various query types. Here's a list of the ways to set a boost factor:

- `Fieldable.setBoost(float boost)`   The `Fieldable` interface is implemented by two classes, `org.apache.lucene.document.AbstractField` and `org.apache.lucene.document.Field`, so this is the method to use to set a boost factor on a field object.
- `Document.setBoost(float boost)`   This method sets a boost factor for query matches on any field of a particular document.

- `Query.setboost(float b)` This method sets a boost factor for a particular query clause to b. For a single-clause query this doesn't do you any good, but for queries with multiple clauses this will cause an increase in the score of documents that match the boosted clause.
- `MultiFieldQueryParser(String[] fields, Analyzer analyzer, Map boosts)` This constructor allows passing a map with keys of field names and values of boost factors. Each named field will have the corresponding boost applied to it.
- `MoreLikeThis.setboost(Boolean b)` A little different than what we worked with so far, this method accepts a Boolean that turns boosting on and off. The default value is false. Once turned on, boosting is based on the ratio of the score of a particular document and the top score of the total query results.

The BoostingQuery

One additional query that you should be aware of is the `BoostingQuery`. This `Query` class originally started out in the Lucene *sandbox*, which is discussed along with the `BoostingQuery` class in section 13.1.2. This is why we decided to discuss it there. It's an easy way to change the scoring of matching documents and can be made to work in ways you're probably not expecting.

7.4 Summary

The `QueryParser` class gives us a lot to work with when we want the user to be able to enter free-form text as a query. The syntax it generates to perform searches is not difficult to learn and is invaluable when it comes to finding out why query results are not exactly as we expected them to be. An example of this problem is having a – (dash) in a name. This dash can be interpreted as a Boolean NOT and change the results unexpectedly. Luke can come to our rescue by showing us exactly how our query was interpreted.

For more sophisticated search engines where the complexity is hidden from the user, as in the consumer websites (Amazon, eBay, and Google), you need to fine-tune your queries and hide the query syntax complexity from the user. Lucene provides a programmatic API and a plethora of `Query` classes for us, including the `TermQuery`, `RangeQuery`, `FuzzyQuery`, `WildcardQuery`, and `BooleanQuery`. The latter is usually the type of query we end up with when queries are rewritten by the system for simplification. We can use many combinations of these query types programmatically to create custom queries that achieve things the `QueryParser` cannot do by itself.

These queries can also accomplish other things for us. For example, utilizing the `FuzzyQuery` can help eliminate misspelling problems.

We now know that `MultiTermQuerys` (wildcard and prefix) are not magic, and it's possible to examine the list of terms that they generate by using the various `TermEnum` classes that are provided. These terms are combined eventually into a `BooleanQuery`.

The order of precedence of specified analyzers from highest to lowest is as follows:

1 `@Field` analyzer
2 `@Entity` analyzer
3 The analyzer specified in the configuration via `cfg.setProperty( Environment.ANALYZER_CLASS, `*`Specific Analyzer`*`.class.getName());`.

    This is known as the global analyzer. It can also be set via the hibernate.properties or hibernate.cfg.xml files, whichever you use.

The information in this chapter demonstrates that we have many ways to manipulate queries to provide us the data we're looking for. We're limited only by our ingenuity in how we ask the user for the pertinent query and how we employ what the user gives us. If you wish to delve deeper into this subject, we recommend Manning Publishing's *Lucene in Action* and digging into the Javadoc and source code of the `Query` subclasses.

Filters: cross-cutting restrictions

This chapter covers

- Configuring and using dynamic filters
- Caching filters
- Various filter examples

Full-text queries are great for answering a question formulated by a user. However, in some situations, you'll need to add restrictions that don't belong to the core of the user question. These are cross-cutting restrictions: restrict by security, restrict by category, restrict by availability, and so on. This is what a filter is for.

What is a filter? A *filter* restricts results of a query after the Lucene query has been executed, usually based on rules that aren't directly related to the query. Filters can be adjusted independently of the original query and don't affect the relative score of a document against another; the ordering defined by the original query is respected. Filters can be applied on top of each other. In Lucene, a filter is very much like a bit mask, which removes part of the results from a query; each

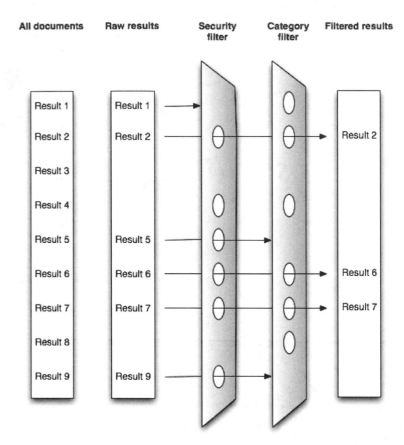

Figure 8.1   Filters selectively remove elements from a result set without affecting the order.

Lucene document is represented by a bit, which can be on or off. Figure 8.1 shows how filters selectively remove elements from the result set.

Filters offer the ability to apply cross-cutting restrictions on matching elements returned by queries. Numerous use cases can benefit from cross-cutting restrictions. A search engine might hide results a given user doesn't have access to (security filter); the results might be restricted to a certain period of time (temporal filter); the results might need to be restricted to a certain category or type of data (category filter). Think about your last application, and you'll likely find one or two use cases for filters.

Let's explore how filters are implemented in Lucene and what benefits Hibernate Search brings to the table.

8.1   Defining and using a filter

Nothing prevents you from changing your query to apply additional restrictions and simulate the behavior of filters. You can, for example, use a Lucene `BooleanQuery` that wraps the original user query and the restriction query. This approach, while quite easy, has a few problems:

- The restriction query is executed over and over. There's no way to cache the result of this restriction independently of the user query.
- Each process that applies the restriction is aware of its details, or, at least, the approach is fairly procedural. A new person on your team might forget to apply the restriction on a new piece of code or apply it incorrectly.
- The code that executes the query must manually chain various restrictions.
- Constraints are limited to the data indexed in the filtered `Documents`.

A Hibernate Search filter provides an elegant answer to these drawbacks by using a declarative approach. After explaining how to write and use a Lucene filter, we'll show how to declare one in Hibernate Search, what it brings us, and how to activate it.

8.1.1 *Lucene filter*

Filters in Lucene are implemented as a subclass of `org.hibernate.lucene.search.Filter`, whose main method takes an `IndexReader` and returns a `DocIdSet` (see listing 8.1). A `DocIdSet` is a structure that returns the ordered list of matching document ids via an iterator. The most common `DocIdSet` implementation (`DocIdBitSet`) uses a structure named `BitSet` to store the list of matching results. `BitSet` is a compact structure that returns `true` or `false` for a given Lucene `Document` id; `false` means the element is filtered out. A `BitSet` uses one bit per `Document`. If your index contains ten million `Documents`, the `BitSet` structure will require 1.2 MB of memory. The `DocIdSet` is computed and returned for an `IndexReader` instance.

NOTE Lucene comes bundled with a faster implementation of the `BitSet` class but which exposes more of its internal state. If you're looking for performance, consider using `OpenBitSet` instead of `BitSet`.

Likewise, if your filter returns a very small subset of matching (or nonmatching elements), or if your filter can determine the list of matching documents based on a very compact structure, consider writing your own `DocIdSet`. Your own implementation of `DocIdSet` can save memory.

An `IndexReader` instance represents the state of the index at the instant the `IndexReader` is opened by Hibernate Search. For a given `IndexReader` instance, the list of `Documents` is fixed, and a `Document` cannot change its id number. The same `DocIdSet` can be returned for the same `IndexReader` instance provided that the filter conditions don't change. But a different `IndexReader` instance works potentially on a different set of `Documents` (either from a different index or simply because the index has changed and a new `IndexReader` has been opened). The `DocIdSet` then has to be rebuilt. Listing 8.1 shows the `Filter` superclass. Every filter subclasses it and implements the necessary logic.

Listing 8.1   The `Filter` superclass

```
public abstract class Filter implements java.io.Serializable {

    /**
     * @return a DocIdSet that provides the documents which should be
     * permitted or prohibited in search results.
     * @see DocIdBitSet
     */
    public DocIdSet getDocIdSet(IndexReader reader) throws IOException;
}
```

Lucene Filter ❶
contract

Return the `DocIdSet` filter ❶ for a given `IndexReader` instance.

NOTE   `Filter` used to return `BitSet` objects instead of `DocIdSet` objects. While you can still write your filters using the old method, the authors recommend against it. Your implementation will not be supported in Lucene 3.0.

Lucene comes with built-in `Filter` implementations, but you can implement your own strategy quite easily. We'll walk through a few practical examples in the next section, but now let's have a look at some of the built-in `Filter` implementations to become more familiar with the concept:

- `QueryWrapperFilter`—A Lucene query result defines the `DocIdSet` applied on subsequent filtered queries.
- `RangeFilter`—The `DocIdSet` contains the id for all documents where a given field is within the range; the field must not be tokenized.
- `CachingWrapperFilter`—Wraps a `Filter` implementation and caches the `DocIdSet` per `IndexReader` instance in a `WeakHashMap`. Don't use this implementation with Hibernate Search. Use a hard–reference-based or at least a soft–reference-based cache mechanism instead. Even better, use the Hibernate Search built-in cache mechanism.

If you intend to filter based on some data stored in the index, `QueryWrapperFilter` is one of your best and most flexible choices. Filtering is built on a Lucene query; building a query is now a familiar operation for us. One of the use cases is to apply a query to the result set of a previous query, allowing a user to refine the search. `RangeFilter` is an alternative approach to `RangeQuery`, as we discussed in chapter 7. It restricts results to documents that match a given range. `RangeFilter` doesn't suffer from the `TooManyClauses` exception syndrome, because range is applied after the Lucene query execution.

Filters really shine from a performance point of view when they can be cached and reused, that is, when the filter `DocIdSet` is built once (or occasionally) and reused by many queries. As you've seen previously, a cached `DocIdSet` is valid for only a given `IndexReader` instance. Practically, it means that you cannot cache a filter efficiently if too many updates occur on your index data.

In a plain Lucene environment, the application developer needs to handle instances of filters and apply them to the queries manually. This imperative approach can be quite cumbersome, especially when the code tries to benefit from filter caching.

8.1.2 Declaring a filter in Hibernate Search

Hibernate Search goes a step further and handles filters as resources. Just as you don't need to manually open index readers when using Hibernate Search, filter instances are managed transparently and declaratively for you.

Let's assume your `Filter` implementation is ready to be used. Hibernate Search lets you associate a name with it. Later we'll show how to enable filters declaratively on queries using their names, but for now look at listing 8.2, which describes how to define a filter in Hibernate Search. A filter definition annotation (`@FullTextFilter-Def`) is placed on any of the indexed entities but is not specific to the entity it's placed on. Each definition has a name that must be unique in the deployment unit.

Listing 8.2   Declare a filter using the `@FullTextFilterDef` annotation

```
@Entity @Indexed @Table(name="PRODUCTS")
@FullTextFilterDef(
    name="distributor",            ◁───────  Filters have a
                                             name (reference)
    impl=DistributorFilter.class)  ◁───  Filter
public class Item {                      implementation
    ...

}
```

You can define more than one filter per class by using `@FullTextFilterDefs`; this annotation accepts an array of `@FullTextFilterDef`.

`DistributorFilter` in listing 8.2 must have a no-arg constructor. This constraint can be cumbersome in some situations; for example, you might want to reuse a `Filter` implementation that doesn't provide a no-arg constructor (like `QueryWrapper-Filter`). Hibernate Search lets you provide a `Filter` factory implementation instead of a `Filter` implementation. Simply set `FullTextFilterDef.impl()` to the filter factory class. A filter factory class is a class where one of the methods is annotated with `@Factory`. Listing 8.3 is an example of such an approach; a `DistributorFilterFactory` provides a properly initialized `QueryWrapperFilter`.

Listing 8.3   Use a `Filter` factory to build filters needed for initialization

```
public class WarnerDistributorFilterFactory {  ◁───  Has a no-arg constructor

    @Factory                                   ◁──────❶ Factory method
    public Filter buildDistributorFilter() {
        Term term = new Term( "distributor.name", "Warner" );
        Query query = new TermQuery( term );

        Filter filter = new QueryWrapperFilter( query );  ◁───┐
                                                   Build the  │
        return filter;                       QueryWrapperFilter ❷
    }
```

```
    }
@Entity @Indexed @Table(name="PRODUCTS")
@FullTextFilterDef(
    name="category",
    impl=WarnerDistributorFilterFactory.class)        ◀┐      Define a Filter
public class Item {                                   ❸      factory
    ...
    }
```

❶ The factory method must return `Filter` instances and be annotated with `@Fac-`
`tory`. ❷ A `QueryWrapperFilter` is initialized with the distributor-filtering query. ❸
The filter definition takes a filter factory as an implementation.

The method providing the filter instance must be marked as `@Factory`.

Filters show their real power when they are cached. Hibernate Search offers you
two layers of caching:

1 Caching of the `Filter` instances themselves
2 Caching the `DocIdSet` result from the filter execution (for a given
   `IndexReader`)

Let's have a deeper look.

CACHING FILTERS
Caching the actual filter instances allows a given filter to be used across many (concurrent) `filter.getDocIdSet()` calls. This is especially useful if the creation of the filter
is costly or if it does a costly evaluation.

On top of filter-instance caching, `DocIdSet` results can be cached by Hibernate
Search. There are some conditions for returning the same `DocIdSet` instance:

- The same filter instance is targeted.
- The same parameters are used to initialize the query and the filter instance.
- The same `IndexReader` (think of a view in Lucene directories) is used.

This `DocIdSet` caching is known in the Lucene world as filter caching, and in Hibernate Search it's essentially implemented by wrapping the filter instance around a customized version of Lucene's `CachingWrapperFilter`. The benefit of caching the
`DocIdSet` is, of course, that expensive recomputations can be avoided. Caching results
and caching `DocIdSet` are synonymous.

TIP   Make sure your `Filter` implementation is thread-safe when you enable
        caching.

In most cases, enabling both levels of filter caching is the right choice, and for that
reason it's the default in Hibernate Search (`FilterCacheModeType.INSTANCE_AND_`
`DOCIDSETRESULTS`). Note that to cache results, you must also cache the instance.

In some situations, however, it might be useful to cache only the `Filter` instance.
For example, a filter could use its own specific caching mechanism, or the filter results
could change dynamically because of application-specific events, making `DocIdSet`
caching unnecessary or even harmful. You can keep filter instance caching enabled

while disabling result caching with the following declaration: `@FullTextFilter-Def(cache=FilterCacheModeType.INSTANCE_ONLY)`.

Finally, on rapidly changing data sets or a heavily memory-constrained environment, it might not be necessary to cache filters at all. Likewise, if the filter factory dynamically chooses one filter implementation over another at runtime, caching `Filter` instances is not an option. Instead, use the following declaration: `@FullTextFilterDef(cache=FilterCacheModeType.NONE)`.

> **NOTE** For Hibernate 3.0 users, Hibernate Search did not have the second level of caching, and so results were not kept around. If you wish to cache results, make sure you manually cache filter `BitSets`. To enable instance caching in Hibernate Search 3.0, use `@FullTextFilterDef (cache=true)`.

By default, Hibernate Search caches the last 128 instances of filters used (using a most-recently-used algorithm). Additional filter instances are added to a soft reference cache. If you need to reclaim memory, the virtual machine can release those additional instances. You can adjust the number of instances that will not be reclaimed by using the following property in your configuration file: `hibernate.search.filter.cache_strategy.size`.

For each filter instance, and if you've kept result caching enabled, Hibernate Search caches the last five results used (using a most–recently-used algorithm). Additional `DocIdSet` results are added to a soft reference cache. The garbage collector can reclaim these results to save memory. You can adjust the number of results not reclaimed by using `hibernate.search.filter.cache_bit_docidresults.size`.

If the idea of a hard-reference-capped cache overflowing to a soft-reference-based cache is not your cup of tea, you can provide you own caching strategy by implementing the `FilterCachingStrategy` interface and declaring it in your configuration file, as shown here:

```
hibernate.search.filter.cache_strategy =
     com.manning.hsia.dvdstore.util.NeverReleasedFilterCachingStrategy
```

Hibernate brings additional flexibility compared to a plain Lucene filter.

INJECTING PARAMETERS

If you pay close attention to listing 8.3, you'll realize that this approach is not very flexible when the application needs to deal with more than a handful of distributors. Writing one class per specific distributor is not very appealing and simply does not work if the list of distributors is not known at development time.

Hibernate Search can inject parameters into a filter when the filter is enabled on a query, as we'll show in the next section. Each parameter has a name and a value. For each parameter provided, the `Filter` implementation (or the `Filter` factory implementation if you use the factory strategy) must have a corresponding setter in order for Hibernate Search to inject it.

Using parameters in filters has consequences on filter caching. A filter that receives two different sets of parameters should return a different `DocIdSet` instance. Let's say the parameter represents the security level the user is allowed to access, and different security levels should restrict different sets of documents and return different `DocIdSets`. When your filter receives parameters and you use caching (the default in `@FullTextFilterDef`), you need to give Hibernate Search a way to recognize whether two filters can be considered equal if two filters share the same class and have been initialized with the same set of parameters.

Each instance of `Filter` is cached by `FilterKey` in the Hibernate Search `Filter` cache. By default, Hibernate Search caches filters by class. The `FilterKey` implementation ensures that the `equals()` and `hashCode()` methods consider equal two `Filter` instances of the same class. You should provide your own implementation of `Filter-Key` that will ensure that two `Filter` instances are cached under the same key when they're from the same type and if their significant parameters are equal.

While you can subclass the `FilterKey` class yourself, Hibernate Search provides a default implementation that compares parameters using `equals()/hashCode()` for each parameter value. The default implementation provided by `StandardFilterKey` is used in listing 8.4 to ensure that distributor filters are cached per category. This implementation should be good enough for most use cases. The method generating the `FilterKey` is annotated with `@Key`. The key implementation ensures that each filter is cached by its category parameter.

Listing 8.4   Using parameters in filters

```
public class DistributorFilterFactory {

    private String distributor;

    public void setDistributor(String distributor) {     ①  Parameters are
        distributor = distributor;                              injected in setters
    }

    @Factory
    public Filter buildDistributorFilter() {              ②  Use injected
        Term term = new Term( "distributor.name",               parameters
                    distributor );
        Query query = new TermQuery( term );
        Filter filter = new QueryWrapperFilter( query );
        return filter;
    }                           ③  Method generating
                                    the FilterKey
    @Key
    public FilterKey getKey() {
        StandardFilterKey key = new StandardFilterKey();
        key.addParameter( distributor );                 Default
        return key;                                       implementation  ④
    }
}
```

Each possible parameter has a corresponding setter ❶. The Filter implementation uses parameters to configure itself ❷. If the filter is cached and uses parameters, a method returning a FilterKey must be annotated as @Key ❸. StandardFilterKey receives the significant parameters and ensures that the same Filter instance won't be shared between calls involving different parameter values ❹.

TIP If you set @FullTextFilterDef.cache to FilterCacheModeType.NONE, or if the filter doesn't have any parameters, you don't need to provide an @Key method.

You now know how to implement a Filter, either a simple one or one using parameters, declare it to Hibernate Search, and benefit from the cache. But you don't know yet how to use filters or how to set the parameters. Let's explore this process.

8.1.3 Applying filters to a query

You can choose to enable or disable filters per query declaratively, thanks to Hibernate Search. Each filter is enabled by name. A query can enable more than one filter; the result must pass all filters to be returned by the query. In practice, filters are chained and applied one after the other; a DocSetId that takes into account all DocSetIds in the chain is used to filter the query results. Listing 8.5 enables two filters on a query.

Listing 8.5 Activation of two filters on a Hibernate Search query

```
public List<Item> searchItemWithinDistributor(String search, Distributor
distributor) {
    FullTextSession ftSession = SessionHolder.getFullTextSession();
    org.apache.lucene.search.Query luceneQuery =
        buildLuceneQuery( search );

    FullTextQuery query = ftSession.createFullTextQuery(
        luceneQuery, Item.class );

    query.enableFullTextFilter( "security" );               ← A filter is activated by name
    query.enableFullTextFilter( "WarnerDistributor" );      ← Several filters can be activated

    List results = query.list();
    return results;
}

@Entity
@Indexed                                    Declare filters on any
@Table(name="PRODUCTS")                      of the indexed entities
@FullTextFilterDefs( {                  ←
    @FullTextFilterDef(name="WarnerDistributor",
                impl=WarnerDistributorFilterFactory.class),
    @FullTextFilterDef(name="distributor",
                impl=DistributorFilterFactory.class),
    @FullTextFilterDef(name="security",
                impl=SecurityFilter.class)
} )
```

```
public class Item {
    ...
}
```

Filters can be activated or deactivated using `fullTextQuery.enableFullTextFilter(String name)` or `fullTextQuery.disableFullTextFilter(String name)`. Both methods are available for the Hibernate Core and Java Persistence extensions of `FullTextQuery`.

Remember, for each parameter that a filter needs, you must have a corresponding setter in the `Filter` class or the `Filter` factory class. When the `Filter` instance (or its factory) is built, parameters are injected into their respective setters and are available to the `getDocIdSet()` method as well as to the `@Factory` and `@Key` methods when they are present. Listing 8.6 shows how to apply category filtering on a Hibernate Search query.

Listing 8.6 Parameters are passed to the `Filter` instance or its factory.

```
public List<Item> searchItemWithinDistributor(String search,
    Distributor distributor) {
    FullTextSession ftSession = SessionHolder.getFullTextSession();
    org.apache.lucene.search.Query luceneQuery =
        buildLuceneQuery( search );

    FullTextQuery query = ftSession.createFullTextQuery(
        luceneQuery, Item.class );

    query.enableFullTextFilter( "security" );
    query.enableFullTextFilter( "distributor" )
            .setParameter( "distributor",              ❶ Pass parameters
                    distributor.getName() );

    @SuppressWarnings("unchecked")
    List results = query.list();
    return results;
}

public class DistributorFilterFactory {

    private String distributor;
                                                       ❷ Parameters
    public void setDistributor(String distributor) {      are injected
        this.distributor = distributor;
    }

    @Factory
    public Filter buildDistributorFilter() {
        Term term = new Term( "distributor.name",     ❸ Parameters are
                    distributor );                       available
        Query query = new TermQuery( term );
        Filter filter = new QueryWrapperFilter( query );
        filter = new CachingWrapperFilter( filter );
        return filter;
    }

    @Key
    public FilterKey getKey() {
```

```
        StandardFilterKey key = new StandardFilterKey();
        key.addParameter( distributor );
    return key;
    }
```

Parameters are
4 available

```
}
```

1 One or several parameters can bet set for a given filter. **2** Parameters are injected into the `Filter` instance or its factory. **3** Parameters are available to the `@Factory` method. **4** Parameters are available when `@Key` is built.

Alternatively, you can apply a filter on a query without having to declare it in Hibernate Search. The `FullTextQuery` API can receive `Filter` instances in `setFilter()`. The filter is added and executed after the list of enabled named filters.

TIP   While it can be convenient to use this manual approach in some situations, the authors recommend using the named filter approach because it makes the code more readable and modular and allows filter caching.

You now know all the theory behind filters. This feature is relatively simple, but it is very flexible and useful in a plethora of situations. The next section is a collection of examples showing filters used in various situations. Enough theory—let's practice!

8.2   *Examples of filter usage and their implementation*

This section is by no means a complete list of use cases for filters, but it will give you some advice and inspiration. Before we begin, look back at listing 8.6, which is a good example of category filtering. The `DistributorFilter` builds a query wrapper filter based on the content indexed in Lucene and on parameters provided at query time to the filter.

8.2.1   *Applying security*

Our DVD store website contains a children's selection. Contrary to many websites out there, our website gives power to children, not parents. The children category is reserved for customers who log in and certify they are younger than 13. We want to expand this restriction to our search engine, so that adults cannot find books reserved for our young customers. Filtering is a perfect solution for such a use case. Contrary to the distributor example (listing 8.6), our system does not naturally index an age category. We'll show how to combine a class-level field bridge with a filter to implement this solution.

The list of categories for a given item is available through `item.getCategories()`. We'll first write a class-level field bridge that will store in the index the fact that an item is part of the children category. This approach is very useful for writing queries or filters based on information you wouldn't have put in your indexes. By using a synthetic flag, you minimize pollution in your index. Listing 8.7 shows a possible implementation.

Listing 8.7   Use a class-level bridge to add a category flag

```
/**
 * Add "yes" to the dedicated field if item is
 * contained in the children category
 */
public class ChildrenFlagBridge implements StringBridge {
    public String objectToString(Object object) {
        Item item = (Item) object;

        boolean hasChildrenCategory = false;
        for ( Category category : item.getCategories() ) {        ◀─┐  Retrieve
            if ( "Children".equalsIgnoreCase(                        │  unindexed
        ➥category.getName() ) ) {                                 ❶ data
                hasChildrenCategory = true;
                break;
            }
        }

        return hasChildrenCategory ? "yes" : "no";   ◀──❷ Index useful flag
    }
}

@Entity
@Indexed
@Table(name="PRODUCTS")                         ❸ Declare class-level bridge
@ClassBridge(name="childrenOnly",    ◀─
            impl=ChildrenFlagBridge.class,
            index=Index.UN_TOKENIZED)
public class Item {

    @ManyToMany
    @JoinTable(name="PRODUCT_CATEGORY",
            joinColumns=@JoinColumn(name="PROD_ID"),
            inverseJoinColumns=
    ➥@JoinColumn(name="CATEGORY"))           ❹ Property not indexed
    private Set<Category> categories;   ◀─
    ...
}
```

We access unindexed data ❶, build a synthesized flag to represent the state we're interested in, and index the flag value ❷. The bridge is declared at the class level ❸ and applied to the childrenOnly field. The data that leads to the flag is not indexed directly ❹.

The next step is to write a query-based filter using the flag information, declare the filter definition, and activate it on queries for older members, as shown in listing 8.8.

Listing 8.8   The filter uses the flag to select results

```
/**
 * exclude all items reserved for children
 */
public class NotAChildFilterFactory {

    @Factory                                              ❶ Use flag info
    public Filter getChildrenFilter() {
        Term term = new Term( "childrenOnly", "no" );   ◀─
```

```
                Query query = new TermQuery( term );

            Filter filter = new QueryWrapperFilter( query );

            return filter;
            }
    }

    @Entity
    @Indexed
    @Table(name="PRODUCTS")                           ❷ Define filter
    @FullTextFilterDef(name="notachild",       ←┐
                impl=NotAChildFilterFactory.class)
    @ClassBridge(name="childrenOnly",
            impl=ChildrenFlagBridge.class,
            index=Index.UN_TOKENIZED)
    public class Item {
        ...
    }

    //service implementation
    public List<Item> searchItems(String search, boolean isChild) {
        FullTextSession ftSession = SessionHolder.getFullTextSession();
        org.apache.lucene.search.Query luceneQuery =
            buildLuceneQuery( search );

        FullTextQuery query = ftSession.createFullTextQuery(
            luceneQuery, Item.class );
                                                  ❸ Activate filter
        if ( ! isChild ) {
            query.enableFullTextFilter( "notachild" );   ←┐
        }

        @SuppressWarnings("unchecked")
        List<Item> results = query.list();
        return results;
    }
```

❶ The filter restricts results to elements not flagged "children only." ❷ The filter is declared. ❸ The filter is enabled selectively during the query.

The filter uses the synthetic flag to apply necessary restrictions.

NEGATIVE QUERIES Negative queries (queries excluding a term) are somewhat surprising in Lucene, because they remove elements matching the term from the elements returned by the other parts of the query. By default, you cannot query all elements not matching a given term, but you can work around the problem by using a `MatchAllDocsQuery`. In our example, the filter query excluding `childrenOnly` fields that match `yes` would be written as in listing 8.9.

Listing 8.9 Use `MatchAllDocsQuery` to build negative queries

```
    @Factory
    public Filter getChildrenFilterThroughNegativeQuery() {

        Term term = new Term( "childrenOnly", "yes" );
        Query query = new TermQuery( term );

        BooleanQuery totalQuery = new BooleanQuery();
```

```
totalQuery.add( new MatchAllDocsQuery(),
               Occur.SHOULD );     ⟵─┐  Add a term matching
totalQuery.add( query,                │  all documents
               Occur.MUST_NOT );      └──⟵
Filter filter = new QueryWrapperFilter( totalQuery );

return filter;                              Exclude elements
  }                                    matching a specific term
```

Listing 8.9 must contain this somewhat artificial MatchAllDocsQuery. Otherwise the query results would be empty all the time because the negative term would be applied to nothing.

The security example showed us how to explicitly add information into the index to later query on it or filter it. The procedure is quite simple:

1 Write a bridge injecting the necessary information into the indexes.

2 Apply the bridge to the relevant entity.

3 Write a filter implementation (or a query) using the specific information stored in the index.

The next example shows you how to avoid getting the TooManyClauses exception when using a RangeQuery.

8.2.2 *Restricting results to a given range*

Often a full-text query restricts one of the properties to a given range of values. For example:

- Age must be between 20 and 30.
- Price must be lower than 500.
- Date must be between last month and today.

The classic approach for solving this problem is to use RangeQuery, as explained in section 7.3.6. Unfortunately, RangeQuery is susceptible to the TooManyClauses exception. When Lucene sees a RangeQuery, it replaces it with a series of TermQuerys. Lucene looks for all possible term values matching the range in the index for the targeted field and adds a term query for each of them. This approach is perfectly fine when the number of matching term values is relatively low, but it could quickly lead to TooManyClauses exceptions.

An alternative approach is to use a range filter; the query is executed without range limitations. In the second phase, a filter removes the elements not matching the range. This approach no longer suffers from the TooManyClauses exception. This solution particularly shines in the following situations:

- Term values matching the expected range are numerous.
- The same range is used many times across queries.

Our DVD store site has competitive prices and attracts people on a small budget. One of our features is to provide a search engine that targets prices below $15. The first step is to index prices using the padding technique described in chapter 4, and the second step is to create a filter implementation using `RangeFilter`.

The bridge we used in section 4.1.3, (listing 4.6), suits our needs, and we'll reuse it. Listing 8.10 shows the filter implementation and its usage. Don't forget to apply the same logic applied by the price bridge to the value passed to the `RangeFilter` (in this case padding and rounding). The terms queried must match the terms indexed.

Listing 8.10   Price is indexed using a padding technique and rounding

```
@Entity
@Indexed
@Table(name="PRODUCTS")
@FullTextFilterDef(name="maximumprice",
            impl=MaximumPriceFilterFactory.class)
public class Item {
    @Column(name="PRICE") @NotNull
    @Digits(integerDigits=10, fractionalDigits=2)
    @Field(index=Index.UN_TOKENIZED)
    @FieldBridge(                                          ❶ Pad numbers
        impl=ParameterizedPaddedRoundedPriceBridge.class,
        params= { @Parameter(name="pad", value="10"),
                @Parameter(name="round", value="1") }
            )
    private BigDecimal price;
    ...
}

public class MaximumPriceFilterFactory {
    private static final int PAD = 10;
    private long maxPrice = -1;                    ❷ Inject max
                                                     price parameter
    public void setMaxPrice(long maxPrice) {
        this.maxPrice = maxPrice;
    }

    @Factory
    public Filter getMaximumPriceFilter() {
        if ( maxPrice == -1) {
            throw new IllegalStateException(
                "MaximumPriceFilterFactory.maxPrice is mandatory"
            );
        }                                       ❸ Build a range filter
        Filter filter = RangeFilter.Less(
            "price",
            pad( maxPrice ) );
        return filter;
    }

    @Key
    public FilterKey getKey() {
        StandardFilterKey key = new StandardFilterKey();
        key.addParameter( maxPrice );
```

```
            return key;
        }
        private String pad(long price) {          ⬅─┐   ❹ Apply same
            String rawLong = Long.toString( price );         padding as bridge
            if ( rawLong.length() > PAD )
                throw new IllegalArgumentException(
                    "Try to pad on a number too big" );

            StringBuilder paddedLong = new StringBuilder();
            for ( int padIndex = rawLong.length();
                    padIndex < PAD;
                    padIndex++ ) {
                paddedLong.append( '0' );
            }
            return paddedLong.append( rawLong ).toString();
        }
    }

    public List<Item> searchItemsLowPrice(String search) {
        FullTextSession ftSession = SessionHolder.getFullTextSession();
        org.apache.lucene.search.Query luceneQuery =
            buildLuceneQuery( search );

        FullTextQuery query = ftSession.createFullTextQuery(
            luceneQuery, Item.class );                  ❺ Enable filters

        query.enableFullTextFilter( "maximumprice" )   ⬅─┐
            .setParameter( "maxPrice", 15 );

        @SuppressWarnings("unchecked")
        List<Item> results = query.list();
        return results;
    }
```

❶ The bridge transforms price into a padded number rounded to the next integer.
❷ The maximum price is passed to the filter as a parameter. ❸ `RangeFilter` has a
generic constructor and a few helper methods to build the right range; we want prices
lower than or equal to `maxPrice`. ❹ Be sure to apply the same logic (in this case, padding) to the bridge and to the term value passed to `RangeFilter`. ❺ Enable the filter
on queries.

You can use the generic `RangeFilter` constructor to define lower and upper
boundaries and decide whether or not these boundaries are included or excluded
from the range. Alternatively, you can use one of the two static helper methods available; refer to the JavaDoc for more information.

WARNING   The field used in a `RangeFilter` or a `RangeQuery` must not be token-
          ized because the field would appear to have multiple values. Only one
          term per field is allowed to ensure proper range comparison.

This filter is particularly efficient when the same range is used by most, if not all,
users. In our case, the Marketing Department decided that 15 was the psychological
price to apply but wanted the flexibility to change it down the road. We used a param-
eterized filter to achieve this flexibility.

Our next example is a tool that can be quite useful for certain specialized websites to allow the user to refine the queries.

8.2.3 Searching within search results

In some situations, a user might want to execute a search within the results of a previous search. This approach can be a nice way to refine results by incrementally restricting them. Another advantage (or behavior) is that results are ordered based on the score of the last query executed. In other words, the relevancy based on the previous query is simply forgotten. If your search user typically searches generically and refines his search to the specific topic he's interested in, this solution becomes quite attractive because the order by relevance will be based on the last search.

TIP An alternative solution to searching within a search is to use a Lucene `BooleanQuery` to enforce both the previous query and the refined query. When you use this approach, relevance is computed based on both queries.

Implementing this solution is quite easy with Hibernate Search. You need to keep the previous Lucene query around in some kind of conversational context. In a simple architecture, `HTTPSession` can fulfill that role; if you use JBoss Seam, a standard conversation is your best bet. Listing 8.11 shows a possible implementation.

Listing 8.11 Implementing search within a search

```
public class SearchWithinSearchFilterFactory {
    private Query previousQuery;

    public void setPreviousQuery(Query previousQuery) {
        this.previousQuery = previousQuery;
    }

    @Factory
    public Filter getSearchWithinSearch() {
        return new QueryWrapperFilter(
            previousQuery );            ◁─┐  Wrap previous
    }                                     ❶  query in filter
}

@Entity @Indexed @Table(name="PRODUCTS")
@FullTextFilterDef(name="searchWithinSearch",
            impl=SearchWithinSearchFilterFactory.class,
            cache=FilterCacheModeType.NONE)    ◁─
public class Item {                          ❷  Disable cache
    ...
}

public class ItemRetrievalActionImpl
        implements ItemRetrievalAction {
    private org.apache.lucene.search.Query
 ➥previousLuceneQuery;                ◁─   Keep previous
                                       ❸  query around
    @SuppressWarnings("unchecked")
```

```
public List<Item> searchItems(String search) {

    FullTextSession ftSession = SessionHolder.getFullTextSession();
    org.apache.lucene.search.Query luceneQuery =
        buildLuceneQuery( search );

    previousLuceneQuery = luceneQuery;
    FullTextQuery query = ftSession.createFullTextQuery(
        luceneQuery, Item.class );

    @SuppressWarnings("unchecked")
    List<Item> results = query.list();
    return results;
}

@SuppressWarnings("unchecked")
public List<Item> searchWithinSearch(String search) {

    if (previousLuceneQuery == null) return searchItems( search );

    FullTextSession ftSession = SessionHolder.getFullTextSession();
    org.apache.lucene.search.Query luceneQuery =
        buildLuceneQuery( search );

    FullTextQuery query = ftSession.createFullTextQuery(     ❹ Pass
        luceneQuery, Item.class );                             previous
                                                               query to
    query.enableFullTextFilter( "searchWithinSearch" )  ◁──┘ filter
            .setParameter( "previousQuery", previousLuceneQuery );

    @SuppressWarnings("unchecked")
    List<Item> results = query.list();
    return results;
}
}
```

❶ Use a `QueryWrapperFilter` to build a filter out of the previous Lucene query. ❷ Do not cache the `Filter` instance because most queries and filters are user specific. ❸ Keep the previous query around in a conversational context (for example, a JBoss Seam conversation context). ❹ Apply the named filter to pass the previous query.

One interesting note: This filter is not cached by Hibernate Search. Most users perform queries unrelated to each other, and it makes little sense to cache previous query filters in memory. It's more efficient in our system to reapply the original query each time.

TIP   Be careful to not abuse searching within a search. Very few search websites expose such a feature in their user interface because it can be very confusing for users. Search websites tend to use a slightly different technique. After the initial query, the search engine proposes various refinement possibilities to the user, who can then decide whether or not to refine his query, based on those choices. Yahoo! Search uses such a technique, called Search Assist.

So far, all the examples have been extracting information from the Lucene index to build the filter `DocIdSet`. This is not a requirement.

8.2.4 *Filter results based on external data*

A filter implementation doesn't have to build its DocIdSet from the data stored in the Lucene index. It's perfectly possible to extract information from an external service and use that information to compute the filter.

Back to our DVD store example: Around Christmas, customers become upset when the items displayed in the results are out of stock. Our website needs to filter out items that are no longer in stock. Stock information is updated per batch every half day. It's possible to build a filter that removes items that are out of stock.

Listing 8.12 shows a more complex Filter implementation than what we've seen so far. It makes use of an external service, holds an internal cache, and rebuilds data when needed. It also shows some of the techniques used to find a Lucene document id based on indexed information (that is, correlating unique information indexed in a document to a document id).

Listing 8.12 Use an external service to build the appropriate DocIdSet

```
public class StockFilter extends Filter {                           ① Update timestamp

    private volatile long lastUpdateTime;

    @SuppressWarnings("unchecked")                                  Keep cache in a  ②
    private final Map<IndexReader, DocIdSet> cache =               SoftHashMap
        Collections.synchronizedMap(
            new ReferenceMap(ReferenceMap.SOFT, ReferenceMap.HARD) );

    @Override
    public DocIdSet getDocIdSet(IndexReader reader) throws IOException {
        StockAction action = getStockAction();                     Retrieve the
        long lastUpdateTime = action.geLastUpdateTime();          ③ service
        if ( lastUpdateTime != this.lastUpdateTime ) {
            cache.clear();          Clear
        }                        ④ outdated cache          ⑤ Check if in cache
        DocIdSet cached = cache.get( reader );
        if (cached != null) return cached;

        //not in cache, build info
        final BitSet bitSet = getAllPositiveBitSet(     By default all
                        reader.maxDoc() );              documents pass

        Term clazzTerm = new Term( DocumentBuilder.CLASS_FIELDNAME,
                        Item.class.getName() );
        if ( reader.docFreq( clazzTerm ) == 0 ) {           No need
            //index does not contain Item objects        ⑥ to filter
            //no-op
        }
        else {
            //for each item out of stock, find the
            //corresponding document id by item id
            //and switch off the corresponding bit
            for ( String ean : action.getEanOfItemsOutOfStock() ) {
                Term term = new Term( "ean", ean );
                TermDocs termDocs =                  Invoke external service ⑦
```

```
                          reader.termDocs( term );     ◄── ❽ Document by ean
                  while ( termDocs.next() ) {
                      bitSet.clear( termDocs.doc() );    ◄── Filter them out
                  }
              }
          }
          DocIdSet docIdSet = new DocIdBitSet( bitSet );   ◄──  ❾ Build DocIdSet
          cache.put( reader, docIdSet );         ◄──┐         from BitSet
          this.lastUpdateTime = lastUpdateTime;  ◄──┤     ❿ Put results in
          return docIdSet;                                   the cache
      }                              Update timestamp │

      private BitSet getAllPositiveBitSet(int maxDoc) {
          BitSet bitSet = new BitSet( maxDoc );
          bitSet.set( 0, maxDoc - 1 );      ◄──┐ New BitSet
          return bitSet;                     ⓫ with all bits on
      }

      private StockAction getStockAction() {
          return Container.getService( StockAction.class );
      }
  }
```

❶ A synchronization flag detects when the external service has updated stock data and needs to refresh cached `BitSets`. ❷ `DocIdSets` are cached per `IndexReader` instance in a `SoftHashMap`; when the `IndexReader` instance is dereferenced, the entry can be garbage collected. `ReferenceMap` is a class from the Apache Commons Collection project. ❸ The `Filter` implementation makes use of an external service; the service is provided by your method of choice, in this case by looking up the service from the container. ❹ If the external service is updated, the `DocIdSet` cache is cleared. ❺ Try to find precomputed `DocIdSets` first. ❻ Make sure the index contains `Item` documents; `docFreq` returns the number of documents containing the given term. This is a small optimization that avoids calling the service and looping though the documents when it's not needed. ❼ Invoke the external service that returns all EANs for out-of-stock items. ❽ `termDocs` finds all document ids matching a given EAN (there should be only one), and we mark these documents out in the `BitSet`. ❾ A `DocIdBitSet` wraps a `BitSet` structure in the `DocIdSet` contract understood by Lucene. ❿ Add the newly computed `DocIdSet` into the cache. ⓫ Build a `BitSet` and let all documents pass. Its size corresponds to the number of documents in the index.

Depending on the number of items out of stock, `BitSet` initializations could take some time to process in a real system. It's important to cache `Filters` and `DocIdSets` to maximize performance.

An alternative implementation could avoid using the `BitSet` structure and use the `OpenBitSet` structure or even implement a customized `DocIdSet`.

NOTE The `IndexReader` methods used in listing 8.12 use indexed properties. These properties do not have to be stored in the Lucene index (as in `@Field(store=Store.YES)`).

Listing 8.12 implements its own caching system and stores the results by `IndexReader` in a map. `StockFilter` has better information than Hibernate Search and can adjust caches more appropriately. If we were using the regular Hibernate Search results caching, we could not clear the cache when the data sent by the external service is updated.

TIP   Do not use a `WeakHashMap` to store your results. To share `IndexReader` instances among different requests and allow polymorphic queries, Hibernate Search wraps the shared `IndexReaders` with a per-query `IndexReader`. The wrapper instance, which is passed to the filter instance, is discarded after the query and would be reclaimed too quickly by a weak reference. Instead, use either a soft-reference-based map or a regular map limited in size and coupled with a most-recently-used algorithm or a timeout algorithm. You can typically find such solutions in cache libraries such as JBoss Cache or EHCache.

Since `StockFilter` caches the results itself, make sure you disable the Hibernate Search results caching layer, as shown in listing 8.13. Filter instance caching should still be enabled because otherwise the `StockFilter` instance and its cache would be discarded after each usage.

> **Listing 8.13   Disable filter result caching and keep filter instance caching**

```
@FullTextFilterDef(name="stock",
            impl=StockFilter.class,
            cache=FilterCacheModeType.INSTANCE_ONLY )   ◁──┐  Disable result
public class Item {                                         caching but cache
    ...                                                     instances
}
```

This example is by far the most complex, but remember that you write the `Filter` implementation only once and use it declaratively at query time. Also in most cases, the built-in filters like `QueryWrapperFilter` keep `Filter` implementations really simple. If you want to know more about the `IndexReader` methods used in listing 8.12 and available to you in a `Filter`, check *Lucene in Action* from Manning and the `IndexReader` JavaDoc.

8.3   *Summary*

Filter is a very powerful feature provided by Lucene. It allows an application to decouple some restriction logic from the core query implementation, making filters a cross-cutting concern. Hibernate Search makes this feature easy to use by adding a declarative layer on top of it; you can declaratively enable and disable filters on a full-text query. Filters are cached by Hibernate Search transparently for the application, increasing query performance.

Filters are very useful is a wide variety of use cases. This chapter and its examples have hopefully given you the necessary knowledge to explore filters and make the best use of them in your applications. Unleash your imagination!

The next part of *Hibernate Search in Action* explores more advanced concepts, touching on performance, scalability, and optimization.

Part 4

Performance and scalability

The previous parts of this book covered all of the fundamental concepts and practical knowledge necessary to index a domain model and query it. The next two chapters focus on performance and scalability.

Chapter 9 is a performance cookbook that's full of tips and tricks to apply to optimize various areas of Hibernate Search: indexing, querying, and optimizing index structures. Chapter 10 covers scalability and particularly focuses on using Hibernate Search in a cluster of servers.

Performance
considerations

9

This chapter covers

- Optimizing the indexing process and the index structure
- Optimizing queries
- Index partitioning (named sharding)
- Testing

While full-text search technology, also called information retrieval, offers many features not attainable by a pure relational database, it's also well known for retrieving information quickly. People are accustomed to retrieving search results in fractions of a second and grow impatient if it doesn't happen that fast. Blame Google!

This chapter is a collection of information, tips, and tricks for making the best of your Hibernate Search application and understanding why some operations are expensive. You have some of this knowledge already if you've read the previous chapters carefully; some of it will be new to you. The authors thought it would be quite convenient to collect all of these techniques into a single chapter.

Performance is always a double-edged sword problem. As Donald Knuth (the author of *The Art of Computer Programming*) phrased it: *Premature optimization is the root of all evil.*

Before running into optimization cycles and before applying every single trick in this chapter, you should be very clear about what your goals are. Ask yourself:

- Is the application fast enough already?
- If it's slow, which use case should be made more efficient?
- Is the cost of this optimization worth the gain?

First and foremost, is the application too slow for your use case? In many cases, Lucene and Hibernate Search are doing a good job out of the box. If some searches are considered too slow or if indexing is taking too long, be sure to identify the problem clearly and define your goal in terms of performance. Finally, try to understand the cost of optimization. Optimization can be costly in many different ways: the time you, as a developer or architect, spend on the problem; the effect on code readability; the use of additional resources (you might optimize response time by using more memory or CPU); and so on.

We're now clear about our goals, so let's go boost Hibernate Search performance!

9.1 Optimizing indexing

Indexing is an operation that doesn't get all the attention it deserves; people are more focused on search speed. They can accept indexing not being a Formula 1 or NASCAR car because it doesn't affect their system much. In some situations, however, it's good to know how to index faster. Indexing time depends on many factors:

- Size of the data indexed
- Index strategy used
- Database access and performance
- Network performance
- Input/output performance

The rest of this section will describe how to optimize some of these factors.

9.1.1 What influences indexing time for a single entity

Several factors influence the indexing operation for a given object. Let's walk through some of the factors you can easily influence:

- Number of properties indexed
- Type of analyzer used
- Properties stored
- Properties embedded

The more properties are indexed on a given object and the bigger they are, the longer the indexing process takes. Make sure to index only those properties you need to search by. This will also reduce the size of your index and make the search faster.

Properties marked for tokenization are passed through the relevant analyzer implementation, which splits the property into individual words and applies additional logic, this logic being either simpler or more complex. This operation takes time. Stemming a word or finding its phonetic approximation can be quite consuming of time and CPU compared to an analyzer that simply passes the words to the index. Make sure you need the feature, or, more accurately, if you need the feature, make sure indexing time is still within your acceptable range.

When you mark a property for `Store.YES` or `Store.COMPRESS`, Lucene needs to do some additional operations (which can be costly in terms of input/output and CPU if you choose to compress it). Provided that Hibernate Search doesn't need you to store properties in the index unless you want to project them, think twice before storing a property.

Be a bit cautious with `@IndexedEmbedded` properties. Hibernate Search lets you embed information about associated objects so that you can later apply queries on these associations. There are a couple of drawbacks with this approach:

- Associated object(s) must be loaded (if they're not already) to be indexed.
- More data is indexed, especially when collections are marked as `@Indexed-Embedded`.

Make sure to not embed an association if you don't need the information at query time (especially collections). Also make sure to keep your database access efficient. Section 9.1.3 gives good advice on this subject.

These tips are helpful for reducing the indexing time of a given object. What happens when many objects are indexed concurrently?

9.1.2 *Optimizing many concurrent indexing operations*

Lucene is not a relational database. In particular, its concurrency behavior isn't what you'd expect from an ordinary relational database. Every time an index is updated, a pessimistic lock is acquired for the duration of the update. Other writers have to wait until the lock is released to apply their own changes. Only one writer can work at a given time on the index.

This limitation is perfectly acceptable on applications where updates are relatively infrequent (read-mostly applications) but can produce huge contentions and limit the system's scalability for more write-intensive applications. During heavy index writing, all application threads will end up waiting on each other for the index lock acquisition. This will essentially transform your multiuser application into a single-threaded application, which will be quite disappointing. Don't panic; this catastrophic scenario happens only on heavy write applications.

Test your system before deciding to go for an asynchronous approach. Lucene is fast enough, and the synchronous approach is probably perfectly fine for you.

Two solutions are available to reduce or eliminate this contention problem:

- Index asynchronously.
- Index on a different machine.

By default, Hibernate Search indexes your object changes at commit time. Once changes are indexed, the commit operation ends. This approach can lead to the contention problem because indexing is done synchronously. The lock is acquired synchronously with the application flow during the precommit phase and can become a hot spot for the whole application.

You can configure Hibernate Search to index data asynchronously, at commit time. Changes are passed to a different thread for later execution, and the commit operation finishes right away. This approach decouples index lock acquisition from the main application flow. This is particularly useful when the application temporarily suffers from heavy writing time. During a heavy writing moment, update operations queue up because the indexing process cannot keep up with the load. When the heavy writing period diminishes, Hibernate Search continues to write to the index until it has emptied the queue.

You can tune some aspects of the asynchronous process. For example, you can define the maximum number of elements in the waiting queue and the number of concurrent threads processing the queue. If the queue limit is reached, the caller thread (commit operation) will process indexing synchronously. Setting a limit has two advantages:

- It prevents filling up the queue until an OutOfMemoryException occurs.
- It provides feedback to the system that limits the indexing load (by forcing producer threads to wait).

The ideal number of concurrent threads depends on the number of Lucene indexes written concurrently in your system. Since a pessimistic lock is acquired per index, having two concurrent threads working on the same index is only marginally beneficial (at least for the current version of Hibernate Search). The default value is 1; one thread is used globally for indexing. Be sure to experiment on your system to find the sweet spot, starting with one thread per index used in a typical transaction. The configuration shown in listing 9.1 configures Hibernate Search for an asynchronous process using `hibernate.cfg.xml`. You can, of course, use `persistence.xml` as well.

Listing 9.1 Configuring Hibernate Search to index asynchronously

```
<hibernate-configuration>
  <session-factory>
    <property name="hibernate.search.default.indexBase">
          ⮡ ./build/indexes</property>

    <property name="hibernate.search.worker.execution">       | Execute
          ⮡ async</property>                                   | asynchronously
    <property name="hibernate.search.worker.thread_pool.size"> | Concurrent threads
          ⮡ 2</property>                                       | processing
    <property name="hibernate.search.worker.buffer_queue.max"> | Queue size limit
          ⮡ 100</property>

    <session-factory>
  </hibernate-configuration>
```

An alternative approach pushes asynchronism even further. Instead of pushing work onto a local queue processed by a local pool of threads, you can ask Hibernate Search to push indexing work onto a JMS queue, which is remotely processed on a different machine (the index master server). We won't describe this approach in detail here because chapter 10 is fully dedicated to it. Here are some of its benefits from a performance point of view:

- The indexing load is transferred to a different machine, freeing CPU, I/O, and memory to the main application processes.
- Lock contention is delegated to the index master and entirely absent from the flow in the main application, regardless of the load.

For more information about indexing backend strategies, read section 5.3.3. When you first index your database, or if you reindex your data set entirely every night, you want the massive indexing process to be as fast as possible. Let's explore some of the techniques available for that.

9.1.3 *Optimizing mass indexing*

Reindexing your entire data set or a significant part of your data set can be a long process if you do it the wrong way. This section will help you to make it as efficient as possible.

Indexing a huge data set involves two distinct but interwoven operations: You need to read objects from the database, and then you need to index them. Most of the performance problems arise on the first operation. Hibernate Search needs to have access to the object and all its associated indexed objects during the indexing operation. The object, its `@IndexedEmbedded` associations, and its `@ContainedIn` associations (recursively) form the object graph used during indexing. Use the following techniques to load this graph as efficiently as possible:

- Write the appropriate query using joins.
- Use `@BatchSize` or `FetchMode.SUBSELECT` when a direct join cannot be used.
- Load lazy properties if they are indexed (for example, use the "fetch all properties" syntax in HQL).

If you don't pay attention, Hibernate Search might trigger some $n+1$ load problems while indexing your data. Listing 9.2 is an example of the query needed to load Item objects provided that their `Distributor` association is marked as `@IndexedEmbedded`.

Listing 9.2 When indexing objects, load using a query to minimize *n+1* problems

```
Criteria query = session.createCriteria( Item.class )      1 Load necessary
        .setFetchMode( "distributor", FetchMode.JOIN )        associations
        .setResultTransformer(
            CriteriaSpecification.DISTINCT_ROOT_ENTITY      2 Distinct them
        );                                                    (collection load)
```

You need to fetch associations involved in the indexing process for this entity by using FetchMode ❶ (you can also use static mappings such as @BatchSize). If you load collections, make sure you distinct the results to avoid indexing the same object multiple times ❷. (SQL loads the data for your main object for each element in your collection.)

How to make sure all necessary data is fetched

Several strategies are available to make sure you haven't missed an association. The first one is to enable Hibernate Core logging and check queries going through. An *n*+1 pattern is readily recognizable; after a given query, you'll see a second query executed many, many times.

The second approach is to use the Hibernate Core statistics API (available in SessionFactory.getStatistics()). When an entity is loaded under the cover, Hibernate increases getEntityFetchCount(). Be sure to enable statistics before testing by using statistics.setStatisticsEnabled(true).

The second most common problem occurs because your indexed data set cannot fit all data in memory (usually). If you attempt to load all objects, then index them, you'll likely face an OutOfMemoryException before you even finish loading objects. Make sure you use a scrollable result set and flush your index work queue and clear the session on a regular basis. This will limit the number of objects loaded into memory at a given time. Listing 9.3 demonstrates a typical mass indexing routine.

Listing 9.3 Mass indexing routine limiting objects loaded into memory

```
private static final int BATCH_SIZE = 1000;
private static final int FETCH_SIZE = 100;

public void indexAllItems() {          ◁── Run in a transaction

    FullTextSession session = SessionHolder.getFullTextSession();

    Criteria query = session.createCriteria( Item.class )
            .setFetchMode("distributor", FetchMode.JOIN)
            .setResultTransformer(
    ➥CriteriaSpecification.DISTINCT_ROOT_ENTITY)    ❶ Minimize cache
            .setCacheMode(CacheMode.IGNORE)   ◁──┘      interaction
            .setFetchSize(FETCH_SIZE)                  ◁──
            .setFlushMode(FlushMode.MANUAL);  ◁──          ❷ Align batch
    ScrollableResults scroll = query.scroll(    Disable     size and JDBC
    ➥ScrollMode.FORWARD_ONLY);        ◁──   flush          fetch size
                                      Scroll in forward
    int batch = 0;                  ❸ mode only
    scroll.beforeFirst();
    while ( scroll.next() ) {
        batch++;
        session.index( scroll.get(0) );
        if (batch % BATCH_SIZE == 0) {
```

```
            //no need to session.flush()
            //we don't change anything
             session.flushToIndexes();
             session.clear();
        }
    }
    //the remaining non flushed index work
    //processed at commit time
}
```

④ Flush index
works and clear
the session

❶ It is a good practice to ignore the cache when dealing with a huge amount of data. The benefit doesn't overcome the cost of maintaining cache coherence. ❷ Align JDBC fetch size with the batch window size so that FETCH_SIZE = BATCH_SIZE/n to minimize memory consumption and database round trips. ❸ Scrolling in forward mode loads objects on demand and makes sure objects (and their JDBC row representation) are garbage collectable. ❹ After every BATCH_SIZE operations, flush changes to the indexes (flushToIndexes()) and free objects from the session (clear()). This will limit memory consumption.

Be sure to run the indexing process in a transaction. If you don't, Hibernate Search needs to apply index changes when fullTextSession.index() is called, leading to expensive Lucene index opening and closing for each Item.

Reindexing and old content removal

If you plan to completely refresh an index and reindex the entire content, be sure to delete the old indexed information by using searchFactory.purgeAll(Class). Otherwise, removed objects will still live in the index. To save space, you can call searchFactory.optimize(Class) after purgeAll. The old content will be physically removed from the index structure. Listing 9.4 shows the process.

Listing 9.4   To reindex a data set, remove the old content first

```
public void indexAllItems() {

    FullTextSession session = SessionHolder.getFullTextSession();

    session.purgeAll( Item.class );                          ❶ Remove obsolete content
    session.flushToIndexes();                                ❷ Apply purge before optimize
    session.getSearchFactory().optimize( Item.class );

    //read and index the data                                Physically clear space ❸

}
```

Remove the old content to make sure no orphaned document remains ❶. If you're short on space, call flushToIndexes ❷, then optimize. optimize will physically remove the old content ❸. This operation is generally unnecessary.

You can find additional information in section 5.4.2.

Indexing is the first half of Hibernate Search's job. Let's now see how to optimize search queries.

9.2   *Optimizing searches*

The most prominent part of a search engine is the search. Slow searches are the first problem your users will notice. But just as with any part of the system, don't try to prematurely optimize. Lucene and Hibernate Search are pretty good at providing results efficiently out of the box. That being said, let's walk through the elements that influence query time.

9.2.1   *Optimizing the way you write queries*

You can change a few things in the way you write queries to make the most of Hibernate Search:

- Limit the number of targeted classes.
- Limit the number of clauses in your Lucene query.
- Use pagination to limit the number of objects loaded.
- Use criteria to define the fetching strategy.
- Use projection.

Let's have a look at each technique.

LIMIT THE NUMBER OF TARGETED CLASSES

When you write a Hibernate Search query, you can define one or more targeted classes. Returned objects will match only these classes (and any of their subclasses). Under the hood, Hibernate Search optimizes Lucene resources and runs the query only on the relevant Lucene indexes, reducing unnecessary input/output and file opening. Be sure to explicitly define the list of classes your query is targeting, as shown in listing 9.5.

Listing 9.5   Explicitly listing targeted classes improves query performance

```
public List<Item> getMatchingItems(String words, int page) {

    FullTextSession ftSession = SessionHolder.getFullTextSession();
    org.apache.lucene.search.Query luceneQuery =
        buildLuceneQuery( words );

    org.hibernate.Query query =
        ftSession.createFullTextQuery(
                luceneQuery,
                Item.class );     <──❶ Restrict query

    @SuppressWarnings("unchecked")
    List<Item> results = query.list();
    return results;
}
```

Performance is at its best when a single class is targeted ❶, because Hibernate Search can issue a single database query.

LIMIT THE NUMBER OF CLAUSES

In the same line of thought, let's try to further optimize our use of Lucene. Lucene query performance is a function of the number of clauses (that is, individual restrictions). If you can, try to limit the number of clauses.

By default Lucene limits you to 1024 clauses and raises a `TooManyClauses` exception if the query goes beyond that. You might think that you will never write a query complex enough to reach the 1024 clause limit. After all, that would be a huge query!

This is not true. Remember that a range query, a prefix query, and a wildcard query among others are rewritten as Boolean queries that encompass all the matching terms in the index. Provided the range is large enough and populated enough, you'll reach this limit in a heartbeat. Fortunately, there's a way to work around this problem.

Use a filter to exclude elements that are out of range. Filters are applied independently of the core query process and don't suffer from the clause limit problem. Filters especially shine when the same range is reused by many concurrent queries (for example, a filter showing only changes that happened in the last month). Check section 8.2.2, for more information on how to set up and use a filter.

The next tricks are focused on optimizing interactions between Hibernate Search and the Hibernate persistence context. This typically happens after the Lucene query execution.

USE PAGINATION TO LIMIT THE NUMBER OF OBJECTS LOADED

The first trick is to not load information you don't need. Why would you load 1000 objects if your customer looks at only the first 20 elements 95 percent of the time? The process of limiting the number of matching results returned is called *pagination*. Not only does it limit the number of domain model objects loaded by Hibernate Search, it also limits the number of `Document` objects loaded by Lucene. Listing 9.6 shows pagination used to display Item objects by batches of 20.

> **Listing 9.6 Use pagination to limit the amount of data loaded**

```
private static final int WINDOW = 20;

public List<Item> getMatchingItems(String words, int page) {

    FullTextSession ftSession = SessionHolder.getFullTextSession();
    org.apache.lucene.search.Query luceneQuery =
        buildLuceneQuery( words );

    org.hibernate.Query query = ftSession.createFullTextQuery(
        luceneQuery, Item.class );

    @SuppressWarnings("unchecked")
    List<Item> results = query
        .setFirstResult( (page - 1) * WINDOW )          ← ❶ First result
        .setMaxResults( WINDOW )          ←
        .list();                                    ❷ Number of results
     return results;
}
```

❶ First result

❷ Number of results

When paginating, you define the first element retrieved ❶ (the first element of the page in this case) and the number of elements retrieved ❷. Section 6.4 has more in-depth information about pagination.

LOAD THE APPROPRIATE OBJECT GRAPH

We now load exactly the number of results we want, but the objects matching the query and returned as a result might not be all the data we need. What if your screen needs to display information from an associated entity? By default, and if your associa-tion is marked as lazy, Hibernate Search will not load this information when retrieving the matching object. This can potentially trigger an *n+1* problem, where multiple sub-sequent queries are fired to load these associated objects.

Hibernate Search lets you override the fetching strategy of your object graph. Section 6.8 has more information on the subject, but let's refresh your memory with listing 9.7.

Listing 9.7 Use a `Criteria` API to define a fetching strategy

```
public List<Item> getMatchingItemsWithDistributor(String words, int page) {
    FullTextSession ftSession = SessionHolder.getFullTextSession();
    org.apache.lucene.search.Query luceneQuery =
        buildLuceneQuery( words );

    FullTextQuery query = ftSession.createFullTextQuery(          ❶ Define
        luceneQuery, Item.class );                                  fetching
                                                                    strategy
    Criteria criteria = ftSession.createCriteria( Item.class )  ⟵
                .setFetchMode( "distributor", FetchMode.JOIN );

    @SuppressWarnings("unchecked")
    List<Item> results = query
        .setFirstResult( (page - 1) * WINDOW )
        .setMaxResults( WINDOW )
        .setCriteriaQuery(criteria)      ⟵  Set fetching strategy
        .list();                         ❷  to the query
    return results;
}
```

Use a Criteria query to define which associations should be fetched ❶ and associate the Criteria query with the full-text query ❷. Note that the full-text query and the Cri-teria query both target `Item`.

TIP   You can define the fetching strategy only when you target one class (and its subclasses) in your full-text query. This class must be the same as the class used to build the Criteria query. Also remember, you must not use the Criteria query to apply a restriction.

More information about overriding fetching strategies is in section 6.8.

USE PROJECTION

Our last tip related to query writing is useful when you find yourself displaying a very small portion of the object properties. If loading the matching object takes too long, and you expect to display only a couple of properties, consider using projection.

Projection will rehydrate specific properties from the index instead of delegating the object load to Hibernate Core. This can save the overhead of loading the object (graph) from the database. The catch is that you must store the property values in the index (see section 3.3.3), and the bridge used to convert the object property into a string consumable by Lucene must be two-way (see section 4.1). Because of these additional stored properties, your index will become bigger and slower. Using property projection is a trade-off; don't use it unless you gain significant performance improvements.

TIP   If you use pagination, the difference between projecting and loading the full object should be fairly minimal. If you load a huge number of objects, the difference could be more significant. But in general, returning a lot of objects should be questioned.

Section 6.5 gives you a more in-depth explanation, but let's look at a small example here (see listing 9.8). Using projection to retrieve only the necessary properties can increase performance significantly but has trade-offs.

Listing 9.8   Using projection to retrieve only necessary properties

```
@Entity @Indexed
public class Item {

    @Id @GeneratedValue
    @DocumentId
    @Column(name="PROD_ID")
    private Integer id;

    @Field(index=Index.TOKENIZED, store=Store.YES)      ❶ Projected properties
    @Column(name="TITLE")                                  are stored
    @NotNull @Length(max=100)
    private String title;
    ...
}

public List<String> getTitleFromMatchingItems(String words) {

    FullTextSession ftSession = SessionHolder.getFullTextSession();
    org.apache.lucene.search.Query luceneQuery =
        buildLuceneQuery( words );

    FullTextQuery query = ftSession.createFullTextQuery(
        luceneQuery, Item.class );

    @SuppressWarnings("unchecked")
    List<Object[]> results = query        ❷ List projected
        .setProjection( "title" )           properties
        .list();

    List<String> titles =
        new ArrayList<String>( results.size() );    ❸ Retrieve arrays
    for(Object[] objects : results) {                 of objects
        titles.add( (String) objects[0] );
    }
    return titles;
}
```

① Projected properties must be stored in the index and must use a two-way bridge. **②** This defines the list of projected properties. **③** Results are returned as `Object[]`. The conversion code could be replaced by a `ResultTransformer` (see section 6.6 for more information).

We've walked through a few tips to write full-text queries efficiently. Let's now see how to tweak the Hibernate Search engine to optimize even further.

9.2.2 *Maximizing benefits from the caching mechanisms*

Hibernate Search caches resources to maximize query performance. This section will describe some of these caching strategies and let you make the best of them.

DEFINE A READERSTRATEGY

For queries, Hibernate Search interacts with Lucene through one or multiple `IndexReaders`. As their name implies, `IndexReader` objects are used to read indexes. They see the state of the index at the time they are opened as if they were taking a snapshot of the index. The way Hibernate deals with index readers is fully customizable through the `ReaderProvider` interface.

By default, Hibernate Search ships with two strategies:

- `not-shared`
- `shared`

The `not-shared` strategy opens the necessary index readers for every query. This is the least-efficient strategy and should rarely be used, if at all.

The `shared` strategy shares `IndexReader` instances across many concurrent queries and keeps the segment readers open as long as the underlying index segment doesn't change. This solution turns out to be very efficient for these reasons:

- The cost of opening and closing the index files is virtually eliminated.
- Index readers are kept warm for many queries.

The first few queries applied to an `IndexReader` are slower because some internal data is cached by the `IndexReader` object and needs to be loaded by the first few queries. Sharing `IndexReaders` eliminates the cost for all subsequent queries.

`shared` is the default strategy used by Hibernate Search, but you can override it by setting a configuration property, as shown in listing 9.9. If you're not satisfied with the reader strategies Hibernate Search provides, you can write your own `ReaderProvider` implementation and pass the fully qualified class name to the same configuration property.

Listing 9.9   Changing default reader provider

```
hibernate.search.reader.strategy not-shared      ⟵  Use the not-shared strategy

#alternatively
hibernate.search.reader.strategy                      Use a custom reader
   ⇨ com.acme.application.util.OtherReaderProvider  ⟵┘  provider strategy
```

The shared strategy is the right choice most of the time and should rarely be overridden. It is important to understand how this strategy works in order to make the best of it. When a change happens to an index, you should reopen the IndexReaders to see this change. When a full-text query is executed, the shared strategy identifies the readers that need to be used, verifies that they are up to date, and reopens them if required (or more precisely reopens the segments that changed). The less writing to indexes there is in your application, the longer IndexReaders will be shared.

One possible custom ReaderProvider implementation could warm up IndexReaders in the background before using them. This would prevent the first few slow queries and would come at the cost of seeing the latest version of the index all the time. The old IndexReaders would have to be served while new readers are warmed up.

TIP If you write a custom ReaderProvider implementation, remember that a ReaderProvider is accessed concurrently. Look at the default implementations, and you will learn a lot about how to guard against concurrent accesses while maintaining a cache of IndexReaders.

In chapter 10, we'll show a way to minimize the number of times indexes are updated without changing how your application updates data. By updating the index asynchronously and pushing back index changes from time to time, you can keep an IndexReader open for a longer period of time. The catch is that changes are not visible immediately in full-text queries.

NOTE By default, entities are indexed in different Lucene indexes. If one entity is updated frequently but another is rarely updated, the caching system will perform very well for queries targeting the entity that's updated infrequently. The IndexReader object for this entity will rarely have to be updated.

Another cache system offers benefits when index changes are infrequent, and we'll discuss it now.

FILTER CACHING

Filters are used to eliminate some results from a query after the query execution and apply some cross-cutting restrictions such as those pertaining to security, time ranges, or categories. A filter is essentially a bit mask indicating whether or not a Document in the index should be included in the final result. Building this bit mask (often represented by the memory-efficient BitSet object through the DocIdSet API) can be quite expensive. But Hibernate Search can cache DocIdSet objects, making subsequent filter applications very cheap. DocIdSets are cached for a given set of elements:

- The IndexReader the DocIdSet has been created for
- The filter type (its definition)
- The optional parameters injected into the filter

When the index changes, the bit mask is likely to be obsolete and needs to be rebuilt. A filter that uses different parameters is unlikely to return the same bit mask and must not share the same DocIdSet object. Those three elements guarantee that the DocIdSet will be applied to the relevant data.

If your index doesn't change frequently and your filter doesn't use parameters or uses the same set of parameters often, you'll make the most of filter caching. Here are a few good examples:

- *A temporal filter shows only the DVDs released in the last 30 days.* This filter can be computed once a day and its `DocIdSet` reused.
- *A category filter restricts some categories to customers.* Because the number of categories is limited, Hibernate Search can cache the `DocIdSet` for each category.
- *A security filter applies restrictions to the visible documents.* If the system contains five levels of security, keeping filter results for the five different parameters in the cache is likely to be quite efficient.

By default, caching is enabled, but you can adjust that in the filter definition (`@Full-TextFilterDef`). Explore chapter 8 for more information. Also remember that caching trades speed for memory; keep an eye on memory consumption.

The speed of a Lucene query is directly dependent on the index structure. We'll now explore how this structure evolves over time during indexing and how you can optimize it to speed up your queries.

9.3   *Optimizing the index structure*

Lucene tries very hard to make searches as fast as possible. In some information-retrieval systems, it means the index cannot be updated. The index has to be entirely recreated for every change. Fortunately for us, Lucene is not such a system and can update information in the index. Not only that, but you can also query the index while new information is added to it. To achieve this, Lucene doesn't change the index files but rather creates new sets of files containing the newly indexed information. These files are a kind of mini-index called a *segment*, which together form the global index. Likewise, instead of physically deleting a document from the index, Lucene flags it as deleted and ignores it during queries. In Hibernate Search, indexing is executed per transaction. One mini-index is created per transaction and per index (unless merging occurs).

This file-structure approach results in the creation of numerous small files in the Lucene directory and a constant increase in space used because no record is physically deleted. To query an index, Lucene must open many different files. This poses three problems:

- Opening many files is slower than opening a smaller number of files.
- Because records are not physically deleted, Lucene has to read more information.
- The total number of files you can open simultaneously is limited in some operating systems (particularly Linux).

If you want to know more about the index structure, either check the Lucene documentation or have a look at *Lucene in Action* from Manning, which talks in depth on this subject.

NOTE INCREASING THE MAXIMUM NUMBER OF FILES OPENED When you use Lucene, you can quickly reach the maximum number of files opened simultaneously on Linux systems. You can adjust this limit by using the `ulimit -n <limit>` command.

To circumvent those problems, Lucene can optimize the index structure. This operation is very similar to file system defragmentation. The mini-indexes are merged into a single, bigger index, and the deleted records are removed from the new index.

This results in a file structure that's much more efficient for Lucene queries:

- Fewer files have to be opened.
- The amount of data to be read is smaller.
- The risk of hitting the file system limit of simultaneous opened files fades away.

Note that optimizing an index has a few drawbacks. `IndexReaders` have to be reopened to see the new structure, and an index copy from master to slaves in the JMS replication model will likely be a full copy. In general, these drawbacks are acceptable considering the benefits.

Let's see how to apply this optimization with Hibernate Search.

9.3.1 *Running an optimization*

You can run the optimization process in two ways in Hibernate Search: manually or automatically.

MANUAL OPTIMIZATION

The `SearchFactory` method exposes two methods for optimizing your indexes. The first one optimizes the index(es) for a given class. Listing 9.10 shows how to call this method.

Listing 9.10 Optimizing index(es) hosting a given class

```
public void optimize(Class clazz) {
    FullTextSession session = SessionHolder.getFullTextSession();
    session.getSearchFactory().optimize( clazz );        ◁┐
}                                                   Optimize a given class
```

When this method is called, the optimization operation is immediately executed. Contrary to index operations, `optimize` does not wait until the end of the transaction. You can still query while an optimization is in progress, but queries tend to be much slower for the duration of the optimization process.

TIP When using JMS mode (see section 10.1.2), optimization is not applied when run on the slaves. Slaves have read-only indexes. Be sure to apply optimize calls on the master instance.

You can also optimize all the indexes by calling the `searchFactory.optimize()` method, as shown in listing 9.11.

Listing 9.11   Optimizing all indexes

```
public void optimize() {
    FullTextSession session = SessionHolder.getFullTextSession();
    session.getSearchFactory().optimize();      ◁──┐
}                                                   │  Optimize all indexes
```

When should you call `optimize`? Optimizing is useful when many insertions or deletions have been made, particularly after initial data indexing or when you have reindexed a significant part of your data set.

TIP   There's no need to optimize when you're about to index a large section of data unless you need to reclaim disk space. Optimization doesn't make indexing faster. On the other hand, when you've finished a massive indexing, it's a good time to optimize. Subsequent queries will execute faster.

A nice tool to see if an optimization is necessary is Luke. One of the panels shows how many files the index contains and the size of each (see section 2.6). Listing 9.12 shows how to use `optimize` after a complete reindexing.

Listing 9.12   Run `optimize` after indexing all data to speed up queries

```
public void reindex() {

    FullTextSession session = SessionHolder.getFullTextSession();
    session.purgeAll( Item.class );
    session.flushToIndexes();
    session.getSearchFactory().optimize( Item.class );      ◁──┐  ❶ Run after purge
                                                               │     to save space
    Criteria query =
        session.createCriteria( Item.class )
                .setFetchMode( "distributor",
                        FetchMode.JOIN )
                .setResultTransformer(
                    CriteriaSpecification.DISTINCT_ROOT_ENTITY )
                .setCacheMode( CacheMode.IGNORE )
                .setFetchSize( BATCH_SIZE );

    ScrollableResults scroll = query.scroll( ScrollMode.FORWARD_ONLY );

    scroll.beforeFirst();
    int batch = 0;
    while ( scroll.next() ) {
        batch++;
        session.index( scroll.get(0) );
        if (batch % BATCH_SIZE == 0) {          │  flush() is not called;
            session.flushToIndexes();      ◁──┘  no change is made
            session.clear();
        }
    }                                      ❷ Flush the final changes
                                              before optimizing
    session.flushToIndexes();          ◁──┘
    session.getSearchFactory().optimize( Item.class );   ◁──❸ Run optimization
}
```

❶ To save space, you can run optimize after purging your data. Make sure you call flushToIndexes between purgeAll and optimize to apply the purge to the Lucene index. This set of operations is not mandatory. ❷ Be sure to finish flushing all index changes before optimizing. ❸ Optimize operations after making big changes in the index to speed subsequent queries.

Don't forget that optimizing is a fairly expensive operation, especially if there is a lot to optimize. It's preferable to do it on offline indexes, when only few queries are run, or to execute it frequently enough to have small sections of work.

Hibernate Search offers a more transparent way to optimize your indexes, which we'll explore next.

AUTOMATIC OPTIMIZATION

Hibernate Search can take care of running the optimization process for you on a regular basis. Optimization can be triggered when the following metrics reach a certain limit:

- The number of operations applied to an index
- The number of transactions applied to an index

If you set these numbers to a reasonably low value, small optimizations will be applied regularly and transparently for you. You can define these settings for all indexes or override them per index. The configuration mechanism is similar to the one you saw in section 5.1.1. A property name is composed of the following:

- hibernate.search.
- The index name or default to share these configurations for all indexes
- A dot (.) followed by the property suffix

The two interesting suffixes are optimizer.operation_limit.max and optimizer.transaction_limit.max. When more than optimizer.operation_limit.max operations are executed on a given index (one index per entity type by default), an optimize operation is executed, and the operation and transaction counters are reset. Likewise, when optimizer.transaction_limit.max transactions are executed on a given index, an optimize operation is executed, and the operation and transaction counters are reset. Hibernate Search is smart enough to run automatic optimizations only at the end of the transaction. This is useful because an optimize operation is better done after all indexing is complete.

Listing 9.13 shows a configuration where we optimize every 100 operations by default and every 30 transactions (or 100 operations, whichever comes first) for items.

Listing 9.13 Setting transparent optimization limits

```
<session-factory>
  ...
  <property name="hibernate.search.com.manning.hsia.dvdstore.
➥model.Item.optimizer.transaction_limit.max" >30</property>
  <property name="hibernate.search.default.
➥optimizer.operation_limit.max">100</property>
  ...
</session-factory>
```

You know how to trigger an optimization. Now let's see if you can configure Hibernate Search to tune the index structure.

9.3.2 *Tuning index structures and operations*

Hibernate Search allows you to tune its indexing performance through a set of configuration parameters that control how the underlying Lucene `IndexWriter` utilizes memory and disk file structures. A Lucene index is composed of mini-indexes (each of them being an atomic structure containing the necessary information). These mini-indexes are called *segments* in Lucene.

The two sets of parameters allow for different performance settings depending on the use case. During indexing operations triggered by database modifications, the following parameters are used:

- `hibernate.search.<indexname>.indexwriter.transaction.merge_factor`
- `hibernate.search.<indexname>.indexwriter.`
  `↪transaction.max_merge_docs`
- `hibernate.search.<indexname>.indexwriter.`
  `↪transaction.ram_buffer_size`

The `indexname` can be replaced by `default` if you want to define global values.

`merge_factor` determines how often segments are merged with each other when insertions in the Lucene index occurs. The lower the `merge_factor`, the fewer segments are allowed at a given time and the more frequently merging happens. With small values, less RAM is used because fewer documents are kept in memory before being merged. But more file creations and merges are performed while indexing, making indexing speed slower. On the other hand, searches on unoptimized indexes are faster because fewer segments are present at a given time. With larger values, indexing is faster, but searches on unoptimized indexes are slower because of more segmented files. By default, Hibernate Search uses the Lucene default value (currently 10).

`max_merge_docs` defines the largest number of documents allowed in a segment. When Lucene is about to add a new document to a given segment, it will create a new segment if the `max_merge_docs` limit is reached. This limit has priority over the `merge_factor`. A segment containing `max_merge_docs` will never be merged again. By default, Hibernate Search uses the Lucene default value (currently no limit).

> **TIP** While `max_merge_docs` can be useful for ensuring smaller merges, don't use it as a way to control memory usage; `ram_buffer_size` is a better way. If you happen to use both at the same time, a new segment is created as soon as one of the limits is reached.

`ram_buffer_size` controls the amount of memory used to buffer documents during indexing. This property is expressed in megabytes and defaults to 16. When this value is large, it takes longer for a new segment to be created, and merges happen less often. However, merge operations are slower and involve more documents.

You can see from their definitions that these parameters are interrelated. The higher a `merge_factor` is, the less often a merge happens, because Lucene lets the number of segments increase. At the same time, when `ram_buffer_size` is high, a single segment can contain many documents, which leads to fewer segment files being created. Finally, a nondefault value for `max_merge_docs` could force Lucene to trigger a merge earlier.

When indexing occurs via `fullTextSession.index()`, `purge()`, or `purgeAll()`, the following properties are used and have the same effect as those discussed previously:

- `hibernate.search.<indexname>.indexwriter.batch.merge_factor`
- `hibernate.search.<indexname>.indexwriter.batch.max_merge_docs`
- `hibernate.search.<indexname>.indexwriter.batch.ram_buffer_size`

Unless the corresponding `.batch` property is explicitly set, the value will default to the `.transaction` property.

Why is there a need for two modes: a transaction mode and a batch mode? During transactional operations (entity insertions, updates, and deletions), you likely want to limit memory consumption to leave more resources for the rest of the system. You also want to limit the response time. Keep the merge factor relatively low to limit the number of concurrent files (segments) opened. In practice, because Hibernate Search batches changes per transaction, segment files tend to be small, and `ram_buffer_size` is rarely attained. During batch mode (that is, when you index or reindex a significant part of your data), you want to maximize memory consumption and limit the number of merges to keep index speed as high as possible. You also want to maximize throughput. Subsequently, you'll run an `optimize()` operation to reduce the number of segments. Unfortunately, there's no magic formula to estimate the best value for each setting. Start with the default values, and run performance tests to find the best strategy for your application.

> **NOTE** To gain a better understanding of how these parameters affect searching and indexing speed, remember these general principles concerning parameters: Search speed is dependent on the number of files (segments) the index is spread across. The larger the segment file count, the slower the search. Indexing speed also is dependent on segment file count but inversely to the way search speed is affected. That is, as search speed goes up, indexing speed goes down, and vice versa. The amount of RAM available also affects these speeds.

By default, Lucene and Hibernate Search store the information on a given segment in a single file. This approach is named *compound file format*. It's possible to store segments differently. The alternative format spreads information of a given segment across multiple files. While this approach requires more files and thus more file handlers, it is faster at indexing time (5 percent to 33 percent depending on the conditions) and requires less temporary storage. To build a compound segment, Lucene creates the individual files and compounds them, temporarily requiring twice the space. If you aren't constrained by the number of concurrent file handlers, you can activate multifile support by using `hibernate.search.<indexname>.indexwriter.use_compound_file = false`. Notice that we didn't use the transactional or batch prefix. While this is possible, it makes little sense to mix compound and noncompound segments.

A couple of additional properties are worth mentioning:

- `hibernate.search.<indexname>.indexwriter.max_field_length`
- `hibernate.search.<indexname>.indexwriter.`
  ↪`transaction.term_index_interval`

`max_field_length` limits the number of terms (words) that will be indexed for a given field. If a property contains more terms than allowed by `max_field_length`, the extra ones are silently ignored and are not indexed. This sounds like bad behavior, but this limit is put in place to avoid receiving `OutOfMemoryException`. If you happen to have properties with large numbers of terms, and you want to index all of them, make sure you adjust this setting so that you won't run into an `OutOfMemoryException`. This setting should not be prefixed by either `transaction` or `batch`. The default value is 10000.

`term_index_interval` is an expert setting that lets you trade memory for faster queries. When this number is low, more memory is consumed but access to a term in the index is faster. When this value is high, less memory is consumed but finding a term in the index is slower. The default value is 128. This means that you can have a maximum of 128 terms to scan before finding the expected one. In large indexes where queries usually involve the same subset of terms (typical of a user-entered query), this setting will have little impact because Lucene will spend more time processing frequency and positional data. On a small index involving numerous uncommon query terms (for example, those generated by a `RangeQuery` or a `WildcardQuery`), looking for terms in the index is a costly operation. This setting can impact performance in this case. It's unlikely that you'll need to tune this property. The configuration can be different between `transaction` and `batch`.

Some additional configurations such as `max_buffered_docs` and `max_buffered_delete_terms` are available but are considered fairly advanced and rarely useful. Refer to the Hibernate Search reference documentation and the Lucene documentation for the latest information.

By default, Hibernate Search uses one Lucene index per entity type. While this default is good enough most of the time, you might need to split your index data into more than one index per entity. Hibernate Search calls this operation *sharding*, and we'll look at it next.

9.4   *Sharding your indexes*

Sharding is the idea of splitting a set of data across multiple physical storage places instead of one while still making data access behave as if there were a single storage place. In the case of Hibernate Search, we split indexed data for a given entity type into several physical Lucene indexes.

NOTE WHAT DOES SHARDING MEAN? The definition of *shard* is "a piece of a broken pot or ceramic or glass vessel." Surely you don't want your data to look like broken pottery. Sharding is a term widely used at Google to describe partitioning (data, CPU, team, bread, and so on). This term seems to be slowly spreading into the data partitioning industry as a whole.

Why would you need to do that? There are several reasons for splitting index data and many reasons for not doing it. The best advice is to avoid sharding altogether unless you need to use it. Generally speaking, Hibernate Search needs to apply a query to multiple indexes at the same time, which tends to slow down queries. In addition, Lucene needs to open more indexes (and more files) at the same time. The warning being given, let's look at the benefits of sharding:

- Working around performance limits
- Enforcing legal or security partitioning
- Increased maintainability

Some people use Lucene indexes as a massive database (they store values in the index) and have found Lucene more efficient for large-scale use when the index data is split into several subindexes. While this is an interesting approach for specific situations, the authors want you to guard against considering Lucene as a database. Lucene is not a database for many reasons (see section 1.4.2). This is not the best use case for sharding.

Another performance-related factor affected by sharding is locking. Every time an index is changed, Lucene requires a global lock. Only one thread can update an index at a given time. As you will see in chapter 10, this can be quite problematic for systems that are heavily written to. Using sharding makes the lock more specific: If Hibernate Search needs to update one shard, it doesn't have to lock the other ones and will push the scalability barrier a bit further. This is particularly applicable if you use in-memory distributed Lucene directories.

Not all use cases are related to performance. For legal or practical reasons, you might have to separate data of a given category from the data of another category (see figure 9.1):

- Data related to different geographical regions (one index per country)
- Data related to different customers (privacy laws)
- Data related to different companies

For reasons the authors have yet to understand, these kinds of physical separations tend to keep lawyers and customers happier, especially in a software as a service environment.

The third reason why sharding might be beneficial is maintenance. Splitting index data among several physical indexes makes each individual index smaller. Copying an

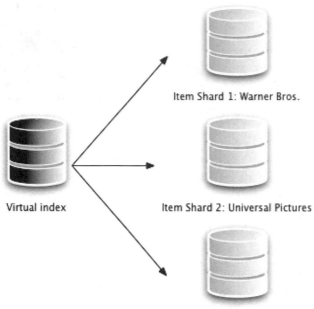

Item Shard 1: Warner Bros.

Virtual index

Item Shard 2: Universal Pictures

Item Shard 3: Sony Pictures

Figure 9.1   Use one physical index per distributor to index items.

index is faster (and thus simpler), and rebuilding an individual index, if needed, is faster as well and does not impact other indexes.

Let's explore the configuration side of sharding.

9.4.1 Configuring sharding

Sharding is disabled by default but can be enabled per entity type. The first step is to determine the number of shards you'll split your data into. The number of shards is a relatively static choice that requires you to restart the Hibernate `SessionFactory` or `EntityManager` when changed and can possibly require reindexing. We recommend that you choose an appropriate value up front.

TIP   Don't use too large a shard number. Reading from multiple shards is slower than reading from a single index.

You can configure the number of shards through the `sharding_strategy.nbr_of_shards` property. This property is defined per index, as shown in listing 9.14.

By default, Hibernate Search will create one Lucence index per shard and name it *index_name.index_nbr*. For example, if you use an `FSDirectoryProvider`, the directory names for `Item` indexes assuming three shards will be:

- `com.manning.hsia.dvdstore.model.Item.0`
- `com.manning.hsia.dvdstore.model.Item.1`
- `com.manning.hsia.dvdstore.model.Item.2`

It's possible to override these defaults and even change the root directory for each shard. Listing 9.14 shows how to do that. Each shard configuration is held under `hibernate.search.`*`index_name.shard_nbr`*. All the configuration properties discussed in section 5.1.1 and earlier in this section can be used on each individual shard.

> **Listing 9.14 Configuring index sharding, placing each shard on its own disk**
>
> ```
> hibernate.search.com.manning.hsia.dvdstore.model.
>   Item.sharding_strategy.nbr_of_shards 3          ◁─── Number of shards
>
> hibernate.search.com.manning.hsia.dvdstore.model.Item.0.indexBase
>   /mnt/shard0/indexes/virtdir0          ◁─── Shard specific property
>
> hibernate.search.com.manning.hsia.dvdstore.model.Item.0.indexName
>   Item0
>
> hibernate.search.com.manning.hsia.dvdstore.model.Item.1.indexBase
>   /mnt/shard1/indexes/virtdir1
>
> hibernate.search.com.manning.hsia.dvdstore.model.Item.1.indexName
>   Item1
>
> hibernate.search.com.manning.hsia.dvdstore.model.Item.2.indexBase
>   /mnt/shard2/indexes/virtdir2
>
> hibernate.search.com.manning.hsia.dvdstore.model.Item.2.indexName
>   Item2
> ```

Overriding defaults can be useful if you wish to store shards on different physical hard drives. Each root directory pointing to each individual hard drive is configured by the `indexBase` property. Running on different physical hard drives has the benefit of reducing contention for input/output and can increase performance. This is heavily dependent on your hardware. If you don't like the default index-naming scheme, you could change the directory names using the `indexName` property suffix.

Sometimes you want to define the same configuration for all shards of a given entity type. You can do just that by using the prefix `hibernate.search.[index_name]` (notice the absence of a shard number). The common property will be available to each shard, just as a property shared across all indexes is placed under `hibernate.search.default`.

Now that we're using several shards, Hibernate Search needs to decide in which shard a new object must be indexed.

9.4.2 *Choosing how to shard your data*

Hibernate Search needs to decide in which shard a given object instance will be indexed. This task belongs to the `IndexShardingStrategy` object. By default, Hibernate Search hashes the string representation of your id and applies to the hash a modulo by the number of shards. This should ensure a fairly even distribution of data entries among all the shards.

This approach likely won't satisfy your needs and has a few drawbacks. For example, adding more shards to an index requires a complete reindexing (because the hash method will no longer return the same shard number for a given id). Fortunately, you can customize how Hibernate Search chooses the right shard by implementing your own `IndexShardingStrategy`. This interface is responsible for returning the shard in which an object has to be indexed and the list of shards to consider when an object has to be removed from the index. Typically, as shown in listing 9.15, a strategy chooses a given shard based on a business property.

Listing 9.15   Implementing a property-based sharding strategy

```
# Configuration file
hibernate.search.com.manning.hsia.dvdstore.model.
➥Item.sharding_strategy.nbr_of_shards 3

hibernate.search.com.manning.hsia.dvdstore.model.
➥Item.0.indexName  Item-Universal          ◄──① Functional sharding

hibernate.search.com.manning.hsia.dvdstore.model.
➥Item.1.indexName Item-Sony

hibernate.search.com.manning.hsia.dvdstore.model.
➥Item.2.indexName  Item-Warner
                                                    ② Sharding strategy
hibernate.search.com.manning.hsia.dvdstore.model.        implementation class
➥Item.sharding_strategy               ◄──┘
    com.manning.hsia.dvdstore.util.DistributorShardingStrategy

hibernate.search.com.manning.hsia.dvdstore.model.Item.
➥sharding_strategy.distributors.1 0
                                                    ③ Properties used
hibernate.search.com.manning.hsia.dvdstore.model.Item.       by the strategy
➥sharding_strategy.distributors.2 1    ◄──┘

hibernate.search.com.manning.hsia.dvdstore.model.Item.
➥sharding_strategy.distributors.3 2

public class DistributorShardingStrategy
        implements IndexShardingStrategy {
    private static final String RADIX = "distributors.";
    private DirectoryProvider<?>[] providers;
    private HashMap<String, Integer> providerIdPerDistributor;

    public void initialize(    ◄── Initialize the strategy
            Properties properties,
            DirectoryProvider<?>[] providers) {     ④ One directory
                                                       provider per shard
        this.providers = providers;        ◄──┘
        this.providerIdPerDistributor =
            new HashMap<String, Integer>();

        //find all properties starting with 'distributors.'
        //the suffix is the distributor id,
        //the value is the shard id
                                            ⑤ Read available
        Enumeration<?> propertyNames =          property names
            properties.propertyNames();    ◄─┘

        while ( propertyNames.hasMoreElements() ) {

            Object key = propertyNames.nextElement();
```

```
        if ( ! String.class.isInstance( key ) ) {
            continue;        ⬅──┐   Work around the poor
        }                    ❻   design of Properties
        String propertyName = (String) key;
        if ( propertyName.startsWith(RADIX) ) {
            String distributorId =
                propertyName.substring(
                    RADIX.length(),
                    propertyName.length() );

            String providerId =
⇒properties.getProperty(propertyName);
            providerIdPerDistributor.put(
                distributorId,
                Integer.parseInt(providerId)
            );
        }
    }
}

public DirectoryProvider<?>[] getDirectoryProvidersForAllShards() {
    return providers;    ⬅──┐  Providers for queries
}                        ❼   and optimize
public DirectoryProvider<?> getDirectoryProviderForAddition(Class<?>
⇒entityType,
        Serializable id, String idInString, Document document) {

    //make sure it is used on the right class
    assert entityType.getName().equals( Item.class.getName() );

    String distributorId =              ❽ Read discriminator
        document.get("distributor.id");  ⬅──┘  from document
    Integer providerIndex =
      providerIdPerDistributor.get( distributorId );

    if ( providerIndex == null ) {
        throw new IllegalArgumentException(
            "Distributor id not found: " + distributorId);
    }

    if ( providerIndex > providers.length ) {   ⬅── Write defensive code
        throw new IllegalArgumentException(
            "Shard " + providerIndex + " does not exists");
    }
                                    ❾ Provider where the
    return providers[providerIndex];   ⬅──┘  document is added
}

public DirectoryProvider<?>[] getDirectoryProvidersForDeletion(
        Class<?> entity, Serializable id, String idInString) {
    return providers;    ⬅──┐  Providers where the
}                        ❿  document is deleted
}
```

❶ Assign a functional subset of the data per shard. ❷ This is the fully qualified class name of the IndexShardingStrategy implementation. ❸ Assign one distributor id to a shard id. You can use the property-naming scheme of your choice. ❹ The initialize method is provided a list of ordered `DirectoryProviders` (one per shard). (**5** Properties can be read. A property name is composed of only its suffix (that is, it excludes `hibernate.search.`*`index_name.shard_nbr.`*). You can access all property names through the `Properties` API. **6** The `Properties` API is neither the most intuitive nor the most type-safe. Be sure to use defensive code. **7** You must return the list of providers on which queries (or the optimize operations) are run, usually the full list of providers. **8** `Documents` can be used as a payload to pass the discriminator value (in our case the distributor id). **9** Return the `DirectoryProvider` the document will be added to. **10** Return the list of providers an entity deletion will be applied to, generally all the providers because the strategy usually doesn't have enough information to restrict the list further.

When Hibernate Search indexes an object, it lets the strategy determine which directory provider to use (see figure 9.2). In our case, this choice is driven by configuration.

Make sure you embed in the document the field or fields on which you want to base your shard strategy. Unfortunately, Hibernate Search cannot pass around the entity instance; that would prevent Hibernate Search from playing nicely in a clustered environment, as we will show in chapter 10. This isn't a problem, because the `Document` instance will help you carry on the information.

The delete operation is applied to all `DirectoryProviders` returned by the `get-DirectoryProvidersForDeletion()` method. A safe implementation returns all shards (because of the lack of knowledge). But if your implementation knows where a given object is indexed, it's preferable to return the specific directory provider (or a subset of directory providers) to speed up the delete operation (see figure 9.3).

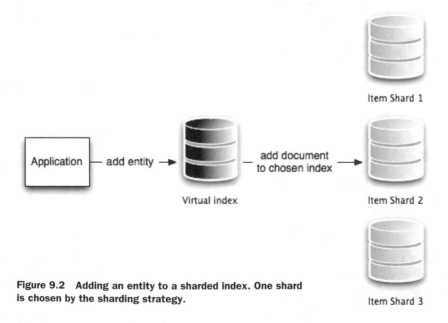

Figure 9.2 Adding an entity to a sharded index. One shard is chosen by the sharding strategy.

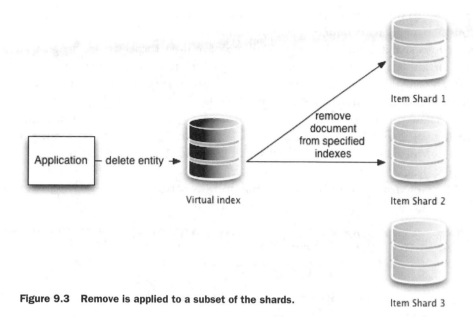

Figure 9.3   Remove is applied to a subset of the shards.

When querying, Hibernate Search applies the Lucene query on all `DirectoryProviders` returned by `getDirectoryProvidersForAllShards()` (see figure 9.4). This is also the list of directory providers on which optimization is applied.

Sharding in Hibernate Search suffers from one main drawback. It's not possible to create shards on the fly. The number of shards must be defined at configuration time and their respective `DirectoryProviders` configured. It's preferable to shard by a set of properties whose value set is fairly small and evolves in a controlled manner. Also

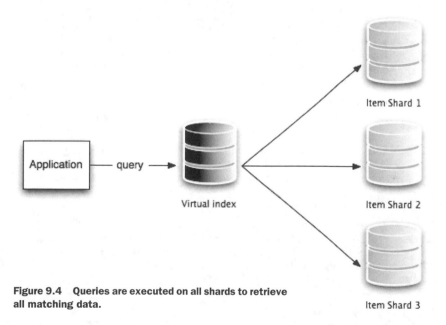

Figure 9.4   Queries are executed on all shards to retrieve all matching data.

make sure your strategy can add new shards over time. A sharding strategy based on a business property can meet these constraints. A new value will be indexed in a new (or existing) shard, but existing values still point to their respective existing shard. This is important because it doesn't require that you reindex everything when a new shard is added. The default hash implementation doesn't satisfy this criteria and requires complete reindexing when new shards are added.

When you need to add a new shard, you must change the configuration (see listing 9.15) and build a new `SessionFactory` or `EntityManagerFactory` to ensure the new properties are used. It's possible to avoid this explicit change and reloading by creating enough shards to absorb the load and by using a sharding strategy that's both stable for existing values and able to transparently compute a shard id for new values. Listing 9.16 is an example of such a strategy.

Listing 9.16 A sharding strategy that can absorb new shards transparently

```
public class AutomaticDistributorShardingStrategy implements
        IndexShardingStrategy {

   private DirectoryProvider<?>[] providers;
   private int shardNbr;

   public void initialize(Properties properties,
      DirectoryProvider<?>[] providers) {
         this.providers = providers;
         this.shardNbr = Integer.parseInt(
            properties.getProperty( "nbr_of_shards" ) );
   }

   public DirectoryProvider<?>[] getDirectoryProvidersForAllShards() {
         return providers;
   }

   public DirectoryProvider<?> getDirectoryProviderForAddition(
      Class<?> entityType, Serializable id,
      String idInString, Document document) {
         assert entityType.getName().equals(            ⟵─┐ Ensure correct
            Item.class.getName() );                          class is used

         String distributorId = document.get( "distributor.id" );
         int providerIndex =                         ❶ Automatically build
            Integer.parseInt(distributorId) - 1;    ⟵─┘ shard number

         if (providerIndex < shardNbr) {  ⟵──❷ Ensure we never go over
            throw new IllegalShardException(
      "The number of distributor are higher than available shards");
         }
         return providers[providerIndex];
   }

   public DirectoryProvider<?>[] getDirectoryProvidersForDeletion(
      Class<?> entity, Serializable id, String idInString) {
         return providers;
   }
}
```

An automatic rule builds the shard number from the distributor id. This rule is stable and doesn't change over time ❶. The total number of shards must be high enough to avoid out-of-bounds settings ❷.

Sharding is an advanced concept that's useful in specific scenarios. This approach can be quite hard to handle, and some subtle bugs can occur in the sharding strategy. Don't jump too early to such a design, and make sure you have a compelling reason before sharding your index.

In this chapter, the authors have insisted on not doing premature optimization. One of the key tools for avoiding premature optimization and for ensuring that an optimization doesn't break things is testing. This is the focus of the next section.

9.5 *Testing your Hibernate Search application*

Testing has become an essential part of development. However, the more frameworks and libraries your application uses, the harder it usually becomes to test parts of the application in isolation. In this chapter we'll explore various techniques for testing the behavior of your application once you decide to use Hibernate Search. Your choice will depend on your goals and to a great extent your testing philosophy. We'll also explore testing as a tool for measuring performance. Finally we'll look at how your search engine reacts to real users.

9.5.1 *Mocking Hibernate Search*

Unit testing ensures that individual pieces of software behave as expected. Their contract is tested individually. Depending on the design of your code, this kind of test can be achieved with a limited amount of pain by using a mock approach. Mocking is the idea of simulating objects by mimicking the behavior a real implementation would do in a particular environment. The Hibernate Search API (querying, indexing) consists of interfaces and can be easily mocked either manually or by using mock libraries such as EasyMock (http://www.easymock.org/).

For Hibernate Search, you'd typically mock the FullTextSession and FullText-Query APIs in a given test. The tested class will call both the FullTextSession and FullTextQuery APIs and receive the results from the mock object. This isolates the tested class from the Hibernate Search library. Listing 9.17 shows an example of Hibernate Search mocking in a unit test.

Listing 9.17 Mocking Hibernate Search in unit tests

```
import static org.easymock.EasyMock.*;          ⟵┐ Static imports make
                                                    EasyMock easier
...

@Test(groups="hibernatesearch")                       Create raw service
public void testSearch() throws Exception {           implementation to
                                                          be tested
    SearchingAction action = new SearchingActionImpl();   ⟵┐ Create mock
                                                            for each
    FullTextQuery query = createMock( FullTextQuery.class );  ⟵┘ object used
    FullTextSession session = createMock( FullTextSession.class );
```

```
SearchFactory factory = createMock( SearchFactory.class );      | Define how
expect( session.getSearchFactory() ).andReturn( factory );  ◁  | SearchFactory
expect( factory.getAnalyzer( Item.class ) )                    | is called
            .andReturn( new StandardAnalyzer() );  ◁─  and the expected
expect( session.createFullTextQuery(                               results
                 isA( Query.class ),
                 eq( Item.class ) )  ◁─ 
       ).andReturn( query );                  Potentially restrict
expect( query.setProjection( "title" ) )      input parameters
     .andReturn( query );  ◁─  Should call projection and return self

List<Object[]> results = new ArrayList<Object[]>();  ◁─ Build query results
results.add( new Object[] {"The Incredibles"} );
expect( query.list() ).andReturn( results );  ◁─ 
                                            Associate them to
                                            query execution

SessionHolder.setFullTextSession( session );  ◁─
                                            Pass mock objects to
replay( factory );  ◁─  Prepare mocks for   the service
replay( query );        listening
replay( session );
                                                        Service
List<String> titles = action.                           executed
    getTitleFromMatchingItems("title:incredibles");  ◁─ using mocks

assert 1 == titles.size()  ◁── Check results based on mock
    : "should have two match, not " + titles.size();
assert "The incredibles".equals( titles.get(0) ) : "The Incredibles";
}
```

Mocking a service requires the following steps:

1 Create mocks for all objects used by the service you want to test.

2 Define expected calls on the various interfaces and the objects that will be returned by the mock implementation. This is where you ensure that the Hibernate Search API is used properly (for example, that projection is called on the right property). This is also where you define fake results. This part is a bit tedious and can go very deep in the service stack; you might end up mocking a lot of services.

3 Pass the mock objects to the service. If you use inversion of control, this will be as simple as calling the appropriate constructors or setters from your service.

4 Activate mock objects. They will listen to specific actions and ensure everything is used as expected or raise assertion failures otherwise.

5 Execute the service. Mock objects will be called by the service.

6 Test the service results. Part of the contract is tested by the mock objects (the right methods called with expected parameters and so on), but you can assert the service output too.

In the authors' opinion, mocking is not always the best approach. It typically requires a significant amount of extra work and a deep knowledge of the library you're mocking, and it doesn't replace adequate integration tests. EasyMock isn't easy for someone new to mocking to use, and error reports are quite confusing, but this library is very flexible.

9.5.2 *Testing with an in-memory index and database*

Unit tests and integration tests are complementary tools that cover slightly different aspects of the application. Beyond the philosophical difference between a unit test and an integration test, the key differences between a test suite that people run and a test suite that people don't run are speed and ease of configuration (zero configuration being ideal). While some teams mandate running test suites before committing and back that up with a continuous integration tool, most don't. If the test suite is too slow or doesn't work right out of the box, developers well known for their laziness (a quality in most cases) will simply skip it and commit broken code.

It's possible to do integration testing with Hibernate and Hibernate Search while keeping speed up and configuration low. By using an in-memory database like:

- H2 (http://h2database.org)
- HSQLDB (http://hsqldb.org)
- Derby (http://db.apache.org/derby)

you can get away with the heavy configuration of a (remote) database, and execution speed is very fast.

TIP   On versions tested by the authors, Derby is significantly slower than the other two at executing DDL statements (schema and table creation). This is problematic for unit tests because most of them start with a schema drop and creation. Derby is significantly faster than an external database though.

Hibernate shields you from the database differences for the most part by switching dialects. In the same spirit, instead of using a filesystem-based Lucene directory provider, use the in-memory directory provider when testing. In this approach, tests are isolated from one another; a different database instance and a different Lucene directory instance are created for each test. Before each test, you should populate the database and the index with the data you need to run. You have essentially two approaches:

- Run SQL statements using import.sql and manually index the data inserted. Hibernate Core executes all statements placed in the file named import.sql, but remember that this file must contain database-specific SQL.
- Create new objects and persist them through Hibernate. Both the database and the index will be populated.

To run SQL statements, you can create an /import.sql file in your classpath that contains the various SQL insert statements that initialize the database. Hibernate Core will execute them when the `SessionFactory` is created. Alternatively, you can use tools like DbUnit to define your SQL statements for each test. DbUnit is a JUnit extension that lets you put a database into a known state before running your tests and lets you assert the database state after the test has run. You can find more information at http://www.dbunit.org. When your database is initialized, don't forget to manually index data in Lucene, as we've shown in section 5.4.2. Otherwise, your index will be outdated or simply empty.

Alternatively, you can create an object graph at the beginning of your test and persist it using the Hibernate Core APIs. Both the database and the index will be properly initialized. With your database in a known state, you can start testing.

The authors tend to use the latter approach. Hibernate Search handles object indexing for you, the data population process is independent of the underlying database and database schema (thanks to Hibernate), and a change in the data structure will be adjusted quickly in your IDE (class refactoring) rather than being manually tracked.

Listing 9.18 shows an integration test and its configuration. We use TestNG in this example, but the principles can easily be applied to JUnit or your favorite unit test framework. Make sure you place H2 and TestNG in your classpath.

Listing 9.18   Running the test suite in memory

```
<hibernate-configuration>
 <session-factory>
   <!-- database configuration -->
   <property name="hibernate.connection.driver_class"
➥>org.h2.Driver</property>
   <property name="hibernate.connection.url"              In-memory
➥>jdbc:h2:mem:</property>                                 database instance
   <property name="hibernate.dialect"
➥>org.hibernate.dialect.H2Dialect</property>
   <property name="hibernate.connection.pool_size">1</property>

   <!-- regenerate DDL -->
   <property name="hibernate.hbm2ddl.auto"                Generate schema
➥>create-drop</property>                                 every time

   <!-- in-memory index -->
   <property name="hibernate.search.default.directory_provider">
org.hibernate.search.store.RAMDirectoryProvider          In-memory Lucene
   </property>                                            directories

   <mapping class="com.manning.hsia.dvdstore.model.Item"/>
   <mapping class="com.manning.hsia.dvdstore.model.Distributor"/>
   <mapping class="com.manning.hsia.dvdstore.model.Category"/>
 </session-factory>
</hibernate-configuration>

public class HibernateSearchIntegrationTest {

    protected SessionFactory factory;
                                                          Executed before
    @BeforeTest(groups={"hibernatesearch"})              every test
    protected void setUp() throws Exception {
        AnnotationConfiguration configuration =
            new AnnotationConfiguration();
```

```
        factory = configuration                          Build the
            .configure( "hibernate-test.cfg.xml" )       session factory
            .buildSessionFactory();
        postSetUp();              ◄─┐   Run post
    }                                 initialization
    @AfterTest(groups={"hibernatesearch"})
    protected void tearDown() throws Exception {    ❶  Clear the factory
        factory.close();                            ◄─┘    after every test
    }

    public void postSetUp() throws Exception {      ◄─┐
        Distributor distributor = new Distributor();  │ Populate the database
        distributor.setName( "Manning Video" );         before each test
        distributor.setStockName( "MAN" );

        Item item = new Item();
        item.setTitle( "Hibernate Search in Action" );
        item.setEan( "1234567890123" );
        item.setDescription(
          "Video version of HSiA, go through tutorials." );
        item.setPrice( new BigDecimal(20) );
        item.setDistributor( distributor );

        Session session = factory.openSession();
        session.getTransaction().begin();
        session.persist( distributor );
        session.persist( item );                Database and indexes
        session.getTransaction().commit();   ◄─┘ are populated
        session.close();
    }
                                      Actual test
    @Test(groups="hibernatesearch")   ◄─┐
    public void testSearch() throws Exception {

        SearchingAction action = getSearchingAction();

        List<String> titles =                    Run test on
            action.getTitleFromMatchingItems(  ◄─┘ prepopulated dataset
                "title:search" );
                                    Assert results based
        assert 1 == titles.size()  ◄─┘ on the dataset
            : "should have one match, not " +.size();
        assert "Hibernate Search in Action"
                .equals( titles.get(0) ) :
            "right book matches";
    }
}
```

Because the SessionFactory ❶ is closed, the in-memory database and Lucene in-memory indexes are discarded. Each test runs with a clear data set.

In a project, you'll likely factor out the setUp() and tearDown() methods in an abstract test case. Each concrete test case will then override postSetUp() to populate the data as needed for each test case. This test suite executes fast (no input/output is performed), each test is isolated from the other, and the whole chain is effectively tested (Hibernate, Hibernate Search, Lucene).

Unit or integration testing is one thing, but you also need to test in an environment that's close to production, which we'll discuss next.

9.5.3   *Performance testing*

Performance testing is important for guaranteeing a level of service to customers and avoiding last-minute surprises when you're about to launch a new application. There's nothing really specific about performance testing with Lucene and Hibernate Search, but the performance of a search engine is usually closely watched. People are particularly sensitive to speed in this area.

This section is a simple collection of generic advice on the subject. When you're about to prepare a benchmark, make sure you use the same hardware and software the application will run on in production. If you cannot, try to match them as closely as possible. Especially watch the following factors:

- *Use the same database version.*   Optimizers have surprising changes between versions.
- *Use the same server topology (remote or local database, shared filesystem, and cluster of application servers).*   Testing Hibernate Search performance on a local filesystem directory and deploying in production on a network file system directory is a bad idea. The system will behave differently.
- *Use a similar network.*   Network performance has a strong impact on database and Lucene index access times.

When running a performance test, be sure to disable logs, or at least run them at the level they will be in production. Unless you use an asynchronous log appender, logs can become the bottleneck in a system. If you identify a bottleneck, you can then enable logs to refine your measurements.

Test on realistic use cases, and measure as thoroughly as possible (time, CPU, memory, network, and so on) in a repeatable way. Ideally, rerun a typical day for your application. A number of functional focused testing tools are available. Selenium (http://selenium.openqa.org) is one of them. When measuring speed, check the targeted use case in isolation (for minimal response time) and under stress (at the expected peak of concurrent users). Running use cases under stress is very important and shows how the system degrades under pressure. Tools like Apache JMeter (http://jakarta.apache.org/jmeter) let you run the same set of requests and simulate concurrent users.

When you change a setting or apply one of the tips from this chapter, run the same tests on the same bench and measure the differences. Brilliant optimizations on paper don't always materialize in the real world.

9.5.4   *Testing users*

In a whole different category, don't forget to test how users react to your search engine. Simply by logging searches of given users, their subsequent searches on the same subject, and which information they ended up clicking on, you'll receive golden feedback, such as:

- What people are looking for on your search engine
- What query they initially used to find that information
- What workaround they end up using

Design such reporting tools for your search engine, and activate them on a regular basis. Look at these logs, and incrementally improve your search engine by adjusting its variables, such as:

- Creating a list of stop words
- Setting the boost factors of various properties
- Activating or deactivating synonymous or approximation analyzers

Repeat this analysis regularly, because people change and their search patterns do too.

Remember that users don't always do what they tell you they do. Interviewing users to define an initial set of rules for the search engine is a good start, but you'll need to refine this data with real-life feedback. Although your search engine might return query results a bit too slowly, it might nevertheless bring the relevant information to the top each time. This will make your users more productive.

9.6   *Summary*

This chapter showed you how to optimize Hibernate Search. First, we looked at the indexing operation, whether for an individual entity, applied concurrently in an online system, or batched with many other indexing operations. We also looked at how to make fast queries by using both Hibernate Search and Lucene tricks. We examined various levels of caching that Hibernate Search uses. Finally, we looked at the Lucene index structure and at ways to keep this structure optimal for the system, either manually or transparently. We also looked at sharding, which helps you split indexing data across several physical Lucene indexes, for either performance, legal, or maintenance reasons. While sharding should not be overused, it can be quite handy in some situations. Finally we explored how to test Hibernate Search. There's no way to optimize a system without a reliable test environment.

The next chapter focuses on Hibernate Search scalability and how to make its search infrastructure scale a cluster of servers.

Scalability: using Hibernate Search in a cluster

This chapter covers

- Strategies for clustering Hibernate Search solutions
- Details of taking the asynchronous approach
- Configuring the slave nodes
- Configuring the master node

Most of the book pays little attention to your application architecture because Hibernate Search is fairly agnostic in that regard. Clustering a Hibernate Search application is worth mentioning because Hibernate Search makes it very easy to do. (You will especially see how easy if you've previously tried to cluster a plain Lucene application!)

When building an application, always keep in mind how well it will scale in the future, if not the present. The two traditional scalability possibilities are to scale up and to scale out. These days, emphasis is on the ability to scale out, and for good reasons. The good old days of doubling performances by increasing the CPU clock are over. Traditional big machines have been replaced by clusters of cheap commodity hardware. Even inside each machine, the war for scaling up is getting lost: Each CPU nowadays is made of two or more cores, sort of mini-independent CPUs. Every application needs to be able to scale out. This chapter describes how applications that use Hibernate Search can scale out.

10.1 Exploring clustering approaches

Out of the box, Lucene offers no special clustering facilities or capabilities. Every serious application using Lucene needs to tackle the problem of clustering. Trust the authors—it can become very complex! Several libraries built on top of Lucene are trying to make clustering easier. Hibernate Search is one of them.

Fundamentally, we have two different ways of clustering a Lucene application. The first one is to let every node in your cluster read and write the index. A pessimistic lock is used to ensure that only one node at a time updates the Lucene index. As you will see, this approach is not that easy to implement and suffers from a fundamental limit. A global pessimistic lock must be shared across all nodes in a cluster that are willing to update a given Lucene `Directory`. This will limit the scalability of your system. The second approach is to process all index-writing operations on a dedicated node (or subset of nodes) and periodically push the information to the nonwriting nodes (either by replicating the index state or by sharing it).

10.1.1 Synchronous clustering

The classic approach for clustering a Lucene application is to share the same Lucene directory or directories among all nodes. Each node can read and write on the shared index. To prevent index corruption, Lucene uses a pessimistic lock, which is acquired when an index is updated. At a given time, only one node can update a given index.

> **NOTE** Concurrent changes can be applied if they belong to different Lucene indexes. If you follow the Hibernate Search default approach, one global lock per entity type is present, and concurrent changes to two different entity types are possible.

Other nodes must wait for the lock. Figure 10.1 shows this problem. If you use a file-system directory provider, the lock is materialized as a lock file. Of course, the index storage must be shared among several nodes, usually on some NFS. Unfortunately, this approach suffers from problems:

- Some NFS implementations cache directory contents for faster file discovery with the assumption that the directory content doesn't change very often and that immediate visibility isn't a concern. Unfortunately, Lucene relies (partially) on an accurate listing of files.
- Some NFS implementations don't implement the "delete on last close" semantic, which is needed by Lucene.

While the situation is much better than it was back in the days of Lucene 1.4, implementing concurrent index writers on an NFS is still quite complex, and bugs in this area show up regularly depending on your NFS client/server configuration. This work in progress is known as the *NFS saga* in the Lucene community. If you go that route, be sure to read the abundant literature on the subject and pay particular attention to lock exceptions during your performance and stress tests.

Some libraries such as Compass propose a database-backed Lucene `Directory`. The index and its lock are stored in a specific set of tables in a database. Databases are known for implementing a good locking scheme, making them less likely to run into the problems encountered by NFS. Unfortunately, this approach suffers from flaws as well:

- *In most implementations blobs are used to represent segment files.* Blobs are well known for not being the fastest structure in a database. This is particularly true of MySQL, which cannot consider a blob as a stream and loads the entire data flow into client memory.

- *A pessimistic lock must be shared among all read-write nodes.* Under intensive write sessions, most nodes will wait for the lock to transform the clustered application into a gigantic nonconcurrent system. The more nodes present, the higher the risk to hit the scalability limit, because more nodes are competing for the single lock.

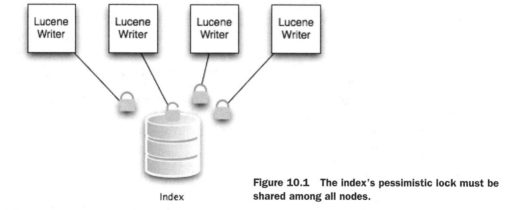

Figure 10.1   The index's pessimistic lock must be shared among all nodes.

An in-memory distributed Lucene `Directory` is another interesting approach that uses the synchronous pessimistic lock solution. You can find a few providers: Giga-Space, JBoss Cache, and Terracotta are all distributed data solutions that support clustering of Lucene directories. You can easily write a Hibernate Search `DirectoryProvider` implementation that wraps any of these solutions. Generally speaking, these solutions do several things:

- They keep a map that represents the current list of Lucene directories locked and guarantee that only one node can acquire a directory lock at a given time cluster-wide.
- They distribute the index content across the cluster.
- If a directory is too big to fit in memory, only part of the content is retrieved from the grid. Some kind of garbage collection ensures that only the latest-used content is kept in local memory for a given node.

This approach still suffers from the theoretical pessimistic lock limit, but advocates have reported good performance and scalability, especially when indexes are sharded. Sharding helps to push the scalability limit a bit further. While it's true that a cluster-wide lock needs to be acquired when updating a Lucene index, you can make smaller indexes. By sharding your indexes, you effectively need a finer-grained lock when updating data. The sharding strategy will acquire locks on only the impacted shards; concurrent nodes will be able to update other shards of the index. On big indexes, the in-memory approach will require more network traffic to load parts of the index that didn't fit in memory. Likewise, filesystem-based approaches require more disk input/output. This book won't cover the configuration details of using an in-memory approach. Check the documentation of the data-clustering project you're interested in.

Note that in production, file-based Lucene indexes are by far the most commonly used deployment mode.

Full-text searching a data grid

JBoss Cache, aside from storing the Lucene directory in memory in a cluster, has an interesting additional feature.

You can combine Hibernate Search and JBoss Cache to enable full-text search capabilities on JBoss Cache distributed objects. A JBoss Cache module named `JBoss-CacheSearchable` has the ability to index and search Java objects stored in JBoss Cache. It uses Hibernate Search to index objects when they are added, updated, or removed from the cache. By reusing the same Hibernate Search mapping annotations, you can make your cached object full-text searchable. Check out the `JBoss-CacheSearchable` project at http://www.jboss.org/jbosscache (the current documentation lives in http://www.jboss.org/community/docs/DOC-10286).

The synchronous approach has the benefit of propagating changes immediately to all nodes. It works best on:

- Small and medium-size indexes (especially if you use the in-memory approach) because network traffic will be needed to retrieve the index.
- Low– to moderate–write-intensive applications. Pessimistic locks still have to be acquired cluster-wise.

The index size depends on a lot of factors, including the amount of RAM you dedicate to indexes. Try it in your environment. You can use Hibernate Search in a synchronized approach by configuring the `DirectoryProvider` on each Hibernate Search node to point to the same physical index storage. However, Hibernate Search comes with an interesting alternative solution.

10.1.2 *Asynchronous clustering*

Hibernate Search is fairly agnostic with regard to your architecture. The software is flexible and extensible enough to support a variety of clustering solutions. The ability to write your own `DirectoryProvider` (see section 5.1.5) gives you the freedom to decide how Lucene indexes are shared among different nodes in the cluster (physically sharing the same location, replicated across all nodes, and so on). A second extension point gives you the ability to customize the backend of Hibernate Search (see section 5.3.4). The backend is responsible for taking a list of indexing operations and performing them. Instead of writing straight to the Lucene index, an implementation could use JGroups (the communication library) to delegate the work to a third-party machine.

That being said, Hibernate Search doesn't leave you alone in this ocean of flexibility. One approach is provided to you out of the box and is promoted by the Hibernate Search team. This approach is an answer to the pessimistic lock problem and its scalability issues. This architecture is shown in figure 10.2.

A single node is responsible for writing in the Lucene index or indexes and pushes changes to all other nodes on a regular basis. This node is named the *master* in the Hibernate Search terminology. The other nodes (known as *slaves*) execute their full-text queries on a local copy of the index and push their changes to a shared queue instead of applying them to their local Lucene indexes. The shared queue is exclusively processed by the master. This approach (one master, many slaves) has quite a few advantages:

- You no longer have to deal with NFS lock madness. The pessimistic lock is no longer shared but used exclusively by the master.
- Slaves that usually host the main application are no longer waiting on the index lock. We've just freed scalability for our application. You can now align many slave nodes without problem.
- Slaves execute their full-text queries on a local copy of the index, keeping performance high and independent of the network. A temporary glitch won't affect the ability to answer full-text queries.
- Resource consumption (CPU, memory, I/O) on slave nodes is lower because indexing is delegated to the master.

Let's have a look at this approach in a more detailed way.

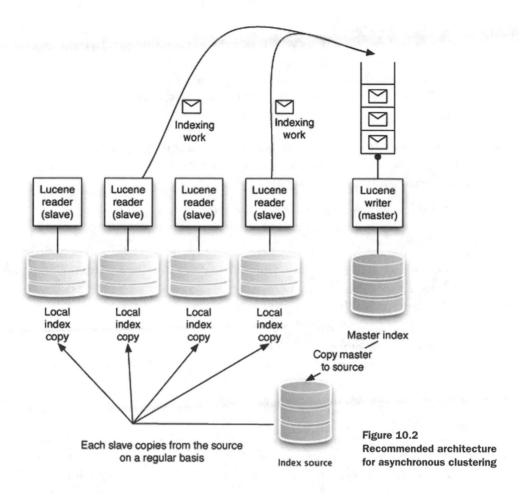

Figure 10.2
Recommended architecture
for asynchronous clustering

ANATOMY OF A SLAVE NODE

A slave node behaves and is in many ways just like a regular Hibernate Search application. The slave node collects all changes applied to indexed entities per transaction. It transforms the entity into its Lucene-friendly structure (a Document object). It executes full-text queries by opening a Lucene index (or indexes).

However, instead of sharing the same Lucene index location with all other nodes, a slave keeps a local copy of the index. Having a local copy guarantees faster query response time (compared to an NFS solution) and ensures that a slave can serve full-text queries autonomously. At regular intervals, a slave node obtains a copy of the master node index from a shared location. Remember, the slave doesn't apply changes to its local index; it passes the work list to the master. The master applies the changes to the Lucene index.

Because of this asynchronous approach, there's a delay between the time an element is changed in the database and the time it's reflected by full-text queries. This delay can be configured, as you will see later in this chapter (it defaults to one hour), and is the only real drawback of this asynchronous technique. In most applications, a small delay (30 minutes) is perfectly acceptable for their search engine. As a matter of fact, many applications update their indexes only once a day. The operation that copies indexes from the master to a shared location, as well at the operation that copies indexes from the shared location to each slave node, is smart (or at least not too stupid); only files that have changed are copied over the network. Because Lucene creates new files when it indexes new elements, most incremental copying will be quite minimal. Also, it's worth noting that copies are done asynchronously; your application is not impacted by the current index copy.

TIP   When you optimize an index, the whole structure is shuffled. A copy of a recently optimized index will take longer than a regular incremental copy.

How does the slave pass the list of changes to the master? Instead of applying the list of changes to the Lucene index itself, a slave delegates this work to the master. A slave sends its work list to a JMS queue. Sending the list of changes to JMS (for consumption by the master node) has a couple of benefits:

- Once the list of work is sent to JMS, the slave node is fully available to execute services for the rest of the application.
- The Lucene pessimistic lock acquisition is no longer connected to the slave operations. You can add many slave nodes to your architecture without facing the scalability problem the pessimistic lock acquisition causes in a synchronous approach.

As you may recall from section 5.3.3, Hibernate Search can enable asynchronous mode inside a single VM. This approach helps to reduce the bonds between the application's main processes and the pessimistic lock acquisition but is inherently limited:

- The VM is still responsible for indexing data into Lucene. This consumes resources from the main application.
- To limit the risks of receiving an OutOfMemoryException, the asynchronous queue has to be limited. When the limit is reached, subsequent indexing is done synchronously until the queue resorbs.

These limitations are not present in an inter-VM asynchronous mode like JMS. Especially there is no risk of OutOfMemoryException errors.

Why did the Hibernate Search team choose JMS over another message service? JMS is an easily accessible standard that's widely adopted and has rock-solid implementations on the market, both proprietary and open source. It's quite easy to introduce it in an organization. Depending on your JMS provider configuration, JMS provides interesting features such as guaranteed delivery, message persistence, transactional support, and so on. If your architecture cannot use JMS, replacing the inter-VM asynchronous mechanism in Hibernate Search is quite easy. On the slave side, two classes are responsible for JMS delivery, currently totalling less than 200 lines of code (import and comments included). Rewriting this part of the code is not an insurmountable task. If you do so, please consider contributing it to the Hibernate Search project!

Slaves have smartly delegated the hard work to the master. Let's have a look at this poor soul.

ANATOMY OF A MASTER NODE

The master node is responsible for updating the Lucene index or indexes and for pushing updated versions of these indexes on a regular basis. In that regard, the master is the only VM that locks the index. All the problems that we'd face by using a filesystem Lucene `Directory` stored on an NFS are gone.

The master listens to the JMS queue through a message-driven bean (MDB), processes each indexing work list (one work list per message), and applies the work to the Lucene index or indexes.

On a regular basis, the master node copies the index onto a shared location, the location where slaves grab the latest version of the index. The copy is usually done with the same frequency as the slave copy (it defaults to one per hour). Note that during the copy operation, the master suspends the indexing operation (for this particular index directory) to prevent any corruption and ensure that a consistent index is copied. Future versions of Hibernate Search will likely lift this limitation.

What's going on if the master node crashes? After all, it looks a lot like a single point of failure in our system. The first thing to notice is that if the master node fails, slave nodes continue to serve full-text queries and push changes that need indexing. For them, it's almost business as usual. The only different is that changes are no longer pushed back to the local index copy. If the master node crashes in the middle of an indexing process, the JMS message corresponding to the indexing work list is rolled back to the queue (more precisely, it's never considered consumed). When the node is brought back online, the same message is reprocessed, and your system quickly catches up. Because there is no true update in Lucene (updates are really deletes followed by inserts), it's safe to run the same set of operations multiple times. If you think that keeping a master node down for too long is a problem in your application, you can prepare a second master node and keep it inactive. For example, the passive master might not listen to the work queue. If your active master node goes down and cannot be brought back online, simply activate the passive node by making it listen to the JMS work queue. Make sure the old active node doesn't go back online (or at least turn it passive by making it no longer listen to the queue).

The master node is really stateless in that regard. What happens if the index directory gets corrupted for whatever reason? You can reindex your data offline using the technique described at section 5.4.2. Place the newly reindexed structure on the master node, and reactivate the JMS queue consumption.

VARIATIONS

While Hibernate Search provides this asynchronous architecture proposal out of the box, nothing prevents you from adjusting it to your needs. Hibernate Search provides the necessary hooks to do just that.

As mentioned before, you can replace the asynchronous mechanism to best suit your needs. If JMS is not your cup of tea, you can implement a `BackendQueueProcessorFactory` (and its `Runnable` companion) and configure it as described in section 5.3.4.

The way Lucene indexes are stored is also customizable if necessary. Perhaps the idea of copying index structures onto every node isn't the strategy you have in mind. You can very well implement you own `DirectoryProvider` object that shares the `Directory` structure on the same physical storage for all slaves (see figure 10.3). While searches might be slower because of the remote I/O cost, you save quite a lot of storage and make slave nodes truly stateless.

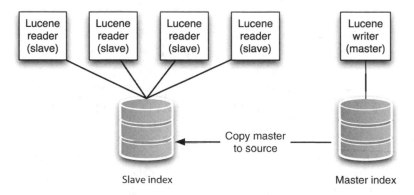

Figure 10.3   Variant where slaves share the same read-only copy of the index

Alternatively, you could consider sharing the read-only version of the index through an in-memory distributed cache such as GigaSpace, Terracotta, or JBoss Cache. All that is required is writing a custom `DirectoryProvider`.

You should have a pretty good understanding of how clustering works in Hibernate Search. Now let's see how to configure it.

10.2   *Configuring slave nodes*

The next two sections will guide you through the configuration of the slave and master nodes. We've chosen to show the configuration using JBoss Application Server (AS) 5, but most of the process is fairly standard Java EE configuration. Refer to your application server or JMS provider for more information. Figure 10.4 describes the network topology we'll use in this configuration example.

We'll now walk through the configuration of a slave node. The first step is to enable the JMS backend in the slave configuration.

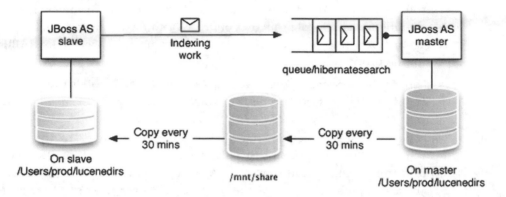

Figure 10.4 Topology of the JMS-based master/slave example

10.2.1 *Preparing the backend*

Slaves send the list of work to a unique JMS queue. Our first step is to configure Hibernate Search to send messages to the right queue using the right JNDI initial context. Let's check the configuration described in listing 10.1.

Listing 10.1 Send message to the right queue

```
<persistence-unit name="dvdstore-catalog">
    <jta-data-source>java:/DefaultDS</jta-data-source>
    <properties>
        <!-- regular Hibernate Core configuration -->
        <property name="hibernate.dialect"
        value="org.hibernate.dialect.H2Dialect"/>
        <property name="hibernate.hbm2ddl.auto" value="create-drop"/>

        <!-- Hibernate Search configuration -->
        <!-- JMS backend -->
        <property name="hibernate.search.worker.backend"
                  value="jms"/>
        <property name="hibernate.search.worker.jndi.url"
                  value="jnp://master:1099"/>
        <property name="hibernate.search.worker.jms.connection_factory"
                  value="/ConnectionFactory"/>
        <property name="hibernate.search.worker.jms.queue"
                  value="queue/hibernatesearch"/>
    </properties>
</persistence-unit>
```

❶ Use the JMS backend

❷ JNDI URL the queue is looked up

❸ Connection factory JNDI name

❹ JMS queue JNDI name

Select the `jms` backend ❶ rather than the default `lucene`. Point to the URL the master JNDI URL is available to ❷. The port can be configured in conf/jboss-service.xml in the master server configuration. Define the JMS `ConnectionFactory` JNDI name ❸. In JBoss AS 5, the connection factory names can be configured in deploy/messaging/connection-factories-service.xml. Configure the JNDI name of the queue the work list will be pushed to ❹. This queue is shared among slaves and master as a communication point.

In some environments (for example, in a plain Java SE environment), you might need to configure additional properties of the JNDI context above what has been done in listing 10.1. You can pass the JNDI factory class name as well as the JNDI URL using the following properties:

- `hibernate.search.worker.jndi.class`, which corresponds to the `java.naming.factory.initial` property (typically `org.jnp.interfaces.NamingContextFactory`).
- `hibernate.search.worker.jndi.url`, which corresponds to the `java.naming.provider.url` property (typically `jnp://server:1099` in JBoss AS). The port can be changed in your JBoss AS server configuration directory in `conf/jboss-service.xml` (check the `org.jboss.naming.NamingService` MBean configuration).

Beyond these default properties, you can pass any property to the JNDI `InitialContext` object by concatenating the property name after `hibernate.search.worker.jndi`. For example, to set `java.naming.factory.url` and pass it to the `InitialContext` object, use the following syntax:

```
# Pass java.naming.factory.url to the InitialContext object
hibernate.search.worker.jndi.java.naming.factory.url
➥ org.jboss.naming:org.jnp.interfaces
```

The approach shown in listing 10.1 sends messages to the queue by connecting to the server queue directly. You can set up more sophisticated approaches that involve sending the message to a local queue and then have the JMS provider bridge messages to the server queue transparently. This more sophisticated approach is recommended to ensure that slave nodes can work even if the master node goes down. The configuration for this solution is dependent on your JMS provider and is beyond the scope of this book. Please refer to your JMS provider documentation for more information.

> ### Running two instances of JBoss AS on the same machine
> If you have to run two instances of JBoss AS on the same machine, you'll need to remap some of the ports (including the JNDI port). This process is described on the JBoss wiki, but the following blog post has a concise how-to description: http://blog.emmanuelbernard.com/2008/08/remotely-send-and-consume-messages-with.html.

Regardless of the approach you choose, the knowledge you gained from this chapter is still relevant because the technique doesn't fundamentally change the configuration of Hibernate Search.

The next step is to make sure slaves get the latest index directory from the master.

10.2.2 *Preparing the directory providers*

We discussed how to use DirectoryProviders in a cluster in section 5.1.4. If you want a more detailed explanation of the configuration, refer to chapter 5. We'll simply complete our slave node configuration (see listing 10.2). Let's assume that /mnt/ share is a shared drive where the master node pushes stable versions of the index directories.

Listing 10.2 Completing the slave node configuration

```
<persistence-unit name="dvdstore-catalog">
    <jta-data-source>java:/DefaultDS</jta-data-source>
    <properties>
        <!-- regular Hibernate Core configuration -->
        <property name="hibernate.dialect"
                value="org.hibernate.dialect.H2Dialect"/>
        <property name="hibernate.hbm2ddl.auto"
                value="create-drop"/>

        <!-- Hibernate Search configuration -->
        <!-- JMS backend -->
        <property name="hibernate.search.worker.jndi.url"
                value="jnp://master:1099"/>
        <property name="hibernate.search.worker.backend"
                value="jms"/>
        <property name="hibernate.search.worker.jms.connection_factory"
                value="/ConnectionFactory"/>
        <property name="hibernate.search.worker.jms.queue"
                value="queue/hibernatesearch"/>
        <!-- DirectoryProvider configuration -->
        <property name="hibernate.search.default.directory_provider"

value="org.hibernate.search.store.FSSlaveDirectoryProvider"/>
        <property name="hibernate.search.default.refresh"
                value="1800"/>
        <property name="hibernate.search.default.indexBase"
                value="/Users/prod/lucenedirs"/>
        <property name="hibernate.search.default.sourceBase"
                value="/mnt/share"/>
    </properties>
</persistence-unit>
```

Annotations:
- Slave directory provider
- Copy from the master every 30 minutes
- Local directory where indexes are copied to
- Directory where master indexes are read from

In this scenario, we read all our indexes from /mnt/share; this directory contains one subdirectory per entity indexed because we use the default Hibernate Search configuration. Every 30 minutes (1800 seconds), the master directories are copied to the local slave.

NOTE Each DirectoryProvider (one per index) is responsible for copying its master version. This is not a global operation that copies all indexes. For example, you could decide that the distributor index can be copied only every three hours, whereas the item index is copied every 30 minutes.

The copy is performed asynchronously and doesn't affect queries processed by the slave. When the copy is finished, the new version becomes the one actively used by the slave node. This means that at a given time, your hard drive contains two versions of the index: the active version and the version being copied. These two versions are placed in the index directory under the directories named 1 and 2. The `Directory-Provider` determines which directory is the active one.

Our slave nodes are configured and ready, but they need the master to do the actual indexing work. Let's see how to configure the master node.

10.3   Configuring the master node

The master is typically a stripped-down version of your application that contains the message consumer (an MDB), your domain model (the Hibernate Search mapping configuration), and the persistence unit (either the `SessionFactory` or the `Entity-ManagerFactory` configuration). The master can alternatively be the complete version of your application and also act like a slave (that is, answering HTTP requests from your customers). Be careful, because the configuration of a master is different than that of the slave. If you deploy the master node but still configure it to use the JMS backend, the MDB will simply consume a message, re-create it, and put it back into the queue. Not so useful.

> **TIP**   You can deploy both a slave node and a master node in the same JBoss AS instance. While you technically lose the CPU, memory, and input/output isolation, you still benefit from the ability to avoid receiving an `OutOf-MemoryException` during heavy write periods provided that your JMS provider overflows messages on disk. Be careful not to deploy the MDB on the slave nodes.

We'll walk through the master node configuration. First we'll see how to build the MDB, then we'll explain how to configure the backend, and finally we'll show how to enable the right directory providers.

10.3.1   Building the message consumer

Slave nodes send their work list into a JMS message. The easiest way to consume these messages in a Java environment is to use a message-driven bean. While Hibernate Search doesn't provide the MDB code, it provides an abstract class your MDB can extend. Let's have a look at a typical MDB implementation in listing 10.3.

Listing 10.3   MDB implementation consuming slave messages

```
@MessageDriven(activationConfig = {                    Read messages from a JMS queue
        @ActivationConfigProperty(propertyName="destinationType",
            propertyValue="javax.jms.Queue"),
        @ActivationConfigProperty(propertyName="destination",
            propertyValue="queue/hibernatesearch")         JNDI name of
        } )                                                the queue
public class MDBSearchController
```

```
        extends AbstractJMSHibernateSearchController   ◁──┐ Extend abstract
        implements MessageListener {              ◁──────┘ helper class
    @PersistenceContext private EntityManager em;
                                    Implement the Java EE interface
    @Override
    protected void cleanSessionIfNeeded(Session session) {   ◁──┐ Clean the
        //nothing to do container managed                         │ session if
    }                                                             │ needed

    @Override                              Provide access to
    protected Session getSession() {   ◁──┘ the session
        return (Session) em.getDelegate();
    }
}
```

AbstractJMSHibernateSearchController extracts the index work list from the message and passes this work list to the right SearchFactory. To access the SearchFactory object, this class needs to access the Hibernate Session and requires you to override two methods: getSession() and cleanSessionIfNeeded(). In a managed environment like Java EE, it's quite easy to get the Session or the EntityManager injected for you, and you just need to pass it along. If you happen to run your application in a non-managed environment, simply create a new session in getSession().

When AbstractJMSHibernateSearchController is done with the session object, it passes it back to cleanSessionIfNeeded(). If you passed a session managed by the environment, you have nothing to do here. If getSession() explicitly created a session object, this session should be closed and discarded in cleanSessionIfNeeded().

In Java EE and EJB 3.0, it's quite easy to mark a class as an MDB; use the @Message-Driven annotation and point to the queue that needs to be consumed. Make sure you mark your class as implementing MessageListener in order for the container to pick it up as an MDB. You do not need any additional deployment descriptor. Bundle your domain model classes, your Hibernate or Java Persistence configuration file, and the MDB class into a JAR. Bundle this JAR into an EAR that contains Hibernate Search and Lucene JARs (and Hibernate Core dependencies if you run outside JBoss AS) in a directory named lib. See listing 10.4 for a description of the structure.

Listing 10.4   Structure of the deployment unit for the master node

```
dvdstore.EAR      ◁──┐ Deploy an EAR without a
   |- dvdstore.JAR    │ deployment descriptor
      |- com/manning/hsia/dvdstore          Include the domain
         |- model ...                   ◁──┘ model classes
         |- master
            |- MDBSearchController.class   ◁──── MDB class
      |- META-INF
         |- persistence.xml      ◁──── Hibernate and Hibernate Search configuration
   |- lib
      |- hibernate-search.jar      ◁──── Hibernate Search and Lucene JARs
      |- lucene-core.jar
      |- (other dependencies)      ◁──── Hibernate dependencies if outside JBoss AS
```

The next step is to configure the queue into which messages are sent.

10.3.2 *Preparing the master queue*

Configuring the master queue is entirely dependent on your JMS provider. Make sure you carefully evaluate criteria such as message persistence, reliability, and security when you configure the queue.

The following configuration is a simple queue declaration in JBoss AS 5.0 based on a fresh install. This description doesn't cover advanced topics such as message persistence or security. To add a new queue in JBoss AS, go to your configuration directory. Configuration directories are located in $JBOSS_HOME/server. In most cases, you'll use the default configuration directory ($JBOSS_HOME/server/default). Open deploy/messaging/destinations-service.xml, and add the following code fragment inside the server tag:

```
<server>

    <mbean code="org.jboss.jms.server.destination.QueueService"
       name="jboss.messaging.destination:service=Queue,
    name=hibernatesearch"                          <──────┐  Defines the
       xmbean-dd="xmdesc/Queue-xmbean.xml">               ┘  queue name

       <depends optional-attribute-name="ServerPeer">
    jboss.messaging:service=ServerPeer</depends>
       <depends>jboss.messaging:service=PostOffice</depends>

    </mbean>
    ...
</server>
```

Defining the queue is necessary only on the master node. You can pretty much add this fragment without change. If you want to rename the queue, be sure to replace hibernatesearch in the MBean name with the queue name of your choice. By default, queues are exposed in JNDI in queue/[queue name]. You can override this if needed, but the authors recommend against it. Doing so makes it harder for other people to understand your JBoss AS configuration, and the benefits aren't clear. Please refer to the JBoss AS documentation for more information.

You can also change the JNDI name where the JMS connection factory is published. By default, it's published at /ConnectionFactory, and this is where we look it up in the slave nodes (hibernate.search.worker.jms.connection_factory). To change it, edit the file deploy/messaging/connection-factories-service.xml and add a new binding name.

```
<mbean code="org.jboss.jms.server.connectionfactory.ConnectionFactory"
    name="jboss.messaging.connectionfactory:service=ConnectionFactory"
    xmbean-dd="xmdesc/ConnectionFactory-xmbean.xml">
    <depends optional-attribute-name="ServerPeer">
 jboss.messaging:service=ServerPeer</depends>
    <depends optional-attribute-name="Connector">
        jboss.messaging:service=Connector,transport=bisocket
    </depends>
    <depends>jboss.messaging:service=PostOffice</depends>
    <attribute name="JNDIBindings">
```

```
        <bindings>
            <binding>/HSearchJMSConnectionFactory</binding>    ◁──── Add a new
            <binding>/ConnectionFactory</binding>                     binding
            <binding>/XAConnectionFactory</binding>
            <binding>java:/ConnectionFactory</binding>
            <binding>java:/XAConnectionFactory</binding>
        </bindings>
    </attribute>
</mbean>
```

Once again, it's usually better to use the default values because it makes your configuration more readable to your users.

The final step configures directory providers to share index changes with the slaves.

10.3.3 *Preparing the directory providers*

We have the right piece of software in place, but we do not yet propagate index directories to the slaves. Contrary to the behavior of slave nodes, the master will physically interact with Lucene indexes. You don't need to change the default backend configuration. However, the DirectoryProviders must copy indexes to a shared location on a regular basis. Listing 10.5 shows a configuration example.

Listing 10.5 `DirectoryProviders` must copy indexes to shared location

```
<persistence-unit name="dvdstore-catalog">
    <jta-data-source>java:/DefaultDS</jta-data-source>
    <properties>
        <!-- regular Hibernate Core configuration -->
        <property name="hibernate.dialect"
                value="org.hibernate.dialect.H2Dialect"/>
        <property name="hibernate.hbm2ddl.auto"
                value="create-drop"/>

        <!-- Hibernate Search configuration -->
        <!-- no change in backend configuration -->                     Master
                                                                directory provider
        <!-- DirectoryProvider configuration -->
        <property name="hibernate.search.default.directory_provider"
                value="org.hibernate.search.
            ➥ store.FSMasterDirectoryProvider"/>        ◁
        <property name="hibernate.search.default.refresh"      Copy from the
                value="1800"/>                          ◁      master every
        <property name="hibernate.search.default.indexBase"    30 minutes
                value="/Users/prod/lucenedirs"/>        ◁
        <property name="hibernate.search.default.sourceBase"
                value="/mnt/share"/>  ◁          Local directory where
    </properties>         Directory where master    indexes are written
</persistence-unit>       indexes are shared
```

The sourceBase for the master must be the same as the sourceBase for the slaves. It is the shared location where indexes are passed along. The shared location will contain two versions of each index at a given time: the active version slaves copy their value from and the passive version the master copies the value to. When the master is finished with its copy, it switches the active and passive versions. For more information on the directory provider configuration in a cluster, you read section 5.1.4. Also take time to run the code examples provided.

10.4   Summary

This chapter discussed clustering approaches and gave you the keys for understanding their pros and cons. It described in detail the standard method for clustering Hibernate Search asynchronously. Don't forget that this is only the recommended approach, and you can always use variations of this technique or even a totally different approach. The key is to make sure you limit the number of nodes waiting on the global pessimistic lock held at the index level.

The standard approach has a few important features:

- It keeps slaves working even when the master node goes down.
- It keeps searches fast. Indexes are copied locally, and queries trigger only local I/O.
- It prevents `OutOfMemoryException` errors even during heavy index-writing loads.
- It keeps the master noncritical to the application's main operations and easily switchable to another machine.

We've now shown you pretty much all that you need to know about Hibernate Search. The next part of the book will explore Lucene in a deeper way. While not directly influencing how you work daily with Hibernate Search, this knowledge is quite useful because Hibernate Search relies on Apache Lucene for the full-text search engine. You will soon gain a better understanding of how query results are produced.

11

Accessing Lucene natively

This chapter covers

- Utilizing the `SearchFactory`
- Accessing Lucene directories
- Working with
- `DirectoryProviders`
- Exploiting projections

If you have not realized it by now, or you just started reading this chapter first, Lucene is the driving force behind the Hibernate Search framework. The entire book up to this point has been dedicated to helping you understand how to implement Hibernate Search in your application. Eventually, everyone has questions related to working with Lucene directly. We hear questions similar to the following all the time:

- Hibernate Search's default constructs won't work for me. Now what do I do?
- I know Hibernate Search takes care of a lot of things for me, but I need to get at Lucene itself and work with its native constructs. How can I do that?

327

- Can I get an instance of a Lucene `Directory` object so I can work at a lower level?

- Hibernate Search has sharded my entity into three separate directories. Is it possible to work with them as a single object? Can I improve retrieval performance?

Do any of these sound familiar? We're going to answer these questions in this chapter. We'll start by looking at Hibernate Search's `SearchFactory`, which is the key entry point to Lucene. It allows access to `Directory` objects and `IndexReaders`. We'll look at the effects that sharding has on these classes, and along the way we'll also see what goes on when indexing multiple entities.

One of the things that developers must assess is whether or not the default `DirectoryProviders` included with Hibernate Search are sufficient for their purposes. In the event they are not, you can write a custom one. We'll discuss what you must take into account in this situation.

We'll also show you how to access the legacy Lucene document and several related values by utilizing a projection, and we'll demonstrate how it can affect performance.

We believe you'll be pleasantly surprised, because accessing native Lucene is much easier than you think.

11.1   *Getting to the bottom of Hibernate Search*

Getting under the covers to interact directly with native Lucene constructs is not difficult. The most important class here is Hibernate Search's `org.hibernate.search.SearchFactory` class. It's the gateway to native Lucene.

The `SearchFactory` keeps track of the underlying Lucene resources for Hibernate Search. The contract for `SearchFactoryImpl` is maintained by the `SearchFactory` and `SearchFactoryImplementor` interfaces.

You can access the `SearchFactory` from an `org.hibernate.search.FullTextSession` instance, which is obtained from a Hibernate session, as shown in the following code:

```
FullTextSession fullTextSession =
    Search.createFullTextSession(SessionFactory.openSession());
SearchFactory searchFactory = fullTextSession.getSearchFactory();
```

Once you have an instance of the `SearchFactory`, you have all you need to work directly with Lucene. From here you can obtain references to Lucene's `Directory` object and also Lucene's `IndexReader`. We'll look at these in the following sections.

11.1.1 *Accessing a Lucene directory*

Lucene has a notion of a `Directory`, which it uses to store its indexed information. A `Directory` is a list of flat files that may be written to once, when they are created. Once created, a file can be opened only for reading or deleting. Random access to the files is permitted at all times.

All file I/O goes through Lucene's API, so that it's nicely encapsulated, but you still retain all needed flexibility. This allows Lucene's indexes to be manipulated and stored several ways, such as these:

- A set of flat files on some type of persistent storage
- A RAM-based directory
- implementation
- A database index implementation, via JDBC

NOTE The authors do not recommend implementing the JDBC configuration. We'll discuss why in section 11.3.

You can always access the native Lucene directories through plain Lucene. The `Directory` structure is in no way different with or without Hibernate Search. However, there are more convenient ways to access a given `Directory`.

The `SearchFactory` we discussed previously keeps track of all of the `org.hibernate.search.store.DirectoryProviders` that an indexed class may utilize. You obtain access to directories via the `DirectoryProvider`. Notice the use of the plural of `DirectoryProvider` here. A given entity can have several `DirectoryProviders`, one per shard, if the index is sharded (see the discussion on index sharding in section 9.4). In the opposite vein, one `DirectoryProvider` can be shared among several indexed classes if the classes share the same underlying index directory. Section 11.1.5 provides an example of this index merging. The `DirectoryProvider` class's main aims are to:

- Set up a Lucene directory for an index
- Serve as an abstraction separating Hibernate Search from the Lucene directory implementation

    This implementation could be in any form, even that of a server cluster and not just of a single file system directory.

Assuming we have an index built from `Order` information, here is a code example showing how to obtain an instance of a Lucene `org.apache.lucene.store.Directory`.

```
DirectoryProvider[] providers =
searchFactory.getDirectoryProviders(Order.class);
org.apache.lucene.store.Directory directory =
providers[0].getDirectory();
```

In this example code, `directory` points to the Lucene index storing `Order` information.

WARNING When utilizing the Hibernate Search framework to obtain an instance of a Lucene `Directory`, do not call `close()` on the obtained `Directory`. This is the responsibility of Hibernate Search. The one opening the resource has to ensure it gets closed; in this case you borrow a Hibernate Search managed instance.

Let's look at some examples so you'll better understand what to expect from the default `DirectoryProviders` that come bundled with Hibernate Search. We will accomplish this by the following steps:

1. Creating an index of a single entity and retrieving its `DirectoryProvider`(s) to see what we get
2. Creating a sharded index of a single entity and again retrieving the
3. `DirectoryProvider`(s) to compare with our first result
4. Creating a single index of two entities and examining how the
5. `DirectoryProvider`(s) have changed in this instance

11.1.2 *Obtaining DirectoryProviders from a non-sharded entity*

Listing 11.1 shows the simple `Animal` entity we'll use for the first example. This is nothing more than a simple JavaBean-style class and will work well for our example.

Listing 11.1 The simple `Animal` entity used in the examples

```
@Entity
@Indexed
@Analyzer(impl = StandardAnalyzer.class)
public class Animal {
  @Id
  @DocumentId
  private Integer id;

  @Field(index = Index.TOKENIZED, store = Store.YES)
  private String name;

  public Integer getId() {
    return id;
  }

  public void setId(Integer id) {
    this.id = id;
  }

  public String getName() {
    return name;
  }

  public void setName(String name) {
    this.name = name;
  }
}
```

NOTE All of the examples in this chapter are based on the example tests included with the Hibernate Search source code. These tests are located in and around the `org.hibernate.search.test.shards` package.

We do not show all of the code in the examples that's necessary to make these examples work, although the complete code is included with the book's accompanying source files. For example, we provide scaffolding code that must be in place for the setup and so on. To examine this code refer to the tests included with the Hibernate Search sources, specifically the code located in the `org.hibernate.search.test.shards.ShardsTest` class.

Listing 11.2 is the single non-sharded entity example. We create instances of our entity and build the index. Then we search for all records so we can clean up after ourselves by deleting everything we added. Finally, we retrieve the `DirectoryProviders`.

Listing 11.2 Indexing an entry to a non-sharded index

```
public class NonShardsTest extends SearchTestCase {          Extend for
  Transaction tx;                                            scaffolding code

  public void testNoShards() throws Exception {
    FullTextSession session = Search.getFullTextSession(openSession());
    buildIndex();

    tx = session.beginTransaction();
    QueryParser parser =
      new QueryParser("id", new StopAnalyzer());

    List results =                                           Make sure
      session.createFullTextQuery(parser.                    everything
    parse("name:bear OR name:elephant")).list();             worked properly

    assertEquals("Either insert or query failed", 2,
    results.size());

    SearchFactory searchFactory =
      session.getSearchFactory();                            ❶ Get the
    DirectoryProvider[] providers =                             DirectoryProvider
      searchFactory.getDirectoryProviders(Animal                for Animal
    .class);

    assertEquals("Wrong provider count", 1,                  ❷ Check DirectoryProvider;
    providers.length);                                          should have only one

    org.apache.lucene.store.Directory directory =           ❸ Retrieve the Lucene
      providers[0].getDirectory();                              Directory object

    try {
      IndexReader reader =                    Use a Directory to
        IndexReader.open(directory);          get the documents
      assert reader.document(0).get("name").equals("Elephant")
        : "Incorrect document name";
      assert reader.document(1).get("name").equals("Bear")
        : "Incorrect document name";
      for (Object o : results) session.delete(o);
      tx.commit();
    }
    finally {
      if (reader != null)        ❹ Explicitly close the
        reader.close();             created reader
      session.close();
    }
  }

  private void buildIndex(FullTextSession session) {
    tx = session.beginTransaction();
```

```
      Animal a = new Animal();
      a.setId(1);
      a.setName("Elephant");
      session.persist(a);
      a = new Animal();

      a.setId(2);
      a.setName("Bear");
      session.persist(a);
      tx.commit();
      session.clear();
    }

    @Override
    protected void setUp() throws Exception {
      File sub = locateBaseDir();
      File[] files = sub.listFiles();
      if (files != null) {
        for (File file : files) {
          if (file.isDirectory()) {
            delete(file);
          }
        }
      }
      buildSessionFactory(getMappings(),
                  getAnnotatedPackages(),
                  getXmlFiles());
    }
```

❶ shows that once we have an instance of SearchFactory, it is only one step to a DirectoryProvider. Because there's only one entity and no sharding, ❷ confirms that there's only one DirectoryProvider. Once we have an instance of a provider, we can easily obtain access to the Lucene Directory object ❸. Finally, ❹ demonstrates that we must close the readers we generated because these were created outside the Hibernate Search framework and it knows nothing about them. In section 11.2 we'll show you a situation where you *must not* call close on a reader.

11.1.3 *And now for sharding one entity into two shards*

In listing 11.3 we'll reuse the same code and make some simple changes. We'll add sharding to the MergedAnimal entity and divide one index into two different directories. The test code will confirm these changes. We're using the MergedAnimal entity here because it specifies the index name in the @Indexed(index = "Animal") annotation. The partial MergedAnimal entity showing the index name is given here:

```
@Entity
@Indexed(index = "Animal")
@Analyzer(impl = StandardAnalyzer.class)
public class MergedAnimal {
  @Id
  @DocumentId
  private Integer id;
  @Field(index = Index.TOKENIZED, store= Store.YES)
  private String name;
```

Listing 11.3   Indexing a single entity to a sharded index

```
public class TestShards extends SearchTestCase {
  Transaction tx;

  @Test
  public void testShards() throws Exception {
    FullTextSession session = Search.getFullTextSession(openSession());
    buildIndex();

    ReaderProvider readerProvider = null;

    IndexReader reader0 = null;
    IndexReader reader1 = null;
    List results;

    try {
      tx = session.beginTransaction();
      FullTextSession fullTextSession =
        Search.getFullTextSession(session);
      QueryParser parser = new QueryParser("id",
                            new StandardAnalyzer());

      results = fullTextSession.createFullTextQuery(
      parser.parse("name:bear OR name:elephant")).list();
      assert results.size() == 2:"Either insert or query failed";

      SearchFactory searchFactory =
        fullTextSession.getSearchFactory();
      DirectoryProvider[] providers =
        searchFactory.getDirectoryProviders(MergedAnimal.class);
      assert providers.length == 2
        : "Wrong provider count";          Check DirectoryProviders;
                                           better be two
      readerProvider =
        searchFactory.getReaderProvider();

      reader0 = readerProvider.openReader(providers[0]);   ① Instantiate
      reader1 = readerProvider.openReader(providers[1]);      individual readers

      assert reader0.document(0).get("name").equals
      ("Bear"): "Incorrect document name";                ② Check for splitting
      assert reader1.document(0).get("name").equals          into shards
      ("Elephant"): "Incorrect document name";
    }
    finally {
      for (Object o : results) session.delete(o);
      tx.commit();
    }

    finally {
      if (reader0 != null)
        readerProvider.closeReader(reader0);
      if (reader0 != null)                    ③ Explicitly close
        readerProvider.closeReader(reader1);     the readers
      session.close();
    }
  }
}
```

```
    private void buildIndex() {
      tx = session.beginTransaction();

      MergedAnimal a = new MergedAnimal();
      a.setId(1);
      a.setName("Elephant");
      session.save(a);

      a = new MergedAnimal();
      a.setId(2);
      a.setName("Bear");
      session.save(a);
      tx.commit();
      session.clear();
    }

    @BeforeClass
    protected void setUp() throws Exception {
      File sub = locateBaseDir();
      File[] files = sub.listFiles();
      if (files != null) {
        for (File file : files) {
          if (file.isDirectory()) {
            delete(file);
          }
        }
      }
      buildSessionFactory(getMappings(),
                  getAnnotatedPackages(),
                  getXmlFiles());
    }

    @Override
    protected void configure(Configuration cfg) {
      super.configure(cfg);
      cfg.setProperty("hibernate.search.default
 ➥.directory_provider", FSDirectoryProvider.class.getName());
      File sub = locateBaseDir();
      cfg.setProperty("hibernate.search.default.indexBase",
 ➥sub.getAbsolutePath());
      cfg.setProperty("hibernate.search.Animal.         ❹ Define two shards
 ➥sharding_strategy.nbr_of_shards", "2");    ◁──┘    for entities

      cfg.setProperty("hibernate.search.Animal.0.indexName",
                  "Animal00");    ◁──┐  Override the
    }                            ❺ default shard name
  }
```

We retrieve index readers for both of the indexes ❶. ❷ shows that our two entities
were split into separate shards. We close the readers ❸, returning them to the ReaderProvider; in this case we have to avoid IndexReader.close(); we didn't open it
directly but got it from the ReaderProvider, so this is necessary to manage its lifecycle.

   To configure multiple shards we define the nbr_of_shards configuration quantity
❹ and decide to override the default shard name of the first shard ❺.

11.1.4 *Indexing two non-sharded entities*

In the final example, we'll index two different entities and not shard either of them. We'll use the `Animal` entity that we used in the previous two examples and add the `Furniture` entity that follows as the second entity. As with the `Animal` entity, this is nothing more than a simple JavaBean-style class.

```
@Entity
@Indexed
public class Furniture {
  @Id
  @GeneratedValue
  @DocumentId
  private Integer id;
  @Field(index= Index.TOKENIZED, store= Store.YES)
  private String color;

  public Integer getId() {
    return id;
  }

  public void setId(Integer id) {
    this.id = id;
  }

  public String getColor() {
    return color;
  }

  public void setColor(String color) {
    this.color = color;
  }
}
```

Listing 11.4 contains the code for this last example. The `protected void config-ure(Configuration cfg)` method in this example is identical to that shown in listing 11.2.

Listing 11.4 Indexing two entities to non-sharded indexes

```
public class TwoEntitiesTest extends SearchTestCase {
  FullTextSession session;
  Transaction tx;

  public void testTwoEntitiesNoShards() throws Exception {
    session = Search.getFullTextSession(openSession());
    buildIndex();

    tx = session.beginTransaction();
    FullTextSession fullTextSession =
      Search.getFullTextSession(session);
    QueryParser parser =
      new QueryParser("id", new StopAnalyzer());

    List results =
      fullTextSession.createFullTextQuery(parser.parse
➥ ("name:elephant OR color:blue")).list();
```

```
        assert results.size() == 2: "
          Either insert or query failed";
        SearchFactory searchFactory =
          fullTextSession.getSearchFactory();
        DirectoryProvider[] provider0 =
          searchFactory.getDirectoryProviders(
        Animal.class);
          assert provider1.length == 1: "Wrong provider count";
        org.apache.lucene.store.Directory directory0 =
          provider0[0].getDirectory();

        DirectoryProvider[] provider1 = searchFactory.
      getDirectoryProviders(Furniture.class);
        assert provider1.length == 1: "Wrong provider count";
        org.apache.lucene.store.Directory directory1 =
          provider1[0].getDirectory();

        IndexReader reader0 = IndexReader.open(directory0);
        assert reader0.document(0).get("name")
          .equals("Elephant"):"Incorrect document name";
        IndexReader reader1 = IndexReader.open(directory1);
        assert reader1.document(0).get("color")
          .equals("dark blue"): "Incorrect color";
        for (Object o : results) session.delete(o);
        tx.commit();
    }
    Finally {
        session.close();
    }

    private void buildIndex() {
        tx = session.beginTransaction();

        Animal a = new Animal();
        a.setId(1);
        a.setName("Elephant");
        session.save(a);

        Furniture fur = new Furniture();
        fur.setColor("dark blue");
        session.save(fur);
        tx.commit();

        session.clear();
    }
    ...
```

① Ensure we have a result from each entity

② Retrieve the DirectoryProvider

③ Retrieve a directory instance

④ Check for the correct Animal entity

⑤ Check for the correct Furniture entity

Persist the second entity

After persisting one instance each of Animal and Furniture, we query for both of the instances ①. We subsequently check for the correct number of results, getting the DirectoryProviders ② for each entry, and from them we retrieve instances of the Directory objects ③. Then we create IndexReaders and open them on the directories ④ and ensure that the entities were placed in the correct directories by examining their Lucene documents ⑤.

We can draw several conclusions from the previous three examples. It seems that each entity is assigned its own directory and therefore its own DirectoryProvider. If the entity is sharded, each of the shards also receives its own `DirectoryProvider`. That makes sense, and our examples prove it. So we're finished, right? As my old coach would say, "Not so fast, my friend!" Although this is the default behavior, Hibernate Search gives you the flexibility to combine entities into the same directory. We'll look at that next.

11.1.5 *Shoehorning multiple entities into one index (merging)*

Merge two entities into the same index? Why would we want to do this? Because we want to reuse the same `Directory`. Another example is to reuse an index that previously contained combined entities by completely deleting one of the entities it contains and replacing it with another.

> **NOTE** The authors are presenting this technique so that you know the option is available. We do not feel that there's enough benefit in merging an index. The example we're presenting here will show that you have to do more work to accomplish the same thing you did in the previous examples.

There are actually two ways to accomplish merging an index:

- Configuring the property `hibernate.search.(fully qualified entity name).indexName=(relative directory from indexBase)`.
- Setting the `@Indexed` annotation's `index` property of the entity you want to merge to the directory you want the entity indexed into.

Look back at the partial `MergedAnimal` entity in 11.1.3. The `@Indexed` annotation shows the `index` property pointing to `Animal`. Now look at the `Furniture` entity shown just before listing 11.4. As is, it points to the `Furniture` directory, because that's the default value. If we wanted all `Furniture` instances to be indexed in the `Animal` index along with all instances of `Animal`, we would specify `@Indexed(index="Animal")`.

This does present a problem. Let's assume that the `id` value for the `Furniture` entities is actually a part number. What happens when we index both a piece of furniture and an animal with the same `id` value? We no longer get a single result back, and we must take into consideration the entity type we're searching for.

Let's look at an example where the additional concern of how to take entity type into consideration will become clear. We'll use an *entity filter* to make sure we work only the entity we need. We'll also use the `MergedAnimal` entity shown in section 11.1.3 as is, and we'll use the `Furniture` entity shown just before listing 11.4. The configuration will handle putting it in the same index as `Animal`. Listing 11.5 shows these two methods of merging entities into the same index.

Listing 11.5 Combining two entities into one index by setting configuration parameters

```
public class IndexMergeTest extends SearchTestCase {
    Transaction tx;

    public void testTwoEntitiesNoShards() throws Exception {
```

```
FullTextSession session = Search.getFullTextSession(openSession());
buildIndex(session);

tx = session.beginTransaction();
FullTextSession fullTextSession =
  Search.getFullTextSession(session);
QueryParser parser =
  new QueryParser("id", new StandardAnalyzer());

List results =
  fullTextSession.createFullTextQuery(parser
.parse("id:1")).list();
assert results.size() == 2:"Either insert or
query failed";                                    ← ❶ Returns two results
                                                      from unfiltered query
SearchFactory searchFactory =
  fullTextSession.getSearchFactory();
DirectoryProvider[] provider =
  searchFactory.getDirectoryProviders(
MergedAnimal.class);
assert provider.length == 1                        ❷ Check only one
  : "Wrong provider count";              ←            provider exists
org.apache.lucene.store.Directory directory =
  provider[0].getDirectory();
                                                   ❸ Remove
BooleanQuery classFilter = new BooleanQuery();        CLASS_FIELDNAME
classFilter.setBoost(0);                        ←     scoring impact

Term t = new Term(DocumentBuilder.CLASS_FIELDNAME,
MergedFurniture.class.getName());                  ❹ Build the filter
TermQuery termQuery = new TermQuery(t);               query boolean
classFilter.add(termQuery, BooleanClause.Occur        clause
.SHOULD);

Term luceneTerm = new Term("id", "1");
Query luceneQuery = new TermQuery(luceneTerm);

BooleanQuery filteredQuery = new BooleanQuery();   ❺ Assemble the
filteredQuery.add(luceneQuery,                        full query
BooleanClause.Occur.MUST);
filteredQuery.add(classFilter,
BooleanClause.Occur.MUST);

IndexSearcher searcher = null;
try {                                              ❻ Returns only one
  searcher = new IndexSearcher(directory);            result from
  Hits hits = searcher.search(filteredQuery);         Filtered query
  assert hits.length() == 1: "Wrong hit count";  ←

  Document doc = hits.doc(0);
  assert doc.get("color").equals("dark blue");   ←   Check for
                                                      correct color
  for (Object o : results) session.delete(o);     ❼  value
  tx.commit();
}
finally {
  if (searcher != null)
    searcher.close();
  session.close();
```

```
            }
        }
        private void buildIndex(FullTextSession session) {
            Transaction tx = session.beginTransaction();

            MergedAnimal a = new MergedAnimal();
            a.setId(1);
            a.setName("Elephant");
            session.save(a);

            MergedFurniture fur = new MergedFurniture();
            fur.setColor("dark blue");
            session.save(fur);

            tx.commit();
            session.clear();
        }

        @Override
        protected void configure(Configuration cfg) {
            super.configure(cfg);

            cfg.setProperty("hibernate.search.default.
        directory_provider",
        FSDirectoryProvider.class.getName());
            File sub = getBaseIndexDir();

            cfg.setProperty("hibernate.search.default.
        indexBase", sub.getAbsolutePath());

            cfg.setProperty("hibernate.search.com.manning
        .hsia.ch11.Furniture.indexName", "Animal");
        }
    }
```

8 **Put Furniture into the Animal index**

1 and **2** are here solely to demonstrate that there are two results to a single query of id=1 and there is only one `DirectoryProvider` for the merged index.

At **3** we are canceling the effect that the `DocumentBuilder.CLASS_FIELDNAME` has on the scoring of the returned document. Remember that Hibernate Search adds a field by the name of _hibernate_class to all indexed documents. This field contains the class name of the indexed entity as its value.

NOTE As you will discover in chapter 12, having multiple documents in an index containing the same term (in this case the id) changes the score of a returned document. The scoring factor this affects is known as the *Inverse Document Frequency* (*idf*).

After this, **4** builds our filter portion of the query by requiring that the DocumentBuilder.CLASS_FIELDNAME field should contain an instance of org.hibernate.search.test.shard.Furniture. This filter is combined with the other half of the query **5** by specifying that the id should be 1. After the query is issued, **6** confirms that, thanks to our restriction, there is now only one result instead of the two pointed out at #1. **7** corroborates that the color field does indeed contain the term *blue.* ⑧ contains the configuration parameters that tell Hibernate Search to put the `Furniture` entity into the `Animal` index.

We hope you noticed that, as we said earlier, you need to do additional work here to obtain your answer. A `BooleanQuery` is now necessary because you are searching on two fields. The first is the _hibernate_class field, having a value of the entity you're searching for. The second is the actual field and value you're querying for, in this case `id` with a value of `1`.

To find out how these two entities merged into a single index, let's turn to Luke and examine the two documents in the index. First look at figure 11.1, which shows document 0 in the index.

Several things should be apparent from this figure:

- Hibernate Search has automatically added the <_hibernate_class> field.
- The <_hibernate_class> value is `MergedAnimal`.
- The <color> field is marked as <not available> because `Animal` does not contain this field.
- This is not the document we're looking for.

Now let's look at figure 11.2, which shows the second document in the index shown in listing 11.2.

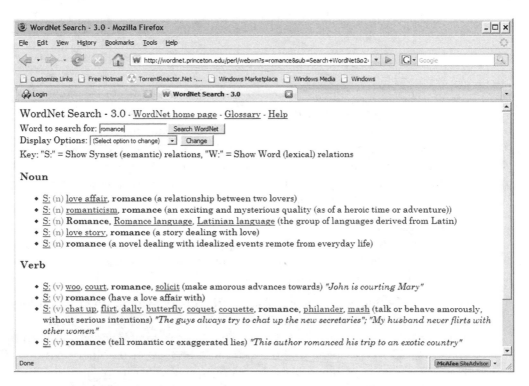

Figure 11.1   Examining document 0 of our example index. Even though this shows fields from both entities being present, if a particular entity doesn't contain one of the fields, it isn't available. Here <color> isn't available because `Animal` doesn't contain that field.

Several things should be apparent from this image also:

- The <_hibernate_class> value is `Furniture`.
- The <name> field is marked as `<not available>` since `Animal` does not contain this field.
- The <color> field is available in this document, and its value is `dark blue`.
- This is the document we are looking for because <color> contains the term `blue`.

These figures show that in merged indexes the individual entities are stored as is, and any fields that are not in a particular entity are ignored.

NOTE Future versions of Luke may not show the index contents exactly as shown here. The actual contents will, however, be as described.

That's enough of working with `DirectoryProviders` and directories. It's time to move on to our next topic concerning Hibernate Search's method of obtaining index readers. Do you remember what we talked about at the end of 11.1.2 concerning closing `IndexReaders`? We explained that because the `IndexReaders` that we instantiated in

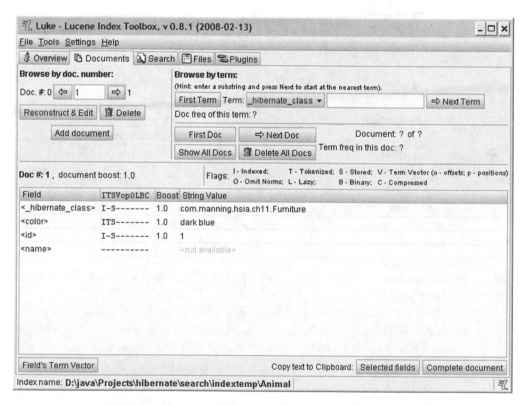

Figure 11.2 Examining document 1 of our example index. In this document <name> is not available since `Furniture` does not contain that field. The <color> field is available though, and it contains the value we're looking for, `blue`.

the examples were generated outside the Hibernate Search framework, we were required to explicitly close them. In the next section, we'll show you how to obtain an instance of an IndexReader within the confines of Hibernate Search so that the *framework* will take care of closing the reader for you.

11.2   Obtaining and using a Lucene IndexReader within the framework

Looking at listing 11.6 you can see that before you obtain an instance of an IndexReader you must first get a reference to a ReaderProvider instance.

Listing 11.6   Obtaining an instance of a Lucene IndexReader

```
DirectoryProvider orderProvider =
  searchFactory.getDirectoryProviders(Order.class)
  [0];
DirectoryProvider clientProvider =                    Obtain
  searchFactory.getDirectoryProviders(Client.class)   DirectoryProviders
  [0];

ReaderProvider readerProvider =
  searchFactory.getReaderProvider();
IndexReader reader =                                  Obtain a reader from
  readerProvider.openReader(orderProvider,            a ReaderProvider
  clientProvider);
try {
  //do read-only operations on the reader
}
finally {
  readerProvider.closeReader(reader);    ◁──┐  Close in a
}                                             │  finally block
```

When ReaderProviders are created, they take into account the ReaderStrategy configuration property hibernate.search.reader.strategy, which can have any full classname of an implementation (see 9.2.2.1 for details), or use the shared and not-shared keywords, the default value being shared. This option is present because one of the most time-consuming operations in Lucene is opening an IndexReader on a particular index. If your code has many users, and the reader strategy is set to not-shared, this could result in performance problems depending on how often new index readers are needed. Using the shared IndexReader will make most queries much more efficient.

To solve this problem and maximize performance, Hibernate Search caches all instances of IndexReader when the ReaderProvider is set to shared. This means that there are some simple additional "good citizen" rules that you'll have to follow:

- Never call indexReader.close() on a reader that was obtained via a Reader-Provider, but always call readerProvider.closeReader (reader); a finally block is the best place to do this, as shown in listing 11.6.

- This `IndexReader` must not be used for modification operations (it's highly likely that in a future release we won't allow this to happen). If you want to use a read/write `IndexReader`, create an instance of one by calling the static `IndexReader.open(Directory directory)` method, like this:

```
DirectoryProvider[] provider =
   searchFactory.getDirectoryProviders(Order.class);
org.apache.lucene.store.Directory directory =
   provider[0].getDirectory();
IndexReader reader = IndexReader.open(directory);
```

WARNING Failure to follow these simple rules will result in clients not being able to access indexes. Worse, clients will fail at unpredictable times, making this a very difficult problem to track down. Also, and most important, if you create your own read/write `IndexReader`, you are responsible for closing it.

Aside from these rules, you can use the `IndexReader` freely.

On some occasions you may be required to furnish a custom `DirectoryProvider`. In the next section we will examine a couple of use cases from Emmanuel's customers who had specific storage requirements. This example shows what you must consider when writing a custom `DirectoryProvider`.

11.3 *Writing a DirectoryProvider your way*

It's impossible to cover even a small number of permutations with persistent storage configurations present in business today. First we'll discuss the `FSSlaveDirectoryProvider` classes' methods and what you must take into consideration for each of them. Then we'll talk about two situations that exemplify what you must take into account when writing your own `DirectoryProvider`. We won't go into detail with code, but we will discuss the use case requirements.

The `FSSlaveDirectoryProvider` is configured with these two directory settings:

- `hibernate.search.default.sourceBase` = *directory of master copy*
- `hibernate.search.default.indexBase` = *directory of local copy for querying*

These settings specify where the master index is located and also where the copies of the master index are to be placed.

Now let's investigate the `FSSlaveDirectoryProvider` class hierarchy. Examining figure 11.3 we see that there are four methods of the `DirectoryProvider` interface that it must implement:

- `void initialize(String directoryProviderName, Properties properties, SearchFactoryImplementor searchFactoryImplementor);` This method is a lightweight initialization that determines the location of the master index from the `sourceBase` setting and the slave index location(s) from the `indexBase` setting. It also determines the index name to allow the `equals` and `hashCode` to work as they must.

- `void start()` This method acquires the resources necessary for index copies. It determines the refresh period and creates the timed task for copying.
- `void stop()` This method is executed when the search factory is closed.
- `TDirectory getDirectory();` This method retrieves the appropriate directory based on the current copy operation being performed.

Figure 11.3 illustrates the class relationships.

In addition to these four method implementations, the comparator methods `equals(Object obj)` and `hashCode()` must also be implemented. These two methods are very important because they must guarantee equality between any two or more providers pointing to the same underlying Lucene store.

```
@Override
public boolean equals(Object obj) {
   if ( obj == this ) return true;
   if ( obj == null || !( obj instanceof FSSlaveDirectoryProvider ) ) return
   false;
   return indexName.equals( ( (FSSlaveDirectoryProvider) obj ).indexName );
}

@Override
public int hashCode() {
   int hash = 11;
   return 37 * hash + indexName.hashCode();
}
```

Shown in figure 11.4 are the two inner classes of `FSSlaveDirectoryProvider`: `CopyDirectory` and `TriggerTask`.

It's possible that you may be required to write one or both of these classes to accomplish whatever is necessary for your implementation. The authors recommend that you examine the source code to see exactly what's going on in these classes.

Now let's take a look at the two use cases we told you about. In the first situation, Emmanuel had a client with a data storage problem, and it's quite possible that you may have experienced a similar difficulty. This customer had a Lucene index of several hundred million records. Planning estimates were that they should provide for build-out to one billion or so within the next three years.

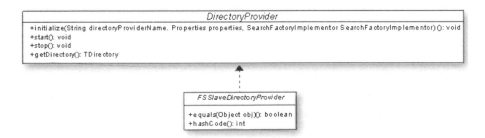

Figure 11.3 The class hierarchy diagram of `FSSlaveDirectoryProvider` shows the six methods of `DirectoryProvider` that must be implemented when writing a new implementation.

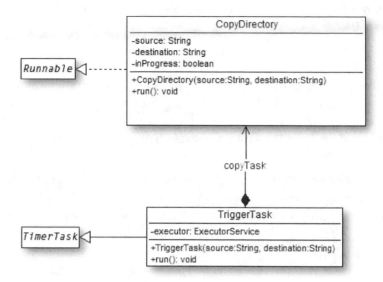

Figure 11.4 **The two inner classes of `FSSlaveDirectoryProvider` showing their relationship**

Problems arose when the customer revealed that the index was actually warehoused in a storage area network (SAN) that fed a 10-node server cluster. A typical SAN configuration is shown in figure 11.5. This cluster provided index query access for the user along with additional functionality. Their concern was that this would become an n-node problem. As the number of cluster nodes (n) grew, it would have been counterproductive to copy the index (`sourceBase`) from the SAN to each of the nodes of the cluster (`indexBase`). The SAN was faster, and the copying would generate much more network traffic than desired. As n increased, so would the traffic and maintenance of the copies.

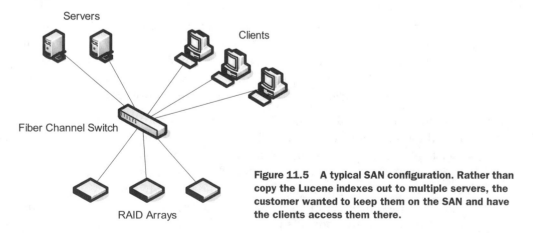

Figure 11.5 **A typical SAN configuration. Rather than copy the Lucene indexes out to multiple servers, the customer wanted to keep them on the SAN and have the clients access them there.**

NOTE   For the following discussion, if necessary, refer to chapter 10 and specifically figure 10.2.

The customer wanted to know if it were possible to configure the FSSlaveDirectory-Provider to not have an indexBase (slave copies of the master index from the index source located on the server cluster) and configure only a sourceBase (index source location) to prevent the copying cycle from reaching the outlying servers. This would make the index source copy of the master index in figure 10.2 the slave index. This is possible but not out of the box. The customer would have to write its own Directory-Provider. Emmanuel's recommendations were:

- Remove the actual copy to the cluster by modifying the run method of the inner CopyDirectory class and copy it to one slave index on the SAN.
- Leave the rest of the code alone: TriggerTask, marker determination, and so on.
- Set the refresh period to a small value to keep the slave index (the index source) up to date. This was now local I/O to the SAN and would be very fast.

Since the slave index was read-only and therefore would not have any Lucene locking issues, the slave directory could be easily shared. This prevents future scaling issues, and SANs are fast enough that they should not become bottlenecks. In the event they should, they also can be easily scaled up. We're sure that you'll probably come up with a different way of doing this—there always is—but that's up to you.

The second use case involved a user who wrote a custom DirectoryProvider that stores an index in a database.

The authors recommend against doing this for several reasons:

- *Lucene index segments are usually stored as blobs in a database.*   Those of you who have stored data this way know that this isn't an efficient manner of storage, especially for frequent access.
- *Because of the way Lucene indexes work, a database would still need a global pessimistic lock for writes.*   This does not scale well.
- *Indexes that mirror database tables and are used to increase search speed instead of using slow SQL queries are somewhat "disposable" for the following reason:*   There is no strong incentive for them to be transactional because they can be fairly easily rebuilt. (No one wants their order-entry system to fail, for example, because they cannot update their order index synchronously with the database.)

Emmanuel discusses these issues with the user on the Hibernate forum at http://forum.hibernate.org/viewtopic.php?t=980778&highlight=lucene+directory+database. This is an informative discussion, and we recommend that you read it.

By now you have probably realized that supplying your own version of a DirectoryProvider is not as simple as in some situations where you provide your own implementation of a method. You may have to change or write one of the inner classes or rewrite several methods. It's not that difficult a task, but it is more than a simple method change.

As one last example of how you can access Lucene natively from Hibernate Search, we're going to work with projection in the next section. This concept comes from Hibernate and allows access to several entity-related values.

11.4 *Projecting your will on indexes*

Hibernate Search (and Hibernate itself for that matter) has a concept called *projection*. Utilizing a projection allows access to several underlying Lucene entity values, which are enumerated in the interface `ProjectionConstants`:

- `public String THIS` Represents the Hibernate entity itself returned in a search.
- `public String DOCUMENT` Represents the Lucene (legacy) document returned by a search.
- `public String SCORE` Represents the legacy document's score from a search.
- `public String BOOST` Represents the boost value of the legacy document.
- `public String ID` Represents the entity's id property.
- `public String DOCUMENT_ID` Represents the Lucene document id, which can change over time between two different `IndexReader` openings.
- `public String EXPLANATION` Represents Lucene's `org.apache.lucene.search.Explanation` object describing the score computation for the object/document. This feature is relatively expensive, and we recommend that you not use it unless you return a limited number of objects (using pagination). To retrieve an explanation of a single result, we recommend retrieving the explanation by using `fullTextQuery.explain(int)`. If you need to, refer to chapter 12 for a review of the `explain` method.

In addition to the items listed in `ProjectionConstants`, any of the fields contained in the indexed entity can be requested by the projection. The following code shows the `Employee` entity that we will use in the example:

```
@Entity
@Indexed
public class Employee {
   private Integer id;
   private String lastname;
   private String dept;

   public Employee() {
   }

   public Employee(Integer id, String lastname, String dept) {
     this.id = id;
     this.lastname = lastname;
     this.dept = dept;
   }

   @Id
   @DocumentId
   public Integer getId() {
```

```
      return id;
    }

    public void setId(Integer id) {
      this.id = id;
    }

    @Field( index = Index.NO, store = Store.YES )
    public String getLastname() {
      return lastname;
    }

    public void setLastname(String lastname) {
      this.lastname = lastname;
    }

    @Field( index = Index.TOKENIZED, store = Store.YES )
    public String getDept() {
      return dept;
    }

    public void setDept(String dept) {
      this.dept = dept;
    }
  }
```

Listing 11.7 demonstrates the use of a Hibernate Search projection. As explained in the note at the beginning of this chapter, the scaffolding code principle still holds for this example. In this case, we examine the tests in the org.hibernate.search. test.query package.

Listing 11.7   Utilizing a Hibernate Search projection to retrieve values

```
public class ProjectionQueryTest extends SearchTestCase {
  FullTextSession session;
  Transaction tx;

  public void testLuceneObjectsProjectionWithScroll() throws Exception {
    session = Search.getFullTextSession(openSession());
    buildIndex();

    tx = session.beginTransaction();
    QueryParser parser =
      new QueryParser("dept", new StandardAnalyzer());

    Query query = parser.parse("dept:ITech");
    org.hibernate.search.FullTextQuery hibQuery =
      session.createFullTextQuery(query, Employee.class);
    hibQuery.setProjection("id", "lastname", "dept",      ❶ Applying a
      FullTextQuery.THIS, FullTextQuery.SCORE,               projection to the
      FullTextQuery.DOCUMENT, FullTextQuery.ID);             query

    ScrollableResults projections = hibQuery.scroll();
    projections.beforeFirst();
    projections.next();
    Object[] projection = projections.get();
```

```
            assert (Integer)projection[0] == 1000
               : "id incorrect";
            assert ((String) projection[1]).equals("Griffin")
               : "lastname incorrect";
            assert ((String)projection[2]).equals("ITech")
               : "dept incorrect";

            assert session.get(Employee.class,
                        (Serializable) projection[0])
               .equals(projection[3]): "THIS incorrect";

            assertEquals("SCORE incorrect", 1.0F, projection[4]);
            assert (Float)projection[4] == 1.0F
               : "SCORE incorrect";
            assert projection[5] instanceof Document
               : "DOCUMENT incorrect";
            assert ((Document) projection[5]).getFields()
               .size() == 4: "DOCUMENT size  incorrect";
            assert (Integer)projection[6] == 1000
               : "legacy ID incorrect";
            assert projections.isFirst();

            assert ((Employee) projection[3])
               .getId() == 1000: "Incorrect entity returned";

            for (Object element : session.createQuery("from "
               + Employee.class.getName()).list())
               session.delete(element);
            tx.commit();
        }
        finally {
            session.close();
        }

        private void buildIndex() {
            Transaction tx = session.beginTransaction();
            Employee e1 =
               new Employee(1000, "Griffin", "ITech");
            session.save(e1);

            Employee e2 =
               new Employee(1001, "Jackson", "Accounting");
            session.save(e2);
            tx.commit();

            session.clear();
        }
    }
```

❶ applies a projection to our "dept:ITech" query. The results of the test query are then checked: ❷ checks the id, lastname, and dept fields from the Employee entity, ❸ checks the validity of the requested ProjectionConstants values, and ❹ retrieves the FullTextQuery.THIS entity of ProjectionConstants and validates that the lastname field corresponds to the correct value.

Assertions on entity fields (❷)

Assertions on ProjectionConstants values (❸)

Checking a value of the returned entity (❹)

Projections are one of the performance improvements that we recommend. You should not make a round-trip to the database to retrieve data if you can retrieve it from the index. Lucene is incredibly fast at locating data, and that's where a projection comes in. It allows you to specify exactly the data you want to examine and skip loading any of the data from the database you're not interested in. This can increase performance, but as usual, you need to test to be sure.

Native Lucene emulates this process through a combination of the `org.apache.lucene.document.MapFieldSelector` and the `org.apache.lucene.document.FieldSelectorResult` classes, to prevent loading data that you're not interested in.

11.5 *Summary*

You've seen that accessing Lucene natively is a straightforward task as long as you have an instance of the `SearchFactory` object to start things off. Once you have an instance of this class, you can get references to Lucene `Directory`s and `DirectoryProvider(s)`.

These classes make creating `IndexReader`s and `ReaderProvider`s a straightforward operation, although section 11.2 lists some rules you will have to live by to utilize them safely. Sometimes, but not often, it's necessary to write your own `DirectoryProvider`. We examined that process and found that it may be necessary to provide overriding implementations of the following:

- `void initialize(String directoryProviderName, Properties properties, SearchFactoryImplementor searchFactoryImplementor);`
- `void start();`
- `void stop();`
- `TDirectory getDirectory();`

The `equals` and `hashCode` methods must also be overridden, but these are certainly not insurmountable tasks.

Remember, implementing projections can increase result-retrieval performance. We recommend you test for performance gains and use them as you see fit.

Next we're going to talk about a subject that's a little more difficult to grasp but not overly so: document scoring and changing how it is calculated so that it fits our needs. This is a lengthy topic, but we're sure that when you finish it you'll understand a lot more about Lucene and information retrieval in general.

Part 5

Native Lucene, scoring, and the wheel

In this final section of the book we will examine a veritable hodgepodge of topics.

Chapter 11 considers how to get to the native Lucene constructs that exist underneath of and are used by Hibernate Search. Chapter 12 discusses at length how documents are scored, utilizing the vector space model of information retrieval. A short discussion of document relevance is also included. Chapter 13 demonstrates some of the classes provided for you that were contributions from various sources and finishes with a lengthy discussion of how to index different document formats, such as Microsoft Word documents and XML files.

Following chapter 13 is an appendix, a quick reference guide of Hibernate Search artifacts. Here you can find annotations, APIs and Lucene query APIs, and where in the book the discussion is found.

Document ranking

12

This chapter covers

- The vector space model
- Extending the `DefaultSimilarity` class
- Writing your own `Scoring` and `Weight` classes
- Relevancy

Have you ever found yourself saying something like, "I need to score the results of my queries slightly differently. How do I go about that?" Or maybe, "I don't care about how many times what I'm looking for occurs in a result; I just want to know whether or not it does." The authors have even heard, "The lengths of the documents I'm querying should have nothing to do with the scores of the results."

How documents are scored when they are retrieved during a search is a very hot topic among users. Questions appear every day on the Lucene mailing list at java-user@lucene.apache.org echoing these same concerns. If you wish to subscribe to this list, you can do so at http://lucene.apache.org/java/docs/mailinglists.html.

We're going to answer many of those questions here, and in doing so we'll cover one of the most difficult topics in the information-retrieval realm. We'll start by utilizing the classic vector space model to score documents against a query. We'll then cover Lucene's scoring methodology and run through examples of how to change document scores. We'll build our own classes and extend others to score things the way we want them. Finally, we'll talk about document relevance and how to improve it. There's a lot to cover here, so let's get started.

12.1   Scoring documents

Lucene offers a plethora of ways to adjust the scoring of documents returned from queries. You can adjust the way a document's individual fields are scored when queried against by boosting the scoring value of those fields. The scoring for an entire document can be changed by boosting at the document level. The sole purpose of the classes `Similarity`, `Weight`, and `Scorer` is to allow you to change various calculations that determine how documents are scored. Even the explanation of exactly how a document's score was achieved is available. We'll start with that exercise by using a complete example of calculating document scores. Section 12.2 will cover Lucene's modifications to the classic model and show you how to modify it to adjust scores.

> **NOTE**   Even though this is an "in Action" book, the authors deem that a discussion of scoring methodology is a needed addition. Scattered references and citations concerning information-retrieval scoring theory abound on the internet, but we'd like to put the facts in one place. This will make things much easier to understand for anyone wanting to adjust how documents are scored. It will also help those who want to comprehend what is involved in the scoring process. If you consider yourself to be mathematically challenged, please do not let the formulas intimidate you. At the same time, this discussion is not an absolute necessity for understanding the process. If you wish, you can skip the theory portion and work directly with the related classes. Hopefully, you'll revisit the theory later to see why it worked that way!

We'll start by introducing the classic vector space model. This has become the basic building block of several scoring techniques, including Lucene's. Along the way, we'll talk about the shortcomings of this approach. Then, after working through a complete example, we'll move on to how Lucene deals with these shortcomings, how it implements its variations of this model, and how you can manipulate the scoring process.

12.1.1   Introducing the vector space model

First and foremost, let's define exactly what a score is.

> *A document's score is a ranking of the relevancy of the retrieved document relative to other retrieved documents in response to a query against a repository of documents.*

An important thing to remember about this score is that it is completely unrelated to any score returned by a different query on the same repository. It is relevant only to scores of other returned documents for the same query.

Several methodologies are in use today for ranking the information returned from data repositories. Hibernate Search's engine, Lucene, is based on the vector space model first proposed by Salton et al in 1975 with their paper "A Vector Space Model for Automatic Indexing." Lucene also uses Boolean retrieval methods to narrow the number of documents that need to be scored, but by far the vector space model is the scoring methodology it uses.

In the paper, Salton states that documents and queries can be expressed as vectors and as such should be comparable in such a way that a *similarity coefficient* that measures the similarity between them can be computed. This coefficient turns out to be a measure of the angle between the vector representing the document and the one representing the query. This is the elusive score we're looking for. See figure 12.1.

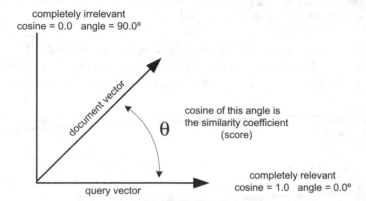

Figure 12.1   Documents and queries can be represented as vectors. A similarity coefficient that is the cosine of the angle between these vectors could represent the relative ranking (score) of the document compared to others.

The vector space model of Salton refers to a query term's weight as the result of his formula, so we will stay with his nomenclature for this discussion. It also considers documents from two different perspectives: information from individual documents (local information) and document repositories (global information). The reason for this distinction will make sense in a minute.

The classic formula is shown in equation 12.1.

$$w_i = tf_i * \log\left(\frac{D}{df_i}\right)$$

w_i = term weight

tf_i = term frequency or the number of times a term i appears in a document

df_i = document frequency or the total number of documents in the repository containing term i

D = number of documents in the repository

Equation 12.1   The classic vector space model formula for calculating the weight (score) of a document by multiplying the term frequency (tf) by the log of the inverse document frequency (idf).

Considering the local information that is the first term on the right side of the equals sign in equation 12.1 and temporarily ignoring the second term, as tf increases, so does the score. The second term on the right side of the equals sign of equation 12.1 was introduced to take global information into account by considering the total number of documents in the repository. This term is known as the *inverse document frequency (idf)*. A closer look at this portion of the equation shows that holding the number of documents in the repository constant and increasing the document frequency results in a lower weight. For example, equation 12.2 shows that with a repository of 1000 documents, if 5 documents contain the term queried for, then the idf is 2.3.

$$\log\left(\frac{1000}{5}\right) = 2.3$$ **Equation 12.2**   **With a repository of 1000 documents, if 5 documents contain the term queried for, then the idf is 2.3.**

If the number of documents containing the term increased to 20, equation 12.3 shows the idf would become 1.7. This shows that queried terms found in an excessive number of documents cause those documents to receive a lower score than those that do not.

$$\log\left(\frac{1000}{20}\right) = 1.7$$ **Equation 12.3**   **If the number of documents containing the term increased to 20, the idf would become 1.7.**

How does this equation of tf, idf, and term weight translate into a document score? To understand that we will look at a complete, albeit somewhat trivial, example of how document scores are calculated in the vector space model.

CALCULATING THE PRELIMINARY VALUES

This example was originally developed by Professors David Grossman and Ophir Freider from the Illinois Institute of Technology for use in their book *Information Retrieval: Algorithms and Heuristics* from Springer Publishing and is used here with permission of the publisher. Our thanks to Professor Grossman and Springer.

Assume that we have a document repository of three documents:

- D1: "shipment of gold damaged in a fire"
- D2: "delivery of silver arrived in a silver truck"
- D3: "shipment of gold arrived in a truck"

The query against this repository is `"gold silver truck"`, and the resulting calculations between the query and documents are shown in table 12.1.

The last row of table 12.1 is the column numbers, which are referenced in the following discussion.

In columns (1) to (5) we list the terms in the document repository and determine the term counts (tf) for each of the documents and also the query.

In columns (6) to (8) we determine the idf by summing the number of documents in which the individual term occurs. Then we divide these totals into the total number of documents in the repository, 3, and take their logarithm. Notice that for the term

Table 12.1 A listing of all document and query terms and their frequency counts that are used to calculate the inverse document frequency and term weights. The last row in the table provides the column numbers referred to in the text.

	D = 3 (the number of documents in our repository)										
	Term counts (tf)							**Weights (w = tf * idf)**			
Terms	**Query**	**D1**	**D2**	**D3**	**Df**	**D/df**	**idf**	**Query**	**D1**	**D2**	**D3**
A	0	1	1	1	3	3/3=1	0	0	0	0	0
Arrived	0	0	1	1	2	3/2=1.5	0.1761	0	0	0.1761	0.1761
Damaged	0	1	0	0	1	3/1=3	0.4771	0	0.4771	0	0
Delivery	0	0	1	0	1	3/1=3	0.4771	0	0	0.4771	0
Fire	0	1	0	0	1	3/1=3	0.4771	0	0.4771	0	0
Gold	1	1	0	1	2	3/2=1.5	0.1761	0.1761	0.1761	0	0.1761
In	0	1	1	1	3	3/3=1	0	0	0	0	0
Of	0	1	1	1	3	3/3=1	0	0	0	0	0
Silver	1	0	2	0	1	3/1=3	0.4771	0.4771	0	0.9542	0
Shipment	0	1	0	1	2	3/2=1.5	0.1761	0	0.1761	0	0.1761
Truck	1	0	1	1	2	3/2=1.5	0.1761	0.1761	0	0.1761	0.1761
(1)	(2)	(3)	(4)	(5)	(6)	(7)	(8)	(9)	(10)	(11)	(12)

silver the df (document frequency) is still only 1, because even though it appears twice, both occurrences are in the same document.

In columns (9) to (12) we compute term weights with `tf * idf`.

The final step is to take these weights and perform a similarity analysis, treating these weights as vector coordinates.

PUTTING IT ALL TOGETHER

The full similarity equation for a query *Q*, documents *i*, and terms *j* is given in equation 12.4.

$$sim\left(Q, D_i\right) = \frac{\sum w_{Q,j} \, w_{i,j}}{\sqrt{\sum_j w_{Q,j}^2}}$$

Equation 12.4 The full similarity equation between a query and a document

Don't let this equation worry you; it's not as complicated as it looks. We can rewrite this equation as shown in equation 12.5, which shows it as the *dot product* of the query and document weights divided by the product of the lengths of the same quantities, that is, the vector length of the query multiplied by the vector lengths of individual documents.

$$Cosine\theta_{Di} = \frac{Q \bullet D_i}{|Q| * |D_i|}$$ **Equation 12.5   Rewrite of equation 12.4 to the dot product divided by the product of the lengths of the same quantities**

Let's rewrite this equation one more time into the terms that we have from table 12.1. Equation 12.6 should show you exactly how this equation correlates to the quantities we have to this point.

$$Cosine\theta_{Di} = \frac{\sum(weight_{termi} * weight_{query})}{\sqrt{\sum weight_{termi}^2} * \sqrt{weight_{query}^2}}$$ **Equation 12.6   Breaking down equation 12.4 to the weights we have from table 12.1**

To calculate the similarity we'll take the numbers we've calculated so far and plug them into this formula for each document. Equations 12.7 through 12.13 show how different terms are calculated (refer to table 12.1 as necessary). We first calculate the vector length of the query:

$$|Q| = \sqrt{0.1761^2 + 0.4771^2 + 0.1761^2} = \sqrt{0.2896} = 0.5382$$

Equation 12.7   Substituting the numbers from table 1 for the query into the formula in equation 12.4

Next, for each of the three documents in the repository we calculate their vector lengths:

$$|D_1| = \sqrt{0.4771^2 + 0.4771^2 + 0.1761^2 + 0.1761^2} = \sqrt{0.5173} = 0.7192$$

$$|D_2| = \sqrt{0.1761^2 + 0.4771^2 + 0.9542^2 + 0.1761^2} = \sqrt{1.2001} = 1.0955$$

$$|D_3| = \sqrt{0.1761^2 + 0.1761^2 + 0.1761^2 + 0.1761^2} = \sqrt{0.1240} = 0.3522$$

Equations 12.8, 12.9, and 12.10   Substituting the numbers from table 12.1 for documents 1, 2, and 3 to calculate the vector lengths

Now that we have the products of the lengths, we calculate the dot products. These calculations are shown in equations 12.11 to 12.13.

$Q \bullet D_1 = 0.1761 * 0.1761 = 0.0310$

$Q \bullet D_2 = 0.4771 * 0.9542 + 0.1761 * 0.1761 = 0.4862$

$Q \bullet D_3 = 0.1761 * 0.1761 + 0.1761 * 0.1761 = 0.0620$

Equations 12.11, 12.12, and 12.13 Calculating the dot products of the individual documents

Finally, for documents 1, 2, and 3 we calculate the similarity coefficients for document 1, as shown in equation 12.14, followed by equations 12.15 and 12.16 for documents 2 and 3, respectively.

$$sim\left(Q,D_1\right)=\frac{Q\bullet D_1}{\mid Q\mid * \mid D_1\mid}=\frac{0.0310}{0.5382 * 0.7192}=0.0801$$

$$sim\left(Q,D_2\right)=\frac{Q\bullet D_2}{\mid Q\mid * \mid D_2\mid}=\frac{0.4862}{0.5382 * 1.0955}=0.8246$$

$$sim\left(Q,D_3\right)=\frac{Q\bullet D_3}{\mid Q\mid * \mid D_3\mid}=\frac{0.0620}{0.5382 * 0.3522}=0.3271$$

Equations 12.14, 12.15, and 12.16 Similarity coefficient calculations between documents 1, 2, and 3 and the query

Sorting these values in descending order, we have:

1 Document 2 = 0.8246

2 Document 3 = 0.3271

3 Document 1 = 0.0801

Notice in our table of calculations that terms occurring very often in many documents do nothing to increase the score of a document. For example, *of* and some other words in our example actually calculate to zero. Therefore they aren't included in further calculations. This is due to the global information component, idf. In our example these terms appear in *every* document, which causes their idf value and therefore their weights to calculate to zero. In large repositories if they had not appeared in every document, they still would have appeared in the vast majority of them, and their weights would calculate to very small quantities and therefore have little effect on query outcomes. Common words like *the, and*, and *but* are known as *stop words*. Many indexing and querying schemes allow for their removal both from documents before they are put into a search repository and from queries before they are applied to a search.

Is there still a problem here? The three documents now are for all intents and purposes the same length. What would happen if document 1 were inordinately longer than the other two? Let's say that document 1 reads, "Shipment of gold damaged in a fire, gold was undamaged, gold truck was total loss, gold exchange notified."

It is a natural assumption that long documents concerning a specific topic would probably contain higher term frequencies of the term they were concerned with. Witness the *gold* term in our new document. How can we take that into account? We'll discuss that in the next section.

12.1.2 *Normalizing document length to level the playing field*

Term frequency counts by themselves are not a good measure of relevancy to a term query *Q* because:

- With different length documents, a longer document may be scored higher because *Q* could appear more often.
- Equal-length documents are scored higher for more occurrences of *Q*.

We will discuss the document-length problem first, then examine the term-count problem. Long documents tend to contain higher individual term counts, but the idf remains constant; therefore the term weight *w* increases proportionally. Suppose we have a document D1, which has a certain weight w1 for a given term t1. Now suppose we increase the size of D1 by appending a copy of D1 to itself. What have we accomplished? The document count has not changed and neither has the df, but the term frequency count and therefore the score have doubled.

How do we solve or at least minimize this problem that document length can pose? We normalize the tf weights of all terms occurring in a document by the maximum tf in that document. Formally this is shown in equation 12.17.

$$f_{i,j} = \frac{tf_{i,j}}{\max\ tf_{i,j}}$$

$f_{i,j}$ = normalized frequency
$tf_{i,j}$ = frequency of term *i* in document *j*
$\max tf_{i,j}$ = maximum frequency of term *i* in document *j*

Equation 12.17   Dividing a term's frequency by the largest term frequency value yields a normalized frequency.

Consider a document with the terms and frequencies shown in table 12.2.

The *truck* term occurs most often, so the normalized frequencies are determined as shown in table 12.3.

Table 12.2 Example terms and frequencies

Term	Frequency
delivery	1
shipment	2
silver	4
truck	5

Table 12.3 Terms with their frequencies normalized

Term	Normalized frequency
delivery	1/5 = 0.20
shipment	2/5 = 0.40
silver	4/5 = 0.80
truck	5/5 = 1

The weight of term *i* in document *j* is given in equation 12.18. This is the formula used in normalized frequency term vector calculations.

$$w_{i,j} = \frac{tf_{i,j}}{\max tf_{i,j}} * \log\left(\frac{D}{df_i}\right)$$

Equation 12.18   The weight of term *i* in document *j*.

Queries also can be normalized if necessary. The formal equation for queries is shown in equation 12.19.

$$f_{Q,i} = 0.5 + 0.5 * \frac{tf_{Q,i}}{\max \ tf_{Q,i}}$$

$f_{Q,i}$ = normalized query frequency
$tf_{Q,i}$ = frequency of term i in query
$\max \ tf_{Q,i}$ = maximum frequency of term i in query

Equation 12.19   The formula used in normalized frequency query vector calculations

As an example, suppose you have the following query: Q = shipment silver shipment. The frequencies are

```
shipment   2
   silver   1
```

The *shipment* term occurs most often, so the normalized frequencies are

```
shipment  (0.5 + 0.5 * 2/2) = 1
   silver  (0.5 + 0.5 * 1/2) = 0.75
```

The weight of term i in query Q is given in equation 12.20. This formula was derived entirely from experimentation and measuring the results as the constants were changed to produce the best results.

$$w_{Q,i} = \left(0.5 + 0.5 * \frac{tf_{Q,i}}{\max \ tf_{Q,i}} \right) * \log \left(\frac{D}{df_i} \right)$$

Equation 12.20   The weight of term i in query Q. This is the formula used in normalized frequency query vector calculations.

Now that we've looked at how to minimize the effect of document length on its score, let's see what we can do to minimize the effect that a large term count can have on it. That is the topic of the next section.

12.1.3 *Minimizing large term count effects*

In the early days of the internet, people would insert a large number of identical terms into their HTML page's metadata. Let's say that these terms represented, for example, what their company manufactured. An internet search engine utilizing just term count information would then artificially inflate their page with a higher score and bring it closer to the top of search results. This practice is known as *keyword spamming*.

Our similarity coefficient calculation example at the beginning of this chapter did not demonstrate or even attempt to demonstrate this problem. This was because, first, we did not want to introduce too many things at once. We wanted you to concentrate on the calculations and understand how they are done. Second, it is impossible to illustrate this problem with such a small document repository. Let's face it; our example is totally unrealistic as far as repository size and document frequency are concerned. With that in mind we're going to ramp up our example to a realistic size and at the same time reduce our query to two terms and calculate the weight of two documents in the repository, D1 and D2. The increase in repository size will allow for reasonable number generation, and the query size reduction and weighting of only two documents will simplify the visualization of exactly what these numbers mean. Also, it will demonstrate what we meant when we presented figure 12.1 and how we derived that figure in the first place.

Here are the new quantities we're going to work with:

- repository size of 10,000,000 documents
- query is "gold truck"
- *gold* appears in the repository in 80,000 documents
- *truck* appears in the repository in 120,000 documents
- *gold* appears in D1 two times and in D2 one time
- *truck* appears in D1 three times and in D2 six times

We are simulating keyword spamming by saying that *truck* appears six times in D2. This is exactly how spamming is accomplished: have a term show up in a document many, many times. It is usually even more than six times, but that is good enough for our example. Table 12.4 is generated exactly as table 12.1 was and shows our base calculations. As we promised, things are a little simpler.

Table 12.3   Query and document weight calculations exactly as performed in table 12.1

| | D = 10,000,000, the number of documents in the repository | | | | | | | | |
| | Term counts (tf) | | | | | | Weights (w = tf * idf) | | |
Terms	Q	D1	D2	Df	D/df	Idf	Q	D1	D2
gold	1	2	1	80,000	125.0	2.097	2.097	4.194	2.097
truck	1	3	6	120,000	83.33	1.921	1.921	5.763	11.526

First we calculate the dot product of the documents and the query shown in equations 12.21 and 12.22.

$$D1 \bullet Q = 4.194 * 2.097 + 5.763 * 1.921 = 19.866$$
$$D2 \bullet Q = 2.097 * 2.097 + 11.526 * 1.921 = 26.538$$

Equations 12.21 and 12.22   Calculating the dot product of the documents and the query

Looking at the dot product alone, you might be tempted to say that D2 has the better score, but we're not finished yet. Next we need to calculate the vector lengths of the documents and query. These calculations are given in equations 12.23 through 12.25.

$$|D1| = \sqrt{4.194^2 + 5.763^2} = 7.128$$
$$|D2| = \sqrt{2.097^2 + 11.526^2} = 11.715$$
$$|Q| = \sqrt{2.097^2 + 1.921^2} = 2.844$$

Equations 12.23, 12.24, and 12.25   Calculating the vector length of the documents and query

We now have everything we need to calculate the document weights. The final calculations are given in equations 12.26 and 12.27.

$$\frac{D1 \bullet Q}{|D1| * |Q|} = \frac{19.866}{7.128 * 2.844} = 0.9800$$

$$\frac{D2 \bullet Q}{|D2| * |Q|} = \frac{26.538}{11.715 * 2.844} = 0.7965$$

Equations 12.26 and 12.27 Calculating the weight of documents D1 and D2 using the previously calculated quantities

Now you can see the effects of keyword spamming! Increasing the frequency of the term *truck* in D2 actually caused the document's score to *decrease*. Let's look at a graphical representation of this in figure 12.2. This should also help you to understand what we meant by figure 12.1.

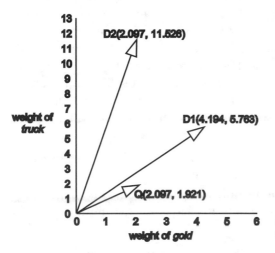

Figure 12.2 Plotting the query and document vectors by their respective weights

As you can see by figure 12.2, increasing the term frequency of *truck* in D2 increased that term's weight and therefore pushed D2's vector away from the query vector *Q*. If you were to measure the angles between the query and the document vectors, you would find that the cosine of the angle between *Q* and D1 is 0.9800, and between *Q* and D2 it is 0.7965. If you had a problem understanding figure 12.1 when you first saw it, take a look at it now, and we bet it will make more sense.

Let's review what we've covered so far. In the classic vector space model of information retrieval, documents and queries are considered to convey meaning based on their respective contents (terms). By counting these terms and performing relatively simple mathematical manipulation on them, it is possible to represent them as vectors. Once these vectors are developed, they can be utilized to calculate similarity coefficients between documents and a query. This coefficient can be interpreted as a relative score for returned documents against the query.

This model is not without its problems. A simple count of the number of occurrences of a term is not a good measure of relevancy because of the possibility of keyword spamming. The equating of queries and documents to vectors and calculating the angle between them solves this problem. Document length can adversely affect the model because as length increases, so do the term counts. Term count normalization for both documents and queries helps to offset these problems.

There are other problems with the classic model, but this discussion was not intended by any means to be an exhaustive canvass but only a gentle introduction. Let's move on to Lucene and how it performs its document scoring. We will look at the `DefaultSimilarity`, `Similarity`, `Weight`, and `Scorer` classes that are used to manipulate scoring and how to change their default behavior.

12.2 Exploring Lucene's scoring approach and the DefaultSimilarity class

As stated earlier, Lucene uses a combination of the Boolean model and the vector space model to respond to queries. Lucene's approach to document scoring is to score only those documents that have at least one term that matches a query. It does not implement a pure vector space model whereby all documents are scored whether matching or not. The Boolean model is first utilized to filter matching documents (remember all the `BooleanQuery` occurrences in chapter 7?), and then the vector space model is used in the scoring calculations of those documents. The Boolean model utilizes the standard Boolean terms `AND`, `OR`, `NOT`, and so on. This is a good marriage of two very different approaches to retrieval for two reasons:

- Conventional Boolean retrieval contributes little to relevance ranking. A document either matches a query or does not match a query.
- Having to calculate a score for only those documents that match the Boolean query greatly reduces the number of calculations that must occur, resulting in faster response.

The `Similarity` class is an abstract class that defines the methods necessary for a subclass to override whether the user wishes to modify the way Lucene scores documents. `Similarity` has two subclasses: `DefaultSimilarity` and `SimilarityDelegator`. For this discussion we are interested only in `DefaultSimilarity`. As it name suggests, the `DefaultSimilarity` class is in effect if the user does nothing to modify the scoring calculation and lets Lucene work. Before we cover how to utilize this class, a discussion of Lucene's scoring methodology is in order.

Lucene utilizes the formula in equation 12.28 for scoring document d against a particular query q.

$$score(q,d) = \\ coord(q,d) \cdot queryNorm(q) \cdot \sum \left(tf(t \text{ in } d) \cdot idf(t)^2 \cdot t.getBoost(\,) \cdot norm(t,d) \right)$$

Equation 12.28 Lucene's interpretation of the vector space scoring formula, which takes much more into account

Some of these terms should appear familiar from the earlier discussion of the vector space model. Let's examine each in some detail before moving on to examples of what happens when they are manipulated:

- *coord(int overlap, maxOverlap)* A query time score adjustment that takes into account the number of query terms that are matched by a document. *Overlap* is the number of matched terms, and *maxOverlap* is the total count of terms in the query. The default implementation is given in equation 12.29.

$$coord = \frac{overlap}{\max Overlap}$$ **Equation 12.29** **The number of matched terms divided by the total number of terms in the query**

- *queryNorm(float sumOfSquaredWeights)* Applied at query time. This quantity is multiplied against all returned documents so that it does not affect a document's ranking (the order of returned results), but it will affect its score. If the weight of a term increases, the `queryNorm` value will decrease, thereby decreasing the score. Its main purpose is to make scores comparable between dissimilar queries or even different indexes. We'll show an example of this in section 12.2.2. The default implementation is shown in equation 12.30.

$$queryNorm = \frac{1}{\sqrt{sumOfSquaredWeights}}$$ **Equation 12.30** **The query normalization factor**

The `sumOfSquaredWeights` value is taken care of by the `org.apache.lucene.search.Weight` object, which we'll discuss in section 12.3.1.

- *tf (float frequency)* This is the term frequency of the vector space model. Normally, higher term frequencies produce higher scores. Lower term frequencies produce lower scores. The default implementation is shown in equation 12.31.

$$tf = \sqrt{frequency}$$ **Equation 12.31** **The term frequency factor. This is equivalent to the term frequency of the vector space model.**

- *idf(Term term, Searcher searcher)* The idf of the vector space model. It computes a score factor for a term. The default implementation is shown in equation 12.32.

$$idf = 1 + \log\left(\frac{numdocs}{docFreq + 1}\right)$$ **Equation 12.32** **Lucene's inverse document frequency calculation**

- *term.getBoost(t)* A query time score adjustment for a particular term in a query. It is set by `Query.setBoost(float b)`. In Lucene there is no direct way to get at the boost factor of a single term in a multiterm query, so it is not part of the following formula, but since a query contains multiple `TermQuery` objects, one each for the terms, `Query.getBoost()` can be used for accessing a term's boost factor.
- *norm(t, d)* Applied at indexing time, hence the need to apply the same `Similarity` at both indexing and querying time. Norm encases several boost and length factors.

- *document boost* Established by `Document.setBoost(float b)`. This applies a separate boost factor to a particular document before it is added to the document index, allowing it to be scored differently from the rest of the documents.
- *field boost*—Established by `Field.setBoost(float b)`. This functions the same way as document boost, except it is applied to a single field in the document.
- *lengthNorm* Similar to document normalization, which was discussed in the previous normalization section, except that it applies to individual document field instead of the entire document. Its effect is to decrease the scoring contribution of fields with many terms and to increase scoring for shorter fields.

The default implementation is given in equation 12.33.

$$norm = doc.getBoost(\ ) \bullet lengthNorm \bullet \prod_{\substack{field\ f\ in\ d \\ named\ as\ t}} f.getBoost(\ )$$

Equation 12.33 Lucene's document length normalization factor applied at index time

This is definitely not the easiest `Similarity` calculation to understand, especially because of the way it is stored in the index. This formula translates to the `field.get-Boost()` value being multiplied by `Document.getBoost()` of the document containing this field. If a document has multiple fields with the same name, all such values are multiplied together. This product is then multiplied by the value `Similarity.lengthNorm(String, int)` and encoded by `Similarity.encodeNorm(float)` as a single byte to reduce its storage size. It is then stored in the document index. If you are interested in the algorithm used to accomplish this, refer to the JavaDoc for `Similarity.encodeNorm(float)`.

At query time, this value is read from the index and decoded back to a float value by the static method `Similarity.decode(n)`. There will be a loss of precision here resulting from rounding factors of the encoding algorithm to and from the byte representation. Remember, there's no contract anywhere stating that `decode (encode(x)) = x`.

That is enough of equations and theory for a while. Let's take this information and apply it by exploring several examples and examining how scores change as we vary the quantities.

12.2.1 *DefaultSimilarity examples*

Let's see how Lucene puts all of the terms into action to determine a document's score.

To analyze how the scoring process works, we'll utilize the `org.apache.lucene.search.Searcher` class, which contains the `explain (Query query, int hitId)` method. The first parameter of this method is the original query we employed to generate results. The second is the Lucene `Hit.Id` number of the document we want to examine. This is available from the document's `Hit` object, which is obtained by iterating through the returned `Hits` object. Once you examine the code, you'll see how easy it is.

NOTE   All of the examples in this chapter utilize the DVD Store example provided with the Seam framework download available at http://www.seam-framework.org/Download. We decided to use the DVD Store because of the long descriptions of each of the DVDs, which helps in showing the length influence on normalization. Plus they make the examples more realistic. To make things a little easier on you, this index is available for download on the book's internet site.

First we'll search on one term to obtain a baseline value to compare changes against. Then we'll change the term frequency calculation. Next we'll search on two terms and examine the differences in the explain printout; finally we'll adjust the coord factor and see exactly what it can do to a score.

SEARCHING ON ONE TERM

We'll query the Product index for all occurrences of the term *salesman* in the description field in listing 12.1.

Listing 12.1 Searching Product.description for `salesman`

```
public class TestSalesmanSearch extends SearchTestCase {

  @Test
  public void searchProduct() throws Exception {
    FullTextSession session = Search.getFullTextSession(openSession());
    Transaction tx = session.beginTransaction();

    try {
      Query query = new TermQuery(new Term("description"           ❶ Query for
        "salesman"));                                                single term,
      System.out.println(query.toString());                         salesman

      org.hibernate.search.FullTextQuery hibQuery =
        session.createFullTextQuery(query,
          com.jboss.dvd.seam.Product.class);
      hibQuery.setProjection(FullTextQuery.DOCUMENT,            ❷ Declare a
        FullTextQuery.SCORE,                                       projection
        FullTextQuery.DOCUMENT_ID);

      List<Object[]> results = hibQuery.list();

      assert results.size() > 0: "no results returned";
      for (Object[] result : results)                          ❸ Iterate the matching
        System.out.println("score => " + result[1]);             documents
        System.out.println(hibQuery
          .explain((Integer) result[2]));             ❹ Call explain on
      }                                                  the results
      tx.commit();
    }
    finally {
      session.close();
    }
  }
}
```

First, declare a single `TermQuery` on the description field for *salesman* ❶. Next, declare a projection of the document, score, and document id ❷. This projection is necessary since we're using a bare index: the index is not backed by a database, so we must prevent Hibernate Search from querying it. At ❸ we iterate over the results and print the explain method's contents ❹. The explain method returns an instance of the org.apache.lucene.search.Explanation class.

❹ shows one of the ways to access the contents of the explain method. The other way is to declare the explanation in the projection shown at ❷. We'll demonstrate this in the next example, which is shown in listing 12.4. The Explanation class overrides its toString() method and supplies a nicely formatted description of how a document is scored against the query, as shown in listing 12.2. A first-rate feature of this generated description is that the printout is not cluttered with information we're not interested in (yet). Similarity values that remain at their default are not reported on by the explain method.

NOTE   The contents of the description field of each document are quite large. Consequently, the five resulting product descriptions we'll be working with are not reproduced here. It's an easy process for you to display the description fields. That way you can examine them and see exactly what each one contains. We'll even reduce the results to the top three because they show us all we need to see.

Listing 12.2   Formatted printout of the explain method

```
score => 0.84061575
0.84061575 = (MATCH) fieldWeight(description:salesman
              in 108), product of:
  1.0 = tf(termFreq(description:salesman)=1)          ❶ The score and
  5.379941 = idf(docFreq=5)                             its calculation
  0.15625 = fieldNorm(field=description, doc=108)


score => 0.5944051
0.5944051 = (MATCH) fieldWeight(description:salesman
              in 471), product of:                     Higher term
  1.4142125 = tf(termFreq(description:salesman)=2)  ◁─ frequency
  5.379941 = idf(docFreq=5)
  0.078125 = fieldNorm(field=description, doc=471)  ◁─ The
                                                       fieldNorm
score => 0.58843106                                    value
0.58843106 = (MATCH) fieldWeight(description:salesman
              in 57), product of:
  1.0 = tf(termFreq(description:salesman)=1)
  5.379941 = idf(docFreq=5)
  0.109375 = fieldNorm(field=description, doc=57)
```

Listing 12.2 is the output of the Searcher.explain() method for each of the first three matching documents. ❶ contains a lot of information in just four lines. The first line contains the document's fieldWeight (score) value along with the query description:salesman followed by the Hit.Id of the document in the repository. In this case the tf, the idf, and the fieldNorm values were multiplied together. In the second line is the term frequency value, which is the number of times the term appears in the document. The third line is the idf, showing that there were five matching documents in the repository. In line 4 is the field normalization value, which translates to the `lengthNorm` value discussed in 12.3.

NOTE   You may be wondering why we bothered to print the score for each of the explained results. This printed score is the normalized score returned by `Hit.Id`, whereas the score listed in ❶ is a raw score. It's possible that the raw score of ❶ can be greater than 1, in which case a normalized result for each score is produced, dividing each one by the highest. Think back to our discussion of normalization in section 12.1.2. We'll present an example of this shortly.

Looking at listing 12.2 we can see that our earlier statement concerning the `explain` method producing uncluttered output is true. This is a concise listing of exactly what went into scoring the documents. Some may say that this listing can be misleading because it doesn't show *all* of the factors, but what it does not show are those values that remained at their defaults, and that's where we're going next.

Let's override the `DefaultSimilarity` class, change some values one at a time, and see how document scores are affected.

CHANGING THE TERM FREQUENCY CALCULATION

You're free to extend `Similarity` and override the classes' abstract methods in any way you deem fit to adjust document scoring, but `org.apache.lucene.search.DefaultSimilarity` makes this task a little easier.

Extending the `DefaultSimilarity` class allows it to function in a manner analogous to what an adapter class does for an interface. It supplies default implementations for the abstract methods of the `Similarity` class that you're not interested in, while allowing you to override whichever methods you wish to change.

Let's start with a simple scoring adjustment. We'll assume for this scenario that we aren't interested in how many times a term appears in a document. In other words, term frequency doesn't matter to us. Instead of the normal term frequency, our `ScoringTestSimilarity` class will return the value 1.0F instead of the normal square root of the actual term frequency. First we define our `ScoringTestSimilarity` class in listing 12.3.

Listing 12.3   Extending the `DefaultSimilarity` to override frequency calculation

```
public class ScoringTestSimilarity            Extend the
  extends DefaultSimilarity {                 DefaultSimilarity class
  @Override
  public float tf(float freq) {               Override the
    return 1.0F;                              tf(float freq) method
  }
}                            ❶ The returned value
```

In ❶ we've replaced the default term frequency calculation of the square root of the frequency to return a float of 1.0.

Once we have our implementation changed to the way we want it, we have to replace the `DefaultSimilarity` class with our class before we perform the query. This is done with one line of code, as shown in listing 12.4.

Listing 12.4   Replacing the `DefaultSimilarity` class with our own implementation

```
public class TestSalesmanSearch extends SearchTestCase {

  @Test
  public void searchProduct() throws Exception {

    FullTextSession session = Search.getFullTextSession(openSession());
    Transaction tx = session.beginTransaction();

    try {
      Query query = new TermQuery(new Term("description",
                                 "salesman"));
      System.out.println(query.toString());

      org.hibernate.search.FullTextQuery hibQuery =
        session.createFullTextQuery(query,
          com.jboss.dvd.seam.Product.class);
      hibQuery.setProjection(FullTextQuery.DOCUMENT,
                  FullTextQuery.SCORE,
                  FullTextQuery.DOCUMENT_ID,
                  FullTextQuery.EXPLANATION);

      List<Object[]> results = hibQuery.list();

      assert results.size() > 0: "no results returned";
      for (Object[] result : results) {
        System.out.println("score => " + result[1]);

        System.out.println(result[3].toString());
      }
      tx.commit();
    }
    finally {
      session.close();
    }
  }

  protected void configure(org.hibernate.cfg
    .Configuration cfg) {
    cfg.setProperty("hibernate.search.default
    .directory_provider",
             FSDirectoryProvider.class.getName());
    cfg.setProperty("hibernate.search.default.indexBase",
    locateBaseDir().getAbsolutePath());
    cfg.setProperty("hibernate.search.similarity",
    "com.manning.hsia.ch12.ex12_4.ScoringTestSimilarity");
  }
}
```

❶ Declare projection including explanation

❷ Print the explanation

❸ Change the scoring similarity

We declare a projection that contains the `FullTextQuery.EXPLANATION` element ❶. This is the second method of providing an explanation, as opposed to calling the `explain` method from the query as we did in listing 12.1 at ❹. ❷ presents the results

Implementing different similarities per entity

Listing 12.4 demonstrates how to set the similarity when you want to override what is provided by default. This applies across all entities unless you override it for a particular entity or entities. To override the similarity for an entity, use the @Similarity annotation. This annotation has a target of @Target(ElementType.TYPE), meaning that it is applicable only at the entity level. The following code snippet demonstrates its use:

```
@Entity
@Indexed
@Similarity( impl = MySimilarity.class)
public class Dvd {
...
}
```

Please be warned that in changing similarities we're addressing a difficult topic at best! The more similarities you override, the more difficult it becomes to assess the results. A lot of time goes into testing score adjustments and ensuring that they produce the results you're expecting. Even if you override only a single similarity trying to move results up or down the scoring ladder, you can expect a lot of testing time to assess results.

of the explanation projection. The `DefaultSimilarity` class is replaced at ❸ by the `ScoringTestSimilarity` class.

Executing this code produces the results in listing 12.5.

Listing 12.5 The results showing that the score of several documents has changed

```
score => 0. 84061575
0.84061575 = (MATCH) fieldWeight(description:salesman
                   in 108), product of:
 1.0 = tf(termFreq(description:salesman)=1)
 5.379941 = idf(docFreq=5)
 0.15625 = fieldNorm(field=description, doc=108)

score => 0. 58843106
0.58843106 = (MATCH) fieldWeight(description:salesman
                   in 57), product of:
 1.0 = tf(termFreq(description:salesman)=1)
 5.379941 = idf(docFreq=5)
 0.109375 = fieldNorm(field=description, doc=57)

score => 0. 42030787
0.42030787 = (MATCH) fieldWeight(description:salesman
                   in 217), product of:
 1.0 = tf(termFreq(description:salesman)=1)
 5.379941 = idf(docFreq=5)
 0.078125 = fieldNorm(field=description, doc=217)

score => 0. 42030787
0.42030787 = (MATCH) fieldWeight(description:salesman
                   in 471), product of:
```

❶ No change to document 108

❷ fieldNorm value

❸ Moved here from 3rd place

❹ fieldNorm value

❺ Moved here from 4th place

❻ fieldNorm value

❼ Moved here from 2nd place

```
1.0 = tf(termFreq(description:salesman)=2)
5.379941 = idf(docFreq=5)
0.078125 = fieldNorm(field=description, doc=471)
```

8 **Term frequency changed**

9 **fieldNorm value**

The fourth result was included here to help show the changes that have taken place. Notice how much the documents (**3**, **5**, and **7**) have shuffled; but not **1**. Even though the printout still shows the actual term frequency with (description:salesman)=2, the term frequency at **8** has changed from 2 to 1 as we expected from our overriding of the term frequency method. This changed the term frequency value from 1.4142125 to 1, reducing the overall score and dropping it lower in the results.

We need to discuss one last thing about this explanation printout. Take a close look at the fieldNorm values **1**, **4**, **6**, and **9**. Hopefully you have noticed that the field normalization value has a huge impact on the final score. When the field you are searching is long (read that as "has many terms"), the fieldNorm value can become quite small, reducing the score by a large amount.

There are several ways around this normalization effect if you wish to eliminate it from your method of scoring:

- *Implement your own Similarity class, overriding the lengthNorm calculation.* We're overriding the Similarity class in these examples. If you're going to override this calculation with your own, you must do so both at indexing time by employing the IndexWriter.setSimilarity(Similarity similarity) method and at query time by utilizing the same technique employed in listing 12.4.

- *Write your own IndexReader class that ignores index norm values.* This is the most difficult of these choices to implement and outside the scope of this book. The authors recommend you search the Lucene mailing list archives for examples.

- Add the Field.Index NO_NORMS constant to eliminate norm calculations on a particular field.

- *Call setOmitNorms(boolean omitNorms) on the appropriate field.* This, along with the NO_NORMS method mentioned in the previous bullet, is the easiest way to prevent normalization effects for a particular field.

WARNING   Beware when disabling norms: you must disable norms for every single occurrence of that field in any document in your index. If even one document exists in which you did not disable norms for that field, that will spread to all other docs anytime index segments merge.

Let's go through our third example to demonstrate querying by more than one term and the resulting changes that occur to the explain method's printout. This will utilize a BooleanQuery to effect the change.

SEARCHING ON MULTIPLE TERMS

When querying on more than one term, documents matching more of the query's terms will normally receive a higher score than those matching on a lesser number. In other words, high match counts increase scores, while low match counts do not. This does not have to be the case. Since these values can be whatever the developer chooses, their ratio could actually be reduced with a high match count.

To demonstrate this we'll look at the coord(int overlap, maxOverlap) calculation and how changing it can affect document scoring. Listing 12.6 is the query code we're going to use for this example.

Listing 12.6   Querying on more than one term with `DefaultSimilarity`

```
BooleanQuery query = new BooleanQuery();
query.add(new BooleanClause(
  new TermQuery(new Term(FIELD_NAME,
                "spielberg")),
                BooleanClause.Occur.MUST));          ❶ Query description
                                                        for spielberg

query.add(new BooleanClause(
  new TermQuery(new Term(FIELD_NAME,
                "war")),
                BooleanClause.Occur.SHOULD));         ❷ Query description
                                                         for war

System.out.println(query.toString());         ◁─────

org.hibernate.search.FullTextQuery hibQuery =        ❸ Print the explanation
  session.createFullTextQuery(query,
                    Product.class);
hibQuery.setProjection(FullTextQuery.DOCUMENT,
                FullTextQuery.SCORE,
                FullTextQuery.DOCUMENT_ID);

List<Object[]> results = hibQuery.list();

assert results.size() > 0: "no results returned";
for (Object[] result : results) {
  System.out.println("score => " + result[1]);

  System.out.println(hibQuery          ❸ Print the explanation
    .explain((Integer)result[2]));    ◁──┘
}
```

This query searches for two terms: the description field for the term *spielberg* ❶ and the description for *war* ❷. The explanation is printed at ❸. Once we execute this query, we receive the explanation printout shown in listing 12.7.

Listing 12.7   Results of a query on two terms with `DefaultSimilarity` unchanged

```
score => 1.0                       ❶ The raw score
1.009682 = (MATCH) sum of:    ◁──┘
 0.72382677 = (MATCH) weight(description:spielberg in     ❷ The score for
                    230), product of:        ◁─────────────── spielberg
  0.7705941 = queryWeight(description:spielberg),
                    product of:
   4.338487 = idf(docFreq=16)
   0.17761816 = queryNorm
  0.93931 = (MATCH) fieldWeight(description:spielberg
                    in 230), product of:
   1.7320508 = tf(termFreq(description:spielberg)=3)
```

```
   4.338487 = idf(docFreq=16)
   0.125 = fieldNorm(field=description, doc=230)
 0.2858553 = (MATCH) weight(description:war in 230),
                     product of:
 0.63732624 = queryWeight(description:war), product of:
  3.5881817 = idf(docFreq=35)
  0.17761816 = queryNorm
 0.44852272 = (MATCH) fieldWeight(description:war in 230),
                         product of:
  1.0 = tf(termFreq(description:war)=1)
  3.5881817 = idf(docFreq=35)
  0.125 = fieldNorm(field=description, doc=230)
```

❸ The score for *war*

Listing 12.7 shows that each queried term has it own calculation set, as you'd expect. The individual term scores ❷ and ❸ are composed of the product of the query weight and the field weight. These scores are in turn summed to produce the raw score ❶.

We have space for one last example. We'll override the coord factor to demonstrate how scoring multiterm matches can be altered.

CHANGING THE COORD(INT OVERLAP, INT MAXOVERLAP)

Now we'll modify the coord function that we introduced in section 12.2. Our ScoringTestSimilarity will override the coord(int overlap, int maxOverlap) method of DefaultSimilarity in listing 12.8 so that the higher the overlap value becomes, the lower the value that is returned.

Listing 12.8 Overriding `coord(int overlap, int maxOverlap)`

```
package org.apache.lucene.search;

public class ScoringTestSimilarity extends DefaultSimilarity {
  @Override
  public float coord(int overlap, int maxOverlap) {
    if (overlap == 2) {
      return 0.5F;
    }                         Increasing overlap;
    if (overlap == 1) {       decreasing value
      return 2.0F;
    }
    return 0.0F;
  }
}
```

Executing the code in listing 12.4 produces the explanation printout of listing 12.9.

Listing 12.9 Explanation for document 230 after changing the `coord` method

```
score => 0.427106        ❶ The document score
0.504841 = (MATCH) product of:   ❷ The raw score     ❸ The basic score sum
  1.009682 = (MATCH) sum of:                            of the field scores
    0.72382677 = (MATCH) weight(description:spielberg
                  in 230),      ❹ Field score for spielberg
                  product of:
      0.7705941 = queryWeight(description:spielberg),
```

```
                    product of:
       4.338487 = idf(docFreq=16)
       0.17761816 = queryNorm
     0.93931 = (MATCH) fieldWeight(description:spielberg
                         in 230), product of:
       1.7320508 = tf(termFreq(description:spielberg)=3)
       4.338487 = idf(docFreq=16)
       0.125 = fieldNorm(field=description, doc=230)
     0.2858553 = (MATCH) weight(description:war in 230),
                         product of:
       0.63732624 = queryWeight(description:war), product of:
       3.5881817 = idf(docFreq=35)
       0.17761816 = queryNorm
     0.44852272 = (MATCH) fieldWeight(description:war
                         in 230), product of:
       1.0 = tf(termFreq(description:war)=1)
       3.5881817 = idf(docFreq=35)
       0.125 = fieldNorm(field=description, doc=230)
       0.5 = coord(2/2)
```

5 Field score for *war*

6 The coord(int overlap, int maxOverlap)factor

Document 230 in listing 12.7 was the top result returned. Applying our new `ScoringTestSimilarity` class moved it all the way to fourteenth place. Looking at listing 12.9 you can see that the basic score **3** is the sum of the weight for the *spielberg* query term **4** and the *war* query term **5**, but the raw score is where our change to the `Similarity` class comes into effect. The raw score **2** is the product of the basic score **3** and our returned value **6**. The fact that the score was reduced because more of the terms matched (two) cut the raw score in half, which is exactly what we wanted to accomplish.

Did you happen to notice the difference between the score contained in the `Hit` object of this result **1** and the raw score **2**? The raw score of the first document returned was 1.1820041. If the top document's raw score is greater than 1, we utilize this value to *normalize* the score of all returned documents by dividing all of their scores by this value. Dividing **2** in listing 12.9 by this value yields 0.4271012.

If you look at listing 12.7 you'll notice the same situation. The only difference is that this is the top document returned for this query. Because its raw score is greater than 1.0, it is divided by itself, yielding 1.0, and all other returned documents' raw scores are divided by it in turn.

Enough on the `Similarity` class. Before we move on to other classes that are used to affect scoring, we'd like to briefly discuss one more thing, query boosting.

12.2.2 *Query boosting*

We briefly mentioned query boosting in the `t.getBoost(t)` paragraph of the `DefaultSimilarity` class. Let's change listing 12.6 slightly and apply a boost factor to our query term of *war* in listing 12.10. Before we apply the boost, we say that *war* should appear in the results, and by adding a boost to it we are saying that if *war* does appear, score it higher than those results where it does not appear.

Listing 12.10   Boosting one term of a two-term query to score it higher

```
BooleanQuery query = new BooleanQuery();
query.add(new BooleanClause(new TermQuery(
  new Term(FIELD_NAME, "spielberg")),
  BooleanClause.Occur.MUST));

TermQuery war =
  new TermQuery(new Term(FIELD_NAME, "war"));        ❶ Double the query
war.setBoost(2.0F);                                        boost factor
BooleanClause c =
  new BooleanClause(war, BooleanClause.Occur.SHOULD);
query.add(c);
System.out.println(query.toString());

org.hibernate.search.FullTextQuery hibQuery =
  session.createFullTextQuery(query, Product.class);
hibQuery.setProjection(FullTextQuery.DOCUMENT,
                FullTextQuery.SCORE,
                FullTextQuery.DOCUMENT_ID);

List<Object[]> results = hibQuery.list();

assert results.size() > 0: "no results returned";
for (Object[] result : results) {

  System.out.println("score => " + result[1]);

  System.out.println(hibQuery        ❷ Examine the
    .explain((Integer)result[2]));         explanation
}
```

Here, in listing 12.11, is the explanation of the results, which we are going to compare with listing 12.7. We are showing only the top two results here.

Listing 12.11   The explanation of the results after boosting a term in a two-term query

```
score => 0.86979103    ❶ The top score has decreased
0.86979103 = (MATCH) sum of:
  0.485959 = (MATCH) weight(description:spielberg in 230),
                  product of:
   0.5173574 = queryWeight(description:spielberg),
                  product of:
    4.338487 = idf(docFreq=16)         ❷ The queryNorm
    0.11924834 = queryNorm             has decreased
   0.93931 = (MATCH) fieldWeight(description:
                        spielberg in 230),
                  product of:
    1.7320508 = tf(termFreq(description:spielberg)=3)
    4.338487 = idf(docFreq=16)
    0.125 = fieldNorm(field=description, doc=230)
  0.383832 = (MATCH) weight(description:war^2.0 in 230),    The queryWeight ❸
                  product of:                                increased for war
   0.8557694 = queryWeight(description:war^2.0), product of:
    2.0 = boost        ❹ Double the query
                         boost factor
```

```
  3.5881817 = idf(docFreq=35)
  0.11924834 = queryNorm
0.44852272 = (MATCH) fieldWeight(description:war in 230),
                    product of:
  1.0 = tf(termFreq(description:war)=1)
  3.5881817 = idf(docFreq=35)
  0.125 = fieldNorm(field=description, doc=230)
```

The queryNorm ❷
has decreased

```
score => 0.6644006
0.6644006 = (MATCH) sum of:
  0.28056857 = (MATCH) weight(description:spielberg in 15),
                       product of:
    0.5173574 = queryWeight(description:spielberg), product of:
    4.338487 = idf(docFreq=16)
    0.11924834 = queryNorm
    0.5423109 = (MATCH) fieldWeight(description:spielberg in 15),
                        product of:
    1.0 = tf(termFreq(description:spielberg)=1)
    4.338487 = idf(docFreq=16)
    0.125 = fieldNorm(field=description, doc=15)
  0.383832 = (MATCH) weight(description:war^2.0 in 15),
                     product of:
    0.8557694 = queryWeight(description:war^2.0), product of:
    2.0 = boost
    3.5881817 = idf(docFreq=35)
    0.11924834 = queryNorm
    0.44852272 = (MATCH) fieldWeight(description:war in 15),
                        product of:
    1.0 = tf(termFreq(description:war)=1)
    3.5881817 = idf(docFreq=35)
    0.125 = fieldNorm(field=description, doc=15)
```

We'd be willing to bet that this isn't what you expected. Comparing this to listing 12.7, you can see that the document scores actually dropped ❶, but the things we expected to change have changed in exactly the way we expected:

- The document's ranking has not changed. Result 1 in listing 12.7 is still result 1 here. Result 2 is still result 2, and so on.
- The 2.0 boost factor ❹ for the *war* term increased the query weight for that term from 0.63732624 to 0.8557694 ❸.

The queryNorm value decreased ❷ since the *war* term weight increased. We weren't expecting it to have that big of an impact. Remember, the queryNorm value doesn't affect document ranking; it affects matching documents' scores equally. Its main purpose is to make scores comparable between dissimilar queries or even different indexes.

This is the example we promised to show you when we talked about the queryNorm quantity. This example doubles your return. It shows both the effect of boosting a term in a query and what that does to the queryNorm calculation.

Some other components also affect document scoring, namely, the Scorer class and the Weight class, and we have to warn you that working with these classes is not for the faint of heart. It will really help you to keep things straight if you remember the following facts about each of these classes:

The `Scorer` class:

- Calculates document scores based on a given `Similarity`
- Is created by a `Weight` class via `Weight.scorer(IndexReader reader)`

The `Weight` class:

- Is created by a query: `Query.createWeight(IndexSearcher searcher)`
- Is an internal representation of the query that allows the query to be reused by the searcher

We'll look first at the `Scorer` class and its responsibilities in the scoring calculation.

12.3   *Scoring things my way*

The `Scorer` class is the focal point of Lucene scoring. If it helps, you can think of this class during the scoring process as functioning similarly to a `JDBC RowSet` having a forward-only cursor with the `RowSet` data as the group of documents that matched a query.

`Scorer` is an abstract class that defines the following abstract methods:

- `public abstract boolean next();`   This method advances to the next matching document *if* one exists.
- `public abstract int doc();`   This method returns the current document id value. Just as with a `JDBC RowSet`, this is not a valid call until the `next()` method has been called one or more times.
- `public abstract boolean skipTo(int target);`   Overriding this method could be as simple as using a basic loop, as shown here, which is fine for our purposes:

```
boolean skipTo(int target) {
  do {
      if (!next())
        return false;
    } while (target > doc());
  return true;
}
```

- `public abstract Explanation explain(int doc);`   This is the method that lays out the scoring explanation so well. It can become quite involved, so we recommend that you examine the `explain` method of the `TermScorer` class and use that as a guide in writing your own `explain` method.
- `public abstract float score();`   This is the method we've been looking for. Here is where the actual scoring procedure is defined, and you're free to change document scoring by overriding this method. For our purposes we'll examine the `TermScorer`'s score method. This method in conjunction with the `TermScorer`'s constructor is a good basic example for us to work with. The constructor and `score()` method are given in listing 12.12.

Listing 12.12 The score() method of the MyTermScorer class

```
MyTermScorer(Weight weight,
          TermDocs td,
          Similarity similarity,                 ❶ The TermScorer
             byte[] norms) {        ◁─────┘      constructor
  super(similarity);
  this.weight = weight;
  this.termDocs = td;
  this.norms = norms;
  this.weightValue = weight.getValue();
                                              ❷ Calculate and
  for (int i = 0; i < SCORE_CACHE_SIZE; i++) ◁─┘ cache score values
    scoreCache[i] = getSimilarity()
      .tf(i) * weightValue;
}
public float score() {  ◁─┘ The score method
  int f = freqs[pointer];  ◁─┐
                          ❸ Cached term
                            frequency (tf) counts
  float raw =
    f < SCORE_CACHE_SIZE                 ◁─┐
    ? scoreCache[f]                        │ Get cached value or
    : getSimilarity().tf(f)*weightValue; ❹ calculate a value

                                          ❺ Return the
  return raw * Similarity.decodeNorm(norms[doc]);  ◁─┘ raw score
}
```

The constructor ❶ caches a number of score values for fast access at ❷. These scores are calculated by retrieving the Similarity.tf() calculation over the range of cache index values multiplied by the weight.getValue() quantity of the query. Since the default implementation of the tf() method is the square root of the passed-in term, the values inserted into the cache are 0.0, 1.0, 1.414, 1.732, and so on, each multiplied by the weight value. The term frequency ❸ is utilized ❹ to look up the score in the cache or calculate the score if the number of terms is greater than the cache size. This calculation is the same as the constructor's calculation ❷, as you would expect. Finally, the raw score ❺ is determined by normalizing the cache score against the decoded normalization value of this document and returned.

NOTE The TermScorer is one of the easiest score implementations to understand. If you followed this even at just a cursory level, you have to have noticed how prevalent the Similarity class is in this calculation. Because of this, the authors recommend that, before you try to implement your own scorer, you determine whether what you want to accomplish can be done through reimplementing the Similarity class. This may save you not only a lot of work but also possibly a lot of long and sleepless nights.

We're going to hold off on an example for a bit until we cover the last important class in the scoring process, Weight. Why we are holding off will become apparent when you see just how intertwined these classes are.

12.3.1 *Modifying a query's Weight class*

An instance of the `Weight` class is specific to a particular query. After all, it has two purposes. First and foremost is to normalize a query so that searching does not modify the query in some way. This allows the query to be reused. Second is to build a `Scorer` class. In other words, a query has an associated `Weight` instance that it utilizes before performing the search process.

We can employ a custom `Weight` class in several ways. The abstract `org.apache.lucene.search.Searcher` class implements the `Searchable` interface, which defines three abstract methods that take a `Weight` instance as one of their parameters. These are:

- `void search(Weight weight, Filter filter, HitCollector results)`
- `TopDocs search(Weight weight, Filter filter, int n)`
- `TopFieldDocs search(Weight weight, Filter filter, int n, Sort sort)`

These methods are very low-level API calls, and each returns matching documents differently, so we suggest you read the documentation to see the strengths and weaknesses of each in relation to what you're trying to do.

WARNING   Lucene is a dynamic project and its code changes constantly with modifications and additions. Consequently, the code shown in the `Weight` class in this section and the `Scorer` class in section 12.3.2 examples probably have changed since this was written. The methods in these classes we are most concerned with likely have not changed but be sure to look at the latest source code.

The last way to change the way weighting is done is to not only develop your own `Weight` class but also to develop your own `Query` class and have your `Query` employ your `Weight`. This isn't as bad as it sounds. `Query` classes can be extended, so a lot of the work in this respect is already done for you. The `Weight` class is different, though. If you've downloaded the Lucene source code (if you have not, we recommend you do so now) and happened to have looked in the `org.apache.lucene.search` package, you'll notice that there are no `Weight` classes there. Many `Weight` class implementations are inner classes of the query they're related to. As mentioned previously, a `Weight` class is specific to a particular query. Making them inner classes assures that this is the case. If you look at the `org.apache.lucene.search.spans` package, you'll see that these queries all use the non-inner class `SpanWeight`. The manner of implementation is up to you.

The sequence of operations for weighting is contained in the `Query.weight(Searcher searcher)` method, shown in listing 12.13.

> **Listing 12.13   The weight(Searcher searcher) method of Query**

```
public Weight weight(Searcher searcher)
  throws IOException {
  Query query = searcher.rewrite(this);
```

```
                                                              Instance of
Weight weight = query.createWeight(searcher);     ←┘         Weight created
float sum = weight.sumOfSquaredWeights();

float norm =                                ❶ Query normalization
   getSimilarity(searcher).queryNorm(sum);  ←┘  factor calculated

weight.normalize(norm);  ←┐ Normalization factor
return weight;              passed to instance
}
```

NOTE For the following discussion the order of the calls in listing 12.13 is critical to understanding the calculations.

A Weight class must implement the Weight interface, which contains the following six method signatures:

- Query getQuery(); This returns the Query that this Weight represents.
- float getValue(); This returns the calculated weight for this query. For a TermQuery this is idf * idf * term boost * queryNorm (queryNorm is calculated by a call to the normalize method).
- float sumOfSquaredWeights(); This calculates and returns idf * idf * boost2.
- void normalize(float norm); The value calculated by sumOfSquaredWeights is passed to the Similarity.queryNorm() method, and then the resulting normalized value is passed to this method. The value returned by the getValue method is then figured and stored in the Weight instance.
- Scorer scorer(IndexReader reader); This constructs an instance of the Scorer class. If you've implemented your own Scorer, you'd retrieve an instance of it here.
- Explanation explain(IndexReader reader, int doc); This is the Weight class's implementation for an explanation printout of its effect on a document's score. We recommend again that you examine the explain() method of the TermScorer class.

NOTE For a single-term query, boosting the term makes little sense. All the matching document's scores would be boosted by the same amount. Where this boost value shines, for example, is boosting one of the terms of a two-term query when the query ORs the terms. Any documents matching the boosted query would have their score increased over documents matching the other term.

For our example we'll stay with the TermQuery class because it's one of the simplest implementations. We'll extend TermQuery and define an inner Weight class where we have replaced the final multiplication by the idf in the normalize method with a constant value of 6, as shown at ❶ in listing 12.14. This will be the only change made, and it should increase the document scores. We also must write a scorer method, but for this example it won't do anything different than the default implementation. We'll work with it shortly.

Listing 12.14   Extending `TermQuery` and implementing an inner `Weight` class

```
public class MyTermQuery extends TermQuery {
  Private Term term;

  public class MyWeight implements Weight {
    private Similarity similarity;
    private float value;
    private float idf;
    private float queryNorm;
    private float queryWeight;

  public MyWeight(Searcher searcher) throws IOException {
    this.similarity = getSimilarity(searcher);
    idf = similarity.idf(term, searcher);
  }

    public Query getQuery() {                    Return the
      return MyTermQuery.this;   ◁──┘            enclosing query
    }

    public float getValue() {
      return value;
    }

    public float sumOfSquaredWeights() throws IOException {
      queryWeight = idf * getBoost()
      return queryWeight * queryWeight;
    }

    public void normalize(float queryNorm) {
      this.queryNorm = queryNorm;
      queryWeight *= queryNorm;          Remove the idf term
      value = queryWeight * 6;   ◁──┘    to change the weight
    }

    public Scorer scorer(IndexReader reader)
      throws IOException {
      TermDocs termDocs = reader.termDocs(term);

      if (termDocs == null) {
        return null;
      }

      return new MyTermScorer(this,
                   termDocs,          ❶ Create an instance
                   similarity,   ◁──┘   of a Scorer class
➥reader.norms(term.field())));
    }

    public Explanation explain(IndexReader reader,
➥int doc)
      throws IOException {
      removed for brevity, identical to
      Query explanation method
```

```
        }
     }
     public MyTermQuery(Term t) {
        super(t);
        term = t;   <— Save the term
     }

     @Override
     protected Weight createWeight(Searcher searcher)
        throws IOException {
        return new MyWeight(searcher);   <—┐ Return an instance
     }                                      │ of the new weight

     public boolean equals(Object o) {
        if (!(o instanceof TermQuery))
          return false;
        MyTermQuery other = (MyTermQuery)o;
        return (this.getBoost() == other.getBoost())
          && this.term.equals(other.term);
     }
  }
}
```

Here are the document explanations with our change in place:

```
        score => 0.9375
        0.84061575 = (MATCH) fieldWeight(description:salesman in 108),
  product of:
           1.0 = tf(termFreq(description:salesman)=1)
           5.379941 = idf(docFreq=5)
           0.15625 = fieldNorm(field=description, doc=108)

        score => 0.6629126
        0.5944051 = (MATCH) fieldWeight(description:salesman in 471),
  product of:
           1.4142125 = tf(termFreq(description:salesman)=2)
           5.379941 = idf(docFreq=5)
           0.078125 = fieldNorm(field=description, doc=471)

        score => 0.65625
        0.58843106 = (MATCH) fieldWeight(description:salesman in 57),
  product of:
           1.0 = tf(termFreq(description:salesman)=1)
           5.379941 = idf(docFreq=5)
           0.109375 = fieldNorm(field=description, doc=57)
```

Compare these explanations with the one given in listing 12.2. Notice how the scores have increased, but all the other calculations have remained the same. How did we know the scores would increase? The constant value we placed in the `normalize` method was higher than the actual idf value of 5, and it is a weight multiplier for scores in the `MyTermScorer` class. Since it was larger than the idf value, the scores went up. What happens if we drop the constant below the idf threshold? Take a look:

```
score => 0.625
    0.84061575 = (MATCH) fieldWeight(description:salesman in 108),
  product of:
```

```
    1.0 = tf(termFreq(description:salesman)=1)
    5.379941 = idf(docFreq=5)
    0.15625 = fieldNorm(field=description, doc=108)

  score => 0.44194174
  0.5944051 = (MATCH) fieldWeight(description:salesman in 471),
product of:
    1.4142125 = tf(termFreq(description:salesman)=2)
    5.379941 = idf(docFreq=5)
    0.078125 = fieldNorm(field=description, doc=471)

  score => 0.4375
  0.58843106 = (MATCH) fieldWeight(description:salesman in 57),
product of:
    1.0 = tf(termFreq(description:salesman)=1)
    5.379941 = idf(docFreq=5)
    0.109375 = fieldNorm(field=description, doc=57)
```

The scores dropped just as expected. This is not a very useful example. It was intended to demonstrate how to modify a weight calculation. The idf is different for every query, so a constant value would quickly become irrelevant. Maybe it should be changed to idf − 1 or idf + 1.

NOTE   Did you notice the `Similarity` class making its way into the calculation again? Our former recommendation still holds. Before writing a full implementation of a `Weight` class and either extending or writing a new `Query` class, examine `Similarity` and see if what you want to accomplish can be done solely with it.

We said earlier that we'd hold off implementing our own `Scorer` class until we explained some other things, namely the `Weight` class. As one last example before we move on to other subject matter, we're going to do just that, implement a `Scorer`.

12.3.2   *Revisiting the Scorer class*

The end is in sight. We have one final matter to take care of before we move on from scoring. Did you tie ❶ in listing 12.14 to the `Scorer` class we wrote in listing 12.12? This is how you employ your own implementation of a `Scorer` class. All that is necessary is to put your modifications in the `MyTermScorer` class, as we do in listing 12.15.

We'll now implement our `Scorer` class, but we won't change the `score` method; we'll change the constructor to fill the `scoreCACHE` by multiplying the `weightValue` by a constant 1.0, as follows in listing 12.15.

> **Listing 12.15   Changing the `scorer` constructor to multiply by a constant tf**

```
MyTermScorer(Weight weight, TermDocs td, Similarity
        similarity, byte[] norms) {
  super(similarity);
  this.weight = weight;
  this.termDocs = td;
  this.norms = norms;
  this.weightValue = weight.getValue();
```

```
for (int i = 0; i < SCORE_CACHE_SIZE; i++)      Multiplying by a
  scoreCache[i] = 1.0 * weightValue;        ◄──┘  constant tf value
}
```

The MyTermQuery class's normalize method returned to using the idf value instead of the constant 6, so we'll see the effect of changing only the scorer constructor.

The top four document explanations then become these:

```
score => 0.84061575
0.84061575 = (MATCH) fieldWeight(description:salesman in 108),
product of:
    1.0 = tf(termFreq(description:salesman)=1)
    5.379941 = idf(docFreq=5)
    0.15625 = fieldNorm(field=description, doc=108)

score => 0.58843106
0.58843106 = (MATCH) fieldWeight(description:salesman in 57),
product of:
    1.0 = tf(termFreq(description:salesman)=1)
    5.379941 = idf(docFreq=5)
    0.109375 = fieldNorm(field=description, doc=57)

score => 0.42030787
0.42030787 = (MATCH) fieldWeight(description:salesman in 217),
product of:
    1.0 = tf(termFreq(description:salesman)=1)
    5.379941 = idf(docFreq=5)
    0.078125 = fieldNorm(field=description, doc=217)

score => 0.42030787
0.5944051 = (MATCH) fieldWeight(description:salesman in 471),
product of:
    1.4142125 = tf(termFreq(description:salesman)=2)
    5.379941 = idf(docFreq=5)
    0.078125 = fieldNorm(field=description, doc=471)
```

Now compare this with listing 12.5. They are identical! How did this happen? By changing the constructor to multiply by a constant 1.0, we, in effect, said that we don't care about term frequency. If a document contains the term, report it. Is that not exactly what we did in listing 12.4 when we changed the DefaultSimilarity's term frequency? Rather than do that, we extended the Query class, wrote our own Weight class, then wrote our own scorer. Hopefully this demonstrates that things can be made simpler. Don't do more work than you have to!

12.3.3 *Is it worth it?*

At the beginning of this chapter we asked a series of questions about the scoring of documents and how we could possibly manipulate the scoring, if at all. The last question in that group was, "Is it worth it to change this scoring mechanism?" To paraphrase one of the core Lucene developers, Lucene's scoring works well right out of the box.

At the same time, Lucene is definitely not all things to all people. Some people are never satisfied. We believe the answer to this question is the same ubiquitous answer that is given to most questions concerning anything to do with computers and data: "It depends." If you feel the need to tweak the way your application scores data, then by all means do it. Just be smart about it.

It's time to move on. We've covered quite an assortment of topics up to this point, but we briefly mentioned one essential topic and then seem to have forgotten it. That topic is the *relevancy* of documents returned from searches. After all, what use are documents concerning the USS *Kitty Hawk* if they were returned in answer to a query pertaining to the details of the Wright brothers' first flight? Let's take a look at document relevance.

12.4   *Document relevance*

Lucene and therefore Hibernate Search focus strictly on what are known as ad hoc queries. That is, they provide responses to user-supplied queries. The problem with relevance is that it is subjective. What may be judged relevant by one person might not be judged relevant by another. Taking our query about the Wright brothers as an example, one person may say that the aircraft carrier document is relevant because it was named after the location of the Wright brothers' first powered flight, and that person was wondering if any U.S. Navy ships had been named after historical events. Another person may say it is completely irrelevant because it has nothing to do with how many flights took place on December 17, 1903, or what the flight distances were. It depends on what information the user is looking for.

One would think that in this day and age Google would have solved the relevancy problem, but effectiveness measurements have not been made available even by Google itself. According to the Text Retrieval Conference (TREC), as of 2003 search accuracy is, at best, in the 40 percent range.

How can a subjective topic like relevance be measured in scientific terms? That's what we'll discuss next. Experimentation has identified some fairly simple formulas for two quantities: *Precision* and *Recall*. The formulas are simple, but manipulating the underlying framework they represent is not.

12.4.1   *Understanding Precision vs. Recall*

Relevance theory identifies and utilizes two terms: Precision and Recall. These terms are defined by comparing a query's returned documents with that portion of those documents that are judged relevant. See figure 12.3.

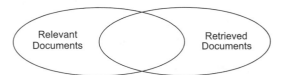

Figure 12.3   The relationship between relevant documents and all retrieved documents. Not all retrieved documents are relevant, and not all relevant documents are retrieved.

Relating to the quantities in figure 12.2, Recall is defined in equation 12.34 as the ratio of relevant retrieved documents to the total number of relevant documents in the repository.

$$Recall = \frac{|\,Ret \cap Rel\,|}{|\,Rel\,|}$$ **Equation 12.34   Formula used to calculate Recall**

Precision is defined in equation 12.35 as the ratio of the number of relevant retrieved documents to the total number of documents retrieved.

$$Precision = \frac{|\,Ret \cap Rel\,|}{|\,Ret\,|}$$ **Equation 12.35   Formula used to measure Precision**

Notice that the size of the document repository has no bearing. We're concerned solely with the ratios of returned and relevant documents.

Applying these concepts to figure 12.3 yields updated figure 12.4.

From the Precision equation you can see that increasing the number of relevant returned documents while keeping the total number retrieved constant increases the Precision proportionally. Can these values be accurately measured? If so, how do we go about it? That is our next topic.

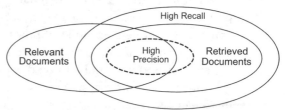

Figure 12.4   High Precision requires returned documents to be relevant; high Recall is concerned only with retrieval.

12.4.2 *Measuring a system's relevance accurately*

How do we go about quantifying how accurate the relevance of a system actually is? As we mentioned, judging search quality is subjective and difficult. Judging the quality of any intricate task can become very labor intensive. To determine accurate relevance of a search system like Lucene, three items are necessary:

- *A standard collection of documents*   Standard document repositories are available free on the internet. As you would expect, non-free ones are available also. One of the free ones is the JRC-ACQUIS Multilingual Parallel Corpus located at http://wt.jrc.it/lt/Acquis/. This corpus is available in 23 different languages. TREC also has repositories available with links on its internet site, but these are not free.

- *A set of standard queries*   Queries against repositories are also available on TREC, and these are free. You can also develop your own.

- *A set of relevance judgments*   This is where the hard labor comes in. You need to specify which of the documents in the corpus are relevant to which standard query *across the entire repository*! TREC offers sets of free relevance judgments and the C source code for a program to aid in determining relevance called trec_eval_latest.tar.gz. Even though you may have to purchase the corpus, the cost saved by the free queries and relevance judgments may make it worthwhile for you.

NOTE   The above bullet points are paraphrased from a presentation given by Grant Ingersoll at ApacheCon 2007. Although this information is quite similar to that given on the TREC website, we want to make sure to recognize him.

Lucene includes utility classes in the contribution package, which we'll be discussing in chapter 13, to utilize TREC information to judge system relevance. You could utilize this to help with generating queries for your application. The benchmark tools are located at *lucene_install_directory*/contrib/benchmark. You'll have to unjar the documentation in the lucene-benchmark-javadoc.jar file. Once you have this uncompressed, start by reading the `org.apache.lucene.benchmark.quality` package file. It contains a complete example of how to quantify search quality. A discussion of these utilities was absent in the first edition of *Lucene in Action* but is included as one of the appendixes in the second edition due out in March 2009.

Information retrieval systems are optimized quantitatively by continuously measuring the effect of system changes through the previous procedures. Once this process is completed, you might ask whether there is any other way that relevant document frequency can be enhanced while still keeping the retrieved document count constant. The document feedback process was formulated to help answer this problem. Basically, it allows the user to determine what is relevant and what is not. Let's examine that process now.

12.4.3 *Document feedback: tell me what you want!*

The process of increasing the relevance of returned documents is known as relevance or document feedback. This methodology, available since the 1960s, assumes that since users usually know little about the details of a particular document repository's makeup, they have difficulty assembling an initial query that produces the results they're looking for.

Think about it. When you call up your favorite search engine in your browser to search for a topic, do you really have any idea what's on the web?

Because of this user-repository mismatch, the initial query should be treated as only a preliminary step in obtaining useful information. The user can then examine the results of this first-round query. Terms from documents that are judged relevant can then be reformulated and applied to new, additional queries, thereby increasing the relevance of the newly returned documents. At the same time, terms in documents considered less relevant can be downplayed in the new queries. The effect of this process after several iterations is to cause more relevant documents to be returned.

An alternative to this manual intervention is known as pseudo or blind relevance feedback. This method does normal retrieval to find an initial set of documents and automatically considers a subset of a certain number of the top documents returned as relevant. Let's say that the top four returned documents in each query round are to be considered relevant documents. The top three terms from each of these documents are to be utilized in the additional queries, and this entire process is to be repeated for a certain number of iterations. At the end of these iterations, the results should be sufficient for the user.

Lucene is capable of emulating this process. Through the use of term vectors, a developer can examine individual terms in documents returned from a query and develop a framework to query for more documents that contain those terms.

Term vectors are collections of term-frequency pairs. To utilize term vectors, you must enable them during indexing so they are stored with documents. To enable them, the `org.apache.lucene.document.Field` class has several overloaded constructors that turn on the storage of term vectors:

- `Field(String name, Reader reader, Field.TermVector termVector)`
- `Field(String name, String value, Field.Store store, Field.Index index, Field.TermVector termVector)`
- `Field(String name, TokenStream tokenStream, Field.TermVector termVector)`

The `org.apache.lucene.document.Field.TermVector` class contains the five static values that `termVector` can have in these methods. These values are given in table 12.4.

Table 12.4 The `Field.TermVector` values and their definition

Value	Definition
`Field.TermVector.YES`	Store the term vectors of each document.
`Field.TermVector.NO`	Do not store term vectors.
`Field.TermVector.WITH_OFFSETS`	Store the term vector plus token offset information.
`Field.TermVector.WITH_POSITIONS`	Store the term vector plus token position information.
`Field.TermVector.WITH_POSITIONS_OFFSETS`	Store the term vector plus token position and offset information.

Notice that in addition to being able to store term frequency counts, it is also possible to store a term's position information and offset information. We'll talk about these shortly.

Let's look at what term vectors can do for us, by examining the additional information we can retrieve from a result. The code in listing 12.16 shows not only the annotation declaration inside the `ElectricalProperties` class but also the code that builds the index consisting of `ElectricalProperties` documents.

Listing 12.16   Declaring term vector information and building a simple index with it

```
@Field(index = Index.TOKENIZED,                                   Include
     store = Store.YES,                                           TermVector
     termVector = TermVector.WITH_POSITION_OFFSETS )   ◁──┐       information

private void buildIndex() throws Exception
{
  tx = session.beginTransaction();

  ElectricalProperties ep =
    new ElectricalProperties();
  ep.setContent("Electrical Engineers measure   ◁───┐
Electrical Properties");
  session.save(ep);

  ep = new ElectricalProperties();                    Build the
  ep.setContent("Electrical Properties are   ◁───┤    index entries
interesting");
  session.save(ep);

  ep = new ElectricalProperties();
  ep.setContent("Electrical Properties are   ◁───┘
measurable properties");
  session.save(ep);

  tx.commit();
  session.clear();
}
```

After the index is built, the code in listing 12.17 can be executed. This queries the index for the term *properties*. The query results broken down by terms per result document are then given.

Listing 12.17   Printing the `TermFreqVector` and position results of query

```
@Test
public void vectorTest() throws Exception {
  FullTextSession session =
    Search.getFullTextSession(openSession());
  Transaction tx = session.beginTransaction();
  buildIndex();

  try {
    Query query =
      new TermQuery(new Term("content", "properties"));
    System.out.println(query.toString());

    FullTextQuery hibQuery =
      session.createFullTextQuery(query,
        ElectricalProperties.class);

    hibQuery.setProjection(FullTextQuery.DOCUMENT,       ❶ Retrieve the
                 FullTextQuery.DOCUMENT_ID,                DOCUMENT_ID
                 FullTextQuery.SCORE);
    reader = getReader(session);
```

```
            List<Object[]> results = hibQuery.list();

        assert results.size() > 0: "no results returned";
        for (int x = 0; x < results.size(); x++) {                    ❷ Get the Lucene
                                                                          document number
            Integer docId = (Integer)results.get(x)[1];   ⬅┘

            TermPositionVector vector =
               (TermPositionVector)reader                             ❸ Get a document's
                 .getTermFreqVector(docId, "content");   ⬅┘             TermPositionVector
            String[] terms = vector.getTerms();
            int[] f = vector.getTermFrequencies();         ❹ Show the document score

            System.out.println(results.get(x)[2]);   ⬅┘

            for (int y = 0; y < vector.size(); y++) {
              System.out.print("docID# =>" + docId);          ❺ Retrieve the arrays of
              System.out.print(" term => " + terms[y]);          terms and frequencies
              System.out.print(" freq => " + f[y]);

              int[] positions = vector.getTermPositions(y);
              TermVectorOffsetInfo[] offsets =
                vector.getOffsets(y);
              for (int z = 0; z < positions.length; z++) {   ❻ Retrieve the
                System.out.print(" position => "                 arrays of
                           + positions[z]);                      positions and
                System.out.print(" starting offset => "          offsets
                  + offsets[z].getStartOffset());
                System.out.println(" ending offset => "
                  + offsets[z].getEndOffset());
              }
              System.out.println("---------------");
            }
        }
        tx.commit();
    }
    finally {
      session.close();
      if (provider != null) {
        provider.closeReader(reader);
      }
    }
  }

  private IndexReader getReader(FullTextSession session) {
    SearchFactory searchFactory = session.getSearchFactory();
    DirectoryProvider dirProvider =
      searchFactory.getDirectoryProviders(
        ElectricalProperties.class)[0];
    provider = searchFactory.getReaderProvider();
    return provider.openReader(dirProvider);
  }
```

In this example we must set a projection on the query ❶ so that we can retrieve the
Lucene document id number at ❷. We need this number to access the term information. ❸ retrieves the `TermPositionVector` for a single document field, utilizing an
`IndexReader` and the document id number we just retrieved.

WARNING If your index is built with `Field.TermVector.NO`, this code snippet will fail with a `NullPointerException`. The explicit cast to a `TermPositionVector` can be done only when position information is available. This information is available only when the index is built with one of the last three `Field.TermVector` values listed in table 12.4. As is, `vector` will be `null`.

In cases where `Field.TermVector.YES` is used to build the index, then ❶ should read as `TermFreqVector vector = reader.getTermFreqVector(x, "content");`.

We show the result item score ❹ to verify the correct order of returned documents. ❺ retrieves a document field's terms as a string array and their frequencies also as an array. These arrays have one-to-one correspondence; that is, in our example `terms[3]` would return a particular term and `freqs[3]` would return that term's frequency.

❻ retrieves the term's position and offset information. These two arrays also have one-to-one correspondence the same way the term and frequency arrays do.

Listing 12.18 shows the results of our query. Notice first that because of document ranking, the document order is not the same as when we entered them in the index. Second, notice that `freq` displays a count of each term in its document. You can compare this to what was entered in listing 12.16 and see that the frequencies do match. Also, for those terms with a frequency count of more than 1, multiple positions and offsets are listed.

Position and offset information starts at 0, so let's interpret the first term of the document with a `docId` of 0. This is the seventh term described in listing 12.18.

- The term *electrical* occurs in document 0 twice.

  `freq => 2`
- It occurs at the first (0) and the fourth (3) positions.

  `position => 0 and position => 3`
- The first occurrence starts at character offset 0 of the content field.

  `starting offset => 0`
- The second occurrence starts at character offset 29 (30th character) of the content field.

  `starting offset => 29`

Listing 12.18   The term frequency and position results of the query in listing 12.17

```
0.5036848
docID# =>2 term => electrical freq => 1 position => 0
starting offset => 0 ending offset => 10
---------------
docID# =>2 term => measurable freq => 1 position => 2
starting offset => 26 ending offset => 36
---------------
docID# =>2 term => properties freq => 2 position => 1
starting offset => 11 ending offset => 21
 position => 3 starting offset => 37 ending offset => 47
```

```
   ---------------
   0.35615897
   docID# =>1 term => electrical freq => 1 position => 0
   starting offset => 0 ending offset => 10
   ---------------
   docID# =>1 term => interesting freq => 1 position => 2
   starting offset => 26 ending offset => 37
   ---------------
   docID# =>1 term => properties freq => 1 position => 1
   starting offset => 11 ending offset => 21
   ---------------
   0.3116391
   docID# =>0 term => electrical freq => 2 position => 0
   starting offset => 0 ending offset => 10
    position => 3 starting offset => 29 ending offset => 39
   ---------------
   docID# =>0 term => engineers freq => 1 position => 1
   starting offset => 11 ending offset => 20
   ---------------
   docID# =>0 term => measure freq => 1 position => 2
   starting offset => 21 ending offset => 28
   ---------------
   docID# =>0 term => properties freq => 1 position => 4
   starting offset => 40 ending offset => 50
   ---------------
```

This data is easy to retrieve, but what does this additional information do for us? It adds a lot of sophistication to queries. Let's say that you'd like to change the formatting (boldface, color highlighting, and so forth) on the queried terms where they appear in the returned documents. Knowing the position of a specific term would allow us to manipulate these terms in this manner. We'll be discussing this in chapter 13 and present a full example.

Let's get back to relevancy. What if we took the three most frequent terms and used them in another query? Then we took the three most frequent terms from that query. Does this sound familiar? There's a lot you can do with this information. Having this data at your disposal allows you the freedom to create applications that help with relevancy issues and with a little ingenuity provide the document feedback we're discussing.

Rather than your going to all this trouble, though, Lucene comes with a contributed class that performs a bit of this manipulation for you. This class is MoreLikeThis. You could use it as a launchpad for your code or as is.

This class comes with an opening comment, which is a portion of an email written by one of the Lucene developers concerning best practices in these circumstances. We suggest you read it because it contains good information. Let's take a quick look at this class now.

12.4.4 *Improving relevance with MoreLikeThis*

Among the contributions to Lucene that were once part of the *sandbox* (you'll learn more about this in chapter 13) and are now part of the core package is the `org.apache.lucene.search.similar.MoreLikeThis` class, which was designed to help in the relevancy process.

WARNING We want you to understand that this is not the easiest class to obtain accurate results with. It contains many variables where small changes in their values can have drastic effects on results. That being said, you'll have to realize that much experimentation with this class will be necessary to obtain results close to what you expect them to be for a given document corpus.

The `MoreLikeThis` API documentation is available at /docs/api/org/apache/ Lucene/search/similar/MoreLikeThis.html. If you download and unpack the Lucene distribution, you'll find that it is packaged in the source code at /contrib/queries/ src/java/org/apache/lucene/search/similar/MoreLikeThis.java. A precompiled version is located in /contrib/queries/lucene-queries.jar.

The `MoreLikeThis` class sprang from an email by Doug Cutting, who is one of the principal Lucene committers. This email is included in the Javadoc API for the class. A summary of the email follows.

Lucene allows retrieval of a term's document frequency through `IndexReader` `.docFreq(Term term)` and term frequencies by counting a document's tokens. The problem is that document frequency calculation for every term in a document would be very slow. Heuristics can improve this speed problem by making approximations.

Assuming that you want a maximum `tf * idf` value, two heuristics could improve search speed:

- *Choose a low tf threshold (2 or 3).*   Terms with lower frequencies will be ignored in the source document.
- *Threshold the terms by their number of characters, say, 6 or 7.*   Terms with a high idf (that is, a low document frequency) tend to be longer.

These heuristics should allow for a small list of, for example, 10 terms to be generated that do a decent job of identifying a document.

What this all means is that we should be able to:

1 Take a document that results from a query.
2 Analyze it by applying various metrics to its terms.
3 Extract terms via the analysis that represent the documents.
4 Utilize these terms to search for additional documents that are more like these terms.

For example, let's say that we were searching a document repository for the term *Kitty Hawk*, and the first three results returned are:

1 Located on the Outer Banks of North Carolina, the town of Kitty Hawk offers year-round residents and visitors alike a unique and relaxing environment.

2 The USS *Kitty Hawk* is the first in a class of three supercarriers constructed by the New York Shipbuilding Corporation at Camden, New Jersey.

3 Kitty Hawk Kites, Inc. was founded in 1974 by John Harris, a pioneer in hang gliding, to provide instruction, products, and service to the burgeoning new sport.

That's a wide variety of results, but we spot the information we're looking for in item 2. Now we should be able to take the result, extract pertinent terms from it, and search again utilizing these terms. This process could be repeated several times. We would utilize the heuristics described in the previously mentioned email to help us determine the relevant terms in our chosen search result. Hopefully, by now you have realized that this is one implementation of document feedback utilized to improve relevancy.

The `MoreLikeThis` class allows us to employ these heuristics programmatically through the included methods:

- `setAnalyzer(Analyzer analyzer)`
- `setMinTermFreq(int minTermFreq)`
- `setMinDocFreq(int minDocFreq)`
- `setMinWordLen(int minWordLen)`
- `setMaxWordLen(int maxWordLen)`
- `setMaxQueryTerms(int maxQueryTerms)`
- `setMaxNumTokensParsed()`
- `setStopWords(Set stopWords)`
- `setFieldNames(String[] fieldNames)`

All of these heuristic variables have default values, which are listed in table 12.5 along with an explanation of each of the quantities.

Table 12.5 Default values of `MoreLikeThis` heuristic variables and their meanings

Variable name	Default value	Setter method
DEFAULT_ANALYZER	StandardAnalyzer	Analyzer to use when querying.
DEFAULT_MIN_TERM_FREQ	2	Ignore words less frequent than this in the like document.
DEFAULT_MIN_DOC_FREQ	5	Ignore words that do not occur in at least this many documents.
DEFAULT_MIN_WORD_LENGTH	0	Ignore words in the like document if less than this length. If zero, this has no effect.
DEFAULT_MAX_WORD_LENGTH	0	Ignore words in the like document if longer than this length. If zero, this has no effect.
DEFAULT_MAX_QUERY_TERMS	25	Return a query with no more than this many terms.

Table 12.5 Default values of `MoreLikeThis` heuristic variables and their meanings (*continued*)

Variable name	Default value	`Setter` method
DEFAULT_MAX_NUM_ TOKENS_PARSED	5000	Maximum number of tokens to parse in each doc field.
DEFAULT_STOP_WORDS	null	Default set of stop words. Null means to allow stop words.
DEFAULT_FIELD_NAMES	new String[] { "contents"}	Field name(s) of like document to examine.

Looking at these default values, you can see that you will want to change some of them when using the `MoreLikeThis` class in your own code. As it is, word length has no effect, and as discussed in the email, different values of these quantities can dramatically affect results.

Let's look at an example of the `MoreLikeThisQuery` class in action. Listing 12.19 demonstrates its use. We will again utilize the `query.toString()` method to show the terms that are extracted from our document and utilized in the additional searches, because this is the crux of the entire process.

Listing 12.19 Utilizing the `MoreLikeThisQuery` to obtain additional documents

```
public class TestMoreLikeThis extends SearchTestCase {
    public List<Object[]> results;
    private FullTextSession session;
    private IndexReader reader;
    private ReaderProvider readerProvider;

    String likeText =
        "Keanu Reeves is completely wooden in this        ❶ Define the like
    ➥romantic misfire. Reeves plays a traveling              document
    ➥salesman and agrees to help a woman"
    String[] moreLikeFields = new String[]{"description"};

    public void testMoreLikeThis() throws Exception {
        session = Search.createFullTextSession(openSession());
        Transaction tx = session.beginTransaction();        ❷ Create a Reader for
                                                               the document
        StringReader sr = new StringReader(likeText);   ◁─┘
        reader = getReader();

        try {
            MoreLikeThis mlt = new MoreLikeThis(reader);
            mlt.setFieldNames(moreLikeFields);
            mlt.setMaxQueryTerms(2);
            mlt.setMinDocFreq(1);
            mlt.setAnalyzer(new StandardAnalyzer());        ❸ Create and fill the
            mlt.setMaxWordLen(8);                              MoreLikeThis class
            mlt.setMinWordLen(7);
            mlt.setMinTermFreq(1);              ❹ Call the
                                                  like(Reader)
            Query query = mlt.like(sr);   ◁─┘     method
            System.out.println(query.toString());
```

```
org.hibernate.search.FullTextQuery hibQuery =
  session.createFullTextQuery(query,
                       Product.class);
hibQuery.setProjection(FullTextQuery.DOCUMENT,
              FullTextQuery.SCORE,
              FullTextQuery.DOCUMENT_ID);
```
Use projection since there is no DB

```
results = hibQuery.list();

assert results.size() == 6:"incorrect result count";
```
5 **Confirm six results**

```
for (Object[] result : results) {
  Document doc = (Document) result[0];
  assertTrue(doc.get("description").indexOf(
➥"salesman") > 0 || doc.get("description").indexOf(
➥"misfire") > 0);
  }
  tx.commit();
}
finally {
  session.close();
}
}
```
6 **Confirm salesman or misfire in all results**

```
private IndexReader getReader() {
  SearchFactory searchFactory = session.getSearchFactory();
  DirectoryProvider provider =
    searchFactory.getDirectoryProviders(Product.class)[0];
  readerProvider =
    searchFactory.getReaderProvider();
  return readerProvider.openReader(provider);
}
}
```

The like document **1** is defined. As we discussed, this could be obtained in a number of ways, especially from a prior query. Once we have this defined, we feed it to a StringReader **2** in preparation for having the MoreLikeThis class analyze it. We instantiate the MoreLikeThis class **3** and set the parameters we want the class to use to extract the terms from the like document. The query is returned after calling the MoreLikeThis.like(Reader) method **4**. In this example the generated query is

```
description:misfire description:salesman
```

Executing this query should produce six results **5**, and each of them should contain either *misfire* or *salesman* **6**.

Now that we have seen our first example, let's change a couple of the variables and see what effect they have on results. Leaving DEFAULT_MIN_WORD_LENGTH and DEFAULT_ MAX_WORD_LENGTH set to their default values of 0 and DEFAULT_MAX_QUERY_ TERMS to its default value of 25 produces 154 results. The query has now become

```
description:reeves description:wooden description:misfire
description:traveling description:agrees description:completely
description:salesman description:keanu description:help description:woman
description:romantic description:plays
```

It should be pretty clear after this single experiment how drastically the parameters affect results. It should also be clear that a lot of experimentation with your repository and the MoreLikeThis class will be necessary for you to achieve the results you desire.

12.5 *Summary*

You have seen that scoring is not an easy topic. Lucene utilizes Boolean-style queries, but a modified vector space model is its heart and soul. You saw how Lucene exposes several classes concerned with the scoring process. DefaultSimilarity, Similarity, Weight, and Scorer provide ways to adjust scoring any way the developer could want. You also saw that it is possible to avoid a lot of work if you take a critical look at what you are trying to accomplish and do a little planning before you jump headlong into generating code. It is not always necessary to develop your own implementations of all of the classes related to scoring. Armed with what you know now, it is quite often possible to cope with a given situation by implementing just one of them, Similarity.

NOTE   Lucene contains the org.apache.lucene.search.function package, which contains classes that allow you to modify scoring. Be warned, though, that all of these classes are, as of version 2.3.1, experimental, and there is no guarantee of what will happen with them in the future. The Lucene documentation itself has the following disclaimer on classes in this package:

WARNING   The status of the search.function package is experimental. The APIs introduced here might change in the future and will not be supported anymore in such a case.

Another important concern exists, which is the issue of document relevancy. The problem with relevance is that it is subjective. To counteract this, the somewhat measurable quantities Precision and Recall have been instituted, and to improve the ratio between these two quantities the concept of relevance feedback has been introduced. Relevance feedback utilizes several of the top-scoring results of a query to generate additional queries and thereby over several iterations improve the results. An aid to the process of improving relevance by utilizing relevance feedback principles is the MoreLikeThis class provided in the Lucene contributions. By changing various parameters of this class, it is possible to obtain additional documents related to a sample document.

In the next chapter we're going to look at a range of seemingly unrelated topics. The Lucene website maintains two separate repositories of code donated by developers, Contributions and the Lucene Sandbox. The Contributions repository contains unsupported code for your use, and the Sandbox contains supported code from the Lucene committers. We'll examine some of the available software in each of these repositories in turn.

Don't reinvent the wheel

13

This chapter covers

- Term highlighters
- The `BoostingQuery` class
- Synonym generation and regex queries
- Extracting and indexing text from different file formats

In this final chapter we're going to look at some of the non-core contributions to Lucene made by developers and interested parties who want to see additional functionality in the product. The authors almost guarantee that one of these libraries will save you time and work in one of your projects.

The Apache Lucene website maintains links to a Lucene Sandbox of contributions that are free to use (within licensing restrictions), open source offerings at http://lucene.apache.org/java/docs/lucene-sandbox/index.html, and third-party contributions at http://lucene.apache.org/java/docs/contributions.html, not all of which are open source or free. Some open source libraries not mentioned on the Lucene website can also help out tremendously depending on the situation. We'll be discussing one of these. You've used several of these contributions before.

Remember the `MoreLikeThis` class in chapter 12? In addition, you've been using the index examiner application Luke throughout this book, and we'll continue to use it in this chapter.

Although we are by no means going to discuss all the libraries and applications available on the Lucene site, we will cover examples of a varied nature to give you a feel for what you will find there. It's not necessary to read this chapter in the order in which it's presented. Feel free to jump directly to any topic of interest and start there.

We'll get started with the Lucene Sandbox and its collection of utility classes. After a section that mainly deals with extracting text from various document formats such as Adobe Systems PDF files and Microsoft documents and finishes with extracting text from a simple text file, we'll go over the contributions.

13.1   *Playing in the Sandbox*

The Sandbox is located at http://lucene.apache.org/java/docs/lucene-sandbox/index.html, and the accompanying code repository is located at http://svn.apache.org/repos/asf/lucene/java/trunk/contrib/. It deals with code donated by the core developers along with others interested in the Lucene project. The code is not actively maintained, so you may have to experiment with it.

In addition to the items we will be talking about, the Sandbox contains such things as a large quantity of analyzers, tokenizers, and filters for many different languages. Also, it contains an ANT task that creates a Lucene index from the files specified by an ANT fileset.

NOTE   As of this writing, the fate of the Sandbox is up in the air. The authors were informed that it is no longer being maintained, and some of the classes there have been adopted into the Lucene core. We're going to discuss two of them—`BoostingQuery` and `RegexQuery`. We still consider these two classes important to discuss so that you can see their inner workings and possibly adapt them to your own code if needed. Besides, that's what the Sandbox is for.

After looking at a term highlighter, we will revisit a topic discussed in chapter 12, scoring and the `BoostingQuery`. Depending on the circumstances, this utility class may save you a lot of work. The last parts of this section, before we move on to the contributions, will cover various types of query classes such as synonym and regular expression (regex) queries.

13.1.1   *Making results stand out with the term Highlighter class*

The first set of classes we'll examine allows us to change the output format of the terms that match our queries. The Lucene source code contains these classes and is located at lucene_install_directory/contrib/highlighter/src/java/org/apache/lucene/search/highlight. These classes are also included in a precompiled .jar file, lucene-highlighter, located at lucene_install_directory/contrib/highlighter, which needs to be placed in your classpath.

In the following example and in several of the remaining examples in this chapter, we'll make use of the Dvd class. This simple class is shown here, and it will allow us to demonstrate the points we're trying to make without overly complicating matters.

```
@Entity
@Indexed
@Analyzer(impl = StandardAnalyzer.class)
public class Dvd {
  private Integer id;
  private String title;
  private String description;

  @Id
  @DocumentId
  public Integer getId() {
    return id;
  }

  public void setId(Integer id) {
    this.id = id;
  }

  @Field(index = Index.TOKENIZED, store = Store.YES)
  public String getTitle() {
    return title;
  }

  public void setTitle(String title) {
    this.title = title;
  }

  @Field(index = Index.TOKENIZED, store = Store.YES)
  public String getDescription() {
    return description;
  }

  public void setDescription(String description) {
    this.description = description;
  }
}
```

Listing 13.1 demonstrates how to use the highlighter classes to make the query-matching terms conspicuous.

Listing 13.1 Using `Highlighter` to make query result terms more conspicuous

```
public class TestHighlighter extends SearchTestCase {
  private IndexReader reader;
  private Analyzer analyzer = new StandardAnalyzer();
  ReaderProvider readerProvider;

  String desc[] = {
    "Keanu Reeves is completely wooden in this romantic misfire.
Reeves plays a traveling salesman and agrees to help a woman",
    "Jamie Lee Curtis finds out that he's not really a salesman
and Bill Paxton is a used-car salesman."
```

```
      };
    public void testSimpleHighLighter() throws Exception {
      FullTextSession session =
        Search.getFullTextSession( openSession() );

      try {
        buildIndex( session );

        Transaction tx = session.beginTransaction();
        QueryParser parser = new QueryParser( "description", analyzer );

        Query query = parser.parse( "salesman" );          ❶ Rewrite multiterm queries
        query = query.rewrite( reader );              ←─┘
        org.hibernate.search.FullTextQuery hibQuery =
          session.createFullTextQuery( query, Dvd.class );
        List<Dvd> results = hibQuery.list();

        Highlighter highlighter =                       ❷ Create a new
        new Highlighter( new QueryScorer( query) );  ←─┘   Highlighter
        highlighter.setTextFragmenter( new SimpleFragmenter( 20 ) );

        int maxNumFragmentsRequired = 3;

        for ( Dvd p : results ) {
          String text = p.getDescription();
          TokenStream tokenStream =
            analyzer.tokenStream( description,
                    new StringReader( text ) );
                                                        ❸ Read the hit field
        String result =                                   content as a stream
          highlighter.getBestFragments(
            tokenStream, text,
            maxNumFragmentsRequired, " ..." );
        assert result != null : "null result";
        assert result.length()>0 : "0 length result";
        System.out.println( result );
      }
      readerProvider.closeReader( reader );
      for ( Object element : s.createQuery( "from "
        + Dvd.class.getName() ).list() )
        s.delete( element );

        tx.commit();
      }
      finally {
        s.close();
      }

    private void buildIndex( FullTextSession session )
        throws Exception {
        getReader( session )
        Transaction tx = session.beginTransaction();

        for ( int x = 0; x < desc.length; x++ ) {
          Dvd dvd = new Dvd();
          dvd.setId(x);
          dvd.setDescription( desc[x] );
          session.save( dvd );
        }
```

```
        tx.commit();
    }

    @Override
    protected void tearDown() throws Exception {
        reader.close();
        super.tearDown();
    }

    private void getReader(FullTextSession session) {
        SearchFactory searchFactory = session.getSearchFactory();
        DirectoryProvider provider =
            searchFactory.getDirectoryProviders( Dvd.class )[0];
        readerProvider =
            searchFactory.getReaderProvider();
        reader = readerProvider.openReader( provider );
    }
}
```

```
not really a <B>salesman</B> …
⇒ is a used-car <B>salesman</B>                    ❹ Results
 a traveling <B>salesman</B>
```

❶ shows that during the search all multiterm queries (prefix, wildcard, range, fuzzy, and so on) must be rewritten or they won't work! This takes care of rearranging the queries behind the scenes. Just remember to do it. ❷ shows the single-parameter `Highlighter` constructor that takes a `Scorer`. If you want to substitute your own `Formatter`, you must call one of the other constructors that also takes a `Formatter` as a parameter. The loop through the resulting hits ❸ shows that the field to be highlighted is read as a stream so that the highlighting code can be inserted where you want it. Results are shown at ❹.

Listing 13.2 shows the default `SimpleHTMLFormatter` class that comes with `Highlighter`. This class controls exactly how the term highlighting should look. It implements the `Formatter` interface, which contains the single method signature: `String highlightTerm(String originalText, TokenGroup tokenGroup);`. In this signature `tokenGroup` contains the token or tokens to be highlighted along with their score, which will determine whether or not they are highlighted. The `highlightTerm` method in listing 13.2 shows an example usage.

Listing 13.2 `SimpleHTMLFormatter` formats code to highlight matches

```
public class SimpleHTMLFormatter implements Formatter {
    String preTag;
    String postTag;

    public SimpleHTMLFormatter(String preTag,          ❶ Constructor for
                        String postTag) {                 insertion of tags
        this.preTag = preTag;
        this.postTag = postTag;
    }
                                          ❷ Constructor with
    public SimpleHTMLFormatter() {   ←       predefined tags
        this.preTag = "<B>";
        this.postTag = "</B>";
    }
```

```
    public String highlightTerm(String originalText, TokenGroup
  tokenGroup) {                          ⟵——— ❸ Formatter method to override
      StringBuffer returnBuffer;
      if ( tokenGroup.getTotalScore() > 0 ) {
        returnBuffer = new StringBuffer();
        returnBuffer.append( preTag );
        returnBuffer.append( originalText );    ❹ Splicing in
        returnBuffer.append( postTag );             formatting tags
        return returnBuffer.toString();
      }
      return originalText;
    }
  }
```

The default constructor ❷ contains predefined tags. As shown in listings 13.1 and 13.2, the default `Formatter` class surrounds the matching terms with HTML bold tags. So how can you modify the highlighting and make matching terms appear the way you want them? There are three ways to accomplish this. The first and easiest way is to create an instance of the `SimpleHTMLFormatter` class by calling the constructor that takes two strings ❶. These two strings are the formatting code placed around the matching terms by the `highlightTerm` method.

If what you want to accomplish is more complicated than that or you want additional functionality, you can do it the second way. It will be necessary to write your own `Formatter` class that's similar to the `SimpleHTMLFormatter` in listing 13.2, making sure that you also implement the `Formatter` interface by overriding the `highlightTerm` method ❷. This way you can add any functionality you wish ❹. Another option would be to extend the `SimpleHTMLFormatter` class and override the `highlightTerm` method ❸.

Once you have your `Formatter` class, you can inject it when creating an instance of the `Highlighter` class by calling one of the two constructors that takes a formatter as a parameter:

- `public Highlighter(Formatter formatter, Scorer fragmentScorer)`
- `public Highlighter(Formatter formatter, Encoder encoder, Scorer fragmentScorer)`

Let's move on to scoring, a topic that is probably near and dear to your heart. As we discussed at length in chapter 12, modifying the way documents are scored can be a painstaking process. The next utility class can help ease that pain.

13.1.2 *Modifying a score the easy way with BoostingQuery*

When we utilize a Boolean query to search for multiple terms, the use of the Boolean keyword NOT eliminates documents containing the NOTed term from the returned results. If we query our DVD index for all documents containing "spielberg and NOT war," we would retrieve movie descriptions of all Steven Spielberg movies except for those that contained the term *war* in their description. So, we would not have *Saving Private Ryan* and *Schindler's List* returned in the query results. What if we wanted these results returned, but we wanted them demoted to further down in the returned list, that is, with a lower score than those documents that did not contain the term *war*? Are we out of luck? No; one of the principal committers to the Lucene project, Doug Cutting, has contributed a class that does exactly that. It demotes documents that contain specific terms.

If you are only interested in the demoting of results, this class is the somewhat non-intuitively named `BoostingQuery`. The source code is located in the *lucene_install_directory*/contrib/queries/src/java/org/apache/lucene/search directory. A precompiled Lucene-queries .jar file is available and located in the *lucene_install_directory*/contrib/queries/ directory. The basic use of this query type is as follows:

```
Query query = new BoostingQuery( match, context, 0.2f );
```

The `match` contains the required, desirable criteria that select all matching documents. The `context` contains the undesirable elements that are used to lessen the scores of matching documents. Documents matching the `context` have their score multiplied by the so-called boost parameter, in this case 0.2f. To achieve a demoting effect, this should be less than 1.0f.

Listing 13.3 is the source listing for the `BoostingQuery` class itself.

Listing 13.3   The code for the `BoostingQuery` class

```
public class BoostingQuery extends Query {
  private float boost;          ⟵── The amount to boost by
  private Query match;          ⟵── The query to match
  private Query context;        ⟵── Boost value when both clauses match

  public BoostingQuery(Query match, Query context,
➡float boost) {
    this.match = match;
    this.context = (Query)context.clone();
    this.boost = boost;                    ┐ Ignore context-
                                           │ only matches
    context.setBoost(0.0f);      ⟵────────┘
  }

  public Query rewrite(IndexReader reader) throws IOException {
    BooleanQuery result = new BooleanQuery() {

      public Similarity getSimilarity(Searcher searcher) {   ❶ Supply a new
        return new DefaultSimilarity() {          ⟵              Similarity

        public float coord(int overlap,
                    int maxOverlap) {    ⟵── Refer to section 12.2.1
          switch (overlap) {
            case 1:
              return 1.0f;         ⟵
            case 2:                                   Matched only
              return boost;   ⟵                       one clause; use
            default:                Matched both    ❷ as is
              return 0.0f;          clauses; multiply
            }                    ❸ by boost
          }
        }
```

```
        };
      }
    };

    result.add( match, true, false );
    result.add( context, false, false );

    return result;
    }

    public String toString(String field) {
      return match.toString(field) + "/" + context.toString(field);
    }
  }
}
```

Remember chapter 12 and overriding the `DefaultSimilarity`? ❶ shows how `Boost-ingQuery` accomplishes its scoring modification. It does the same thing we were doing in chapter 12. The choice of what score to return, ❷ or ❸, determines the multiplying factor to use in scoring the results.

Let's look at an example of the `BoostingQuery` class in action and compare the results obtained from our `TestBoostingQuery` with those from listing 12.2 using the `explain` method.

Listing 13.4 shows the results of querying for the term *salesman*.

Listing 13.4 Results of the `explain` method when querying for *salesman*

```
score => 0.84061575    ◁————❶ The target document score
0.84061575 = (MATCH) fieldWeight(description:salesman in 108), product of:
  1.0 = tf(termFreq(description:salesman)=1)
  5.379941 = idf(docFreq=5, numDocs=479)
  0.15625 = fieldNorm(field=description, doc=108)

score => 0.5944051
0.5944051 = (MATCH) fieldWeight(description:salesman in 471), product of:
  1.4142135 = tf(termFreq(description:salesman)=2)
  5.379941 = idf(docFreq=5, numDocs=479)
  0.078125 = fieldNorm(field=description, doc=471)

score => 0.58843106
0.58843106 = (MATCH) fieldWeight(description:salesman in 57), product of:
  1.0 = tf(termFreq(description:salesman)=1)
  5.379941 = idf(docFreq=5, numDocs=479)
  0.109375 = fieldNorm(field=description, doc=57)

score => 0.42030787
0.42030787 = (MATCH) fieldWeight(description:salesman in 217), product of:
  1.0 = tf(termFreq(description:salesman)=1)
  5.379941 = idf(docFreq=5, numDocs=479)
  0.078125 = fieldNorm(field=description, doc=217)

score => 0.3362463
0.3362463 = (MATCH) fieldWeight(description:salesman in 220), product of:
  1.0 = tf(termFreq(description:salesman)=1)
  5.379941 = idf(docFreq=5, numDocs=479)
  0.0625 = fieldNorm(field=description, doc=220)
```

Document 0 ❶ is the DVD description that starts with "Keanu Reeves is completely wooden…" and is the first one listed simply because it was the first to be indexed. Let's say that we want to query for *salesman,* but we are not interested as much in movies with Keanu Reeves. In other words, any of the salesman movies that have Keanu Reeves in them should be moved toward the bottom of the list. Listing 13.5 shows how to accomplish this using the `BoostingQuery` class. It also shows the resulting `explain` printout.

Listing 13.5   Utilizing the `BoostingQuery` class to demote movies

```
public class TestBoostingQuery extends SearchTestCase {
  public Searcher searcher;

  public void testBoostingQuery() throws Exception {
    FullTextSession session =
      Search.createFullTextSession(openSession());
    Transaction tx = s.beginTransaction();

    Query positiveQuery =
      new TermQuery(new Term("description",           Positive query
                    "salesman"));        ◄───────    creation
    Query negativeQuery =
      new TermQuery(new Term("description",           Negative query
                    "reeves"));          ◄───────    creation
    Query query = new BoostingQuery(positiveQuery,
    negativeQuery, 0.5f);               ◄───────     BoostingQuery
    System.out.println(query.toString());            creation

    org.hibernate.search.FullTextQuery hibQuery =
      session.createFullTextQuery(query,
                    Product.class);
    hibQuery.setProjection(FullTextQuery.DOCUMENT,
    FullTextQuery.SCORE, FullTextQuery.DOCUMENT_ID);

    try {
      List<Object[]> results = hibQuery.list();

      assert results.size() > 0: "no reults returned";
      IndexSearcher indexSearcher = getSearcher ( session );
      for (Object[] result : results) {
        System.out.println("score => " + result[1]);

        System.out.println(indexSearcher.explain(query,
                    (Integer) result[2]).toString());
      }
      tx.commit();
    }
    finally {
      session.close();
    }

    private IndexSearcher getSearcher ( FullTextSession session ) {
      SearchFactory searchFactory = session.getSearchFactory();
      DirectoryProvider provider =
        searchFactory.getDirectoryProviders(Product.class)[0];
      ReaderProvider readerProvider =
        searchFactory.getReaderProvider();
```

```
        IndexReader reader = readerProvider.openReader(provider);

        return new IndexSearcher(reader);
    }
}
```

```
score => 0.5944051
0.5944051 = (MATCH) sum of:
  0.5944051 = (MATCH) fieldWeight(description:salesman in 471),
➡ product of:
   1.4142135 = tf(termFreq(description:salesman)=2)
   5.379941 = idf(docFreq=5, numDocs=479)
   0.078125 = fieldNorm(field=description, doc=471)

score => 0.58843106
0.58843106 = (MATCH) sum of:
  0.58843106 = (MATCH) fieldWeight(description:salesman in 57),
➡ product of:
   1.0 = tf(termFreq(description:salesman)=1)
   5.379941 = idf(docFreq=5, numDocs=479)
   0.109375 = fieldNorm(field=description, doc=57)

score => 0.42030787                              ◄─── ❶ Target document moved
0.42030787 = (MATCH) product of:                         to lower score
  0.84061575 = (MATCH) sum of:
   0.84061575 = (MATCH) fieldWeight(
description:salesman in 108),                    ◄─── ❷ Match on *salesman*
➡ product of:
    1.0 = tf(termFreq(description:salesman)=1)
    5.379941 = idf(docFreq=5, numDocs=479)
    0.15625 = fieldNorm(field=description, doc=108)
   0.0 = (MATCH) weight(description:reeves^0.0 in 108),
➡product of:
    0.0 = queryWeight(description:reeves^0.0), product of:
     0.0 = boost
     5.2257905 = idf(docFreq=6, numDocs=479)
     0.18587564 = queryNorm
    1.1547475 = (MATCH) fieldWeight(
description:reeves in 108),                      ◄─── ❸ Match on *reeves*
➡ product of:
     1.4142135 = tf(termFreq(description:reeves)=2)
     5.2257905 = idf(docFreq=6, numDocs=479)
     0.15625 = fieldNorm(field=description, doc=108)
  0.5 = coord(2/2)                               ◄─── Apply the
score => 0.42030787                                 ❹ boosting factor
0.42030787 = (MATCH) sum of:
  0.42030787 = (MATCH) fieldWeight(description:salesman in 217),
➡ product of:
   1.0 = tf(termFreq(description:salesman)=1)
   5.379941 = idf(docFreq=5, numDocs=479)
   0.078125 = fieldNorm(field=description, doc=217)
```

You should notice several things about these results:

- The document containing *reeves* was indeed moved down the list ❶, in this case to the third position. Its score changed from 0.84061575 to 0.42030787 (multiply

0.42030787 by 2 and see what you come up with—doesn't multiplying a number by 0.5 decrease the score by a factor of 2?).

- The same document matched on two terms, *salesman* ❷ and *reeves* ❸, just as it should have (positive and negative).
- The boosting factor was applied. ❹
- The score of the other documents remained the same.

The authors hope you realize that if you were to put a value greater than 1.0F in the `BoostingQuery` signature, you would cause it to become what it intuitively sounds like it should be. In this case the terms that match the second query in the signature would have their score increased, not decreased. Isn't that what *boosting* means? Also, when you use this class, remember that if the multiplying factor causes the raw score to be greater than 1.0, it will be normalized back to 1.0. In this case the other results' scores will also be adjusted.

The next two sections deal with *query-helper* classes: synonyms and regular expression queries. Some people may find that the first one contains difficult-to-understand concepts, but its implementation is not problematical.

13.1.3 *But I was querying for "flick" utilizing a synonym search*

WordNet is a product of the Cognitive Science Laboratory of Princeton University, New Jersey. It is a lexical database of the English language where words have been grouped into synonyms of distinct concepts. Its homepage is http://wordnet.princeton.edu. This site even has an online page that provides quite a bit of information on any word you enter. Figure 13.2 shows the results of entering the word *romance* into the page.

To get to the point where you can use WordNet to help with Lucene queries, you'll have to take several preliminary steps:

1 Either build the WordNet contribution classes from the source code, which is located at *lucene_install_directory*/contrib/wordnet/src/java/org/apache/lucene/wordnet, or put the precompiled lucene-wordnet .jar file in your classpath. The .jar is located in the *lucene_install_directory*/contrib./wordnet/ directory.

2 Download and expand the Prolog version of WordNet 3.0 as WNprolog-3.0.tar.gz located at http://wordnet.princeton.edu/obtain.

3 Make sure that the WordNet .jar file is in your classpath, and then utilizing the `Syns2Index` Java program included in the Lucene WordNet distribution, build the synonym index as follows:

```
java org.apache.lucene.wordnet.Syns2Index wn_s.pl indexLocation
```

4 wn_s.pl is WordNet's synonym file located in the `WNprolog-3.0.tar.gz` file you downloaded, and `indexLocation` is where you want `Syns2Index` to build the index.

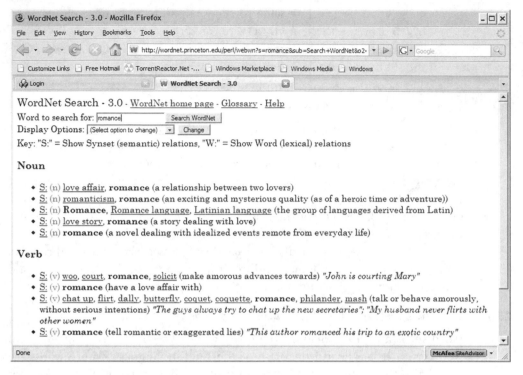

Figure 13.1   A search for the term *romance* on the WordNet online page showing the results

Once you've created the synonym file, you'll be able to use it in your classes to automatically supply synonyms for your queries. Listing 13.6 shows you how to employ this really handy feature.

Listing 13.6   Utilizing the `SynLookup` class to expand a query term with its synonyms

```
public class TestSynonyms extends SearchTestCase {
  String desc[] = {
    "Keanu Reeves is completely wooden in this romantic
misfired flick",
    "Reeves plays a traveling salesman and agrees to help
a woman",
    "Jamie Lee Curtis finds out that he's not really a used
car salesman"
  };

  public void testQuery() throws Exception {
    FullTextSession session =
      Search.getFullTextSession( openSession() );
      Transaction tx = session.getTransaction();
      SynonymHelper helper = new SynonymHelper();       ❶ Build the
    // buildSynonymIndex();                                 synonym index
```

```
     String query = "movie flick";
     Set<String> q =
       helper.getSynonyms(query,
                   session,
                   new StandardAnalyzer());
     assert q.contains( "film" ) : "not found";
     assert q.contains("picture") : "not found";

     try {
       buildDvdIndex(session, tx)
       tx = session.beginTransaction();
       query = "automobile";
       Query expandedQuery =
         helper.expandQuery(query,
                     session,
                     new StandardAnalyzer(),
                     description, 1.0F);

       org.hibernate.search.FullTextQuery hibQuery =
         session.createFullTextQuery( expandedQuery, Dvd.class );
       results = hibQuery.list();

       assert results.size() == 1 : "didn't find the synonym";
       assert results.get( 0 ).getDescription()
         .startsWith( "Jamie Lee Curtis" );
       assert results.get( 0 ).getDescription()
         .indexOf( "car" ) >= 0;

       // uncommenting the following lines will remove all
       // entries in the synonym index and require it to be
       // rebuilt
       // for (Object element : s.createQuery("from "
➥+ Synonym.class.getName()).list()) {
           // session.delete(element);
       tx.commit();
     }
     finally {
       s.close();
     }
   }

   private void buildSynonymIndex( FullTextSession session,
                       Transaction tx ) throws Exception {
     helper.buildSynonymIndex(session, "wn_s.pl");
   }

   public void buildDvdIndex( FullTextSession session,
                      Transaction tx) throws Exception {
     tx = session.beginTransaction();
     for (int x = 0; x < desc.length; x++) {
       Dvd dvd = new Dvd();
       dvd.setDescription(desc[x]);
       dvd.setId(x + 1);
       session.save(dvd);
     }
     tx.commit();
     session.clear();
   }
 }
```

2 Test the synonym generation

3 Expand to include *automobile* synonyms

4 Test result for synonym *car*

5 Delete synonym index

6 Call helper to build synonym index

First and foremost, build the synonym index ❶. In this code it is commented out, but you can uncomment it the first time the test is run and use it as you see fit. The index is deleted at ❺, which is also commented in this code.

We're running two different tests here. The first test ❷ makes certain that synonym generation occurs correctly by querying for the terms *flick* and *movie* and ensuring that other synonyms were generated. The actual query terms generated here are word:movie word:film word:flick word:pic word:picture. Notice that the original term is automatically included in the token list. Using q.toString() will show you the term list.

The second test ❸ queries our DVD description index for the term *automobile*. The query tokens generated for this search are contents:automobile contents:auto contents:car contents:machine contents:motorcar. Notice that the single hit that is returned was on the term *car*. This is a good proof that the synonyms actually work the way they should. ❹ asserts that the synonym *car* was found by the query.

The actual call to the SynonymHelper class to build the index is shown at ❻.

For those of you who said it just could not be done, next up is utilizing regular expressions (regex) in your queries.

13.1.4 *Implementing regular expression searches and querying for "sa.[aeiou]s.*"*

Synonyms are all well and good, but they still won't help with misspellings (this is just one example of how regex could help). If you were able to use synonyms to help with queries of commonly misspelled words, it would be possible to obtain results where you might not otherwise.

NOTE Admittedly this is not the best way to help with misspelled words. Spellcheckers come to mind first, and the Lucene website offers a spellchecking contribution. *N*-grams also come to mind, but they're beyond the scope of this book, other than what is discussed in section 5.3.3. If you're interested in finding out more about them, plenty of documentation is available on the internet.

Listing 13.7 is a standalone unit test that demonstrates the use of regular expressions when querying. You will have to put two .jar files in your classpath for this.

- The lucene-regex .jar located in the *lucene_install_directory*/contrib/regex directory
- The jakarta-regexp .jar located in the *lucene_install_directory*/contrib/regex/lib directory

The authors must warn you that not all of the regular expression syntax is completely supported. So if you're going to use this in your code, be sure to experiment first to see what is and what is not supported.

Listing 13.7   Using queries to help with misspellings

```java
public class TestRegex extends SearchTestCase {
  private FullTextSession s;
  private Transaction tx;
  String texts[] = {
    "Keanu Reeves is completely wooden in this romantic
  misfired flick",
    "Reeves plays a traveling salesman and agrees to help
  a woman",
    "Jamie Lee Curtis finds out that he's not really a
  salesman"
  };

  public void testRegex1() throws Exception {
    try {
      buildIndex();
      assertEquals( 2, regexHitCount("sa.[aeiou]s.*"));
      cleanup();
    finally {
      s.close();
    }
  }

  public void testRegex2() throws Exception {
    try {
      buildIndex();
      assertEquals(0, regexHitCount("sa[aeiou]s.*"));
      cleanup();
    }
    finally {
      s.close();
    }
  }

  public void testSpanRegex1() throws Exception {
    try {
      buildIndex();
      assert spanRegexHitCount( "sa.[aeiou]s", "woman", 5, true ) == 1;
    cleanup();
    }
    finally {
      s.close();
    }
  }

  public void testSpanRegex2() throws Exception {
    try {
      buildIndex();
      assert spanRegexHitCount( "sa.[aeiou]s", "woman", 1, true ) == 0;   ◁─┐
      cleanup();
    }                                                    StandardAnalyzer
    finally {                                            reduces the slop ❶
      s.close();
    }
  }
```

```
    private int regexHitCount(String regex)
       ➡ throws Exception {
      RegexQuery query = new RegexQuery(newTerm(regex));
      query.setRegexImplementation(
  ➡new JakartaRegexpCapabilities());

      org.hibernate.search.FullTextQuery hibQuery =
        s.createFullTextQuery(query, Dvd.class);
      List results = hibQuery.list();
      return results.size();
    }

    private int spanRegexHitCount(String regex1, String regex2,
  ➡int slop, boolean ordered) throws Exception {
      SpanRegexQuery q1 = new SpanRegexQuery(newTerm(regex1));
      SpanRegexQuery q2 = new SpanRegexQuery(newTerm(regex2));
      SpanNearQuery query =
        new SpanNearQuery(new SpanQuery[]{q1, q2},
                    slop, ordered);

      org.hibernate.search.FullTextQuery hibQuery =
        s.createFullTextQuery(query, Dvd.class);
      List results = hibQuery.list();
      return results.size();
    }

    private Term newTerm(String value) {
      return new Term(description, value);
    }

    private void getFullTextSession {
      s = Search.createFullTextSession(openSession());
      tx = s.beginTransaction();

      for (int x = 0; x < texts.length; x++) {
        Dvd dvd = new Dvd();
        dvd.setId(x);
        dvd.setDescription(texts[x]);
        s.save(dvd);
      }
      tx.commit();
      s.clear();
    }
  }
```

2 Create the RegexQuery instance

3 Set the capabilities

4 Create the SpanRegexQuery instances

5 Create the SpanNearQuery instances

The StandardAnalyzer specified in the Dvd class has removed stop words and reduced the slop distance to 1 **1**. **2** creates an instance of RegexQuery for the regular expression sa[aeiou]s.*. Before performing the query, we set the capabilities **3**. RegexQuery comes with two capabilities: JakartaRegexpCapabilities and JavaUtilsRegexpCapabilities. These determine whether Jakarta regular expressions or Java's Utility package regular expressions are used for query expansion.

Utilizing SpanRegexQuerys **4** allows you to search for two different terms separated by a number of intervening terms. This distance is known as the *slop* factor **5**. You can also specify whether the terms are to be searched for in the order you specified them with the ordered parameter **5**.

WARNING Be aware of the effects of analyzers like `StandardAnalyzer` on `Span-RexexQuerys` or any analyzer that utilizes stop word lists. These are lists of common words like *the, of, a, an*, and so forth. These words are eliminated when the index is built and will affect the slop distance. You may not get the results you expect. This design anomaly has caught the authors more than once.

Before moving on to third-party contributions, we want to look at one more utility that can make your life a little easier. Let's examine what a spellchecker can do for you.

13.1.5 *Utilizing a spellchecker*

In sections 7.1.4 and 7.4.5 we discussed the `FuzzyQuery` and the fact that we could utilize it to help us with user-entered misspellings. There is a problem with this. If you've used the `FuzzyQuery` for this purpose, you probably soon found out that setting the minimum similarity correctly to get the results you were expecting is a somewhat time-consuming and tedious process. There is a better and less–time-consuming way to pull this off, and that is to use a spellchecker on the field or fields you are concerned with. It just so happens that Lucene includes a spellchecker in the Contributions section. The spellchecker utility .jar file, lucene-spellchecker.jar, is located in the contrib directory at *lucene-install-directory*\contrib\spellchecker.

NOTE Be advised that the spellchecker, as presented, is not the optimal solution. Because it creates its own index outside the bounds of Hibernate Search, it is an unmanaged index. You'll see this in the example code presented shortly. The authors are working on creating a better solution for Hibernate Search, and by the time you read this it should be available for your use.

The spellchecker supports two types of dictionaries:

- `LuceneDictionary` A dictionary composed of the key terms taken from a field or fields of an existing Lucene index.
- `PlainTextDictionary` A dictionary taken from a list of words contained in a text file. Words in this file must be listed one per line.

The `SpellChecker` class is the main interface to these files of words. We're concerned with three methods of this `SpellChecker` class:

- `void indexDictionary(Dictionary dict)` Indexes the supplied dictionary.
- `String[] suggestSimilar(String word, int numSug)` Provides a sorted numSug-sized list of words similar to Microsoft Word.
- `String[] suggestSimilar(String word, int numSug, IndexReader ir, String field, boolean morePopular)` This is the same method as the second bullet if both the `IndexReader ir` and `String field` are `null`. If they are not `null`, the words are restricted to the specified field in the specified index, and the morePopular parameter takes effect. morePopular restricts the returned word list to words that are more frequent than the searched-for word.

NOTE Both the API documentation and the authors recommend that you do not allow numSug to be less than 5 in either of the calls to SuggestSimilar. Lucene determines the best matches by fetching the most relevant *n-grammed* terms. (this is not the same as the Levenshtein distance strategy). Anything less will not result in the best match being returned.

As always, an example will best demonstrate how the SpellChecker class works. This example will create a DVD index, build a spell-check index from that DVD index, and look for a misspelled word. Listing 13.8 illustrates this process.

Listing 13.8 Building a SpellChecker index and testing its use

```
public class TestSpellChecker extends SearchTestCase {
  public List<String> results;
  private String baseDir;
  private Directory spellDir;

  String texts[] = {
    "Keanu Reeves is completely wooden in this romantic
  misfired flick",
    "Reeves plays a traveling salesman and agrees to
  help a woman",
    "Jamie Lee Curtis finds out that he's not really a
  salesman"
  };

  @Test
  public void testSpellCheck() throws Exception {
    FullTextSession session =
      Search.getFullTextSession(openSession());
    transaction tx = session.beginTransaction();

    Try {
      buildIndex(session, tx);
      SpellChecker spellChecker =
        buildSpellCheckIndex("description",
                    session);

      String misspelledUserInput = "kenu";

      assert !spellChecker
        .exist(misspelledUserInput)
      : "misspelled word found";

      String[] suggestions =
        spellChecker.suggestSimilar(misspelledUserInput,
                    5);

      assert suggestions.length == 1
      : "incorrect suggestion count";

      for (String suggestion : suggestions) {
        System.out.println(suggestion);
        assert suggestion.equals("keanu");
      }

      tx.commit();
```

① Build both indexes

② A misspelled search term

③ Does the word exist as is?

④ Get the suggestions

⑤ Only I should be returned

⑥ Returned word equal to "keanu"

```
    }
    finally {
      session.close();
    }
  }

  private SpellChecker buildSpellCheckIndex(String fieldName,
                             FullTextSession session)
    throws Exception {
    SearchFactory searchFactory =
      session.getSearchFactory();
    DirectoryProvider[] providers =
      searchFactory.getDirectoryProviders(Dvd.class);

    org.apache.lucene.store.Directory DvdDirectory =
      providers[0].getDirectory();

    IndexReader spellReader = null;
    SpellChecker spellchecker = null;

    try {
      // read from the DVD directory
      spellReader = IndexReader.open(DvdDirectory);
      LuceneDictionary dict =
        new LuceneDictionary(IndexReader
    .open(DvdDirectory), FIELD_NAME);

      // build the spellcheck index in the base directory
      spellDir = FSDirectory.getDirectory(baseDir);
      spellchecker = new SpellChecker(spellDir);
      // build the directory
      spellchecker.indexDictionary(dict);
    }
    finally {
      if (spellReader != null)
        spellReader.close();
    }
    return spellchecker;
  }

  private void buildIndex(FullTextSession session, Transaction tx) {
    session = Search.getFullTextSession(openSession());
    tx = session.beginTransaction();

    for (int x = x + 1; x < texts.length; x++) {
      Dvd dvd = new Dvd();
      dvd.setId(x);
      dvd.setDescription(texts[x]);
      session.save(dvd);
    }
    tx.commit();
    session.clear();
  }
```

7 Get the DVD index directory

8 Create dictionary instance

9 Create a spellchecker from the DVD index

10 Make spellchecker available

The first thing to accomplish is to build the DVD index and build the spellchecker index **1** after that. We define a misspelled word **2** to see if it is in the spellchecker index ❸. At ❹ we ask for the top five suggestions from the spellchecker and assert that only one suggestion should be returned ❺, one that is equal to "keanu" ❻.

The next steps show how to build the spell-checking index. We first retrieve an instance of the DVD `Directory` ❼ through the usual Hibernate Search means. ❽ creates a `LuceneDictionary` based on the DVD index, and once we have this we create a `SpellChecker` instance ❾ based on the spell-check directory. In ❿ we call the `spellchecker.indexDictionary(dict)` method to create the spell-check index and return the `SpellChecker` instance for use by the rest of the test.

In the next section of the chapter we're going to look at third-party contributions. Some applications are not free. Luke *is* free. The majority of these contributions deal with extracting text from different document formats such as PDF files and Microsoft documents. Let's take a look.

13.2   *Making use of third-party contributions*

In the remaining sections of this chapter we're going to examine those contributions we mentioned at the beginning: those libraries and applications, some of which are free and some not so free. We'll discuss working with Adobe Systems PDF documents, Microsoft documents, and just plain-old text files. These are common, everyday file formats that you'll work with constantly, so getting a good grasp on how to manipulate them will definitely make your job easier.

13.2.1   *Utilizing PDFBox to index PDF documents*

In this section we're going to show you how to extract the textual content from these PDF documents for insertion into a Lucene index. We'll look first at maintaining total control of the process by developing a class that extracts the text and indexes it. Then we'll look at two different ways that PDFBox makes this process easier for us.

PDFBox is an open source Java library. It was written and is maintained by Ben Litchfield and enables you to work with PDF files. It is located at http://www.pdf-box.org. With this library you can create PDF documents, manipulate existing ones, and extract content from them. The last of these three capabilities is of particular interest to Lucene developers.

We're going to look at two different ways to extract text from PDF documents. We'll start with the more difficult method.

EXTRACTING PDF TEXT AND MAINTAINING TIGHT CONTROL OF THE PROCESS

This is for all of the control freaks out there, and we know who we are, right? If you want to know exactly what's going on in the code while it's executing, this is the text-extraction method for you. It utilizes the base PDFBox classes and not only extracts the text but also builds the Lucene index. We were kidding about control freaks. There are many of us who just want to have more fine-grained control over a program in case something fails. That way we can troubleshoot or debug more easily.

Listing 13.9 shows this class in its entirety.

Listing 13.9   Extracting and indexing text utilizing base PDFBox classes

```
public class TestPDFTextExtractor extends SearchTestCase {
  InputStream istream = null;
  private Analyzer analyzer = new StandardAnalyzer();

  public void testPDFExtractor() throws Exception {
    FullTextSession session =
      Search.getFullTextSession(openSession());
    Transaction tx = session.beginTransaction();

    PDDocument doc = null;
    try {
      File f =
        new File("ch13/src/com/manning/hsia/dvdstore/file1.pdf");
      istream =
        new FileInputStream(f.getAbsolutePath());       ◁─┐ Get the PDF via an
                                                            │ InputStream
      PDFParser p = new PDFParser(istream);
      p.parse();
      doc = p.getPDDocument();   ◁── Parse to a PDDocument

      Pdf pdf = getDocument(doc);
      closeInputStream(istream);
      closeDocument(doc);

      buildIndex(pdf);

      QueryParser parser =
        new QueryParser("description", analyzer);

      Query query = parser.parse("description:salesman");
      org.hibernate.search.FullTextQuery hibQuery =
        s.createFullTextQuery(query, Pdf.class);
      List results = hibQuery.list();
      assert results.size() == 1: "incorrect result size";
      Pdf result = (Pdf) results.get(0);
      assert result.getAuthor().startsWith("John Griffin"):
        "incorrect author";
      assert result.getDescription().startsWith("Keanu Reeves"):
        "incorrect description";

      for (Object element : session.createQuery("from " +
  ➡ Pdf.class.getName()).list())
        { session.delete(element); }
      tx.commit();
    }
    finally {
      session.close();
    }
  }

  private Pdf getDocument(PDDocument pd) {
    String description;
    try {
      PDFTextStripper stripper =
        new PDFTextStripper();                       ❶ Grab the PDF text
      description = stripper.getText(pd);
    }
```

```
      catch (IOException e) {
        closeDocument(pd);
        throw new PDFExtractorException("unable to extract text"
  ➥ , e);
      }
      PDDocumentInformation info =
        pd.getDocumentInformation();
      String author = info.getAuthor();                    ❷ Grab the PDF
      String title = info.getTitle();                         metadata
      String keywords = info.getKeywords();
      String subject = info.getSubject();

      Pdf doc = new Pdf();                          ◁─────
      doc.setDescription(description);              ❸ Create a PDF entity
      doc.setAuthor(author);
      doc.setTitle(title);
      doc.setKeywords(keywords);
      doc.setSubject(subject);
      return doc;
    }

    private void buildIndex(Pdf doc,
                    FullTextSession session,
                    Transaction tx) {
      session.save(doc);
      tx.commit();
      session.clear();
    }

    private void closeDocument(PDDocument pd) {
      try {
        if (pd != null) {
          pd.close();
        }
      }
      catch (IOException e) {
        // live with it
      }
    }

    private static void closeInputStream(InputStream istream) {
      if (istream != null) {
        try {
          istream.close();
        }
        catch (IOException e) {
          System.out.println("unable to close file input stream");
        }
      }
    }
  }
```

Grab the PDF document by opening an InputStream on it. Then create a PDDocument from that stream. The PDFTextStripper class physically extracts the text from the PDDocument ❶. Also the PDF metadata can be extracted with the PDDocumentInformation class ❷. Finally, the Pdf entity can now be created ❸ from the extracted text and metadata.

NOTE The call to getPDDocument fails with the downloadable version 0.7.3. We have included a nightly build with the book's code that fixes this problem.

After executing PDFTextExtractor to build the index, we use Luke to examine it. Figure 13.2 shows that querying the author field for the term *griffin* produces the single record that we indexed. It also shows that PDF metadata is placed into the index if the data exists.

Next we're going to look at a class that accomplishes the same thing but does it in such a way that you're not required to write as much code as in the PDFTextExtractor class.

USING THE LUCENEPDFDOCUMENT CLASS

PDFBox provides support for Lucene out of the box. It includes a class called LucenePDFDocument that will accomplish what we did with PDFTextExtractor but won't require us to write as much code. Most of it will be taken care of automatically. It also provides a command-line utility that we'll discuss in the next section.

As an added bonus, where we had to manually extract the PDF metadata and insert it into the created Lucene document, it will be automatically placed in the index for us if it exists in the PDF document. The fields that will be inserted are listed in table 13.1. We must admit that these are the fields listed in the PDFBox documentation as of the time this book is being written. Future implementations may be different.

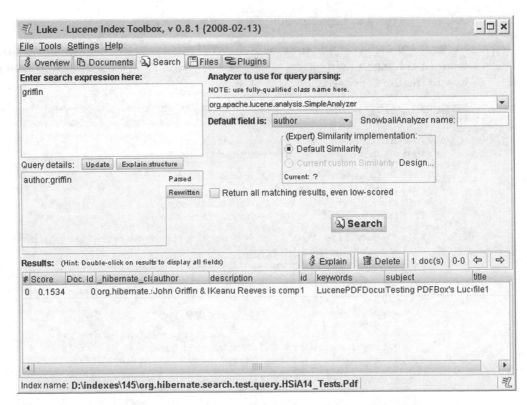

Figure 13.2 Examining the index created with the PDFTextExtractor class, showing the information fields added in addition to the contents field

Table 13.1   A list of the available metadata fields that PDFBox classes will insert into indexes

Lucene field name	Description
Path	File system path if loaded from a file
Url	URL to PDF document
Contents	Not easily accessible; stored as a `StringBuffer`
Summary	First 500 characters of content
Modified	The modified date/time according to the URL or path
Uid	A unique identifier for the Lucene document
CreationDate	From PDF metadata if available
Creator	From PDF metadata if available
Keywords	From PDF metadata if available
ModificationDate	From PDF metadata if available
Producer	From PDF metadata if available
Subject	From PDF metadata if available
Trapped	From PDF metadata if available

In the event that a Lucene document doesn't have any of the metadata fields listed in table 13.1, Luke will display <not available>. Listing 13.10 is a complete example of how to use the LucenePDFDocument class.

Listing 13.10   A complete example of utilizing the `LucenePDFDocument` class

```
public class TestPdfToDoc extends SearchTestCase {
  private Analyzer analyzer = new StandardAnalyzer();

  public void testPdfToDoc() throws Exception {
    FullTextSession session =
      Search.getFullTextSession(openSession());
    Transaction tx = session.beginTransaction();

    File f = new File("ch13/src/com/manning/hsia/dvdstore/file1.pdf");
    buildIndex(f.getAbsolutePath(), session, tx);
    tx = session.beginTransaction();

    try {
      QueryParser parser =
        new QueryParser("description", analyzer);

      Query query = parser.parse("description" + ":salesman");
      org.hibernate.search.FullTextQuery hibQuery =
        session.createFullTextQuery(query, Pdf.class);

      List<Pdf> results = hibQuery.list();
```

```
      assert results.size() == 1: "incorrect result size";
      Pdf result = (Pdf) results.get(0);
      assert result.getAuthor().startsWith("John Griffin"):
        "incorrect author";
      assert result.getDescription().startsWith("Keanu Reeves"):
        "incorrect description";

      for (Object element : s.createQuery("from "
  + Pdf.class.getName()).list())
        { s.delete(element) };
      tx.commit();
    }
    finally {
      s.close();
    }

  private void buildIndex(String filename,
                  FullTextSession session,
                  Transaction tx) {
    Document doc = getDocument(filename);
    Pdf pdf = getPdf(doc);
    session.save(pdf);
    tx.commit();
    session.clear();
  }

  private Document getDocument(String filename) {
    Document doc;
    InputStream istream;
    File file = new File( filename );
    LucenePDFDocument pdf = new LucenePDFDocument();
    try {
      istream = new FileInputStream( file );
      doc = pdf.convertDocument( istream );
    }
    catch (Exception e) {
      throw new PDFExtractorException(
"unable to create document" , e );
    }
    return doc;
  }

  private Pdf getPdf(Document doc) {
    Pdf pdf = new Pdf();
    pdf.setAuthor( doc.get("Author") );
    pdf.setKeywords( doc.get("Keywords") );
    pdf.setSubject( doc.get("Subject") );
    pdf.setTitle( doc.get("Title") );
    pdf.setSummary( doc.get("summary") );
    pdf.setContents( getContents(doc.getField("contents")) );
    pdf.setDescription( pdf.getContents() );
    return pdf;
  }

  private String getContents(Field field) {
    StringReader reader =
```

Create a LucenePDFDocument instance ❶

Get the PDF via an InputStream ❷

Create the Lucene document ❸

```
          (StringReader) field.readerValue();
        BufferedReader br = new BufferedReader(reader);
        String in;
        StringBuilder sb = new StringBuilder();
        try {                                               ④ Get the
          while ((in = br.readLine()) != null) {              Contents field
            sb.append(in);
          }
        }
        catch (IOException e) {
          System.out.println("unable to retrieve contents field");
        }
        finally {
          try {
            br.close();
          }
          catch (IOException e) {
            // Live with it.
          }
        }
        return sb.toString();
      }
    }
```

Create a `LucenePDFDocument` instance ❶, then grab the PDF document by opening an `InputStream` on it ❷. Once you have the stream, creating the Lucene document is one step away ❸.

Listing 13.11 shows the output of the code from listing 13.10. If you compare listing 13.9 with listing 13.10, you'll see that less coding was necessary to produce essentially identical results.

One more thing to cover before we move on to the next topic is the statement we made concerning the Contents field in table 13.1. This field is not stored in the usually easily accessible `Hit.get(fieldname)` format we're used to. It's stored as a Java StringBuffer object. Examining listing 13.10 at ❹, you can see that the Contents field is still accessible albeit not quite as easily as with the `get(fieldname)` method.

Listing 13.11   Example output from listing 13.9 if it were printed

```
contents - Keanu Reeves is completely wooden in this romantic misfire by
    Alfonso Arau
➥  (Like Water
for Chocolate). Reeves plays a World War II vet who hits the road as a
    traveling
➥salesman
and agrees to help a desperate, pregnant woman (Aitana Sanchez-Gijon)

Author - John Griffin & Emmanuel Bernard

CreationDate - 20080120110533

Keywords - LucenePDFDocument; Keanu Reeves; Alfonso Arau

ModificationDate - 20080120113135

Producer - Acrobat Web Capture 8.0
```

```
Subject - Testing PDFBox's LucenePDFDocument.class

Title - file1

summary - Keanu Reeves is completely wooden in this romantic misfire by
    Alfonso Arau
➥(Like Water for Chocolate). Reeves plays a World War II vet who hits the road
    as a traveling salesman and agrees to help a desperate, pregnant woman
    (Aitana Sanchez-
➥Gijon)
```

So which one of these methods should you use to index your documents? That depends on how lazy or how much of a control freak you are. Seriously, the degree of control you need, the amount of time you have to accomplish what you need to do, and many more factors dictate which method you employ. Ultimately you must decide.

It's time to move on to another document format. Like it or not, Microsoft document formats are ubiquitous in today's world. Knowing how to get at their content and being able to put it into an index is a critical skill. Let's see how we can achieve this.

13.2.2 *Indexing Microsoft Word files with POI*

The Apache POI Project exists to create and maintain pure Java APIs for manipulating various file formats based on Microsoft's OLE 2 Compound Document format. In short, it allows you to read and write MS Excel files using Java. As we'll show with example code, you can also read and extract text from Microsoft Word documents. The project is located at http://poi.apache.org/.

Here are the different APIs and the application they are tied to:

- *POIFS*   A set of pure Java APIs for reading and writing OLE 2 Compound Document formats
- *HSSF*   APIs for reading and writing Microsoft Excel 97 (Windows XP) spreadsheets
- *HWPF*   APIs for reading and writing Microsoft Word 97 (Windows XP) documents
- *HSLF*   APIs for reading and writing Microsoft PowerPoint 97 (Windows XP) documents
- *HDGF*   APIs for reading and writing Microsoft Visio documents
- *HPSF*   APIs for reading MFC property sets

POI welcomes anyone who is willing to help with the project, because a lot of work remains to be done. The developers could use help in all aspects, including bug reports, feature requests, and, just like every other project, documentation. If you're interested, join their mailing lists at http://poi.apache.org/mailinglists.html and make yourself known.

NOTE   Since Microsoft has recently (as of this writing) released its file formats to the public domain, the POI projects will likely be changing quite a bit over the next few months.

Let's look at an example of extracting the textual information from a Microsoft Word 2003 document. To run this example you'll need to have both of these .jar files in your classpath along with the usual .jars.

- poi-scratchpad.jar
- poi-3.0.1-FINAL.jar

Listing 13.12 shows how easy it is to accomplish this.

NOTE For the following unit test the document was changed from one paragraph to two by splitting the second sentence into a separate paragraph. This was done to demonstrate the return of individual paragraphs as different elements in the String array.

Listing 13.12 Extracting text from a Microsoft Word 2003 document

```java
public class TestMSDocToIndex extends SearchTestCase {
  private Analyzer analyzer = new StandardAnalyzer();

  public void testExtractFromWordDoc() throws Exception {
    File f = new File("ch13/src/com/manning/hsia/dvdstore/file1.doc");
    buildIndex(f.getAbsolutePath(), session, tx);

    tx = s.beginTransaction();
    QueryParser parser = new QueryParser(decription, analyzer);

    Query query = parser.parse(description + ":reeves");
    org.hibernate.search.FullTextQuery hibQuery =
      s.createFullTextQuery(query, Dvd.class);
    List<Dvd> results = hibQuery.list();

    assert results.size() == 2: "wrong number of results";
    for (Dvd dvd : results) {
      assertTrue(dvd.getDescription().indexOf("Reeves") >= 0);
    }

    for (Object element : s.createQuery("from " +
    DvdFromBridge.class.getName()).list()) s.delete(element);
    tx.commit();
    s.close();
  }

  // The preferred way to do this is via a bridge. For
  // simplicity's sake we chose not to do that here.
  buildIndex( String filename, FullTextSession session, Transaction tx )
    InputStream istream =
      new FileInputStream(new File(filename));       // Get the file via an
                                                     // InputStream
    WordExtractor extractor =
      new WordExtractor(istream);     // ❶ Use WordExtractor
                                      //   to grab the text
    String[] paragraphs =
      extractor.getParagraphText();                  // ❷ Create an array
                                                     //   of paragraphs
    for (int x = 0; x < paragraphs.length; x++) {
      Dvd dvd = new Dvd();
      dvd.setDescription(paragraphs[x]);
      dvd.setId(x + 1);
```

```
                session.save(dvd);
            }
        tx.commit();
        session.clear();
    }
}
```

Once you have an `InputStream` on the Word file, use a `WordExtractor` instance ❶ to get the text as an array of paragraphs ❷. The rest is a Java exercise.

We're not quite done. Before we finish with this chapter we're going to examine the process of indexing a simple text file to Hibernate Search.

13.2.3 *Indexing a simple text file*

This is the simplest example in this chapter for a couple of reasons:

- It has no dependencies other than the Java libraries and obviously Hibernate Search.
- No extraction process is necessary, because it is already plain text.

In the example given in listing 13.13 we're going to use a text file called, ingeniously enough, file.txt. It contains the first text listing of our DVD description files from the end of chapter 12. We'll read the file, construct an entity, and index it.

Listing 13.13 Reading a plain text file and inserting the text into a Lucene index

```java
public class TestReadTextFile extends SearchTestCase {

    public void testTestFile() throws Exception {
        FullTextSession session = Search.getFullTextSession(openSession());
        Transaction tx = session.beginTransaction();

        File f = new File("ch13/src/com/manning/hsia/dvdstore/file1.txt");
        buildIndex(f.getAbsolutePath(), session, tx);
        tx = s.beginTransaction();

        try {
            Query query =
                new TermQuery(new Term("description", "salesman"));
            org.hibernate.search.FullTextQuery hibQuery =
                s.createFullTextQuery(query, Dvd.class);
            List<Dvd> results = hibQuery.list();

            assertEquals("wrong number of hits", 1, results.size());
            assertTrue(results.get(0).getDescription()
     .indexOf("salesman") >= 0);

            tx.commit();
        }
        finally {
            s.close();
        }
    }

    private void buildIndex(String filename ,
                    FullTextSession session,
                    Transaction tx) {
```

```
File in = new File(filename);
BufferedReader reader = null;
StringBuffer sb = new StringBuffer();
try {
  String lineIn;
  reader =
    new BufferedReader(new FileReader(in));       Read the file into
  while ((lineIn = reader.readLine())             a StringBuffer
    != null) {
    sb.append(lineIn);
  }

  Dvd dvd = new Dvd();
  dvd.setDescription( sb.toString() );            Create the entity
  dvd.setId( 1 );

  session.save( dvd );          Write the entity
  tx.commit();                  to the index
}
catch (FileNotFoundException f) {
  System.out.println("unable to locate input file");
}
catch (IOException io) {
  io.printStackTrace();
}
finally {
  if (reader != null) {
    try {
      reader.close();
    }
    catch (IOException io) {
      System.out.println("unable to close file reader");
    }
  }
  session.clear();
  }
 }
}
```

Examining the generated index with Luke in figure 13.3 we can see that the POTF was indexed exactly as we would expect. Searching on *reeves* shows that the index contains one field, contents, and it contains the expected DVD description.

Before we finish we want to examine one last document-extraction methodology, XML. Several ways to accomplish this are possible, and we'll examine two of them, the Serial API for XML (SAX) and the DOM. Each of these methodologies goes about its business in a different way, and we'll examine both with examples and a discussion of their pros and cons.

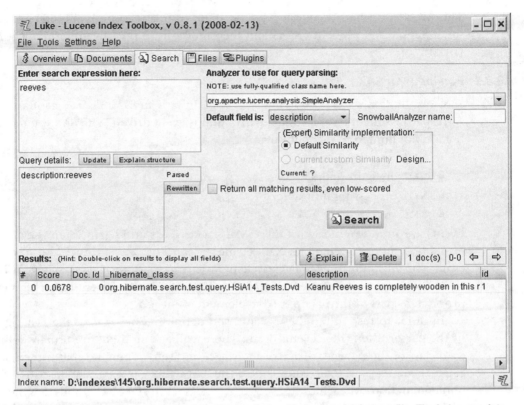

Figure 13.3 **Examining the index created by reading and indexing a plain text file. The index consists of precisely one field, contents, which is exactly what we expected.**

13.3 *Processing XML*

XML, the Extensible Markup Language, has become ubiquitous. There's no getting away from it regardless of how hard you try. Quite a few Integrated Library Systems (ILS) are heavily invested in utilizing XML. Many applications' configuration files are still formatted with it. If you really want to see just how far XML has been able to penetrate the market, search Google with the phrase "systems using xml." We think you'll be surprised not just at how many systems use it but also at the variety of applications.

Hibernate Search doesn't handle XML in the way you'd normally expect. That is, it wasn't designed to take XML documents, parse them into individual entities, and index them. It was, however, designed to parse individual entity properties containing XML and index the extracted content.

NOTE   This doesn't mean that we're saying entities cannot be built from XML documents; they can. All we're saying is that doing so is outside the scope of this discussion, and you'll have to build the entities before calling on Hibernate Search.

This process is what we're going to talk about in this section. We'll discuss both the serial Simple API for XML (SAX) and then move on to the Document Object Model (DOM).

13.3.1 *Parsing with SAX*

SAX was the first widely adopted API for XML in Java and is a *de facto* standard. A SAX XML parser functions as a stream parser and is event-driven. The SAX events include but are not limited to the following:

- XML text nodes
- XML element nodes
- XML processing instructions
- XML comments

Events are fired when each of these XML facets starts and again when they end. For example, suppose we have an XML element `<content>...</content>`. An *element start* event is fired when the `<content>` element is read, and an *element end* event is fired when the `</content>` element is read. Any XML attributes present on an element are provided as part of the data passed to element events.

In order to respond to these events, you define *callback methods* that will be called by the parser when these events occur. These callback methods are usually defined in a subclass of the `DocumentHandler` interface, but we recommend that you extend the `DefaultHandler` class in your code. The `DefaultHandler` class furnishes default implementations of each of the `DocumentHandler` interface's methods analogously to a Java adapter class. Utilizing this will save you quite a lot of work.

Several SAX parsers are available, and a partial list of them is given in table 13.2. Let's look at an example of parsing XML with a SAX parser. For our examples we'll use the Xerces-J parser. The entity we'll use in this example is a CD entity and is shown in listing 13.14.

Table 13.2   SAX parsers available for download and use

Parser Parser class name	Comments
Aelfred2 `Gnu.xml.aelfred2.SAXDriver`	Lightweight nonvalidating parser; free
Oracle's XML Parser for Java `oracle.xml.parser.v2.SAXParser`	Optionally validates; proprietary
Crimson `org.apache.crimson.parser.XMLReaderImpl`	Optionally validates; open source
Xerces-J `org.apache.xerces.parsers.SAXParser`	Optionally validates; open source

Listing 13.14 The CD entity used in the XML SAX parser example

```
@Entity
@Indexed
@Analyzer(impl=StandardAnalyzer.class)
@ClassBridge(name = "",
             index = Index.TOKENIZED,
             store = Store.YES,
             impl = SaxExampleBridge.class)
public class CD {

  private Integer id;
  private String title;
  private String artist;
  private String priceData;

  @Id
  @DocumentId
  public Integer getId() {
    return id;
  }

  public void setId(Integer id) {
    this.id = id;
  }

  @Field(index=Index.TOKENIZED, store=Store.YES)
  public String getTitle() {
    return title;
  }

  public void setTitle(String title) {
    this.title = title;
  }

  @Field(index=Index.TOKENIZED, store=Store.YES)
  public String getArtist() {
    return artist;
  }

  public void setArtist(String artist) {
    this.artist = artist;
  }

  public String getPriceData() {
    return priceData;
  }

  public void setPriceData(String priceData) {
    this.priceData = priceData;
  }
}
```

❶ Declare parsing bridge class

❷ Property holding XML data

At ❶ we specify a bridge class to parse the XML data that's contained in the price-Data property ❷. This property holds the year the CD was released, the company producing it, and the CD's price, as in the following XML fragment:

```
<CD YEAR=\"1985\"><COMPANY>Columbia</COMPANY><PRICE>10.90</PRICE></CD>
```

Bridge classes are a perfect fit for processing this kind of data (refer to chapter 4 if you need to brush up on bridge classes). We'll split the three items of information contained in the `priceData` property into individual fields of a document for storing in the index. Our `SaxExampleBridge` class extends the `DefaultHandler` class we mentioned before and thereby specifies the callback methods that the parser will invoke when the related event occurs. This class is given in listing 13.15.

Listing 13.15 The bridge class that implements callback methods to parse XML

```
public class SaxExampleBridge
extends DefaultHandler                         ❶ Extend the
implements FieldBridge {                           DefaultHandler class

  public void set( String name,
                  Object value,
                  Document document,              ❷ FieldBridge set method
                  LuceneOptions options ) {          implementation
    CD cd = (CD) value;
    String xml = cd.getPriceData();              ❸ Grab the XML data
    if ( xml == null ) {
      return;
    }
    InputSource source =
      new InputSource( new StringReader( xml ) );
                                                 ❹ Create an InputSource
    try {                                           from the XML
      SAXParserFactory factory =
        SAXParserFactory.newInstance();
      SAXParser parser = factory.newSAXParser();
      SaxHandler handler =                       ❺ Create parser
        new SaxHandler( options, document );        and parse XML
      parser.parse( source, handler );
    }
    catch (SAXException s) {
      throw ( new SearchException( "unable to read cd price data", s ) );
    }
    catch (ParserConfigurationException p) {
      throw ( new SearchException( "unable to read cd price data", p ) );
    }
    catch (IOException i) {
      throw ( new SearchException( "unable to read cd price data", i ) );
    }
  }

  /**
   * FieldBridge implementations must be thread safe.
   * So it is necessary to parse the xml in its own
   * instance of a handler to guarantee this.
   */
  private class SaxHandler extends DefaultHandler {

    Map<String, String> attrs;
    List<Field> mFieldList = new ArrayList<Field>();
    Field.Store mStore;
    Field.Index mIndex;
```

```
Field.TermVector mVector;
Float mBoost;
Document mDocument;
StringBuilder text = new StringBuilder();

public SaxHandler( LuceneOptions options,
                Document document ) {
  mStore = options.getStore();
  mIndex = options.getIndex();
  mVector = options.getTermVector();
  mBoost = options.getBoost();
  mDocument = document;
}
public void startElement( String uri,
                    String localName,
                    String qName,
                    Attributes attributes ) {
  text.delete( 0, text.length() );

  if ( attributes.getLength() > 0 ) {
    attrs = new HashMap<String, String>();
    for (int x = 0; x < attributes.getLength();
        x++) {
      attrs.put( attributes.getQName( x ),
            attributes.getValue( x ) );
    }
  }
}
public void endElement( String uri,
                  String localName,
                  String qName ) {
  if ( qName.equals( "CD" ) ) {
    return;
  }
  else {
    Field field =
      new Field( qName.toLowerCase(),
              text.toString(),
              mStore,
              mIndex,
                  mVector );
    if ( mBoost != null ) field.setBoost( mBoost );
    mFieldList.add( field );

    if ( attrs.size() > 0 ) {
      Set<String> keys = attrs.keySet();
      for (String key : keys) {
        String attrValue = attrs.get( key );
        field =
          new Field( key.toLowerCase(),
                  attrValue,
                  mStore,
                  mIndex,
                  mVector );
        mFieldList.add( field );
```

6 startElement event handler

7 Handle any element attributes

8 endElement event handler

9 Generate a field per XML element

10 Generate a field per attribute

```
        }
        attrs.clear();
      }
    }
  }
  public void characters( char[] ch,          ⓫ Process element text
                int start,
                int length ) {
    text.append( ch, start, length );
  }                                           ⓬ documentStart
  public void startDocument() {                  event handler
    mFieldList.clear();
  }
  public void endDocument() {                 ⓭ Add generated fields
    for (Field f : mFieldList) {                 to the document
      mDocument.add( f );
    }
  }
 }
}
```

We start by extending the `DefaultHandler` class ❶ discussed earlier, which, in conjunction with generating an instance of a SAX parser ❺, declares `this` class as the handler of all SAX-generated events. The first event fired is the `startDocument` event ⓬, where we initialize the `FieldList`.

We implement the `set` method required by `FieldBridges` ❷. Here we extract the XML from the `priceData` property ❸ and create an `InputSource` object from it ❹.

❻ is the event handler for each XML element. Here we clear the `StringBuilder` text and then store any attributes of the element in a `HashMap` ❼ for later retrieval. When the `endElement` event is fired, processing continues at ❽. Unless the element is the CD element, we create a field for the element itself ❾ and also individual fields for each attribute ❿, if there were any for this element.

When element text is encountered, the `characters` event is fired ⓫. This fills the `text` buffer for use by other events. Finally, at ⓭ we add each generated `Field` to the document.

Some people have problems conceptualizing callback methods. If you can determine from this example that you are one of those people, this may not be the easiest XML processing model for you to grasp. In that event you could use the DOM, which we discuss next.

13.3.2 *Parsing with the DOM*

In contrast to the SAX processing model, DOM processes XML via recursion. Uh-oh, this is going to be another difficult topic. No, it really isn't that difficult to understand. Let's first look at how DOM visualizes a document as opposed to how SAX does it by examining figure 13.4.

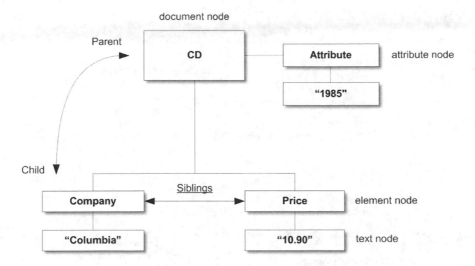

Figure 13.4 Once they are entirely in memory, DOM documents are viewed as a hierarchical tree.

With DOM, everything is a node, and it sees an XML document as a hierarchical tree constructed of these nodes. To accomplish this, it's necessary for the parser to read the entire document into memory before any node processing takes place. This is in contrast to SAX in that SAX processes XML serially as a stream. Notice in figure 13.4 that DOM has its own nomenclature for different types of nodes.

Once a document is in memory, the DOM parser starts processing at the document node, CD in this example, which is the top level of the tree, as shown in figure 13.4. It then continues until all nodes are processed. Just like traversing up and down through a directory tree, the way to accomplish this document traversal is by utilizing recursion.

An example of this recursion should be the best way to demonstrate the process. We will again utilize our CD class, but in this case we have named it CDDOM. This is because we must declare a different bridge class to handle the XML parsing. The only difference is this declaration:

```
@Entity
@Indexed
@Analyzer(impl=StandardAnalyzer.class)
@ClassBridge(name = "",
        index = Index.TOKENIZED,
        store = Store.YES,
        impl = DOMExampleBridge.class)
public class CDDOM {
```

Let's examine listing 13.16, which shows our DOMExampleBridge.

Listing 13.16 Parsing XML with DOM via recursion

```
public class DOMExampleBridge implements FieldBridge {

  public void set( String name,                          Implement FieldBridge
                Object value,                        ① set method
                Document document,
                LuceneOptions options ) {

    CDDOM cd = (CDDOM) value;
    String xml = cd.getPriceData();
    if ( xml == null ) {
      return;
    }

    InputSource source =                                 ② Create an XML
      new InputSource( new StringReader( xml ) );           InputSource

    DOMParser parser = new DOMParser();
    try {                                                Instantiate the
      parser.parse( source );                         ③ Parser and parse
      org.w3c.dom.Document xmlDocument =
        parser.getDocument();
      new DOMHandler( xmlDocument, document, options );
    }
    catch (SAXException e) {
      e.printStackTrace();
    }
    catch (IOException e) {
      e.printStackTrace();
    }
  }

  private class DOMHandler {
    List<Field> mFieldList = new ArrayList<Field>();
    Field mField;
    Field.Store mStore;
    Field.Index mIndex;
    Field.TermVector mVector;
    Float mBoost;

    public DOMHandler( org.w3c.dom.Document xmlDocument,
                  Document document,
                  LuceneOptions options ) {
      mStore = options.getStore();
      mIndex = options.getIndex();
      mVector = options.getTermVector();
      mBoost = options.getBoost();
                                                       ④ Start the
      traverse( xmlDocument.getDocumentElement() );       recursion

      for (Field field : mFieldList) {          ⑤ When finished, add
        document.add( field );                      fields to document
      }
    }

    private void traverse( Node node ) {
      if ( node == null ) {                        ⑥ If no Node, we
                                                      are finished
```

```
      return;
   }

   int type = node.getNodeType();
   switch (type) {
     case Node.ELEMENT_NODE: {            ⑦ Process all XML
       NamedNodeMap attrs =                  document nodes
         node.getAttributes();                              ⑧ Retrieve any
                                                               element attributes
       for (int x = 0; x < attrs.getLength(); x++) {
         Node attrNode = attrs.item( x );              ⑨ Create a Field
         Field field =                                    per attribute
           new Field( attrNode.getLocalName().toLowerCase(),
             attrNode.getNodeValue(),
             mStore,
             mIndex,
             mVector );
         if ( mBoost != null ) field.setBoost( mBoost );
         mFieldList.add( field );
       }

       NodeList children =
         node.getChildNodes();
       if ( children != null ) {              ⑩ Recurse through child nodes
         int len = children.getLength();
         for (int i = 0; i < len; i++) {
           traverse( children.item( i ) );
         }
       }
       break;
     }
     case Node.TEXT_NODE: {   ⑪ Process all XML
                                 text nodes
       if ( node instanceof TextImpl ) {
         if ( !( ( (TextImpl) node )   ⑫ Ignore whitespace
           .isIgnorableWhitespace() ) ) {
                                               ⑬ Create a Field
           Field field =                         per text node
             new Field( node.getParentNode()
               .getLocalName().toLowerCase(),
               node.getNodeValue(),
               Field.Store.YES,
               Field.Index.TOKENIZED );
           mFieldList.add( field );
         }
       }
       break;
     }
   }
 }
   }
 }
}
```

As always, we implement the FieldBridge's set method ❶. Next, we convert our XML to an InputSource ❷ and get an instance of the DOMParser ❸. After parsing the XML document ❹, we start recursing through the nodes by passing the DocumentNode ❺.

If the next node is `null`, we are finished ❻. Remember the recursion principles—it always needs a way out.

All `elementNodes` are processed at ❼. Processing starts by extracting any attributes ❽, converting them to `Document` fields, and storing them in the `Field ArrayList` `mFieldList` ❾. The last step in processing an `elementNode` is to gather its child nodes, if any, and recurse through them ❿.

All `textNodes` (the actual contents of `elementNodes`) are processed at ⓫, and after skipping over any ignorable whitespace ⓬, we convert the text to `Document` fields using its parent node (the `elementNode`) name as the field name.

Once we've processed the last node ⓭ in the document, we transfer all of the generated fields to the Lucene document, and we're finished.

> **PDF and Word extractors as a custom bridge**
>
> Section 13.2, in its entirety, was devoted to explaining how to extract information from various formats. These extractions could very easily have been implemented as custom bridges. You could have byte arrays (for PDFs) or URLs (for Word documents) passed to these custom bridges and the extraction done there. The big benefit of this is that the bridge could be easily reused anywhere you want. What is the title of this chapter, "Don't reinvent the wheel"?

So which one of the parsers do we use? So far we've only shown you how to do the parsing. Is one faster than the other, or more efficient, or more resource intensive? We'll answer these questions in the next section.

13.3.3 *Pros and cons of the different methods*

As with everything else in the world, there are good and bad issues with both SAX and DOM parsing. This section looks at some of these and may aid you in making your decision of which methodology to use when your time comes. Believe us—your time will come! There's no way to avoid it short of passing it off to someone else.

Here are the most prevalent pros and cons:

- *Event-based parsing via SAX provides simple, lower-level access to an XML document.* Documents much larger than available system memory can be parsed, and callback handlers allow construction of specific data structures.
- *DOM parsing is inefficient.* You start by building a memory-resident tree of parse nodes, only to map it onto new data structures and then discard the original tree.
- *SAX parsing is serial (read that as unidirectional).* Previously parsed elements cannot be reread without starting the parsing operation again.

- *DOM parsing is parallel (read that as random access).* Once an element is memory resident, it can be accessed again and again in any order you choose. This includes multithreaded applications accessing the element in parallel to increase performance.
- *DOM-based parsing can put a strain on system resources, especially if the document is large.*

A while back Elliot Rusty Harold, who is well known in XML circles, tested several DOM parsers to see what their memory requirements were, and the results were surprising. The test consisted of loading the XML specification, second edition, into a DOM Document object. This document in file size was 197KB. The simple program he wrote to do this yielded the results given in table 13.3.

DOM parser	Memory requirements
Xerces-J 2.0.1	1489K
Crimson 1.1.3 (JDK 1.4 default)	1230K
Oracle XML Parser for Java 9.2.0.2.0	2500K

Table 13.3 DOM model memory requirements for several DOM parsers

Looking at table 13.3 we can see that there are definitely some things that we should be aware of. *Best-case* memory usage for the document was the Crimson parser, and it required memory with a ratio of 1230/197, or 6.24/1! That's more than six times the size of the document. Worst-case usage required 2500/197, or 12.7/1. That's more than double the best-case usage.

What can we conclude from this? Well, today memory is cheap, but depending on the size of your XML documents, if you use DOM you're going to need a lot of it. The authors realize that this test data is a little dated since the tests were performed in 2002, and the DOM parsers have probably, over time, gotten better at their resource utilization, but we can guarantee that they have not gotten *that* much better!

Hopefully, this discussion of the pros and cons has shed some light on the different parsers and will help you with your decisions, but we believe that you should consider becoming familiar with both. This will also help you decide which one to use under which circumstances.

This chapter has shown that if you have a problem and are in need of a solution, in all probability someone else has had that same problem. It's like that old adage, "No matter how good you are, there is always someone better." Only in this case it is more like, "No matter what the problem is, someone has probably already solved it." Don't just start writing code; look around. With today's search engine capabilities, it's hard to believe someone when he says, "I couldn't find anything on it."

13.4   *Summary*

In this chapter you've seen that Lucene maintains an eclectic mixture of noncore code in two separate repositories, the Sandbox and third-party contributions.

The Sandbox is dedicated to code donated by the core developers along with other personnel interested in the Lucene project, and it is a repository for new ideas. The code is not actively maintained. It consists of such applications as synonym tools, a large variety of foreign language analyzers, and many more utilities that will keep you busy for quite a while.

The third-party contributions section deals mainly with classes and applications that extract text from various file formats such as Adobe Systems's PDF, Microsoft Word and Excel, and XML files. Some of these applications are free and some are not.

We also examined two different methods of parsing XML documents, the serial SAX and the DOM. These two XML parsers utilize completely different methodologies for dissecting XML and have widely varying resource requirements.

As the title of this chapter implies, the Lucene and Hibernate Search projects have made many utilities and classes available for you to use and therefore save time and work. It would be a great benefit to these projects and also to yourself if you were to get involved in improving both projects. The authors recommend it.

We've given you all the fundamental and practical knowledge you'll need to use Hibernate Search efficiently in your application and implement the most suitable search engine for your users. Don't forget, Hibernate is a very dynamic project with lots of new and incremental features coming at each release. Expect the framework to provide more higher-level features with newer versions and probably more control of lower-level features also. Things you're doing manually today might be automated tomorrow. Be sure to check the reference documentation and change logs on a regular basis.

appendix:
Quick reference

This appendix aims at being a quick reference guide of the Hibernate Search artifacts: annotations, APIs, and Lucene query APIs. For each artifact, a quick description and a reference to the book section or URL are provided.

Hibernate Search mapping annotations

Table A.1 describes Hibernate Search annotations.

Table A.1   Hibernate Search annotation summary

Name	Description	Reference
@Analyzer	Defines an analyzer for a given entity, method, attribute, or field. The order of precedence is @Field, attribute/method, entity, default. Can reference an implementation or an @AnalyzerDef definition.	Section 3.4.1
@AnalyzerDef	Reusable analyzer definition. An analyzer definition defines one tokenizer and, optionally, some filters. Filters are applied in the order in which they are defined.	Section 5.2.1
@AnalyzerDefs	Reusable analyzer definitions. Allows multiple @AnalyzerDef declarations per element.	Section 5.2.1
@Boost	Applies a boost factor to a field or an entire entity.	Section 3.4.2, section 7.1.6, section 7.3.8
@ClassBridge	Allows a user to manipulate a Lucene document based on an entity change in any manner the user wishes.	Section 4.1.1, section 8.3.1
@ClassBridges	Allows multiple @ClassBridge declarations per document.	Section 4.1.1
@ContainedIn	Marks the owning entity as part of the associated entity's index (to be more accurate, part of the indexed object graph). This is necessary only when an entity is used as an @IndexedEmbedded target class. @ContainedIn must mark the property that points back to the @IndexedEmbedded owning entity. Not necessary if the class is an embeddable class.	Section 4.2.3

Table A.1   Hibernate Search annotation summary *(continued)*

Name	Description	Reference
@DateBridge	Defines the temporal resolution of a given property. Dates are stored as strings in GMT.	Section 3.3.2
@DocumentId	Declares a property as the document id.	Section 3.2.3
@Factory	Marks a method of a filter factory class as a `Filter` implementation provider. A factory method is called whenever a new instance of a filter is requested.	Section 8.1.2
@Field	Marks a property as indexed. Contains field options for storage, tokenization, whether or not to store `TermVector` information, a specific analyzer, and a `FieldBridge`.	Section 3.3.1
@FieldBridge	Specifies a field bridge implementation class. A field bridge converts (sometimes back and forth) a property value into a string representation or a representation stored in the Lucene `Document`.	Section 4.1
@Fields	Marks a property as indexed into different fields. Useful if the field is used for sorting and searching or if different analyzers are used.	Section 3.3.4
@FullTextFilterDef	Defines a full-text filter that can be optionally applied to full-text queries. While not related to a specific indexed entity, the annotation must be set on one of them.	Section 8.1.2
@FullTextFilterDefs	Allows multiple `@FullTextFilterDef`s per `FullTextQuery`.	Section 8.1.2
@Indexed	Specifies that an entity is to be indexed. An index name that defaulted to the fully qualified class name can be overridden using the `name` attribute.	Section 3.2.1
@IndexedEmbedded	Specifies that an association (`@*To*`, `@Embedded`, `@CollectionOfEmbedded`) is to be indexed in the root entity index. It allows queries that involve associated objects restrictions.	Section 4.2.2, section 4.2.3
@Key	Marks a method of a filter factory class as a `Filter` key provider. A key is an object that uniquely identifies a filter instance associated with a given set of parameters. The key object must implement equals and hashcode so that two keys are equals if and only if the given target object types are the same and the set of parameters is the same. The key object is used in the filter cache implementation.	Section 8.1.2
@Parameter	Basically a key/value descriptor. Used in `@ClassBridge`, `@FieldBridge`, `@TokenFilterDef`, and `@TokenizerDef`.	Section 4.1.1, section 5.3.2

Table A.1 Hibernate Search annotation summary *(continued)*

Name	Description	Reference
`@ProvidedId`	Objects whose identifier is provided externally as opposed to being part of the object state should be marked with this annotation. This annotation should not be used in conjunction with `@DocumentId`. This annotation is primarily used in the JBoss Cache Searchable project.	http://www.jboss.org/jbosscache and http://www.jboss.org/community/docs/DOC-10286
`@Similarity`	Specifies a similarity implementation to use in scoring calculations.	Section 12.2.1
`@TokenFilterDef`	Specifies a `TokenFilterFactory` and its parameters inside an `@AnalyzerDef`.	Section 5.2.1
`@TokenizerDef`	Defines a `TokenizerFactory` and its parameters inside an `@AnalyzerDef`.	Section 5.2.1

Hibernate Search APIs

Table A.2 is a list of the main Hibernate Search APIs and their usage.

Table A.2 Main Hibernate Search APIs

Class	Description	Reference

`Search`
`(org.hibernate.search`
`.Search)`
	Helper method wrapping a Hibernate `Session` object into a `FullTextSession` object.
	Main method:
	`getFullTextSession`
	`(Session)`
		Section 6.2.1

`Search`
`(org.hibernate.search`
`.jpa.Search)`
	Helper method wrapping a Java Persistence `EntityManager` object into a `FullTextEntityManager` object.
	Main method:
	`getFullTextEntityManage`
	`r(EntityManager)`
		Section 6.2.1

`FullTextSession`	Main API used to interact with Hibernate Search in a Hibernate Core environment. Subclasses and wraps a Hibernate `Session`. Main methods: see table A.3.	Section 6.2.1

Table A.2   Main Hibernate Search APIs *(continued)*

Class	Description	Reference
`FullTextEntityManager`	Main API used to interact with Hibernate Search in a Java Persistence environment. Subclasses and wraps a Java Persistence `EntityManager`. Main methods: see table A.4.	Section 6.2.1
`FullTextQuery` (Hibernate Core and Java Persistence)	Subclasses either `org.hibernate.Query` or `javax.persistence.Query` and provides full-text specific query information. Main methods: see table A.5.	Section 6.2.2
`SearchFactory`	Provides application-wide operations as well as access to the underlying Lucene resources. Main methods: see table A.6.	`SearchFactory` instances can be retrieved from `FullTextSession .getSearchFactory()` or `FullTextEntityManager .getSearchFactory()`.
`SearchException`	Exception is raised when an error occurs. This is a runtime exception and is used for all Hibernate Search errors: mapping errors, configuration errors, engine execution errors, and usage errors.	Section 6.2.2
`FullTextIndexEventListener`	Hibernate event listener; listens to entity changes and triggers Hibernate Search indexing.	Section 5.3.1
`DocumentBuilder .CLASS_FIELDNAME`	Name of the Lucene document field in which Hibernate Search stores the class name.	Section 6.2.3

Table A.3 lists the `FullTextSession` methods.

Table A.3   `FullTextSession` methods

Method	Description	Reference
`org.hibernate.Session` methods	`FullTextSession` inherits `Session`. All methods are available, including `persist`, `merge`, `createQuery`, and so on.	Section 2.4
`FullTextQuery createFullTextQuery(org.apache .lucene.search.Query, Class...)`	Creates a `FullTextQuery` based on the Lucene query and restricted to the list of classes passed as a parameter. Entry point for executing a full-text query.	Section 6.2.2

Table A.3 `FullTextSession` methods *(continued)*

Method	Description	Reference
`SearchFactory getSearchFactory()`	Returns the `SearchFactory` object.	
`index(Object)`	Manually triggers indexing of an entity. The entity must be managed.	Section 5.4.1
`purge(Class, Serializable)`	Manually triggers an entity removal from the index. The entity type as well as the id are passed as parameters.	Section 5.4.1
`purgeAll(Class)`	Manually triggers the removal of all index information for a given entity type.	Section 5.4.1
`flushToIndexes()`	Forces the flushing of all pending indexing changes to the Lucene indexes immediately	Section 5.4.2

Table A.4 lists the `FullTextEntityManager` methods.

Table A.4 `FullTextEntityManager` methods

Method	Description	Reference
`javax.persistence.EntityManager` methods	`FullTextEntityManager` inherits `EntityManager`. All methods are available, including `persist`, `merge`, `createQuery`, and so on.	Section 2.4
`FullTextQuery createFullTextQuery(org.apache.lucene.search.Query, Class...)`	Creates a `FullTextQuery` based on the Lucene query and restricted to the list of classes passed as a parameter. Entry point for executing a full-text query.	Section 6.2.2
`SearchFactory getSearchFactory()`	Returns the `SearchFactory` object.	
`index(Object)`	Manually triggers indexing for an entity. The entity must be managed.	Section 5.4.1
`purge(Class, Serializable)`	Manually triggers an entity removal from the index. The entity type as well as the id are passed as parameters.	Section 5.4.1
`purgeAll(Class)`	Manually triggers the removal of all index information for a given entity type.	Section 5.4.1
`flushToIndexes()`	Forces the flushing of all pending indexing changes to the Lucene indexes immediately.	Section 5.4.2

Table A.5 lists the `FullTextQuery` methods.

Table A.5 `FullTextQuery` methods

Method	Description	Reference
`List list()/getResultList()`	Returns the results as a list. All results are loaded up front.	Section 6.3.1
`Iterate iterate()`	Returns an iterator on the results. Only the identifiers are loaded up front.	Section 6.3.2
`ScrollableResults scroll()`	Returns a scrollable object on the results. All resources are only loaded when accessed. Don't forget to call `close()`.	Section 6.3.3
`Object uniqueResult() / getSingleResult()`	Returns a single object. Assumes the query returns one and only one result.	Section 6.3.4
`FullTextQuery setFirstResult(int)`	Pagination API. Sets the first element to retrieve. Starts from 0.	Section 6.4
`FullTextQuery setMaxResults(int)`	Pagination API. Sets the number of elements returned.	Section 6.4
`FullTextQuery setProjection(String...)`	Defines the projected properties. Properties must be stored in the index.	Section 6.5
`FullTextQuery setCriteriaQuery(Criteria)`	Overrides the default fetching strategy using a `Criteria` object.	Section 6.8
`FullTextQuery setSort(Sort)`	Sorts results by a defined order rather than by relevance.	Section 6.7
`FullTextQuery setResultTransformer (ResultTransformer)`	Defines a result transformer. Applied on the query results before they are passed to the user.	Section 6.6
`FullTextFilter enableFullTextFilter(String)`	Enables a full-text filter described by an `@FullTextFilterDef` annotation. The `FullTextFilter` object lets you set the necessary parameters for the filter. More than one filter can be activated.	Section 8.1.3
`disableFullTextFilter(String)`	Disables a full-text filter described by an `@FullTextFilterDef` annotation.	Section 8.1.3
`int getResultSize()`	Returns the total number of matching results regardless of pagination.	Section 6.4.2
`Explanation explain(int)`	Returns the `Explanation` object for a given document id in a query. The document id is not the entity id.	Section 6.9

Table A.6 lists the `SearchFactory` methods.

Table A.6   `SearchFactory` methods

Method	Description	Reference
`ReaderProvider getReaderProvider()`	Returns the `ReaderProvider` used. Allows opening and closing of `IndexReaders`.	Listing 11.6
`DirectoryProvider[] getDirectoryProviders(Class);`	Returns the list of directory providers associated with a given class (one unless sharding is used). Allows you to use Lucene natively.	Section 11.1.1
`optimize()`	Optimizes all indexes.	Section 8.3.1
`optimize(Class)`	Optimizes Lucene indexes associated with the class passed as a parameter.	Section 8.3.1
`Analyzer getAnalyzer(String)`	Returns an analyzer by its `@AnalyzerDef` name. Useful when the analyzer used for indexing should not be used at query time. This is a rare case.	Section 7.2.4
`Analyzer getAnalyzer(Class)`	Returns the scoped analyzer used to index a given entity. In most cases, uses the same analyzer to execute your queries.	Section 7.2.4

Table A.7 lists less-common Hibernate Search APIs.

Table A.7   Other Hibernate Search APIs

Class	Description	Reference
`DirectoryProvider`	Provides access to a Lucene `Directory`. Different `DirectoryProviders` provide access to different `Directory` storage systems or apply some index synchronization.	Section 5.1
`ReaderProvider`	Provides access to the (usually) shared Lucene `IndexReaders`. Lets you use Lucene natively while still benefiting from the Hibernate Search resource-caching mechanism. Be sure to use the `open` and `close` methods together to avoid resource leaking.	Section 11.1.1
`FilterCachingStrategy`	Implements a full-text filter-caching strategy.	Section 8.1.2
`FilterKey`	Class used uniquely to represent a filter and its filter parameters in a cache system. A default implementation, `StandardFilterKey`, is provided.	Section 8.1.2
`StringBridge`	Implements a simple custom field bridge that converts a property value in a string.	Section 4.1.2

Table A.7   Other Hibernate Search APIs *(continued)*

Class	Description	Reference
TwoWayStringBridge	Implements a simple custom field bridge that converts a property value in a string. This bridge is also able to perform the reverse operation. Useful for projected properties and identifier properties.	Section 4.1.2
FieldBridge	Implements a flexible custom field bridge that converts a property value in an indexable structure. It has direct access to the Lucene Document object.	Section 4.1.4
TwoWayFieldBridge	Implements a flexible custom field bridge that converts a property value in an indexable structure and is able to perform the reverse operation as well. It has direct access to the Lucene Document object. Useful for projected properties and identifier properties.	Section 4.1.2
ParameterizedBridge	Implemented by a field bridge that's able to receive parameters.	Section 4.1.3
Worker	Responsible for receiving all entity changes, queueing them by context, and deciding when a context starts and finishes.	Section 5.3.4
QueueingProcessor	Responsible for piling up changes in a given context, preparing the work for Lucene, and triggering the work either synchronously or asynchronously.	Section 5.3.4
BackEndQueueProcessorFactory	Responsible for providing a Runnable instance that will perform the list of Lucene changes. Typical implementations involve direct use of Lucene or sending a message to a JMS queue.	Section 5.3.4

Lucene queries

Table A.8 is a list of the basic Lucene query types accompanied by a brief description. For a comprehensive listing consult the Lucene Javadoc org.apache.lucene.search package.

Table A.8   Main Lucene query classes

Query	Description	Reference
TermQuery	This is the basic building block of queries. It searches for a single term in a single field. Many other query types are reduced to one or more of these.	Section 7.3.1
WildcardQuery	Queries with the help of two wildcard symbols: * (multiple characters) and ? (single character). These wildcard symbols allow queries to match any combination of characters.	Section 7.3.4
PrefixQuery	A WildcardQuery that starts with characters and ends with the * symbol.	Section 7.3.4

Table A.8 Main Lucene query classes *(continued)*

Query	Description	Reference
PhraseQuery	Also known as a proximity search, this queries for multiple terms enclosed in quotes.	Section 7.3.3
FuzzyQuery	Queries using the Levenshtein distance between terms and providing approximate results.	Section 7.3.5
RangeQuery	Allows you to search for results between two values. Values can be inclusive or exclusive but not mixed. Its variant the ConstantScoreRangeQuery does not suffer from the TooManyClauses exception. Check the Lucene Javadoc for more information.	Section 7.3.6
BooleanQuery	Holds every possible combination of any of the other query types including other BooleanQuerys. Boolean queries combine individual queries as SHOULD, MUST, or MUST_NOT.	Section 7.3.7
MatchAllDocsQuery	Returns all documents contained in a specified index.	Section 7.3.7

index

451